THE FIRST
RAILROADS

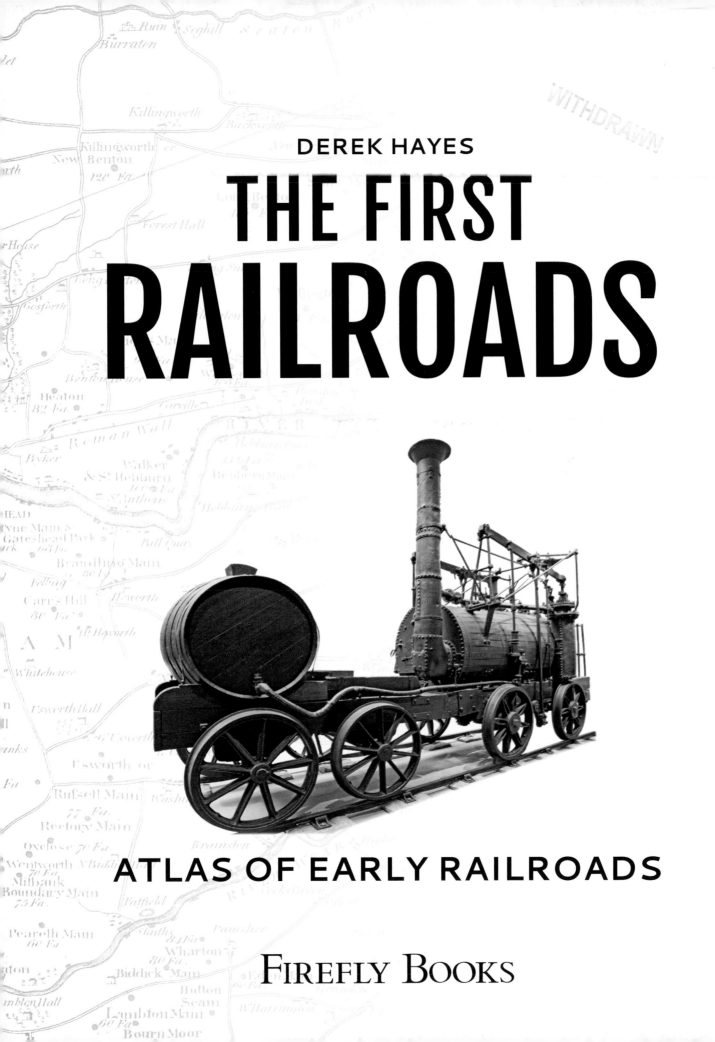

DEREK HAYES

THE FIRST
RAILROADS

ATLAS OF EARLY RAILROADS

FIREFLY BOOKS

A FIREFLY BOOK

Published by Firefly Books Ltd. 2017

Copyright © 2017 Derek Hayes

First printing

Publisher Cataloging-in-Publication Data (U.S.)

Names: Hayes, Derek, 1947– , author.
Title: The First Railroads : Atlas of Early Railroads / Derek Hayes.
Description: Includes bibliographic references and index. | Summary: "An illustrated volume tracing the emergence of modern railways" – Provided by publisher.
Identifiers: ISBN 978-0-22810-009-6 (pbk.)
Subjects: LCSH: Railroads — History. | Railroads – Pictorial works. | BISAC: TRANSPORTA-TION / Railroads / History. | TRANSPORTATION / Railroads / Pictorial.
Classification: LCC TF15.H394 | DDC 385.09 – dc23

Published in the United States by
Firefly Books (U.S.) Inc.
P.O. Box 1338, Ellicott Station
Buffalo, New York 14205

Printed in China

Acknowledgments

As with any book of this sort, I owe a debt of gratitude to many people who helped me.

In particular, I'd like to thank Andy Guy, early railways researcher extraordinaire, for advice and for reading much of the manuscript, allowing me to avoid many mistakes.

Jim Rees, of Beamish Museum, arranged for me to photograph the museum's Steam Elephant replica at work and also provided access to Beamish's extensive archives. Charles Lamont arranged for me to photograph the Catch Me Who Can replica. Others who assisted with access to maps and photographs include Neville Whaler, of the Bowes Railway; Paul Jarman, Beamish Museum; Lucy Arnold, Special Collections, University of Leeds; Jenny Parkerson, Map Librarian, National Library of Scotland; Richard Dean, Cartographics; Martin Routledge, Keeper of History, Sunderland Museums; and Julian Spurrier and Craig Bowen, Canterbury Heritage Museum.

As always, Iva Cheung, my editor, provided invaluable help with her knack for rescuing understandable prose from my unintended gibberish — thank you, Iva!

Thanks too, to Nicola Goshulak for additional proofing.

Finally, thanks to all at Douglas & McIntyre, my Canadian publisher, and to Jethro Lennox and Keith Moore of Harper Collins, UK for the UK and international editions.

MIX
Paper from responsible sources
FSC® C007454
www.fsc.org

Front cover: Steam Elephant (oil painting, artist and date unknown) – Beamish Museum.

Back cover: A contemporary view of the Ludwigsbahn. Adler is seen departing from Nuremberg with a passenger train.

Half-title page: 1927 replica of the Andrew Jackson, first built in 1836. See page 236.

Title page: *Wylam Dilly*, constructed between 1813 and 1815, on a map of the northeast coalfield, 1807. See page 118.

Left: A replica of *Adler* ("Eagle"), the first locomotive to run on a public railway in Germany, the Nuremberg–Fürth line, 1835. Behind it is a modern German Intercity-Express (ICE) train. They were photographed at the Deutsche Bahn Museum in Nuremberg. See page 254.

Contents page, top: A fine engraving of Richard Trevithick's 1803 Coalbrookdale locomotive. Beyond a letter written by Trevithick, there is little evidence for this locomotive—the world's first-recorded run by a locomotive was in 1804 and with a slightly differently designed loco-motive, on the Merthyr Tramroad in South Wales (see page 103). There is, however, a detailed engineering drawing dating from this time that is believed to be of the 1803 Coalbrookdale engine, and this engraving was done from that. It is the model for the Trevithick monument in Merthyr, illustrated on page 104, and, stylized, is used on the left-hand footers throughout this book.

Contents page, bottom: Part of a map of the West Longbenton Colliery and waggonway, in the northeast coalfield, drawn in 1749. The lines shown were of wood. See page 23.

Contents

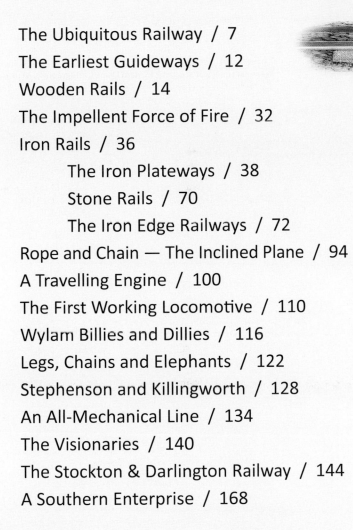

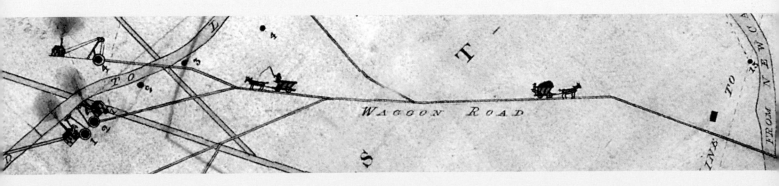

Above.
Robert Stephenson's famous steam locomotive Rocket competed in the 1829 Rainhill Trials held by the Liverpool & Manchester Railway and easily won the contest. With innovative features such as a multi-tube boiler, the design revolutionized railway power and began the process that would make the railway an unbeatable means of transport. The original engine is displayed in the Science Museum in London.

The Ubiquitous Railway

The economy of the modern world revolves much around rails. The movement of freight and, in many countries, the movement of people would be much diminished if the friction-reducing effects of steel wheel on steel rail were not used. It enables the movement of enormous quantities of goods overland at a far lower cost than if rubber-wheeled transport had to be used; it permits the economical export and import of the trade goods on which the world is now so dependent.

The railway only became a worldwide economic force from the middle of the nineteenth century, some forty or fifty years after the first demonstration of a mechanically powered train, and in the popular mind railways began only with George Stephenson's *Locomotion* in 1825 or his son Robert's *Rocket* in 1829. Yet the principles of railed transportation had by that time been used for hundreds of years. What radically changed—in the space of less than three decades—was the method of propulsion, from human or horse power to steam-powered "travelling engines," the forerunners of the modern railway locomotive.

The type of rail that was used to guide the train and reduce friction, making it easier to push or pull, also changed. Here early development was from simple ruts in the ground to wooden slots guiding pins on carts, then to wooden rails of one sort or another on which flanged-wheel rolling stock was required, and then to metal strip–topped wooden rails. Finally, towards the end of the eighteenth century, came all-metal rails, initially sometimes L-shaped, more correctly called plateways, then so-called edge rails— first mere bars, then T-shaped or U-shaped or many other shapes—and all of these required flanged wheels, the system we have today. Then the metal used for rails evolved from cast iron, which broke too easily under the pounding of early engines and wagons, to wrought, or malleable, iron deployed in various shapes, and finally to much more durable and reliable steel.

The world economic impact of the railway was enormous; so too was the social impact, simply by bringing people and things closer together in time. Now the citizen of a grimy interior industrial city could savour the fresh fish of the coast, firmly establishing in Britain the virtual national dish of fish and chips. People could visit the seaside, for a day, for a week. Many large companies laid on annual trips for their employees, who might otherwise never have set foot outside their local area. It promoted harmony and understanding and quelled riot, figuratively and literally. The military significance of the railway would have a great impact on the course of human affairs. The U.S. Civil War and the European First World War could not have been fought without railways supplying the front. Regions of the world opened up to settlement, with railways across continents: North America in 1869 and Asia—the Trans-Siberian Railway—in 1916, the latter the longest rail line in the world at 5,772 miles (9,289 km).

But the railway at the beginning was a local affair, typically carrying coal from a mine or stone from a quarry to the nearest navigable water. In the age of the canal, which preceded that of the railway, lines typically extended the reach of the canal where it was too expensive, too steep to build a canal. Horse-drawn affairs, yes, but still very much railways. No one would argue that a Roman road was not a road simply because no cars drove along it; so likewise with railways. Mechanical power would come, but only after horses had powered the railway for centuries.

Right.
A replica of *Sans Pareil*, Timothy Hackworth's entry to the Rainhill Trials of 1829. The replica is at the Shildon branch of the National Railway Museum, site of the original locomotive works of the pioneering Stockton & Darlington Railway (see page 148).

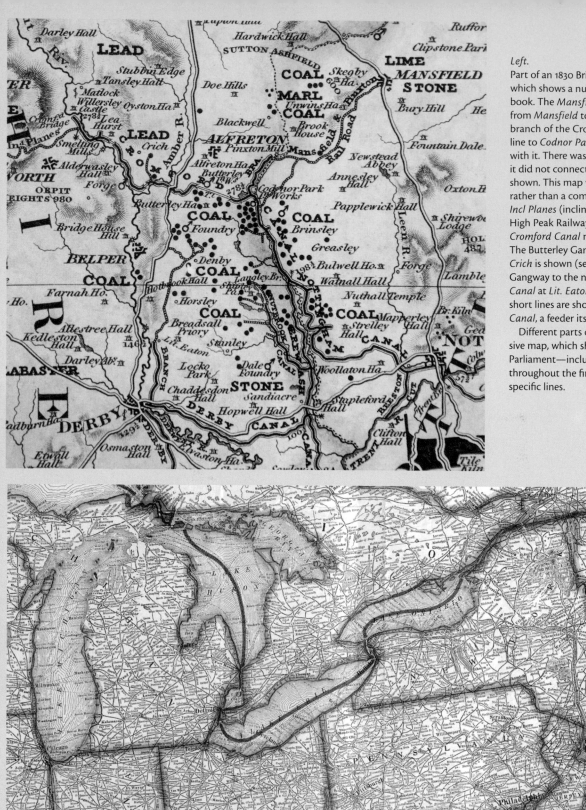

Left.

Part of an 1830 British *Map of the Inland Navigation*, which shows a number of lines covered in this book. The *Mansfield & Pinxton Rail Road* runs from *Mansfield* to *Pinxton Mill*, at the end of a branch of the Cromford Canal (see page 77). A line to *Codnor Park Works* is shown connecting with it. There was a line to the Codnor works, but it did not connect with the Mansfield & Pinxton as shown. This map was based on Acts of Parliament rather than a comprehensive survey of built lines. *Incl Planes* (inclined planes) of the Cromford & High Peak Railway (see page 203) lead to the *Cromford Canal* near its northwestern terminus. The Butterley Gangroad to the quarries near *Crich* is shown (see page 40), as is the Little Eaton Gangway to the northern *Branch* of the *Derby Canal* at *Lit. Eaton* (see page 40). In addition, some short lines are shown leading to the short *Nutbrook Canal*, a feeder itself of the *Erewash Canal*.

Different parts of this large and comprehensive map, which shows routes authorized by Parliament—including some never built—recur throughout the first part of this book, illustrating specific lines.

Above.

With the railway now truly ubiquitous, this 1918 railway map of the northeastern part of the United States shows the system at its zenith. Rail lines cover the land, leaving few areas far from one. Indeed, many lines would prove to have been constructed where demand could not be sustained given the rise of the automobile that began about this time. At its peak, the U.S. had about 254,000 miles of route; today it is about 140,000 miles. Britain, the birthplace of the railway, had just under 20,000 miles at its peak, now reduced to 9,700 miles.

Right.

This interesting juxtaposition of historical elements of the story of rail transport was photographed in the National Railway Museum in York, England, in 2013. To the right is a horse, used for rail power from the earliest days. The horse is standing in a "dandy cart," which gave it a rest while wagons were travelling downhill using gravity, before the horse hauled the empty wagons back uphill. In the background is a stationary winding engine, this one used to haul wagons on the Stanhope & Tyne Railway in northeast England (see page 207). In the foreground left is one of the most powerful steam engines ever built, *Dominion of Canada*, an A4 class locomotive, the same class as its brother, *Mallard*, which broke the world steam speed record on 3 July 1938, at 125.88 miles per hour (202.58 km per hour). All six surviving A4 locomotives had been brought together at the National Railway Museum for an event called "The Great Gathering." *Dominion of Canada*, along with *Dwight D. Eisenhower*, were respectively shipped from Canada and the United States for the event.

Mobile steam on roads failed at the time because of the atrocious state of the roads; had they been the hard-topped, smooth affairs they are today, the battle between road and rail might have had a quite different outcome. Indeed, without relatively smooth rail lines ready to receive the early mechanical monsters, they would likely have hardly moved. The concept was proved by Richard Trevithick in 1804; all that remained was for it to advance to the point where it was generally feasible, the result of improvements in steam propulsion, the reliability and strength of iron boilers, and the durability and design of rails. Events influenced the speed of steam locomotive development too. A tax on horses used for industrial purposes in 1795 and the shortage, and consequent rise in price, of horse fodder during the Napoleonic Wars all encouraged the search for alternatives. And when the war ended in 1815, horses became cheaper, which had the opposite effect.

This book includes the stories—and displays the maps—of two well-known events in railway history: the building of the Stockton & Darlington Railway, opened in 1825, and the Liverpool & Manchester Railway, opened five years later. But arrayed around them are many other stories of smaller lines, less important to be sure, and even ones you may not have heard of, but nevertheless significant in the incremental development of the railway systems that we have today around the world. They were waypoints on the progressive technological wave that would engulf the world by the mid 1800s.

Right.

The power of the railway to transport goods is well illustrated by this photo of an enormous block of slate—you can almost feel the weight—on a diminutive wagon, little more than a set of wheels and a rectangular chassis. The photo was taken at the slate mine at Honister Pass, Cumbria.

Railways were called many things in their early days—waggonways, railways, railroads, iron roads, tramways, tramroads, plateways, and more—generally varying by region and by the type of rail used. I have usually used the term *railway* here because that is what it is called in the majority of the world, the *railroads* of the United States being the major exception.

History is not conveniently linear. One event or discovery did not neatly follow from the previous one. Techniques were used or things invented sometimes completely independent of each other because the flow of knowledge from one time to another or one part of the world to another was far from perfect, quite unlike the modern era where news can be shared instantly anywhere. But a book is necessarily linear. One page has to follow the next. So, while I have tried to make the events described follow a logically reasonable pattern, they sometimes dart forward and then fall backward.

Above, right, and *far right.*
Coal and fire, the basis for the railway revolution. The fuel is actually coke, which was preferred to coal because it produced less smoke. The roaring fire in the firebox is keeping the driver and fireman's tea warm. The photos were taken on a Maunsell Q Class locomotive of 1939 at the Bluebell Railway, a heritage line in southern England, shown in the photo, *right.*

A note on terminology.

Early horse-drawn railways were commonly referred to as waggonways, spelled with a double *g*, and I have retained that spelling here. Wagons were also sometimes spelled with a double *g*, but here I have adopted the more modern form, with a single *g*.

A note on the maps and illustrations.

Contemporary maps have been used to illustrate the stories as much as possible. Occasionally, where no contemporary map was available, later maps are used, sometimes with highlighting added to enhance clarity.
In captions *italics* are used to indicate names *actually shown on the map.* In the main text *italics* are used to indicate page position.
Sources of maps and other illustrations are listed at the back of the book (see page 260).
All photographs are by the author unless noted otherwise on page 260.

Above.
Part of a very large hand-drawn map of the Newbottle Waggonway dated 1817. The individual lines serving collieries can be seen. The waggonway, completed in 1812, linked collieries directly with staiths (coal-loading stages) at Sunderland, accessible to seagoing vessels. Before the waggonway was built, the collieries had to transport coal to the River Wear, where it would be loaded into small barges called keels and transhipped at the mouth of the river. This process broke pieces of coal, and small pieces of coal sold for less than large pieces in the London market.

Right.
Far from being universally accepted, steam traction was actively opposed by many in its early days. This engraving was supposed to warn of the dangers of steam locomotives.

THE STEAM FIEND.

The Earliest Guideways

A "railway" is commonly defined as a *prepared* track that guides vehicles running on it so that they cannot leave the track. In a sense the very earliest railways were simply ruts caused by the passage of carts on softer ground, though these were not deliberately prepared. Such ruts will tend to track those following, particularly if there is a similar distance between the wheels of carts; drivers would have noticed that it was easier to keep in the ruts than to run outside them. And so it was an easy step to artificially create ruts in stone. Rut railways of this nature may have been in use as early as 2200 BC.

The earliest confirmed such rut railway was the Diolkos (or "haul-over") across the Isthmus of Corinth in Greece, a narrow neck of land some 50 miles west of Athens (photo, *right,* and map, *right, bottom*) which allowed cargo and perhaps smaller ships to be hauled between the Saronic Gulf and the Gulf of Corinth, saving a lot of time compared with going round a treacherous coast. It was built about 600 BC. Cargo was hauled over the isthmus by manpower or horse power using some sort of wooden truck. Continuous ruts cut into stone guided the trucks, a system interestingly similar to a much later stone railway on Dartmoor, in England (see page 70).

Below, bottom.
The Diolkos, across the Isthmus of Corinth, Greece, marked in red. Its curved course followed low ground. The much straighter Corinth Canal, completed in 1893, is shown in blue. *Golf Aegina* is the Saronic Gulf. The photo *below* shows a surviving section of the Diolkos today. It was cut off by the canal, seen in the background.

Below, left centre.
This three-dimensional map of Salzburg from the 1580s shows the Hohensalzburg Castle and the Nonnberg nunnery beneath it. The Reißzug carried supplies for the castle up an early railway, the modern version of which is shown in the photo (*left, bottom*).

Left.
A Leitnagel "hund" being pushed along a track on a sort of bridge in the mining district of Erzgebirge, now in Germany. This is an illustration from a mining manual published in 1556, *De Re Metallica*, by Georgius Agricola.

Right, top, and *centre*.
A replica "hund" at the National Railway Museum, York, showing the metal pin between two planks used to guide the wagon. The pin is at the front.

The Romans are known to have used similar rutways, though few definite sites are known. One is underground at Três Minas, a gold mine in Portugal. There are rutways in Malta, in Cornwall, and elsewhere, but it is difficult to determine with any certainty whether the ruts were deliberately cut.

An early European railway was the Reißzug, built by 1504 in Salzburg, now in Austria. It was essentially a cable car pulled up the slope to the Hohensalzburg Castle from the Nonnberg nunnery below. It is likely that the Reißzug was built to transport building materials to the higher parts of the castle. The oldest version of the Reißzug was operated with sleds, beginning in 1496, but by 1504 it had wooden rails, and the Reißzug was turned into something like a railway. For centuries it carried food and other supplies up to the castle, pulled by rope by either men or horses. The power source was changed to an engine in 1910, and the gauge of the rails widened; it is still in use today, bringing up supplies for the castle's restaurants. It is a candidate for the longest more or less continuously operating railway in the world. The railway bears a striking resemblance to an inclined plane at the Dinorwic slate mine in Wales (see page 87).

The broader use of railways began in the mines of central Europe. The Leitnagel "hund" was used to transport ore to the surface along narrow passageways, pushed by a miner. Its claim to being a railway comes from an iron pin on the wagon being guided between two wooden planks, Scalextric-like, while the weight of the load is taken by wheels more akin to rollers on the planks (photos, *right, top*). The resultant barking noise accounts for its name—"hund" or hound.

It was this type of railway that was introduced into Britain by German and Austrian miners mining for copper, lead, and silver in the Lake District in the second half of the sixteenth century. Remains of track have been found at the Silver Gill mine at Caldbeck (photo, *below*).

Caldbeck, Cumbria—the improbable site of the first railway in Britain.

Wooden Rails

Other early railways used something nearer to what might be recognized as a rail to guide their wagons. The most obvious was merely a wooden version of the rut, a channel in which a flat-surfaced wheel would run. A few mines scattered all over Europe used this system in the sixteenth century, and it was also used for short military railways, when fortifications were being constructed. But the channel rail, or another variant that had a wooden rail with a higher flange on its inside edge, thus creating the same sort of channel, was not particularly popular, and especially not underground, perhaps because small pieces of rock would find their way into the channel and require cleaning before the railway would work properly. The very same issues would dog the iron plateway three centuries later (see page 38).

The better solution was to put the flange on the wagon wheel rather than the rail. The rails then did not have to be particularly well laid since the wheels were broad enough to absorb quite a bit of gauge change, and the round rails would not harbour friction-producing soil, rocks, or other detritus (photo, *below, right*). These kinds of railways could be found at scattered locations all over eastern Europe, almost always at mines.

The earliest definitively documented application of a cross-country railed way in Britain is that of entrepreneur Huntingdon Beaumont: his waggonway ran from Strelley to Wollaton, now in the west part of Nottingham. He had obtained a lease on coal pits at Strelley and was desperately attempting to make them profitable. As part of this effort he made a "passage . . . laide with Railes" from the pit to the main road into Nottingham, where it would have been easier to sell the coal at a good price because it could easily be transported by cart from there into the city. Documents fix the date of this first waggonway at between October 1603 and October 1604. His waggonway appears not to have made

much difference to the profitability of his coal mines—interesting, for there would later be many instances of waggonways, or railways, vastly improving coal mine profitability.

Beaumont also had three waggonways built in northeast England to service coal mines in which he had an interest. All three ran down to the River Blythe some 10 miles north of Newcastle, but the exact locations are not recorded. The earliest was likely at Bedlington, where he leased pits from the Bishop of Durham in 1608.

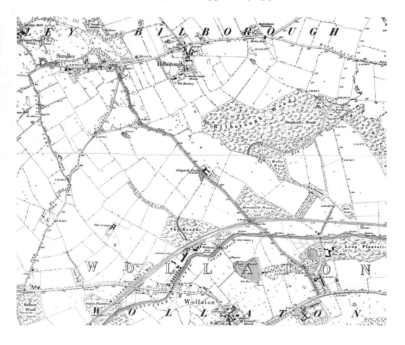

Above and *right* (part).
This is thought to be the world's first surviving railway map! It is dated 1637 and shows the royal manor of Benwell, on the north side of the River Tyne just west of Newcastle. The line of Hadrian's Wall (*The wall*), a Roman defensive work, truncates the manor. Coal had been mined here for a long time before this map was drawn, and coal had been shipped from pits in *Stumple Wood*, near the river. These had become exhausted, and coal was now being mined from *East Feild Or Meadow Feilds*, farther from the river. To more easily transport the coal to the river, a waggonway was built from the southeastern corner of Meadow Fields to *Steathes* (staiths) on the river, a distance of just under half a mile. The waggonway crosses *Lysdon Burn* at right angles. At this time mapmakers had not arrived at a convention as to how to depict railways to differentiate them from roads, so on the map the track route looks much the same as roads. The map was produced for a government hearing into a dispute between Benwell freeholders and tenants over mineral rights.

Left, top.
Miner pushing a truck with apparently flat wheels in channels. This illustration, which dates from 1503, is thought to depict a mine in Saxony.

Far left, bottom.
The likely route of Huntingdon Beaumont's "rayle" way from coal pits at Strelley to the main road into the city of Nottingham, which is off to the right. The approximately 1½-mile route has been marked on an 1880 map as the area is today completely built over with housing. Of course, although his route is shown crossing a railway and a canal, they are much later than Beaumont's rails.

Left, centre, and *left, bottom.*
Two views of a mining truck, called a *riesen*, with massive flanged roller-wheels running on round-edge track that could be little more than selected straighter tree limbs; it came from a sixteenth-century gold mine in Hungary. This *riesen* is displayed at the Deutsches Technikmuseum in Berlin. Crude but workable switching from one line to another was now possible using these rough rails. Huntingdon Beaumont's waggonway probably looked similar to this.

By the 1630s there were several wooden waggonways running to the River Tyne, but the evidence is fragmentary. We know, for example, that burial registers about that time differentiate between road coal carts (wains) and rail coal carts (wagons) as a cause of death. The first waggonway was at Whickham, on the south bank of the Tyne about 2½ miles east of Gateshead. And the first map on which a railway of any sort appears is that of Benwell, on the north bank, dated 1637 (map, *above*).

There is similar evidence of some very early railways in Shropshire, particularly around Broseley, about a mile south of the River Severn, where there were railways by 1605, and where a massive wood wheel much the same as those shown on the *riesen* (*previous page*) has been unearthed. There developed a distinction in type between waggonways in the northeast of England and those in Shropshire and South Wales. The former tended to be wider in gauge, around the 4- to 5-foot width of an average cart, a distance that would, thanks to the influence of George Stephenson, be formalized as the widely used "standard" gauge of 4 feet, 8½ inches; wagons were large and operated singly by one man and a horse to haul the wagon on uphill sections and to return it when empty. Shropshire-type railways tended to be narrower gauge and continue right into the mine where a coal seam outcropped; several wagons might be drawn together.

The first use of a Shropshire-type waggonway in South Wales appears to be in 1697, when Humphry Mackworth acquired collieries at Neath by marriage. They had been abandoned partly because of lack of good transportation, and so he installed a railway "on Wooden Railes from the face of each Wall of Coal twelve hundred Yards under Ground quite down to the Water-side, about three-quarters of a Mile from the Mouth of the Coal-pit . . . by means thereof, great quantities are brought forth and sold to Sea." The map *below* shows Mackworth's estates with the railway.

Scotland's first railway opened in 1722 and ran from coal mines just east of the village of Tranent 2 miles to the coast at Cockenzie, about 7 miles east of Edinburgh, the principal market for the coal. It was based on the Shropshire model, with a gauge of about 3 feet, 3 inches. The coal mines at Tranent had been owned by a supporter of the 1715 Jacobite Rebellion who forfeited them

to the Crown. They were subsequently sold to the York Buildings Company of London in 1719. The company determined to make the most of its investment and reconstructed Cockenzie Harbour and built a waggonway from the pits. It was graded downhill the entire way, and wagons could be dispatched by gravity and the empties pulled back by a single horse. The waggonway is unusual in that in 1745 it found itself right in the middle of a battlefield. The Battle of Prestonpans was fought here at 4 am on 21 September 1745. The English army drew up its cannon behind the embankment of the Tranent to Cockenzie Waggonway, but this was not enough to stop Bonnie Prince Charlie from winning the battle. The waggonway lasted in its wooden-railed form until 1815, when it was rebuilt with iron rails.

The Alloa Waggonway, which was built in 1766 to carry coal from mines some 2½ miles to the River Forth, also had a 3-foot, 3-inch gauge and was based, it is thought, on the Tranent model. As with all these early waggonways, the aim was to carry coal to navigable waters. Rails were being cut to a greater degree of precision than the very early virtual tree limbs; now they were sawn square or rectangular in cross-section and would be able to accept the next development—an iron strip on their top edge to decrease wear and friction. This in fact happened on the Alloa line

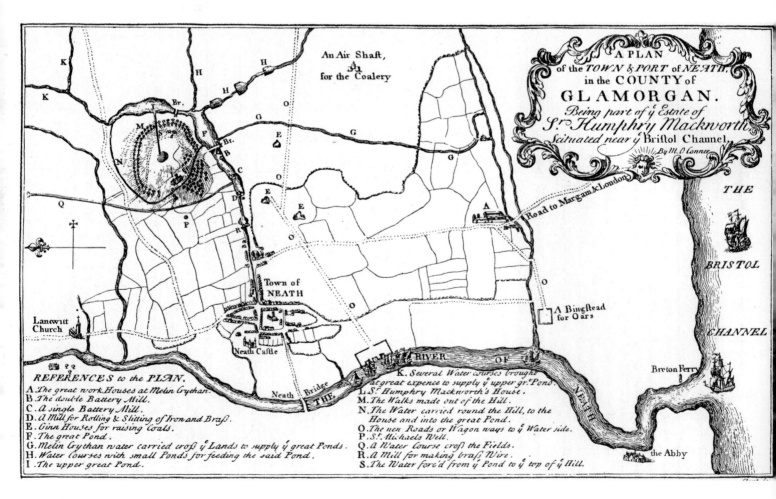

Above.
A map of Sir Humphry Mackworth's estate at Neath, in South Wales, drawn about 1697, shows *The new Roads or Wagon ways to ye Water side* denoted by the letter O. Again, no convention had yet developed for distinguishing railways from roads on maps.

Right.
A rough map drawn in 1737 shows the line of the Tranent to Cockenzie Waggonway as a dashed line from *Tranent* to *Cockeny* [sic].

Far right.
This map, surveyed in 1799, shows how the Tranent to Cockenzie Waggonway traversed the battlefield of Prestonpans, fought in 1745.

Below.
The Tranent to Cockenzie Waggonway is depicted in light green and labelled *Railway* on this 1824–25 map.

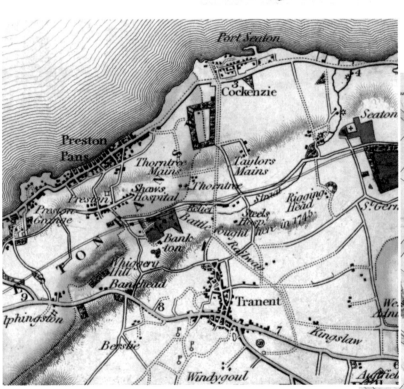

when it was rebuilt in 1785: a strip of malleable (wrought) iron 1¾ inches wide and ¾ inch thick was nailed to the top of 4-inch-square "foreign fir" wood rails.

One waggonway for which there are excellent drawings that enable us to see this was Ralph Allen's wooden railway in Bath, Somerset. Allen was the postmaster of Bath an elegant Georgian town with Roman baths. He owned excellent building stone quarries, and in 1731 he had a wooden railway built to transport the blocks of stone down to the River Avon. The rails were made of square cuts of oak, and the wagons, illustrated here, had cast-iron flanged wheels. They descended by gravity, with the speed being

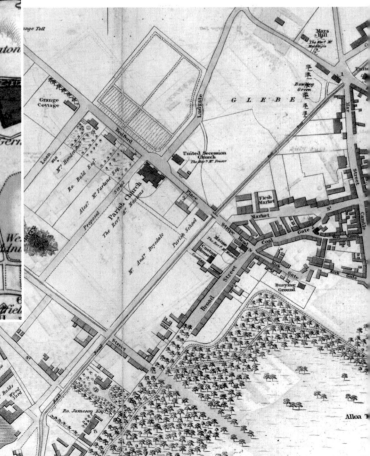

Above.
The Alloa Waggonway is shown running diagonally across this 1825 town plan of Alloa, where it is labelled as a *Rail Road*. The *Quay* at the *Harbour* is on the River Forth.

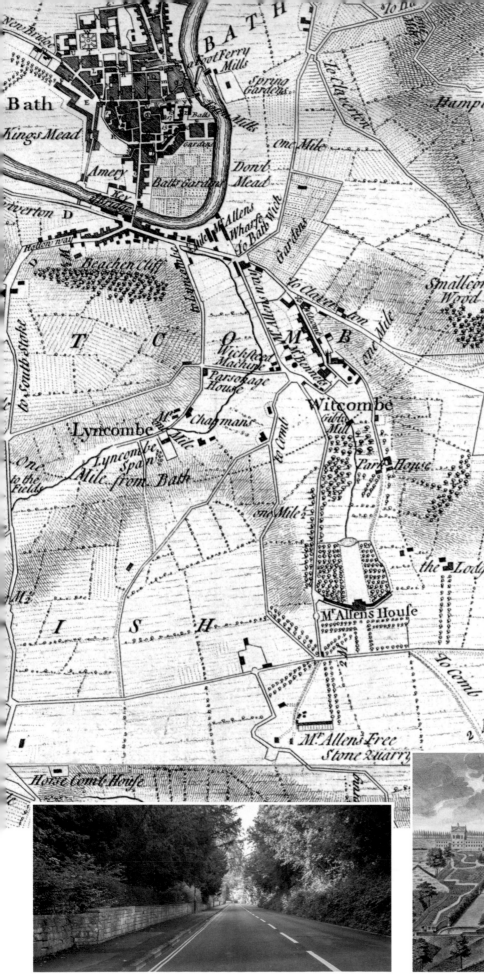

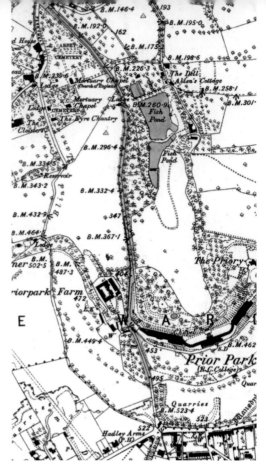

Left.

The route of Ralph Allen's wooden railway can be traced on this 1742 map, with reference to the red highlighted line on the map *above*, which is from 1885. *Mr. Allen's Free Stone Quarry* is where the waggonway began, running downhill, past *Mr Allens House* to *Mr Allens Wharf*, on the River Avon. It is labelled as *Mr Allens Way* near the river. There is no doubt as to whose waggonway it was!

Below.

A coloured engraving from 1752 shows Prior Park, Allen's estate, with the railway running beside it. This is said to be the earliest depiction of a railway in Britain.

Below, left.

Looking up Ralph Allen Drive, Bath, as it is today. This was the waggonway route; Prior Park is on the left.

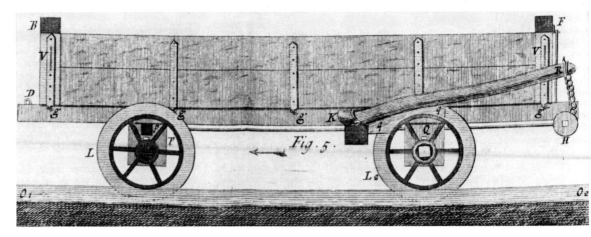

Right and *below*.
We owe these detailed technical drawings of Ralph Allen's wagons to J.T. Desaguliers, a philosopher and engineer who had been one of Isaac Newton's assistants. It clearly shows the flanged wheels running on square-sectioned wooden rails, with a brake to slow descent when necessary; it was quite steep in places, as can be seen from the modern photo of Ralph Allen Drive.

controlled by a crude brake, and empty wagons were hauled uphill again by two horses. If the illustration *below, left,* is to be believed, there was only a single track. Allen's railway was technically advanced for its time, and does not seem to have been copied locally at all; indeed, on Allen's death in 1764 it was dismantled, though that may have been because the quarry was exhausted.

Allen has another distinction. When it became necessary to take stone across the river for use in building in the centre of Bath, he used barges with the same rails on them—the first instance of a train ferry! He also constructed a temporary self-acting inclined plane (see page 98) to transport stone when he was building a Palladian bridge in his estate below his house. Certainly Allen seems to have used all the modern technology he could get his hands on.

At Whitehaven, in Cumbria, the harbour was improved in 1735, and, to better serve the coastal coalfield, waggonways were built converging on staiths—locally called *hurries*—where the coal was loaded onto ships, mainly bound for Ireland. The harbour ends of the *Waggon Roads* and *Waggon Way* are shown on the map, *right*. Wagons descended the hill to the harbour by gravity, and the empties were hauled back up the hill by a horse. There was a substantial increase in capacity by using this system, as compared with the previously used pack horses. Some 32 horses and men delivered 150 loaded wagons a day to the harbour.

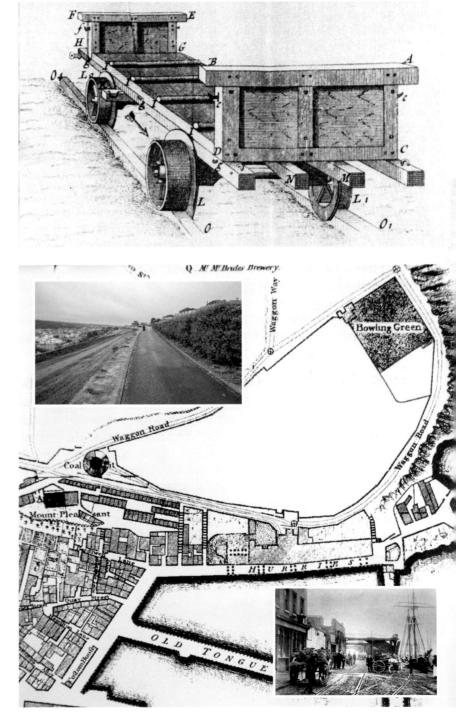

Right.
*Waggon Road*s and a *Waggon Way* are shown leading to the *Hurries* (staiths) with spouts in Whitehaven Harbour in this 1799 map. The circles with crosses are turntable switches. The waggonway at top was extended to make an inclined plane, the Howgill Incline, in 1813 (see page 96).
Inset, top, is the view today looking east (left) from the location of the turntable switch immediately above the hurries.
Inset, bottom, is an undated photo of the Whitehaven hurries.

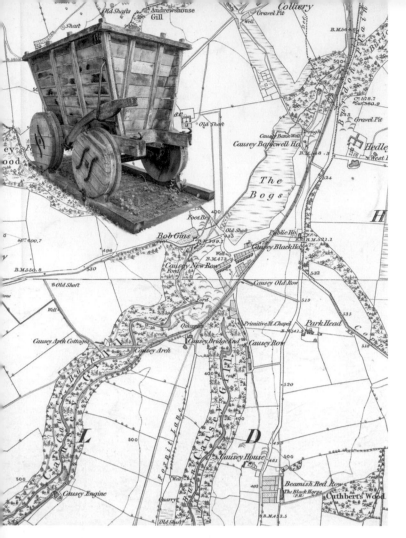

The first Act of Parliament passed to authorize a railway was for a wooden line in Leeds, from the Middleton coal mines of Charles Brandling to staiths in the town, where the coal was transferred to carts. It received Royal Assent on 9 June 1758. A map showing the route is on *page 115*, because this line was also the first to carry a working steam locomotive—that of John Blenkinsop in 1812 (see pages 112–13).

This 1758 legislation is important because a parliamentary act gave permission for the compulsory purchase of land where needed, a critical feature for an engineering work of a linear nature such as a railway. Without it, most lines could not have been built, for there was always at least one landowner in the way thinking he could extort money by being a holdout. Only in the northeast was this system not used very much; there the voluntary wayleave system was usually brought into play (see page 22).

The 1758 act mentions, interestingly, iron rails, but almost certainly oak rails with a renewable strip of beechwood on top were used at Middleton, with wagon wheels also being made of beech, with

Left.
An 1857 map shows the location of the 105-foot span of *Causey Arch* and the main line of the Tanfield Waggonway, by then a standard railway (in red). The line across the arch (green) was one of several branches on that side of *Causey Burn*, and the line joined a main line just beyond the bridge. Causey Arch as it is today, restored and fitted with handrails for the public path, is shown in the photo *below*.

Inset. A possibly not totally accurate replica of a wooden wagon as used on this waggonway. Note the flanged wooden wheels that could not have lasted very long.

Left and *right*.
The Tanfield Waggonway was later used by the North Eastern Railway for a standard-gauge railway line, and it is used today by the heritage Tanfield Railway, seen here. *Left* is track near Causey Arch (*A* on the map, *far left*) and *right* is a train leaving Andrews House, previously the name of a colliery in this location (marked on the map, *far left*, as *B*).

a circular metal plate nailed to the rim of the inner face as a flange, much like those at Ralph Allen's waggonway in Bath (see page 19).

The world's largest concentration of wooden waggonways was on the northeastern England coalfield of Northumberland and Durham. First used around 1608 (and the map on *page 15*, dated 1637, was the first to show one), scattered wooden lines lasted until well into the nineteenth century where it was deemed uneconomical to replace them with iron. Iron straps on top of wooden rails to reduce friction and decrease wear appeared around 1790 and demonstrated the utility of iron rails, the next development.

Below.
Dated 13 May 1761, this map shows the extensive radial network of waggonway branches on Tanfield Moor, upstream of Causey Arch, mainly as they were in the period 1729–61. The main line to the River Tyne from Tanfield Moor is shown on the 1788 map on *page 25*, but that map does not show the detail depicted here. The route to the Tyne on this map is off at top right. The considerable web of waggonways of competing owners sometimes led to lawsuits and even violence; the requirement for wayleaves—permission to cross an owner's land on payment of a rent—meant that colliery owners could sometimes find themselves denied any route to the river and thus were unable to sell their coal anywhere but the pithead, where it had the least value.

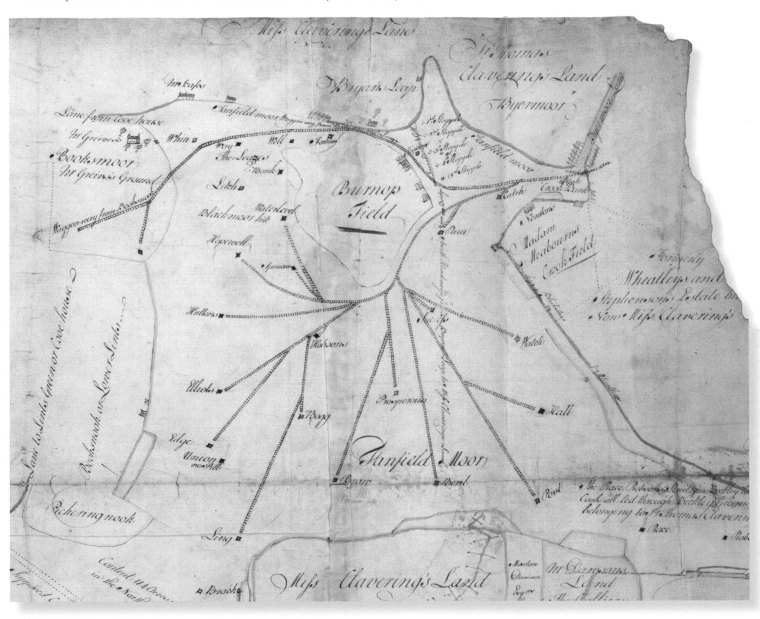

Waggonways made possible the economic exploitation of coal resources that were distant from navigable water. Without them, coal could not find a larger market in Newcastle or be shipped along the coast to London. Waggonways were of major importance, as is demonstrated by the multiple branches and substantial structures built to facilitate them. One waggonway crossed the gorge of Causey Burn—a tributary of the River Team, which flows into the Tyne—by means of a large stone bridge, the famous Causey Arch (map and photo, *previous pages*), sometimes called Tanfield Arch. It was expensive to build and shows that the money expected to be made from its use was substantial. The arch is the oldest surviving railway bridge in the world. It was built in 1725–26 by a powerful group of colliery owners, known as the Grand Allies, to service Tanfield Colliery. It is a measure of the continuing changes to the routes of waggonways—as new pits opened and old ones closed—that there appear to be no maps that show the original route across the arch. It is known that several branches met there and wagons were charged a toll for crossing. Two tracks crossed the arch—one for descending full wagons and one for the returning empties. Yet the colliery the waggonway principally served was closed after its destruction by fire in 1739, so the arch was not in use for very long. This early waggonway also included, farther downstream, a large embankment 100 feet high and 300 feet wide, a huge earthwork for the time.

The use of wayleaves, where a waggonway owner paid the owner of the land it crossed a rent in return for permission to cross the land, was characteristic of the northeast coalfield. There are, naturally enough, many maps showing the land ownership in relation to a waggonway that were drawn for the purpose of calculating, or illustrating, the rents that were due to the various landowners. One such map is on *page 133, top right*, of the Killingworth Waggonway.

Wooden waggonways, as also the iron ones that superseded them, could be quite ephemeral. They often did not require extensive engineering, merely following the lie of the land as much as possible. Where earthworks were needed, it was to maintain an even slope down to the staiths, to avoid the necessity of coupling and decoupling horses every time the line changed from going down to going up, and vice versa. Pitheads often moved quite frequently, too, as the coal strata were worked out, and this explains why some waggonways shown on a map only a few years from another might be quite different. John Gibson's map of the northeast coalfield (*overleaf*) shows some lines in detail, while others, particularly north of the Tyne, are not shown at all, and many of the lines are different from those on the Akenhead map (*pages 28–29*), only nineteen years later.

Two substantial discoveries of old wooden waggonways show exactly how they were made. The first, found in 1996, was at

Below.

Another famous waggonway was that of Wylam Colliery, shown here on an enlargement of part of a 1788 map by John Gibson (*overleaf*). The colliery was too far upstream for the keelboats (which took coal to near the mouth of the Tyne for transhipment onto larger ships). The wooden waggonway was laid down in 1748 to transport coal to *Lemington Staith,* which was the farthest upstream the keelboats could reach. It was converted to an iron plateway in 1808, and it was here that William Hedley's *Puffing Billy* and *Wylam Dilly* first ran (see page 120).

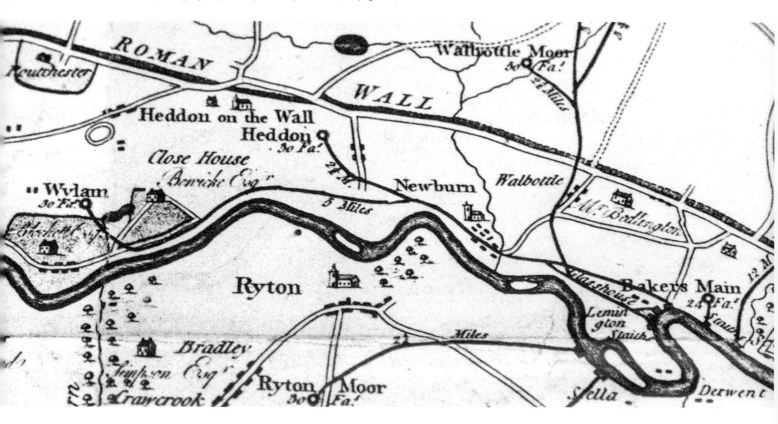

Above.
A section of a 1750 wooden waggonway thought to be from the Grove Rake lead mine at Rookhope, Durham, and now in the National Railway Museum. Wooden rails are held in place with wooden sleepers.

Lambton or Bournmoor D Pit, just west of Houghton-le-Spring in Durham. Over 150 yards of track were exposed. It probably dates to about 1791, when the pit was opened. The gauge was 4 feet, 2 inches. It was found underneath the location of more recent trackwork, consistent with the fact that the pit began replacing wooden rails with iron in 1813.

In 2013 archaeological excavations were carried out at the Neptune Shipyard on north Tyneside prior to redevelopment. They unearthed quite a large amount of well-preserved wooden

Below.
A replica wooden waggonway at Beamish Museum, complete with chaldron wagon and even a carefully placed burned-out stagecoach in the background!

Right.
John Gibson's 1788 map of the northeast coalfield, with many of the principal waggonways shown in red. All are wooden lines. It seems not to be comprehensive, showing only a selection of waggonways rather than all but still gives an appreciation of the large number of lines in existence at that date. One of the earlier long lines, the Plessey Waggonway, ran from *Plessey* to the staiths at *Blyth* and was built in 1699. On this map it is shown only from *Blyth* Pit to the sea, though it was in use until at least 1813. The Killingworth Waggonway (see *page 129*) is not shown at all, despite at least part of it existing as early

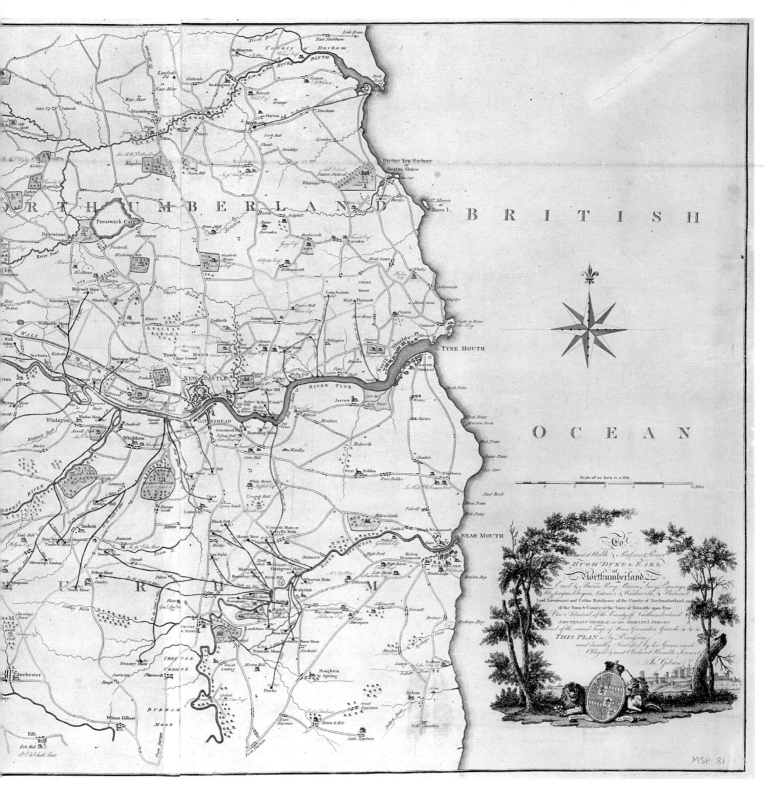

as 1764. Long wooden waggonways to the River Tyne at or near *Dunstan Staiths* (which closed only in 1990) include the Tanfield Waggonway to *South Moor* and *Tanfield Moor*, completed in various sections between 1725 and 1738. Long waggonways trending east to the *River Wear* include those to *Beamish South Moor* (c. 1780), *Pelton Moor* (1746–87), and *Deanry Moor* (1779), and north to the Wear from *Ducks* (West Rainton). The cartouche is interesting, in that it illustrates waggonway operation. A full chaldron wagon is descending the slope to the staith leading a horse (as also in the illustration at *right*; note the smaller wooden back wheel for the brake); and an empty chaldron is going uphill, now being pulled by the horse. A pithead steam engine works at the colliery at right. Note also in the key the tables of dues payable for the use of keelboats to transport the coal from river staith to seagoing ships at the rivers' mouths.

waggonway track; it is shown in the photos on these pages. The track had a gauge of 4 feet, 8 inches—the so-called Stephenson or standard gauge—and is the earliest evidence of that gauge, as it has been identified as part of the Willington Waggonway, built in the 1780s. Some of the wood used was recovered from ships of the time—an example of early recycling! (Incidentally, the timeline of this site, from wooden coal waggonway to shipyard to wind-power-blade production facility, well illustrates changing technologies over time.)

There were two sets of track. A heavy-duty main way had two pieces of wood, one on top of the other, to facilitate repairs due to wear. A loop descended into a dip, which would have been filled with water, the purpose being to try to stop the wooden wheels of the coal wagons from drying out and cracking.

The Kenton & Coxlodge Waggonway was built over this part of the Willington Waggonway between 1808 and 1813.

(Continued on page 30.)

Above.

The location of the wooden waggonway discovered in Neptune Shipyard in 2013 is marked in red on an 1858 map. Here it appears to form part of the later iron-railed *Gosforth & Kenton Wagon Way* (Kenton & Coxlodge Waggonway), which in fact was built over this part of the Willington Waggonway between 1808 and 1813, and today is on the southwest side of Benton Way in Wallsend. Photos *above* and *right* show archaeologists working on the excavation of the waggonway in June 2013. The excellent state of preservation of the wood is likely because of the wet conditions here, which tend to exclude the oxygen necessary for decay.

Above and *right*.

The probable line of waggonway of which the Neptune Shipyards discovery is part is shown on both the 1788 Gibson map (*above*) and the 1807 Akenhead map (*right; see overleaf* for whole map). Both show the line originating at *Biggs Main* Colliery. Note that by the time of the 1858 map (*below, left*) no trace of this wooden waggonway appears, although it is on the line of the *Gosforth and Kenton Wagon Way* (Kenton & Coxlodge Waggonway). Over time, knowledge of the location of wooden waggonways was often lost unless they were mapped.

Plan of the Rivers TYNE & WEAR with the Collieries

Waggon-ways & Staiths, thereon
And the Principal Roads & Villages.
also a Plan of
NEWCASTLE UPON TYNE

N.B. The Waggon ways from the Collieries to the Staiths on each river are represented by dotted lines.

Lambert   Sculpt.

This map published in 1807 by D. Akenhead of Newcastle shows a well-developed system of waggonways existing by that time, the vast majority still wooden railed. The waggonways are marked by thin dotted lines and are thus rather hard to see. The mines in the eastern part of County Durham are not yet developed; they were deeper pits bored through the overlying limestone.

Killingworth
Backworth
Earsdon
Monk Seaton
Killingworth or
New York
Whitley
New Benton
Murton Main
120 Fa.
Shire Moor 45 Fa.
Cullercoates
Long Benton
105 Fa.
Moor House
Forest Hall
Moor Houses
Preston
Gosforth
Tynemouth
Rising Sun
Shipley
Long Benton
Willington
Castle
Landsale
Gosforth
Willington
121 Fa.
Fort Tynemouth
Jesmond
Biggs Main
90 Fa.
Walls-end
SHIELDS
Roman Station
Chirton
Heaton
Benton House
Walls-end
Percy Main or
82 Fa.
105 Fa.
Howdon
119 Fa.
Carville
Dock
Flatworth
S. SHIELDS
Roman Wall
RIVER TYNE
Byker
Hebburn Quay
123 Fa.
Wyril Point
Walker
132 Fa.
Walls-end
Jarrow Slake
Westoe
& S. Hebburn
Hebburn Main
& Temple Main
Park
Marsden Roc
S. Anthons
100 Fa.
Jarrow
GATESHEAD
Hebburn Hall
Low Simonside
Harton
Tyne Main &
Bill Quay
Monkton
High Simonside
Marsden Hall
Gateshead Park
68 Fa.
G. Park
Brandling Main
Hedworth
Beckham
80 Fa.
Biddick
Sunnyside
Hall
Felling
Carr's Hill
Heworth
Wardley
Cleadon
Carrs Hill
80 Fa.
E. Boldon
DURHAM
H. Heworth
Fell Gate
Whitehouse
Laverick Hall
W. Boldon
Whitburn
Com.
N. Tolonsby
Scots House
Main
Usworth Hall
Hilton Bridge
124 Fa.
Roca Point
Sheriff Hill
G. Usworth
Handstone
92 Fa.
Futwell
ghton Banks
L. Usworth
Usworth or
Hilton Castle
Russell Main
Washington
Southwick
MONKW. WEARMOUTH
77 Fa.
Rectory Main
Hilton
Pallion
Battery
Oxclose 70 Fa.
Ferry
Bramston
Highford
B. Wearmouth
SUNDERLAND
Wentworth
N. Biddick Hall
Hendon Lodge
Milbank
RIVER WEAR
High Barns
& Boundary Main
Fatfield
Cocks Green
Low Barns
Blew House
75 Fa.
Offerton
Peareth Main
Staiths
Painsher
60 Fa.
84 Fa.
Wharton
70 Fa.
80 Fa.
Harraton
Biddick Main
Eden Main
Hall
Hutton
60 Fa.
Hope Bay
Lambton Hall
Seam
W. Harrington
Lambton Main
60 Fa.
Bourn Moor
Dean
63 Fa.
Newbottle
Primrose Main
Newbottle Bourn Moor
60 Fa.
60 Fa.
Lumley
Rence House
Seaham
Morton Hall
Houghton le Spring
Scale of Miles
Dalton Tower

Above.
The dandy cart, in which a horse could ride on downhill sections of a waggonway, is said to have been introduced by George Stephenson. Photographs of horses in dandy carts are rare. The one *above right* was taken in 1909, on an iron waggonway. The horse was carried downhill on the dandy cart, the rearmost wagon, here with a load of bricks from Throckley Brickworks (about 5 miles west of Newcastle; *Throckley* is shown on the map, *previous pages*) going generally downward to the River Tyne; the horse would pull the empty wagons back uphill. At left is an example in the National Railway Museum, York.

As both the 1788 Gibson and 1807 Akenhead maps illustrate, a considerable web of wooden waggonway lines that had been built up during the eighteenth century covered the northeast coalfield. Northeast England was certainly the heaviest user of waggonways, but there were many elsewhere, particularly in Shropshire and the Midlands, where wooden railways were considered just as important an adjunct to canals as the iron ones were a little later. Canal companies were empowered to build railways to feed their canals, at first just 1,000 yards from the canal and later 3 miles. But the wooden railways thus constructed tended to be short and local. At least one of these, the first Caldon Low Tramway, built in 1778 to feed the Caldon Branch of the Trent & Mersey Canal, also had iron strips nailed to the top surface of its wooden rails to promote longevity and reduce friction, a development that would eventually lead to the use of iron bars or plates by themselves (see page 36). And, interestingly, the lines in the Midlands tended to be called "railways," or in the case of Nottinghamshire and Derbyshire, "gangways" or "gangroads," rather than the northeastern "waggonways." ("Tramroad" or "tramway" was favoured in South Wales but referred only to plateways.) Wooden railways are often hard to trace on the ground today unless there are major earthworks, because the wood has long ago rotted away; maps can be the only record of their existence and, even then, because of their ephemeral nature they were often not shown on maps either.

It was inevitable that iron rails would supersede wooden ones. Northeast colliery manager and engineer John Buddle did a comparison in 1807. "A horse," Buddle wrote, "will do more work by 30 p. cent on an iron way than on a wooden way; but frequently he will do 50 and even 100 p. cent more." That, and the relative ease of maintenance and longevity of iron railways easily overcame the fact that they cost more to build in the first place. The future lay with iron rails.

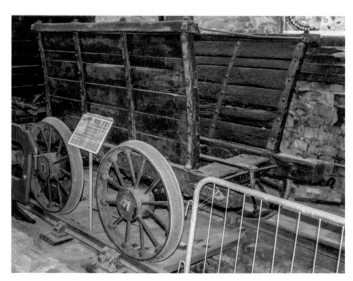

Above, left. A coal chaldron wagon from 1826 that was owned by the Cramlington Coal Company and used to transport coal to the River Tyne. It is now at the Shildon branch of the National Railway Museum.
Above, right. A similar chaldron wagon now at Beamish Museum. These wagons had trapdoors in their bottoms to facilitate unloading.

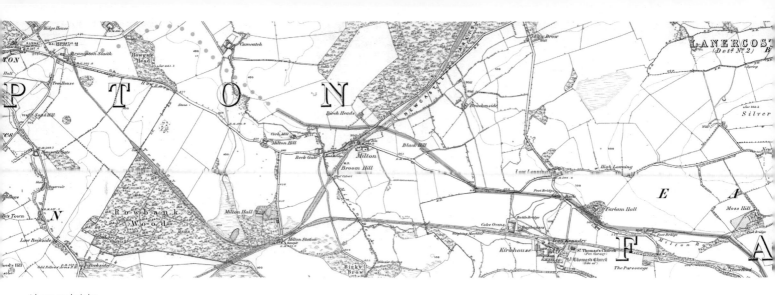

Above and *right*.

Lord Carlisle owned coal mines in the northern part of what was then Cumberland and western Northumberland and wished to develop them by building a railway west to Brampton, his nearest market. In 1798 a wooden waggonway was laid to Brampton from pits at the foot of Tindale Fell, a distance of about 4 miles. The western end of the waggonway is traceable for the most part, and it is shown in red on this 1863-surveyed map. The line was progressively extended eastwards to service coal mines on the face of Tindale Fell; the line is shown in red on the map at *right*, and the cut made across the face of the fell by this wooden railway is still visible today (photo, *below*). By the time Tindale Fell was being laid with wooden rails—1808—the western part of the route had already been relaid with cast-iron rails. That year this railway, which had been a relatively late user of wooden rails, became one of the first to try out new malleable- or wrought-iron rails—and very successfully at that. The railway was later frequently visited by engineers assessing the suitability of malleable iron for their railways. Visiting in 1818, Scottish engineer Robert Stevenson wrote that "malleable iron road is found to answer the purpose in every respect better." In 1836 this railway, relaid on a slightly different routing (shown on the left side of the map *above*, *top*) became home to a locomotive sold by the Liverpool & Manchester Railway as being no longer strong enough to pull its trains—Robert Stephenson's famous *Rocket*.

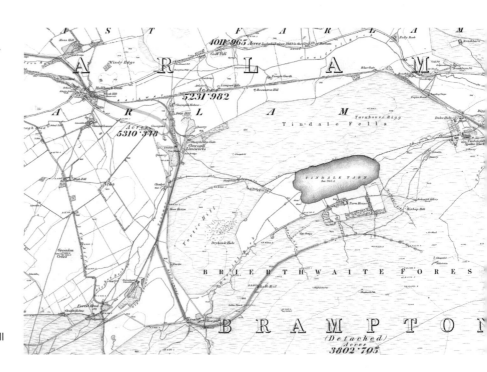

The Impellent Force of Fire

The other component of a modern railway, a source of mechanical motive power, was a concept that had been around for a very long time; its development into something practical had to await the beginning of the nineteenth century. Low-pressure steam required large—and thus very immobile—machines to work at all. Higher-pressure steam was needed, but the technology required to contain such pressures simply was not available. Thus, there were far more designs and concepts than workable machines.

Hero of Alexandria is credited with the first steam engine of any sort, his "aeolipile" of first-century Roman Egypt. It was a metal sphere that contained water. Steam was ejected from four directional spouts when heated by a fire underneath, causing the sphere to rotate.

In 1606 Jerónimo de Ayanz y Beaumont was granted a patent in Spain for a steam-powered water pump, which successfully drained some mines. In the 1690s French inventor Denis Papin devised a way of creating a vacuum in a cylinder using condensing steam, enough to allow a piston to raise weights on a rope and pulley, but he never developed the idea beyond a laboratory working model. He also invented the safety valve.

Above.
One of the first attempts to apply steam at moderate pressure to move a vehicle was this engine by French artillery officer Nicolas Joseph Cugnot, which worked for a while in 1769. Intended to haul artillery, it was near impossible to steer—the boiler is at the front, making it very "front heavy"—and it crashed into a wall on its first outing in Paris. But the concept was sound even if its manifestation was not. This is a replica in the Deutsche Bahn Museum in Nuremberg, Germany; the original survives and is shown *overleaf.*

The first steam engine to be applied industrially was a "fire engine" devised by Thomas Savery of Exeter in 1698. Marketed as the "Miner's Friend," it used a vacuum created by condensing steam to pump water, combined with higher-pressure steam to force the water higher still. His design—"a steam chamber device for raising water by the impellant force of fire"—was patented in 1698. It allowed water to be pumped up as much as 40 feet, but the technology to contain the higher-pressure steam had not yet been perfected, and one of his pumps blew up spectacularly in 1705.

The first commercially successful steam engine, correctly an atmospheric engine since it pumped by means of a vacuum

The ENGINE for Raifing Water (with a power made) by Fire

Right.
This may be the first vehicle driven by steam. Water boiled in a sphere was funnelled to a sort of turbine, which was to drive the wheels using steam pressure. The designer was Ferdinand Verbiest, a Flemish Jesuit missionary in China in the 1670s. It is not clear whether Verbiest ever actually built the vehicle; it is more likely that he built a working model.

Left.
Engraved in 1717, this is Thomas Newcomen's first steam *Engine for Raising Water (with a power made) by Fire*, which was installed at a mine in Devon about 1712. It worked at about twelve strokes per minute.

rather than steam pressure per se, was that of Thomas Newcomen, who sold equipment to the mining industry of southwest England and saw first-hand the problems encountered because of flooding in the mines. Newcomen modified the principles of Savery's engine to create a commercially successful product, but he had to work under Savery's patent, which covered all power produced by "the impellant force of fire," until 1733, when it expired. During that time he installed at least eighty-three of his engines, eight of which were in continental Europe; by 1775 over six hundred Newcomen engines had been built. Newcomen used a cylinder with a piston to which steam was admitted and then condensed by a water spray, creating a vacuum; then atmospheric pressure forced the piston down. The piston was connected to a large beam, which operated the pump in the mine (illustration, *left, bottom*).

Newcomen's engines worked but were not very efficient, largely because the cylinder cooled each time water was injected to condense the steam. Scottish inventor James Watt solved this issue by having a separate condenser so that the main cylinder remained hot. He had hit on this solution after repairing a model of a Newcomen engine belonging to the University of Glasgow. In 1768 he partnered with Matthew Boulton, who owned a "manufactory" in Birmingham that produced iron goods, to build his engine, and the firm of Boulton & Watt was created.

Above.
The oldest surviving Boulton & Watt engine, "Old Bess," built in 1777, on display at the Science Museum in London. Considered a halfway step to a proper factory engine, it does not yet have rotative motion and was used to assist the water wheel at Boulton's Soho manufactory in Birmingham. When the river was low, it pumped water back upstream so that it could be used to drive the water wheel once more, thus achieving rotary motion in a roundabout fashion.

The following year he was granted a patent for "a new method of lessening the consumption of steam and fuel in fire engines," which he would enforce with such vigour in the next few decades as to throttle most other inventors who sought to improve it.

In 1782 Watt, to circumvent an existing patent for a flywheel and crank mechanism, produced a rotative engine that converted up-and-down motion to turn a wheel using a "sun and planet" motion.

By 1804, when Watt's original condensing-engine patent ran out, Boulton & Watt had made about 450 engines. Newcomen engines continued to be made—though less efficient, they were cheaper—so that by this date (notably the year Trevithick would demonstrate his first railway locomotive; see page 104) there were at least a thousand steam engines working in Britain alone. But it would require higher-pressure steam to develop engines that could move themselves.

Left.
Also in the Science Museum is this Boulton & Watt rotative engine built in 1788. The mechanism that converted the vertical motion to a rotation is nearest the camera. This engine drove 43 polishing machines for 70 years.

Such a self-propelled vehicle seems first to have been invented by the French military engineer Nicolas Joseph Cugnot, whose lumbering and virtually unsteerable steam vehicle of 1769 is illustrated on these pages. Though arguably the first automobile, it was not really a practical solution.

One that might have been practical was designed by William Murdoch (anglicized to Murdock), a Scottish engineer who worked with Boulton and Watt as their principal steam-engine installer. About 1784, while resident in Redruth, Cornwall, Murdoch made a model steam road vehicle (photo, *right*) that worked, at first running around his house, and then outdoors. But he was dissuaded from developing the idea further by Boulton and Watt. He was very good at his job, and they did not want to lose him to experimental schemes, but no doubt Watt saw this as a potential threat to his dominance in the steam-engine industry. Watt was also known to have an aversion to anything but very low-pressure steam, perhaps not unreasonably, considering the difficulty of fabricating reliably strong high-pressure boilers at the time.

However, Murdoch had a working concept, and there is little doubt that had he continued to work on his idea, he would have had road steam locomotives and perhaps even railway locomotives before Richard Trevithick finally did. As it was, it was not until fifteen years later that Trevithick reached the same stage as Murdoch was at in 1784. History might have been quite different.

Richard Trevithick's road steam vehicles are illustrated on page 109.

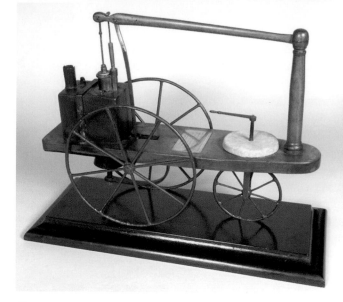

Above.
William Murdoch's 1784 model of a steam road vehicle. Had Murdoch ignored his employers, Matthew Boulton and James Watt, early steam locomotive history might have been quite different.

One other application of mobile steam should be mentioned here, and that was in boats. Unlike a land vehicle running out of necessity on usually atrocious roads, a boat could much more easily house a heavy steam engine and use it to drive a paddle or something similar that would move the boat forward.

The first steam-driven boat was the *Palmipède*, made by a French inventor, the Marquis Claude de Jouffroy d'Abbans, and tested in 1776. The boat had a Newcomen engine that drove paddlewheels. It was barely able to move, and in 1783 he built another boat, the *Pyroscaphe* (photo, *left*), which moved upstream on the Saône River for fifteen minutes before failing. The French Revolution put an end to de Jouffroy d'Abbans's inventions.

In the newly independent United States of America, a surveyor, John Fitch, developed a steamboat of his own design, named *Perseverance*, which he successfully tried out on the Delaware River in 1787. It used an amazing mechanical rowing

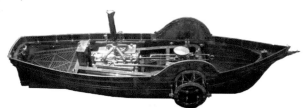

Above.
De Jouffroy d'Abbans's 1783 paddle steamboat, *Pyroscaphe*.
Below.
William Symington's paddle steamer *Charlotte Dundas*.

system to propel itself, but even more amazing was the fact that Fitch built the boat's steam engine to a Watt design using nothing more than illustrations, as Watt engines were not allowed to be exported to Britain's lost colony at that time. Fitch's steamboat was successful, carrying passengers at speeds up to 8 miles per hour for a cumulative total of several thousand miles.

In Britain the first commercially successful steamboat was the *Charlotte Dundas*, which inventor William Symington first demonstrated in 1803 by pulling two barges along the Forth & Clyde Canal to Glasgow against a gale-force wind that would allow nothing else to move. But now we are well into Trevithick territory; he developed his first road steam vehicle in 1797 and in 1804 would demonstrate the first rail steam locomotive (see page 104). His inventions used high-pressure steam, which would become the key to steam traction. And rails would enable the side-stepping of atrocious roads.

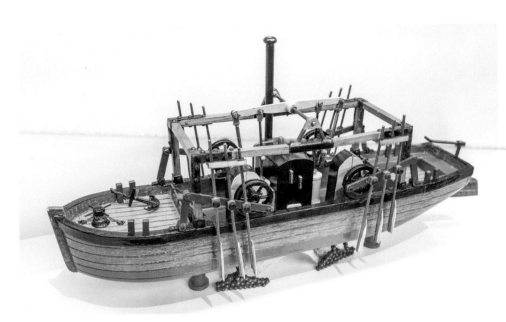

Above.
John Fitch's 1787 steamboat, which used a mechanical rowing system to propel itself. This is a model in the Deutsches Technikmuseum in Berlin.

Below.
The original Nicolas Joseph Cugnot steam vehicle of 1769, now in the Musée des Arts et Métiers in Paris.

Iron Rails

The transition from wooden to iron rails was one of the significant events on the road to the modern railway. The first rails were made of cast iron, then wrought iron (called malleable iron at the time), and finally, from 1857 on, steel. And the form of the rail itself underwent much evolution.

The first use of iron rails was as a strip of iron fastened to the top of wooden rails to provide a more durable running surface with lower friction; it was found that a horse could draw much more weight than it could on a wooden waggonway without the plates. Although there are earlier claims, the first documented use of such strips seems to have been in 1767, when the ironworks at Coalbrookdale in Shropshire cast 5 or 6 tons of rails, flat strips of iron 5 feet long, 4 inches wide, and 1¾ inches thick, which were nailed to existing oak rails. At least 20 miles of such composite rails were in use around Coalbrookdale by 1785. By 1787, probably because of family connections between the two areas, the idea had been transferred to the valleys of South Wales. The first Caldon Low Tramway of 1778 (see page 48), which had iron strips on top of wood, appears to have been the first iron railway approved by an Act of Parliament. Cast-iron flanged wheels, the other half of this low-friction system, appear to have been relatively widespread by the 1750s, and, as we have seen (page 19), were used by Ralph Allen at Prior Park in 1731.

About 1787, a Sheffield colliery manager, John Curr, started using L-shaped plates to guide wagons underground, and although he may not have actually invented them, he did devise a quite complicated system for their use, with crossovers and switches. His system, which he published in a book in 1797, soon once again showed up in South Wales. Canal and railway engineer Benjamin Outram constructed a number of these so-called plate-ways and advised on others (see below). Here the all-important guiding flange was on the rail rather than on the wheel.

By 1794, the Forest Line of the Leicester Navigation (see page 73) had been completed using an edge rail. William Jessop, the line's engineer, is reputed to have devised the inside-flanged wheel to run on a flat rail surface after he had been faced with opposition to the L-rail by turnpike commissioners, whose road he would have to cross, and who believed that the vertical rail surface of an L-plate design would hinder road traffic. Whether this story is accurate is open to debate, but the line was built with edge rails. Another engineer, Thomas Dadford Jr., adopted the edge rail in South Wales for the Blaenavon and Beaufort lines, completed in 1796 and 1799, respectively, though the first order for the rails dates to 1792.

For the next fifty years some railways in South Wales were built as plateways and others as edge railways, depending on the preferences of their owners, and are thus treated separately. In northeast England, however, although plateways were occasionally used (notably at Wylam Colliery from 1808 to 1830; see page 120), most waggonways used edge rails with flanged wheels. Both types of rail evolved to become stronger and fit together better, and the shape of the edge rail changed from a bar of iron to an I shape and many other shapes in between. Both types became longer, and to support the beam a so-called fishbelly shape was sometimes used, so that the rail was thicker in the middle where it was unsupported. The L-plate eventually lost out to the edge rail because it was a weaker design, and friction was caused by stones and earth that were deposited on the horizontal surface. The development that really advanced the world towards the modern railway, however, was the use of malleable or wrought iron, which was considerably less prone to breakage than cast iron.

Iron rails and iron wheels. A is a wheel running on an L-shaped plateway. Although the wheel would in theory also run on a road, in practice this would hardly ever occur, as the narrow rim would quickly sink into the ground. This example is from the Bicslade Tramroad in the Forest of Dean (see page 61). B is a flanged wheel on a flat or I-shaped rail; this is the arrangement we know today. This is a coal wagon wheel at Haig Pit, Whitehaven. C is a double-flanged wheel, running on a flat or rounded rail. Though an unusual development, this configuration was common in the slate quarry railways of North Wales. This one is from the Nantlle Railway (see page 88) and is on display at the Narrow Gauge Railway Museum at Tywyn, Wales.

At *right* is a display of rail cross-sections from Penrhyn Castle's Industrial Railway Museum in Bangor, Wales. The museum does not have record of the origins of each, but it shows an originally round design (at left) from the Penrhyn Quarry Railway (see page 84) and many different designs, including inverted U and T shapes, and more conventional I-shaped rail (at right).

Above.

This index map from a guide to the canals and railways of Britain published in 1830 serves to illustrate the considerable number of iron railways (shown as double black lines) in use by that time. Numbered lines (highlighted in red) were lines for which an Act of Parliament had been required. Some were still under construction at this date. Lines authorized but not built are not highlighted. A few others that were built but did not require an act are shown in red only. The numbers of rail lines (but not canals, which are depicted as single black lines) shown on this map are referenced on page 265. By no means are all rail lines in existence in 1830 shown. There were many more, particularly in northeast England.

The railways in this section were pioneers of the concept of iron rails. The first group were plateways, the second edge railways, and all were horse drawn, at least initially, for it was not until 1830 or so that the notion of steam locomotive power became widespread. But these early iron railways sometimes provided a location for steam power to be tried out—notably on the Merthyr Tramroad in South Wales; Middleton, Leeds; the Orrell Colliery railway in Lancashire; the Butterley Gangroad in Derbyshire; the Kilmarnock & Troon Railway in Scotland; and on some of the northeast waggonways converted to iron rails—the Wylam, Kenton & Coxlodge, Heaton, Lambton, Wallsend, and Killingworth colliery waggonways, which together provided the track on which early steam had its first outings. These, since they are significant to the story of the early railway, are described in separate sections of this book. Notably, all of these uses of steam locomotion on iron rails took place *before* the dates often taken as the beginnings of railways as we know them, whether 1825 (the Stockton & Darlington Railway) or 1830 (the Liverpool & Manchester Railway).

Most of these early iron rail lines, like the wooden waggonways that preceded them, were built to augment the transportation system provided by canals or rivers and typically ran from a quarry, a mine, or works to the water. Many provided a more economical way to extend canals where the terrain had become too steep to warrant the construction of multiple locks. There were probably hundreds of these railways all over Britain, and those described here are but a selection of some of the most important. It was not until the late 1820s that this augmentation concept was broadly exported to other countries, with France (see page 240) and the United States (see page 230) being first.

Two of the leading engineers of the early iron railways were Benjamin Outram and William Jessop, both canal engineers before they were railway engineers. In 1790 Outram, the son of Joseph Outram, a businessman responsible for building the Cromford Canal, founded a iron foundry and ironworks called Benjamin Outram & Company (the name was changed to the Butterley Company in 1805, after Outram's death) with a partner, Francis Beresford, a local landowner. They purchased an estate—the Butterley Estate—along the canal's route, where they hoped to take advantage of the locally available coal, iron ore, and limestone (used for flux) together with the new distribution network provided by the canal. The following year William Jessop, then engineer for the canal, and John Wright, a Nottingham banker (and Beresford's son-in-law from 1791), joined the company as partners. While Outram favoured the L-plate rail, Jessop preferred the edge rail, but their company could just as easily manufacture both types (though the company did not supply the rails for all the rail lines they engineered).

The Iron Plateways

Outram was involved with no fewer than seven plateway railways before 1802: the Butterley Gangroad in 1793; the Little Eaton Gangway in 1795; a line from the Beggarlee Colliery to the Cromford Canal at Langley Mill in 1796 (though Outram engineered the line he did not build it); the Peak Forest Tramway in 1796; the Marple Railway in 1800 (a temporary line linking two sections of the Peak Forest Canal while locks were constructed); with Jessop, the Blisworth Railway on the Grand Junction Canal in 1801 (another temporary railway, connecting the canal while a tunnel was built); and the Ticknall Tramway, in 1802. Outram died in 1805, but other engineers continued to use plateways until 1825–30.

The Butterley Gangroad

Outram and Jessop wanted limestone for their furnaces at Butterley, and their partner Beresford purchased land near Crich, Derbyshire, that contained a suitable deposit. He also purchased land at Bullbridge, on the canal below Crich, for kilns and a wharf, and Outram built a railway line to connect the two, something the Act of Parliament for the canal empowered him to do. The rail line was completed in 1793, the same year as the canal. Running downhill on a sharply curving but relatively evenly graded route, the line passed under the village of Fritchley in a 90-foot-long tunnel, constructed using the "cut and cover" method—it is just below the road. This is considered to be the world's first railway tunnel (other than those in mines).

The L-plates were fastened to stone sleeper blocks laid directly onto the ground. The wagons full of limestone went downhill by gravity, and the empties were pulled back uphill by horses. It was a long-lasting line, being rebuilt and rerouted in 1846–50 with the opening of a new quarry (Hilt's Quarry) nearer to Crich village; the rail was changed from plateway to T-section edge rail. The line acquired a steam locomotive in 1869—a vertical boilered, chain-driven affair, which made the return of the empty wagons uphill a bit faster, though no doubt a lot noisier. Apart from its tunnel, the line's chief claim to fame is as the test site of William Brunton's first interesting and unique "walking horse" engine, which ran on this line in 1813 (see page 126). Brunton worked for the Butterley Company and simply used the gangroad as a convenient test site.

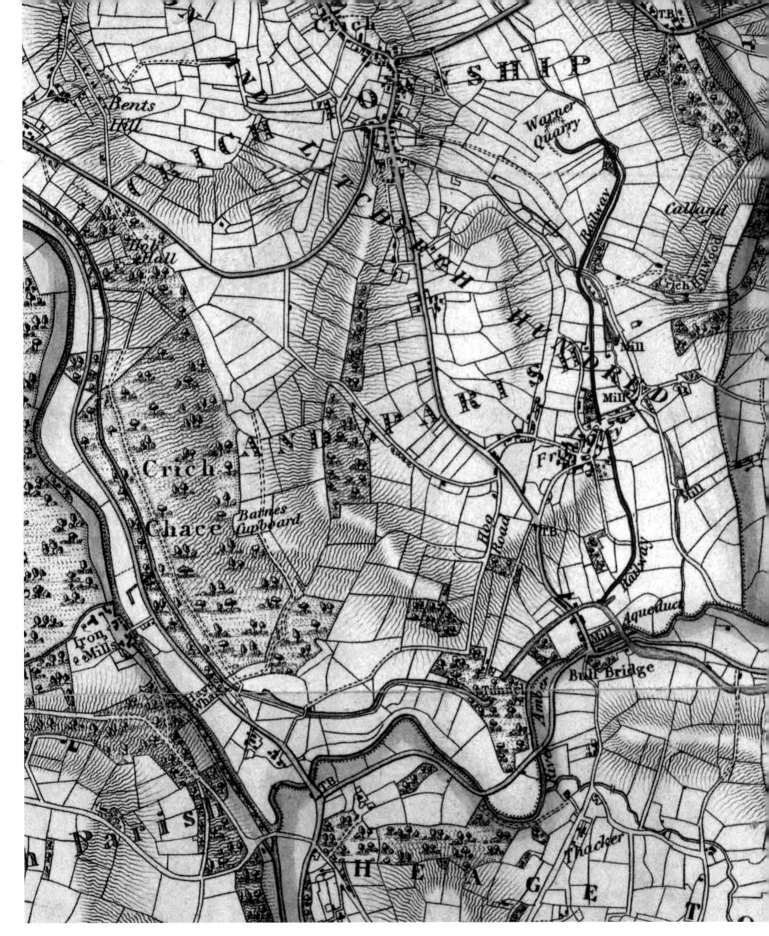

Above.
This map surveyed in 1835 shows the Butterley Gangroad, marked *Railway*, in red, running from *Warner Quarry*, the site of the original limestone quarry, to the Cromford Canal near *Bull Bridge*. At the halfway point there is a gap in the red line, the location of the world's first railway tunnel, at *Fritchley*.

The Butterley Gangroad Project of the Derbyshire Archaeological Society has erected a sign beside the Fritchley Tunnel that displays, along with other information, this photo (*left*) of the inside of the tunnel as excavated in 2013, now resealed. Built in 1793, it is now recognized by the *Guinness Book of World Records* as the world's oldest railway tunnel. Also at the site is this old wagon (*top left*) shown standing on both(!) L-plate rails as initially used by Outram and the flangeless rails installed on the 1846–50 realignment. Unfortunately the wagon has flanged wheels, which do not fit on the L-plate!

Above. This 2015 photo shows the 1846–50 alignment immediately north of the Fritchley Tunnel. The original and more curvy alignment is only the foreground, just before it enters the north end of the tunnel.

The Little Eaton Gangway

The Little Eaton Gangway, also known as the Derby Canal Tramroad, was built as a northward extension of the Derby Canal, and both were constructed at the same time. The canal ended at the village of Little Eaton, a few miles north of Derby, and the wharves built there became the starting point for the gangway.

Benjamin Outram was appointed chief engineer for the railway in 1793. He had previously surveyed a route for the canal to Denby collieries, but a second opinion provided by William Jessop suggested the canal end at Little Eaton and only a rail line be extended to the collieries, which was how it was built. Outram used L-shaped cast plate rails, though they were not supplied by his company. The rail line was partially opened in April 1794 and by May 1795 was complete to the collieries even before the canal was finished the following year. Although the line rose 100 feet over its 4½-mile length, horses were used to haul the wagons in both directions, with the slight downward slope assisting the horses with their full loads. The railway operated until 1908, a period well over a hundred years. It is one of the most photographically documented plateways, and the images reproduced here give a good idea of the way it was operated. Boxes were constructed to fit on each wagon's set of wheels such that the entire load could be lifted off and into waiting barges at the canal. It is thus a very early example of containerization. Outram promoted this concept, which seems to have been invented in 1766 by the canal engineer James Brindley.

Left. Little Eaton Wharf and the Derby Canal. A "container" of coal is being unloaded by crane into a barge.

Right. The fishbelly L-plate rails of the gangway. The top of the wagon is separate from its bottom, allowing the entire load to be lifted off. The ground between the rails has been filled in to provide a walkway for the horses.

The Little Eaton Gangway is well shown on this detailed 1835 map. The *Derby Canal* is at bottom and terminates at *Little Eaton*, some 4 miles north of Derby, at a *Wharf*. The *Railway* runs from there north to *Smithy Houses*, where it divides into two lines, to *Denby Colliery* and *Old Denby Colliery*. Two other branches connect other collieries.

Inset photos:
Top. A "gang" of four horses and eight wagons.
Bottom. Little Eaton Wharf. The fishbelly L-plate rails are clearly shown. Note the "container" crane in the background.

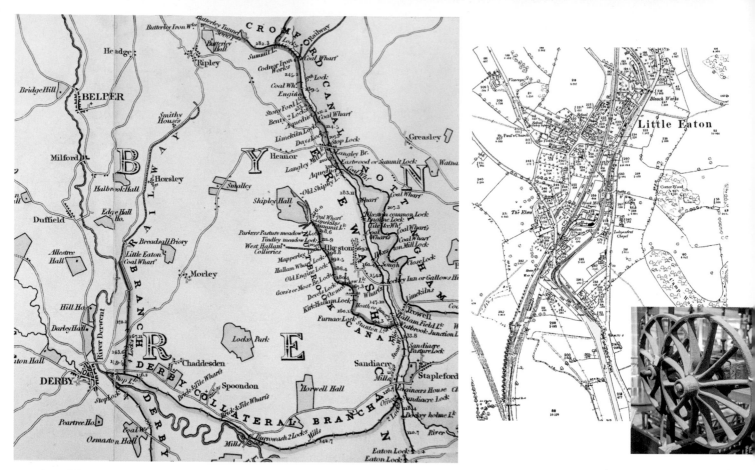

Above, left.
This map from about 1833 shows the Little Eaton Gangway (labelled *Railway*) and its surrounding area. It can be seen how the line connected with the canals of the region. The Derby Canal *Branch* is highlighted in red and connects with the Derby Canal south and east of the city of *Derby*. The *Butterley Iron Wrks.* is at the top of this map, on a tunnel through the *Cromford Canal*. The company used to load its barges in the canal tunnel via a hole from above, surely an unusual way of loading!

Above, right.
This later map (1881) shows in detail the junction of the Little Eaton Gangway with the northern end of the Derby Canal; this is the wharf shown in the photos on the *previous page*. The gangway has been highlighted in yellow.
Inset are a pair of wheels from a Little Eaton Gangway wagon now in the National Railway Museum. The flat rims ran on the L-plate rails.

The Peak Forest Tramway

The Peak Forest Tramway was another canal extension, in this case built where the route became too steep for the economical construction of a waterway. The Peak Forest Canal, authorized in 1794, was planned to connect Manchester with the lime quarries near Dove Holes, north of Buxton, Derbyshire. A railway, here termed a tramway, was authorized for the easternmost part of the route from Chapel Milton. Outram was the consulting engineer for the canal and, after another survey, found that beyond Bugsworth the gradient was unsuitable for a waterway, so he proposed instead to build a plateway.

The Peak Forest Tramway was built from a canal basin at Bugsworth (now Buxworth) to the quarries (map, *right*) and was largely opened by 1796, though not fully completed till three

years later. Parts of the route were so steep that an inclined plane (see page 98) was constructed near Chapel-en-le-Frith, where loaded wagons were let down in a controlled descent by the use a braking drum at the top of the incline; empty wagons were pulled up by the weight of the descending loaded ones. The rest of the line was worked by horses. The wagons, like those at Little Eaton, had detachable bodies, but a side was hinged at one end so that limestone would pour out when the box was tipped (photo, *right*). The tramway clearly worked very well, for it was in use for 130 years, finally ceasing operation only in 1926.

The Peak Forest Canal itself was incomplete until 1805. Until that year, a temporary plateway 1½ miles long had been used to ferry loads around a flight of sixteen locks under construction at Marple, then in Cheshire and now in Greater Manchester. Here the whole line was also an inclined plane.

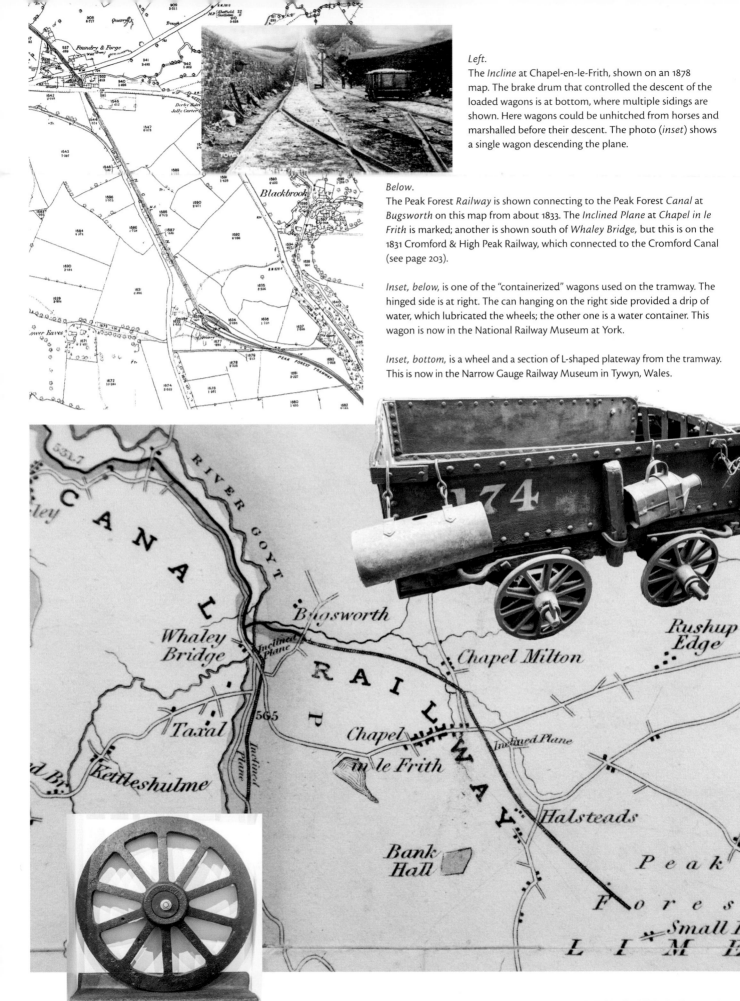

Left.
The *Incline* at Chapel-en-le-Frith, shown on an 1878 map. The brake drum that controlled the descent of the loaded wagons is at bottom, where multiple sidings are shown. Here wagons could be unhitched from horses and marshalled before their descent. The photo (*inset*) shows a single wagon descending the plane.

Below.
The Peak Forest *Railway* is shown connecting to the Peak Forest *Canal* at *Bugsworth* on this map from about 1833. The *Inclined Plane* at *Chapel in le Frith* is marked; another is shown south of *Whaley Bridge*, but this is on the 1831 Cromford & High Peak Railway, which connected to the Cromford Canal (see page 203).

Inset, below, is one of the "containerized" wagons used on the tramway. The hinged side is at right. The can hanging on the right side provided a drip of water, which lubricated the wheels; the other one is a water container. This wagon is now in the National Railway Museum at York.

Inset, bottom, is a wheel and a section of L-shaped plateway from the tramway. This is now in the Narrow Gauge Railway Museum in Tywyn, Wales.

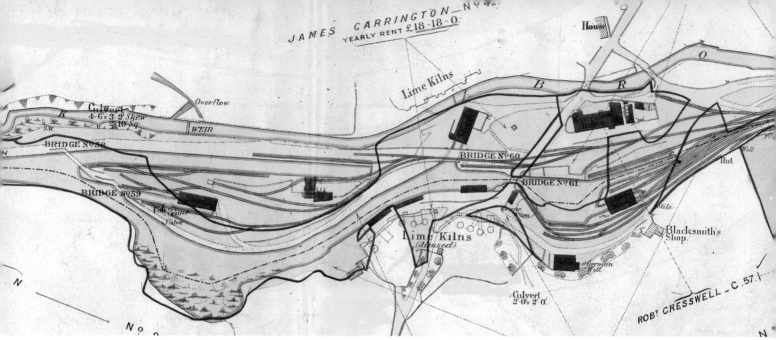

Above.

This is an 1889 map of Bugsworth Basin, the interchange of the Peak Forest Canal and Tramway, and shows how by that time it had become a veritable beehive of activity, with lime kilns as well as transhipment facilities and a maze of plateway tracks. The modern photo (*below*) is taken from just south of *Bridge No. 61* on the map, looking east. The arrays of stone blocks that held the plateway are very much in evidence following restoration. The remains of the *Lime Shed* are at centre top in the photo, overgrown with trees.

The Lancaster Canal Tramroad

The Lancaster Canal Tramroad, also known as the Preston & Walton Summit Tramway, was built not to extend a canal but to link two parts of the same canal over a section that would have cost too much to build as a continuous canal. The Lancaster Canal, authorized in 1792, was to connect Kendal, on the eastern edge of the English Lake District, with the rest of the canal system farther south. Stone, lime, and slate were brought south, and coal north.

Chief engineers to the canal company were John Rennie and William Jessop. Rennie prepared an elaborate plan for crossing the valley of the River Ribble at Preston, but the cost was well beyond the company's means—they already had an expensive aqueduct over the River Lune near Lancaster, farther north—and a railway was then proposed as a temporary measure. In fact it became permanent, as there never was enough money to construct a connecting canal. It is not clear why the company went with the L-plate system, given Jessop's preference for edge rails, but a plateway it was to be. Construction began in 1795, but the 5-mile-long double-track line, which included three inclined planes, a bridge over the river, and a short single-line tunnel in Preston itself (now part of an underground car park), was not finished until 1803. The tramroad was worked by private contractors who paid a toll to the canal company, as was the case with the rest of the canal. The line was not long lasting, and the two parts of the canal were separated again with its partial closure by 1857.

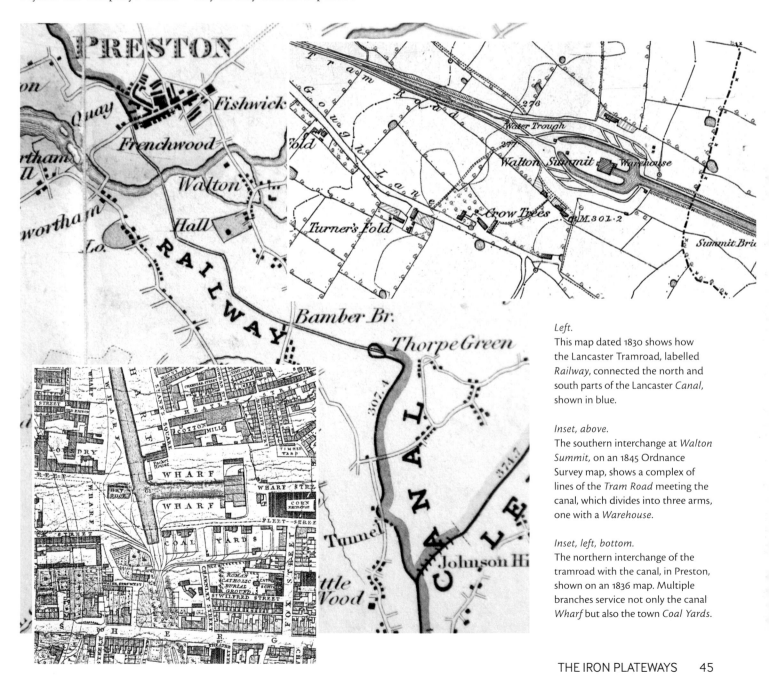

Left.
This map dated 1830 shows how the Lancaster Tramroad, labelled *Railway*, connected the north and south parts of the Lancaster *Canal*, shown in blue.

Inset, above.
The southern interchange at *Walton Summit*, on an 1845 Ordnance Survey map, shows a complex of lines of the *Tram Road* meeting the canal, which divides into three arms, one with a *Warehouse*.

Inset, left, bottom.
The northern interchange of the tramroad with the canal, in Preston, shown on an 1836 map. Multiple branches service not only the canal *Wharf* but also the town *Coal Yards*.

The Ticknall Tramway

South of Derby is another area of limestone. In 1794 the Ashby Canal and railways feeding to it were authorized to connect the area with the Coventry Canal to the south. Benjamin Outram was appointed as the engineer in 1799, and when it became evident that the part of the route from Ashby de la Zouch to the limeworks at Ticknall, Derbyshire, and Cloud Hill, near Breedon, Leicestershire (map, *below*) would be uneconomical for a canal, Outram used the power granted by the act to build two branches of his plateways. Where the two branches met, a double track was provided, but the branches themselves were single track. The branch to Cloud Hill replaced the one provided earlier by the Forest Line of the Leicester Navigation (see page 73).

The lime quarries and lime kilns at Ticknall were within the estate of Calke Abbey, and the landowner, Sir Henry Harpur, despite presumably making a lot of money from his lime, did not want to see them. The quarries were shielded from view by trees and the topography, but the rail line Outram proposed would cross his admittedly rather beautiful driveway, and thus he insisted that it be hidden from view, even though it was only a horse railway. Outram had to tunnel under the driveway (shown on map, *right*). The tramway opened in 1802, even before the canal was totally complete. The line operated for 110 years, finally closing in 1913.

Below.
This 1830 map shows the Ticknall Tramway as *Double Railway* and its two single-tracked branches as *Railway*. The northern branch goes to *Ticknall Limeworks* and the eastern branch to *Cloud Hill Limeworks*. Compare this map with the earlier map on *pages 72–73*. The two lines to *Dimsdale Ironworks* from the Ticknall branch were laid in 1828. The line from the canal to *Swadlincote Colliery* is also later and is an edge-rail line; it was opened in 1827.

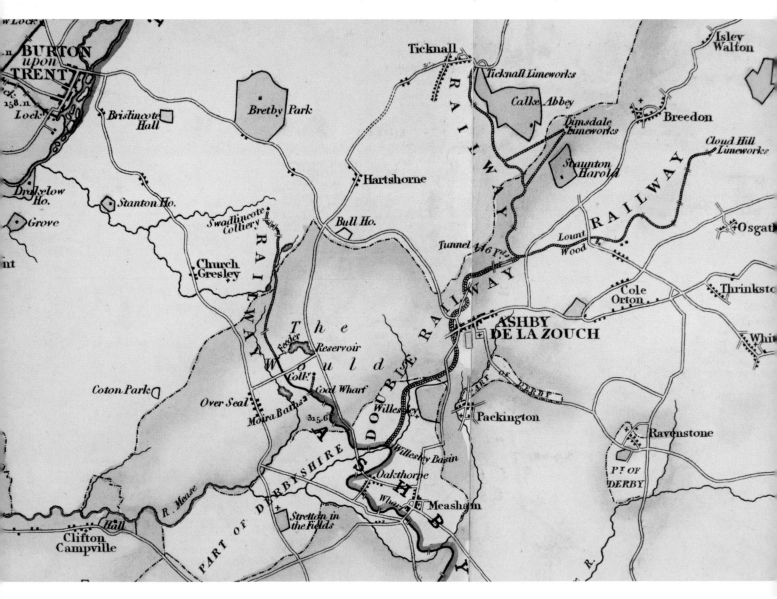

Right.

The detail on this map of the village of *Ticknall* surveyed in 1881 shows both the *Tunnel* under the Calke Abbey driveway (the double row of trees) and the road bridge, photos of which are shown *below*. The tramway line splits into two immediately to the east of the tunnel on its way to the *Lime Works*.

Below, left, is the tramway tunnel today, and *right,* the picturesque driveway to the abbey that it goes under. At *bottom left* is the 1802 bridge across the road, together with a plaque affixed to it (*below, centre*).

Bottom right.

The larger region of the Ticknall Tramway with its resources, mainly *Lime-stone* and *Coal*. The map dates from 1830.

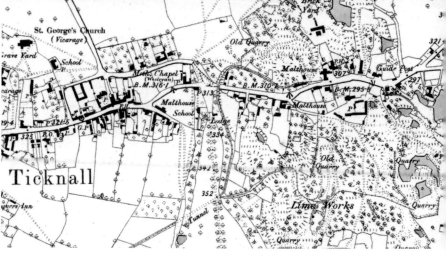

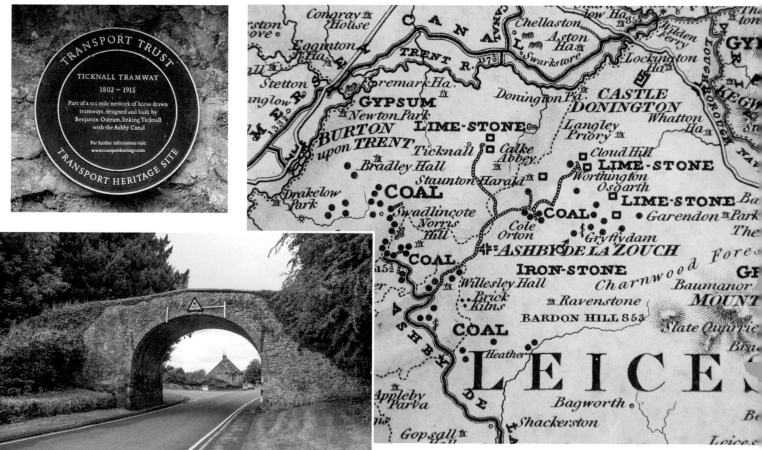

The Caldon Low Tramway

There have been no fewer than four Caldon Low Tramways, all with the same purpose: to connect large limestone quarries near Caldon Low with the Froghall Basin at the eastern end of the Caldon Branch of the Trent & Mersey Canal and hence to the Staffordshire Potteries. The first was completed in 1778, at the same time as the canal, and was authorized by the Trent & Mersey Canal Act of 1776. It had cast-iron strips nailed to wooden rails, the method that appears to have been "invented" a few years before, at Coalbrookdale. The second line, with track built the same way as the first, was completed in 1785 and was really just an improvement in the route of the 1778 line, which had proved to have some unworkable sections.

The third tramway followed a new route designed by engineer John Rennie and used L-plates purchased from Benjamin Outram & Company, soon (1805) to be the Butterley Company. It still involved a number of inclined planes (see page 98), as the quarries were about 670 feet above the canal basin in a distance of only 3½ miles. It was completed in 1804. Rennie much improved the tramway with double track. It was a very busy line, with about 1,000 tons of limestone being loaded into barges every week. Whether full going down or empty going up, one horse could pull twelve of the small wagons used on the sections between the inclined planes. Some coal was also brought up, though this required more horses.

Tracing the route of the line today is made more difficult by the fact that there was yet another railway that replaced Rennie's line in 1849. It is on a different route again, though it crosses the second and third lines, and involved a tunnel, shown on the map at *far right, bottom*. Built by engineer James Trubshaw, who had had some experience building main-line railways, the line was to a higher standard and used edge rails, which by this time had overtaken plate rails as the rail of choice.

Below.
Drawn from a survey done in 1880, this map shows the *Trent & Mersey Canal (Caldon Branch)* ending at *Froghall Wharf* after running through a short *Tunnel*. Also called the Caldon Canal, it runs from Froghall to Etruria, Stoke-on-Trent, in the Potteries, and was opened in 1778. The course of the 1803 tramway has been highlighted in light red. The first part is an inclined plane up from the water's edge, with wagons then being transferred to another incline going southeast, through *Woodcock*. The buildings shown in black just under the wording are brakemen's cottages. The line then continues eastwards through Whiston, where the line is marked *Old Tramway*. The part of the line in *Whiston*, below the elevation 736, is another inclined plane. The rail lines leading south from *Froghall* are those of the Churnet Valley Railway, which became part of the North Staffordshire Railway, and follow the route of the continuation of the Caldon Canal (shown on the map, *right*), sometimes called the Uttoxeter Canal. The North Staffordshire Railway acquired the Trent & Mersey Canal Company and then closed this part of the canal and filled in the channel to be used for the railway.

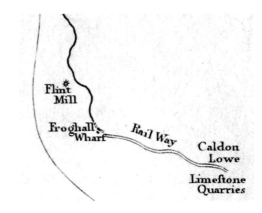

Above.
A map of the Trent & Mersey Canal, published in 1795, had this simple addition at the end of the canal: a *Rail Way*—the second Caldon Low Tramway—to *Limestone Quarries*.

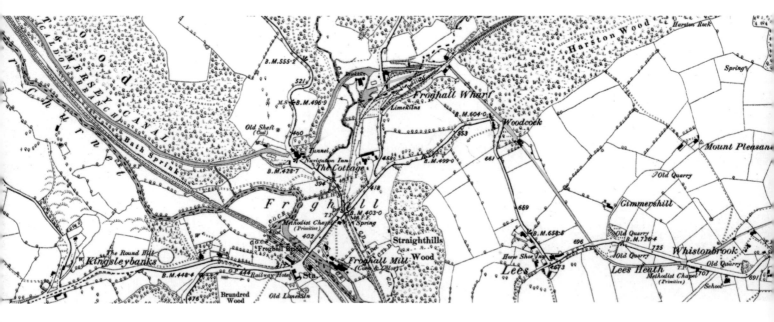

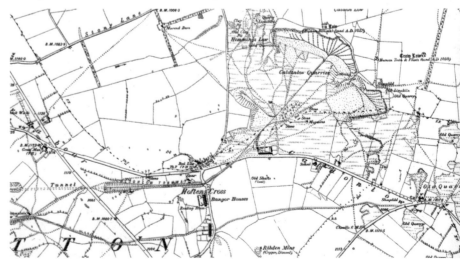

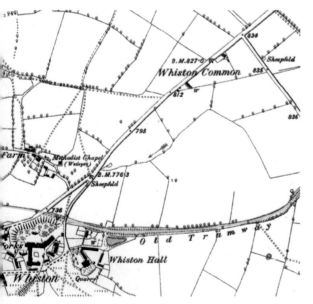

Above.

This 1830 map shows the *Caldon R Rd.* leaving the *Caldon Canal* at *Froghall*. The canal continues east and south; this part of the canal, sometimes referred to as the Uttoxeter Canal, was not completed until 1811, though it was authorized in 1797. The canal company only built it to head off a possible competing canal, and it was never economical. It was closed in 1849 and the route used for a railway, part of which is shown on the map *below*. The resources of the countryside are noted, including *Lime-Stone* at the end of the tramway.

Below.

The eastern part of the 1880 map shows the course of the 1803 line in light red, terminating at the *Old Quarries*. The location of the quarries moved over time. The course of the line to the road south of *Hoftens Cross* is definite, while that east of the road is assumed, based on this map. The 1849 line is shown as *Caldon Low Tramway* and runs though a *Tunnel* (Trubshaw's Tunnel) and now terminates at new *Caldonlow Quarries* to the northwest of the old ones.

The Surrey Iron Railway

Perhaps the best known of all the early plateways is the Surrey Iron Railway. It is often said to be the first public railway—available to all who paid a toll, just like the canals—but this is not correct, for the Lake Lock Rail Road (opened 1798; see page 74) and the Carmarthenshire Railway (opened in May 1803; see page 65) were certainly in operation before it.

It was at first considered as a canal or a horse railroad between London and the South Coast port and naval base of Portsmouth. Sailing through the Strait of Dover was becoming more hazardous because of the war with Napoleon, which would not end until 1815. A link from a southwestern port to the capital better than the existing roads was a strategic answer to this menace. William Jessop was called in to evaluate the possibility of a canal over the first part of the route between Wandsworth, on the south bank of the River Thames, and Croydon, some 7 miles farther south, but he reported in December 1799 that there was not enough water; the only water source was the River Wandle, and all the water there was being used by mills.

The obvious alternative was a railway. An Act of Parliament in 1801 created what was the world's first railway company authorized by a legislature. William Jessop was appointed chief engineer, canal engineer George Leather as resident engineer, and Benjamin Outram as a joint contractor. L-plates were to be used, but Parliament had some reservations and was careful to insist that where the railway crossed a turnpike road, the "ledge or flanch of the railway for the purpose of guiding the wheels of the carriages" should not protrude more than one inch above the surface of the road, so as not to interfere too much with road traffic.

The railway was built quite quickly and "opened to the public for the conveyance of goods" on 26 July 1803. Interestingly, the news reports of the day state that "a gentleman with two companions, drove up the railway, in a machine of his own invention, without horses." (It was a public railway, so all he had to do was pay the toll.) It is tempting to suggest that this might have been some sort of steam engine, but it was more likely a contrivance along the lines of a platelayers trolley, worked by hand; no one knows for sure.

In 1802, while the line was under construction, a meeting was held to discuss the viability of extending the line to the coast, and surveyors, including Jessop, were engaged to survey a route at far as Reigate, Surrey. In October, another meeting resulted in Jessop and his son Josias being asked to prepare a "plan and section" all the way to Portsmouth. From all this, a proposal for another Act of Parliament was put forward for the line as far as Reigate; this was approved in May 1803. Branches to Godstone and Merstham, where there were quarries, were also authorized. Although they were an extension of the Surrey Iron Railway, a separate company, the Croydon, Merstham & Godstone Railway, was created to build and operate the lines.

Right.
A reproduction of the seal of the Surrey Iron Railway Company now adorns a wall of the Ram Brewery in Wandsworth.

The board of the new company included owners of the quarries with which it was to connect. The extension was completed as far as Merstham in 1805. But by then the money—and much of the interest—had run out, and the railway was never completed to Godstone or to Reigate, despite being shown as such on some maps, such as the one *overleaf.*

For the railway soon had competition. The Croydon Canal was completed from Croydon to the Thames farther downstream than Wandsworth in 1809, and although a connection was made to the railway, the canal took some of the latter's business away.

The Surrey Iron Railway did have a further chance of revival, however, when, in 1823, William James published a report espousing the extension of the line not only to Portsmouth, which had been the original long-term intention, but also to Shoreham, another port on the South Coast, near Brighton, and to Rochester. As a railway promoter and visionary, James could perhaps have made it happen, but, as was the case with many of his other schemes, he did not pursue it long enough to get any results. Indeed, his report was written while he was languishing in debtors' prison. The map James produced for this scheme is shown on page 53 (top).

The coming of more modern railways sounded the death knell for the Surrey Iron Railway. The London & Brighton Railway wanted part of the roadbed and purchased the company in 1838, dissolving it the following year.

Above.
An exhibit in the Bluebell Railway Museum at Sheffield Park, Sussex, displays a section of the rail from the 1805 extension of the Surrey Iron Railway, the Croydon, Merstham & Godstone Railway, the initials of which are evident in cast letters on the rail. This is typical L-shaped plateway of the fishbelly type, where the flange is deeper between the stone blocks, where greater strength is required. The stone blocks are from the Surrey Iron Railway.

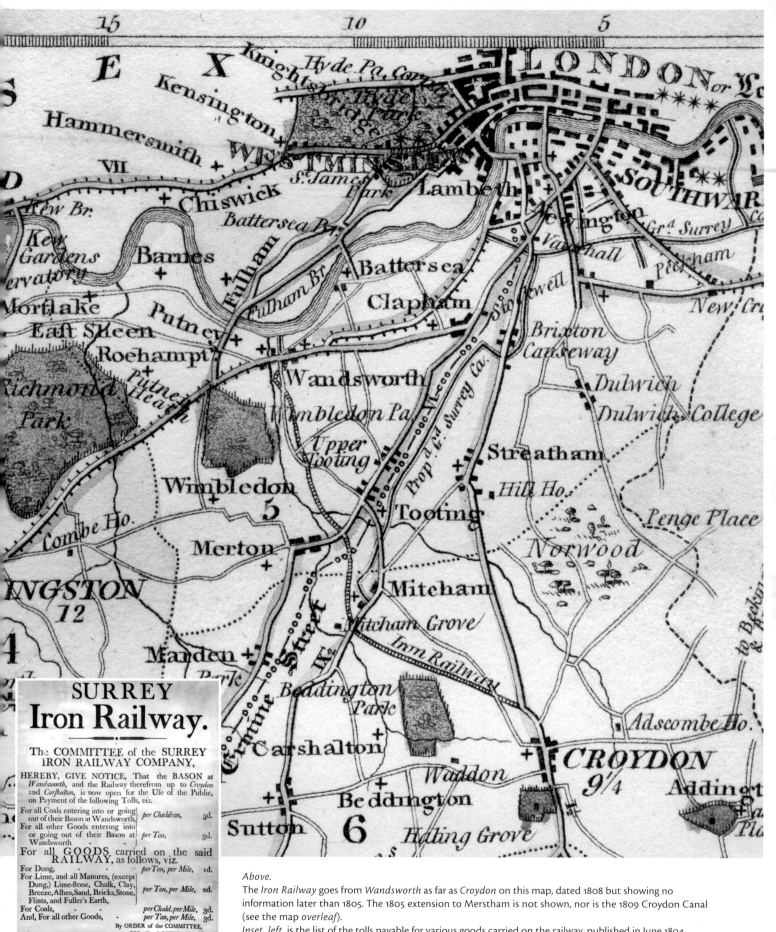

Above.
The *Iron Railway* goes from *Wandsworth* as far as *Croydon* on this map, dated 1808 but showing no information later than 1805. The 1805 extension to Merstham is not shown, nor is the 1809 Croydon Canal (see the map *overleaf*).
Inset, left, is the list of the tolls payable for various goods carried on the railway, published in June 1804.

Right.
An 1830 map shows the Surrey Iron Railway and its extension, the Croydon, Merstham & Godstone Railway, though the line was in fact only completed as far south as quarries at *Merstham*. The *Croydon Canal*, completed in 1809, is also shown; connecting to the G[rand] *Surrey Can*[al], it reaches the Thames considerably farther downstream than the *Surrey Rail Road* at *Wandsworth*.

Below.
Though a much later map (1894) this detail still shows a *Railway Wharf* at the basin constructed where the Surrey Iron Railway met the River Thames at Wandsworth. The view down the road shown in the centre of the map, which was the route of the railway, is the photo at *bottom right.* The view is looking south. The tall chimney is at the *Ram Brewery*, also shown on the map. The plaque and two of the original sleeper stones have been embedded in the wall and can be made out in the street photo beside the nearest tree. A close-up view is *above.* This is all that is left of the Surrey Iron Railway today.

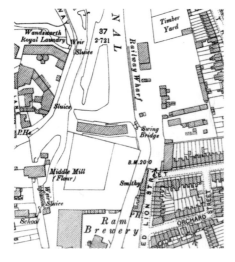

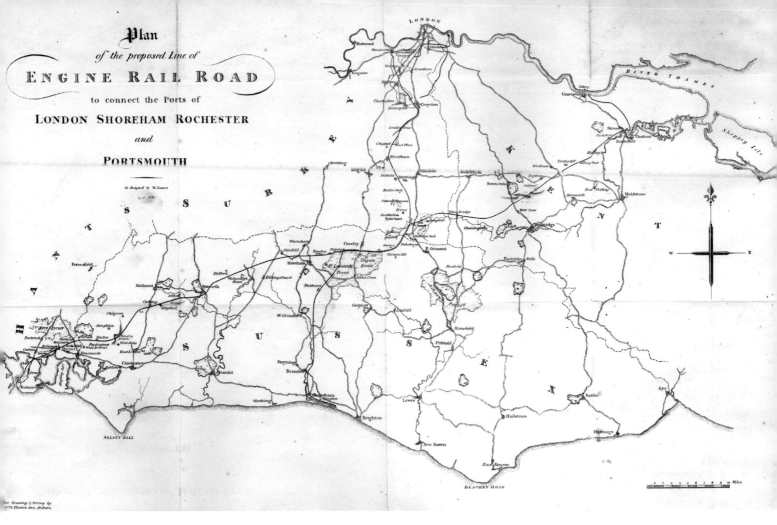

Plan
of the proposed Line of
ENGINE RAIL ROAD
to connect the Ports of
LONDON SHOREHAM ROCHESTER
and
PORTSMOUTH

Above.

William James's 1823 map showing his plans for connecting London and the Surrey Iron Railway with *Portsmouth* and *Shoreham* on the south coast of England and *Rochester* and *Gravesend* on the southeast coast. His line from central London joined the line of the Surrey Iron Railway just south of *Tooting* and then continued south of *Merstham.* The important point of James's plan was that his scheme was to be an "Engine Rail Road" rather than the horse-drawn affair of the original Surrey Iron Railway. James was at this time promoting the use of George Stephenson's locomotives, to which he had gained the marketing rights for all of southern England, and he included an engraving of one of the engines (*below, centre*). James calculated that the government would save £60,000 a year by using his railway to supply the naval depots at the ports, as well as not being exposed to "capture and tempest" if supplied by sea, or "frauds and robberies," "injurious delays from frosts in winter," or "want of water in summer."

Right. The title page of James's report, with its elaborate title in the longwinded style of the times. There could be no mistaking what the report was about!

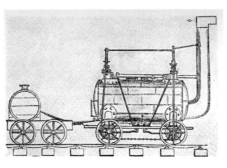

REPORT, or ESSAY,
TO ILLUSTRATE THE
ADVANTAGES OF DIRECT INLAND COMMUNICATION
THROUGH
Kent, Surrey, Sussex, and Hants,
TO CONNECT THE
METROPOLIS
WITH THE PORTS OF
SHOREHAM, (Brighton) ROCHESTER, (Chatham)
AND
PORTSMOUTH,
BY A LINE OF
ENGINE RAIL-ROAD,
AND TO RENDER
THE GRAND SURREY CANAL,
WANDSWORTH AND MERSTRAM RAIL-ROAD,
SHOREHAM HARBOUR, AND WATERLOO BRIDGE SHARES,
PRODUCTIVE PROPERTY:
WITH SUGGESTIONS
FOR DIMINISHING POORS-RATES, AND RELIEVING AGRICULTURE.

" The Real Wealth or Resources of any Nation can evidently be no other than
" the Ability or Means of such Nation, to supply a greater or lesser Number of
" People with whatever shall be requisite for the Performance of the Duties required
" of them in Social Life."

LONDON:
PUBLISHED (FOR THE AUTHOR, No. 3, THAVIES INN, HOLBORN,)
BY J. AND A. ARCH, CORNHILL;
SOLD ALSO BY RICHARDSON, CORNHILL; HARDING, ST. JAMES'S
STREET; AND AT TAYLOR'S ARCHITECTURAL
LIBRARY, HOLBORN.
1823.

Far left, this page.

An 1818 map of canals also showed the Surrey Iron Railway (here highlighted in red). Looking at this map, one can easily see how James and others before him came up with the notion of connecting it with ports on the South Coast.

The First Passenger Railways

In June 1804 Parliament passed an act for a 5-mile-long horse-drawn plateway, to be called the Swansea & Oystermouth Rail-Way, along Swansea Bay in South Wales to the Mumbles peninsula, an area with coal, iron ore, and limestone resources. Construction began later that year, and the line was completed in 1806. It was operated as a public toll road and as such could be used by anyone paying the tolls. The following year Benjamin French offered the company £20 per year in lieu of tolls "for permission to run a waggon or waggons on the Tram Road . . . for conveyance of passengers." The proposal was accepted by the company, and French began his service with what was essentially a stagecoach with the wheels adapted to run on rails on 25 March 1807—thus becoming the world's first documented regular rail passenger service. It seems to have been popular, for French's permission was renewed the following year for £25.

About the same time the passenger service began, an attempt was made to use wind power on the line—for rails gave a hitherto unprecedented low-friction ride. The local newspaper reported that some "jolly sons of Neptune"—presumably sailors—rigged a wagon with a sail and managed to sail to the end of the line in about 45 minutes. However, the experiment does not seem to have been repeated; one imagines that the return journey must have been a bit more difficult!

The mineral traffic on the line did not live up to expectation, and passenger traffic became relatively more important. The line actually closed in 1855 but reopened nine years later. Two companies competed for passenger traffic, one horse drawn and the other steam; they merged in 1898. The line was by now essentially a tourist attraction, and a pier was built at the western end of the line to provide a destination. In 1929 the line was electrified and had 13 tramcars. Popularity grew, and during the depression years of the 1930s 5 million passengers a year were being carried. But the popularity did not last, traffic declined, and the line closed in 1960.

Across page; title above.
The map prepared in 1803 prior to the Act of Parliament for the Swansea & Oystermouth Railway. *Swansea* is at right, *Oystermouth* at left.

Right.
The Swansea & Oystermouth Railway shown on a map from about 1811.

Below.
A horse-drawn passenger tram with passengers, dignitaries, and even a policeman, posing for a photograph about 1865.

Above.
Reconstructed in the Swansea & Mumbles Railway museum in the old station in Swansea, this is what the first passenger "trains" looked like in 1807. The reconstruction is based on several contemporary drawings made by visitors. Behind the coach is a banner proclaiming "The First Passenger Railway in the World." The official name of the company was the Swansea & Oystermouth, but the line soon became known as the Swansea & Mumbles.

Above.
By 1908, the likely date of this photograph, steam had appeared on the railway. This is quite a substantial train and may have been one put on for a special event or excursion. In 1929 the line was electrified, and vehicles more akin to the city trams of the time took over. The Swansea & Mumbles Railway saw five different kinds of propulsion: horse, wind, steam, electric and diesel.

Left.
This exhibit from the National Tramway Museum at Crich, Derbyshire, actually shows a horse tram from about 1904 from the Chesterfield–Brampton line in Chesterfield, Derbyshire, but it is similar to the Swansea & Oystermouth horse trams.

Many early railways carried passengers informally or occasionally. The Sirhowy Tramroad in South Wales had a custom-built passenger carriage by 1810 (see page 65), and the Monmouth Railway Act of the same year specifically authorized tolls for such vehicles, the first reference to passengers in any railway act. The earliest surviving railway carriage for passengers is that of the Portreath Railway in Cornwall, though the carriage in question is actually a directors' inspection wagon.

Passengers often crowded onto trains when a line first opened, and one of the earliest examples of that phenomenon must have been Richard Trevithick's demonstration of his steam engine in 1804 (see page 104), not to mention the famous example of the opening of the Stockton & Darlington Railway in 1825 (see page 148). It has been estimated that by the time the Liverpool & Manchester Railway opened in 1830, 300 to 400 miles of railway line had already carried passengers in some fashion.

Above.
The Portreath Railway (sometimes referred to as the Poldice Tramway) is the line running to the sea at *Portreath* on this 1830 map, which also shows the *Redruth Rl. Rd.*, the Redruth & Chasewater Railway of 1826. Both lines served the copper, lead, and tin mines of Cornwall.
Inset is the directors' carriage from the Portreath line, the earliest surviving rail passenger vehicle, built about 1812.

The Gloucester & Cheltenham Railway

In 1809, authorization was gained for a plateway from the River Severn at Gloucester to Cheltenham, 8¼ miles away. The main reason for the line was to bring coal, mainly from the Forest of Dean across the Severn estuary, to Cheltenham, and also, via a branch line to Leckhampton Quarries nearby, to carry limestone back to Gloucester for transport elsewhere, also principally across the Severn estuary, to South Wales. The owner of the quarries on Leckhampton Hill had by this time already laid tramroads and an inclined plane to get his stone down the hill. The line to Gloucester was in a sense just an extension of this railway. Potential investors were, however, able to see that railways worked before they invested.

Although originally planned to run from the River Severn, the plateway was in fact built from a newly completed basin on the Gloucester & Berkeley Canal, which ran from Gloucester more or less parallel to the twisting and tidal Severn, thus avoiding the river. The canal was not fully opened until 1827; though it had been under construction since 1793, it had stalled because of financial difficulties. A view of the canal basin in Gloucester (*below*) shows the many warehouses that clustered around the transhipment point.

The Leckhampton-to-Cheltenham section was completed in July 1810, and the main line to Gloucester was opened in June the following year. A "great reduction" was immediately seen in the price of coal in Cheltenham. This was, of course, a significant benefit, since coal was the main source of power and heating at the time.

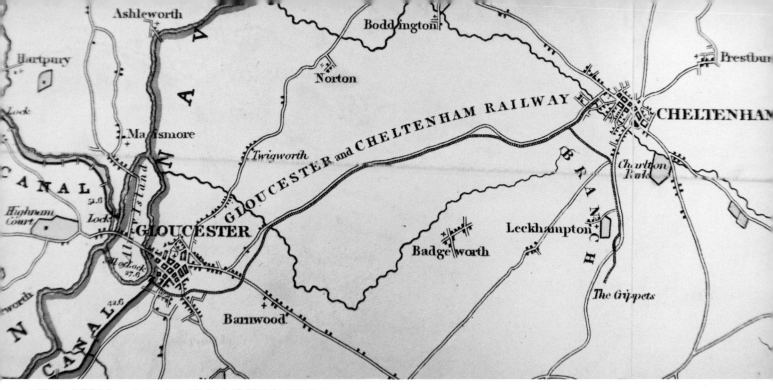

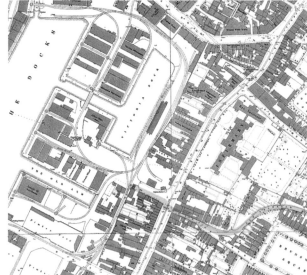

Above.
The *Gloucester and Cheltenham Railway* is shown on this 1830 map running from the (Gloucester & Berkeley) *Canal,* highlighted in red along with a navigable stretch of the River Severn. The line parallels the turnpike road. Near *Cheltenham* is the *Branch* to *Leckhampton;* at the end of the line just beyond the village is Leckhampton Hill, the site of a number of limestone quarries. The quarries are not shown on this map.

Below, bottom, across page, is the location of the plateway's terminus, the canal basin at Gloucester; *below* is a view from about 1850, and the line can be seen on the left approaching the same warehouses as in the modern view.

Left. The dock area of Gloucester on an 1884 map. The route of the plateway, by then long gone, is marked in red. The modern photo was taken more or less from the end of the red line looking north.

Left.
Another map from 1830 shows the *Glou*[r]. *& Cheltenham Rail R*[d]. in the wider context with the *Berkeley & Glou*[r]. *Can.*, with which the railway connected at *Gloucester*. This map shows the way the canal paralleled the tidal estuary of the River Severn.

Left, inset, are two Gloucester & Cheltenham replica wagons that now stand beside the docks in Gloucester. The plate rail is original.

Below, left. A very steep inclined plane at the Leckhampton Quarries. This photo was taken in about 1908; the railways in the quarries continued working for many years after the closure of the Gloucester & Cheltenham.

Below. A plateway in the ominously named Dead Man's Quarry at Leckhampton. The L-shaped rails can be clearly seen. This photo dates from about 1911.

The Gloucester & Cheltenham Railway was operated as a toll road and had a busy though not particularly long life. In 1831 a steam engine named *Royal William* was used on the line. It was built at Neath Abbey Ironworks in South Wales, and it had the distinction of being enclosed in a wooden casing intended to minimize the frightening of horses! The plateway was almost put out of business in 1837 by a new standard-gauge edge railway, the Birmingham & Gloucester, which used a different, more direct route between Cheltenham and Gloucester, but struggled on until 1859, when it was abandoned.

Right.
The line of the Gloucester & Cheltenham plateway is still shown on this 1859 map, though this was the year it ceased operations, a victim of competition from the 1837 Birmingham & Gloucester Railway, the other rail line shown, with a *Station* at Cheltenham, on the right. The plateway, here shown as a single black line and labelled *Rail Way*, follows the route of the turnpike road.

The Middlebere Plateway

The Staffordshire Potteries needed ball clay to manufacture their wares, and there were only three sources in Britain—north Devon, south Devon, and the Purbeck peninsula of Dorset—all inland. The one in north Devon was too far inland and thus uneconomical to extract, and the one in south Devon (after the opening of the Stover Canal in 1792; see page 70) required pack horse transport to the canal and then transhipment into ships. The deposit in Dorset, however, was only 3½ miles from Poole Harbour. Both south Devon and Purbeck clay was shipped to Liverpool or nearby for delivery via the Trent & Mersey Canal. Businessman Benjamin Fayle saw an opportunity and in 1804 leased the Norden clay pits, near Corfe Castle, and built a plateway from them to Poole Harbour, which, completed in 1806, lowered transport costs and enabled him to offer the clay to the Wedgwood Pottery at a reduced price.

The plateway used the Outram L-plate system, but the engineer is not known. Fayle lived in London close to the Surrey Iron Railway and would certainly have seen it in operation, so this is likely what gave him the idea. Although reduced costs enabled him to undercut his competition, his expenses were still more than he had calculated, and he was forced to increase his price two years later. Nevertheless, the potteries were pleased with the reliability of supply as the demand for their pottery was growing, and the plateway lasted for a century, closing only in 1908.

Above.
A *Rail Road* is shown on this map of the whole Purbeck peninsula running from *Norden*—and a large notation *Clay*—to *Poole Harb*ʳ· The map dates from 1830.

Right.
The first edition of the Ordnance Survey map for this region, dated 1811, shows an *Iron Rail Way* from *Nordon* to a *Quay* near *Middlebere*, on the *Middlebere Chan*ˡ·, which flows into Poole Harbour. The plateway branches into two as it crosses the turnpike road to reach the clay pits, which were on the south side of the road. *Corfe Castle* is at bottom, guarding a gap in a line of hills, a good strategic location.

The Silkstone Waggonway

The 2½-mile-long Silkstone Waggonway, just west of Barnsley in Yorkshire, replaced an earlier wooden waggonway in the area and was built with L-shaped plates but still retained the waggonway terminology. The line was built by the Barnsley Canal Company to transport coal from the local collieries to the end of their canal at Barnby Basin (map, *below left*). The canal had been completed in 1799, and the plateway was in operation by 1809. The line has some of the best-preserved sleeper stones from the track route to be found anywhere, but, unusually, some are laid diagonally rather than at right angles to the direction of travel, possibly because it was thought that they were more stable like that.

The waggonway was extended in 1830 to service new collieries, and the extension included an inclined plane and a tunnel. The line operated until 1871 or 1872. The canal basin lasted until the early 1900s.

Below.
The course of the Silkstone Waggonway through the village of *Silkstone* is shown in red on this 1851 map. The waggonway is marked *Tram Road*, and the modern photo of the line today (*left*) was taken just to the north of those words on the map. Note the *Silkstone Old Colliery* adjacent to the line south of the village.

Left.
The Silkstone *Tram Road*, in red, divides into two to access both sides of the *Barnby Basin*, the end of the Barnsley Canal.

Below.
Diagonally set sleeper stones with holes for plugs to hold the track spikes.

The Forest of Dean and Severn & Wye Railways

The interestingly named Bullo Pill Railway, which changed its name to the Forest of Dean Railway in 1826, opened as a plateway, with L-rails, in 1810 to facilitate the transport of coal, iron ore, stone, and wood from the Forest of Dean to Bullo Pill, a little port on the River Severn. The line included a long tunnel and an inclined plane, both shown on the map *below*. The railway thrived until 1815, the end of the Napoleonic Wars. A network of branches was created to service the scattered mines of the region, and, since the Forest of Dean is Crown land, a rent had to be paid—a yearly sum of £100 plus "one guinea per week towards the cost and charges of His Majesty's inspectors." In 1811 the railway company tried to extend its line with a tunnel under the Severn, but water rushed in when the tunnelling reached the halfway mark and it had to be abandoned.

The Severn & Wye Railway, originally incorporated as the Lydney & Lidbrook Railway in 1809, was another plateway, opened in 1813. It connected the Severn with the River Wye and provided more outlets for the resources of the Forest of Dean. In a similar fashion to the Bullo Pill, many branches were built to cover the many mines and quarries of the area. Instead of building the railway all the way to the Severn, the Lydney Canal was dug to cover the final mile to the river. The engineer for the project was Josias Jessop, son of William Jessop.

A branch of the Severn & Wye near Coleford was opened in 1812, serving some quarries and coal pits near that town. Called the Bicslade Tramroad, although it was just one of many branches, it is notable in that when the main line was converted to locomotive power in 1874, it remained horse drawn and continued in this way until the 1950s, becoming the last working horse-drawn tramroad in the region.

Below. Both the *Bullo Pill or Forest of Dean Railway* and the *Severn and Wye Railway* are shown on this 1830 map. The connection between the two is shown. Also shown is the *Monmouth Railway*, another plateway, opened in 1812 to connect the Forest of Dean with *Monmouth*. The branch line coloured green near *Coleford* is the Bicslade Tramroad. The Lydney Canal is that stretch of the red line labelled *Canal* south of Lydney. Part of the *Gloucester and Berkeley Canal* leading to the Gloucester & Cheltenham Railway (see page 56) can be seen on the opposite bank of the Severn.

Inset, below. A pair of wagons like the one shown *below, bottom,* coupled together to enable two horses to pull an 8-ton block of stone. The scene is on the Bicslade Tramroad. The preserved wagon is at the Narrow Gauge Railway Museum in Tywyn, Wales.

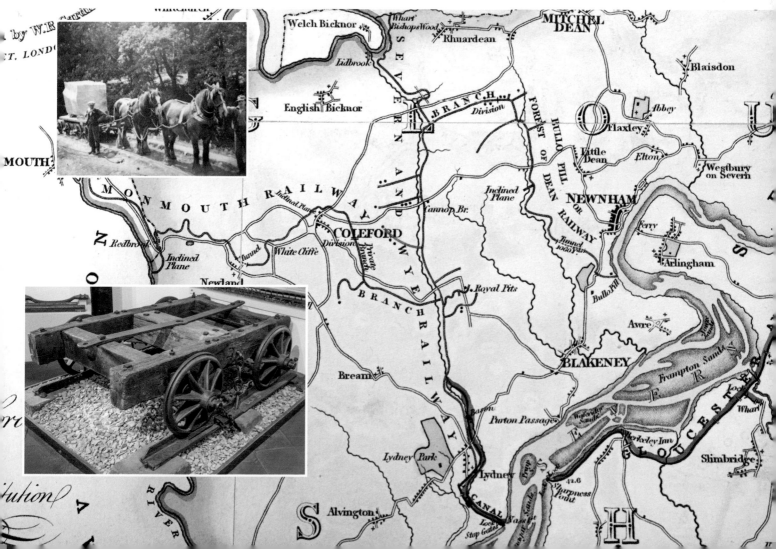

The Somerset Coal Canal Railway

This railway, in Somerset, southwest of Bristol, has an interesting origin. It is a story of not enough water and not enough money.

The Somerset (in full, Somersetshire) Coal Canal was built around 1800 to allow the numerous coal mines of the Somerset coalfield to export their coal. It connected to the Kennet & Avon Canal, completed in sections between 1798 and 1810, which in turn connects to the River Thames—and thus London—via the River Kennet at Newbury.

The Somerset Coal Canal was built with two branches but from the beginning had trouble getting enough water for navigation. The 9-mile-long southern branch met the northern branch at Midford, Somerset, but there was never enough money to pay for the flight of locks that would be necessary to connect it. Instead, the company built one lock, an aqueduct, and a short plateway to bridge the gap. This no doubt contributed to the economic failure of the southern branch, and in 1815 it was closed. The towpath of the canal was used for a plateway, the Somerset Coal Canal Railway.

Even this was never very economical and was replaced in 1874 by a regular railway—the Somerset & Dorset, beloved of railway fans, with nicknames like "Slow & Doubtful"—which itself closed in 1966.

Above.

The *Radstock R*[l.] *R*[d.] is the Somerset Coal Canal Railway, the southern parallel branch of the *Somerset*[shir]e. *Coal Canal* north of it. It joins the Kennet & Avon Canal, which goes from *Bath* eastwards towards London. Also on the map are two other horse-drawn railways authorized by 1830—the Avon & Gloucestershire, or Dramway (1832), and the Bristol & Gloucestershire (1835)—both of which used edge rails.

Above.

The Kilmarnock & Troon *Railway* is shown as a double dashed line from *Kilmarnock* to *Troon Point* on this 1821 map.

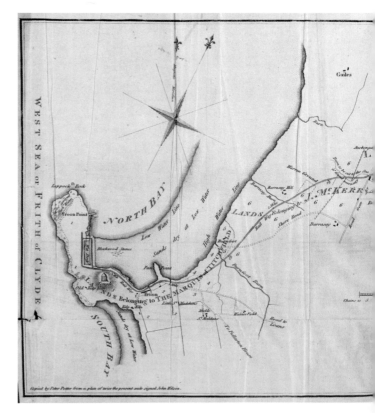

The Kilmarnock & Troon Railway

The Kilmarnock & Troon Railway is better known than most plateways owing to the 1816 trial of a George Stephenson steam locomotive—which failed because of the fragility of the cast-iron plateway track. The line was also the first in Scotland to be built under an Act of Parliament—with its associated powers of eminent domain—and also the first to provide a reasonably regular service for fare-paying passengers, albeit with a horse-drawn coach.

The railway was the initiative of the Marquess of Titchfield, after 1809 the Duke of Portland, who owned collieries in Kilmarnock and wanted to be able to export his coal. He had for some time promoted a harbour at Troon Point, where he also owned land. The Marquess was familiar with the Surrey Iron Railway and basically copied the idea for his line, even employing the same engineer—William Jessop. The Kilmarnock & Troon was, like the Surrey Iron Railway, public—available to all on payment of a toll, an arrangement facilitated by the use of plate rails, which were able to take carts that could also run on roads.

Some difficulties were encountered for about a mile through Shewalton Moss, a soft bog up to 40 feet deep halfway along the route (map, *below, bottom*). The problem, which had a striking similarity to the one later encountered by George Stephenson at Chat Moss on the Liverpool & Manchester Railway, was solved in this instance by a system of drains and sand, with a cover of coal, enough at least to cope with horse-drawn traffic.

The deep-water harbour at Troon Point and the railway were built concurrently and were completed by 1812. As a plateway, the line lasted until 1841, when it was converted to an edge railway and realigned in places.

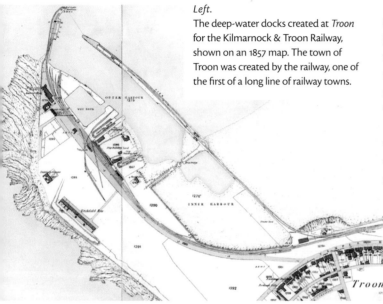

Left.
The deep-water docks created at *Troon* for the Kilmarnock & Troon Railway, shown on an 1857 map. The town of Troon was created by the railway, one of the first of a long line of railway towns.

Below.
An 1811 copy of the original 1807 survey for the line, shown in red, from *Kilmarnock* to *Troon Point*, both owned by the Marquess of Titchfield, the line's promoter. The troublesome *Shewalton Moss* is near the halfway mark.

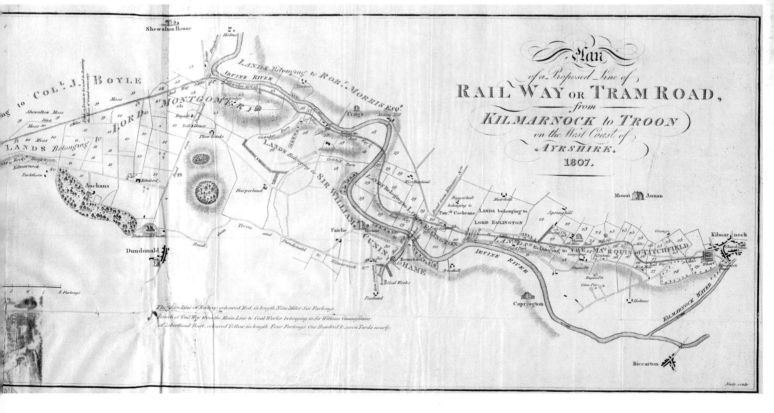

The South Wales Railway and Canal Network

The valleys of South Wales were rich in deposits of both iron ore and coal, so it is unsurprising that an iron industry existed here from the Middle Ages. But the larger-scale ironmakers of the eighteenth and nineteenth centuries faced considerable problems exporting their heavy product in this region of narrow valleys and steep grades. At first, canals solved some of the problems, but there were many places canals could not economically go—the narrow valley sides themselves often preventing the construction of feeder branches. The issue was resolved by the use of railways. Indeed, most of the enabling Acts of Parliament for the canal companies included clauses allowing them to construct feeder rail lines up to 8 miles in length, and land for these could even be acquired, if necessary, by compulsory purchase in exactly the same fashion as land for the canals themselves. If it was longer than 8 miles, a rail line needed separate authorization. One such line, the Merthyr Tramroad, completed in 1802, was to become famous as the venue for Richard Trevithick's pioneer demonstration of steam locomotion (see page 104).

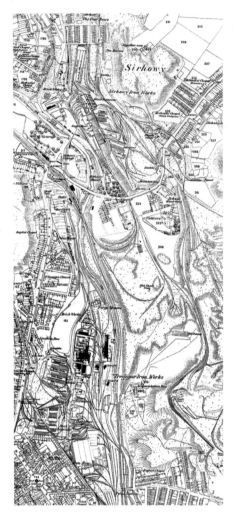

Left. A careful look at the locomotive here reveals its unflanged plateway wheels. The engine is the *St. David*, with the engineer of the Tredegar Iron Works, Tom Ellis, on the footplate. The photo was taken in 1854.

Right.
The maze of, by then, standard edge railway lines serving the *Sirhowy* and *Tredegar Iron Works* in the Sirhowy Valley of South Wales in 1880. Both ironworks are also shown on the map *overleaf*. These works were originally served by the Sirhowy Tramroad.

The first railways here used cast-iron edge rails, with single- or double-flanged wheels running on bars of iron, but from about 1790 the L-shaped plate rail became more commonly used, largely because of the influence of Benjamin Outram and his followers. Plateways in South Wales were typically referred to as tramroads. Some lines became steam locomotive–worked after 1829, and their engines had the unflanged wheels necessary to run on the L-shaped rails.

South Wales had a network of early railways, closely integrated with the canals, second only to northeast England in size and scope. Many of them are shown on the 1830 map *overleaf (pages 66–67)*. But there were many more short lines serving coal mines, ironworks, and quarries that are not marked on a map like this because the scale does not permit it. Overall, the South Wales network was dense and often complex, and became even more so as standard railways replaced plateways between the late 1820s and the 1860s. The tortuous maze of lines around the Tredegar and Sirhowy ironworks in the Sirhowy River valley by 1880 is shown on the map detail at *top right*. Some of the plateway lines are discussed here.

Unusually, the Merthyr Tramroad runs more or less parallel to the Glamorganshire Canal, built in 1790–94. The tramroad originated in a dispute between the ironmasters of the Dowlais, Penydarren, and Plymouth ironworks near Merthyr Tydfil with the Glamorganshire Canal Company over the precedence at locks claimed by the ironmaster at Cyfarthfa Ironworks, just north of Merthyr. Water usage rights and rates were also a source of friction. The three ironmasters determined to become independent of the canal by building their own route past the locks. In 1799 they sent a proposal for an act to Parliament for an extensive tramway in the area, which the canal company opposed. But this was a smokescreen; in the meantime the ironmasters planned a tramroad by obtaining agreements from the landowners over whose land it would pass, thus not requiring an act. The tramroad was engineered by George Overton, who would later carry out the early surveys for the Stockton & Darlington Railway (see page 148). The canal company tried to stop the tramroad from crossing a feeder channel but were out-manoeuvred when the ironmasters bought the land involved. The tramroad (shown on the map, *overleaf*, as the *Cardiff & Merthyr R$^{l.}$ R$^{d.}$*) was completed to Navigation (now Abercynon) in 1802.

In a parallel valley several miles to the east, a similar scene was playing out. Ironmasters in the Sirhowy Valley decided to construct a tramroad all the way down to Newport, rather than to the Monmouthshire Canal at some intermediate point so as to be independent of a canal company. In 1800 they sought the advice of Benjamin Outram, who of course recommended his L-plate rails despite the fact that there were existing railways

Above.
Surveyed in 1878, this map shows the *Long Bridge*, a 32-arch viaduct on the Sirhowy Tramroad, also shown, about 1895, in the photo (*top, right*). The painting (*above*) shows the viaduct as it was about 1810. It shows, at bottom left, a passenger carriage pulled by a single horse.

Right.
An 1867 survey shows the line of the Carmarthenshire *Tram Road* (in red) as it reaches *Llanelly Docks.* The map also shows several later railways.

in the area that used edge rails. The same year they came to an agreement with the canal company to build the last 8 miles of the tramroad to Newport. Sixteen miles of rail were built by the ironmasters, with one further connecting mile over the land of Charles Morgan, a landowner who managed to retain the right to extract very profitable tolls for his single mile, just west of Risca and its viaduct, a 32-arch structure over the Ebbw River and its floodplain. Built in 1805, it lasted exactly a century, being demolished in 1905. The Sirhowy Tramroad (*Sirhowey R*[l]*. R*[d]*.* on the map, *overleaf*) opened the same year.

As might be anticipated with a long railway ending in a major city, a passenger service was soon established, perhaps by 1809 and certainly by 1810, two or three years after the Swansea & Oystermouth, just a few miles to the south, had led the way (see page 54).

Farther to the west the "Carmarthenshire Railway or Tramroad Company"—the confusion of terminology is evident—was incorporated in June 1802 and was the first public railway company in Wales. And the company is thought to have become the first dock-owning public railway in the world when it acquired a dock at Llanelli and a feeder tramroad built in 1799. A 1½-mile length of line from an ironworks to the sea was opened in May 1803, and thus the line lays claim to being the first public railway in use in Britain. The line did not last very long, ceasing operation by 1844. Parts of the trackbed were used by a later standard railway, the Llanelly & Mynydd Mawr Railway, in 1881. The *Carmarthensh. Rail Road* is shown on the map *overleaf.*

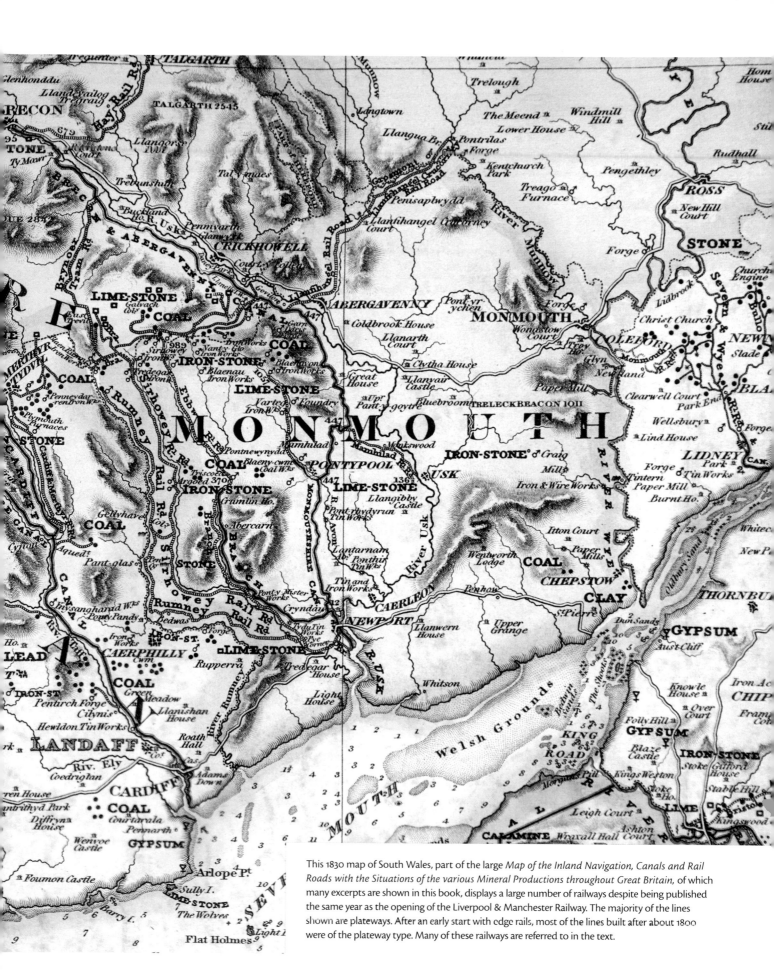

This 1830 map of South Wales, part of the large *Map of the Inland Navigation, Canals and Rail Roads with the Situations of the various Mineral Productions throughout Great Britain,* of which many excerpts are shown in this book, displays a large number of railways despite being published the same year as the opening of the Liverpool & Manchester Railway. The majority of the lines shown are plateways. After an early start with edge rails, most of the lines built after about 1800 were of the plateway type. Many of these railways are referred to in the text.

Above. The Hay Railway plateway wagon wheel and rail from the monument shown *opposite.*

Below. Abandoned trackbed of the Grosmont Railway, which was an extension of the Llanfihangel.

Many railways fed the Monmouthshire & Brecon Canal, in the eastern part of South Wales. The canal was originally two separate canals, the Monmouthshire and the Brecknock & Abergavenny, and canal and railway engineer Thomas Dadford was involved with both. The former opened in 1799, the latter in 1800. They were joined at Pontymoile, near Pontypool, making one 35-mile-long canal with a number of branches. At least thirty-four tramways connected with the combined canal. They included the Llanhiledd Tramroad, which was surveyed by Outram in 1800 and connected the head of a branch of the canal at Crumlin with a line to the Beaufort Iron Works (*Ebbw Rl. Rd.* north from *Crumlin Ho.* on the map, *previous page*); the Monmouthshire Canal Tramway, which connected with the Sirhowy in 1806; the Bryn Oer (or Brinore) Tramway, completed in 1814 from the canal at Talybont-on-Usk to collieries and limestone quarries at Trevil; the 6½-mile-long Llanfihangel and 7-mile-long Grosmont railways, which joined each other to extend a line of communication into Herefordshire, opening in 1818–19; and the Hay Railway, completed in 1816. All are shown on the map on the *previous page.* The map also shows the *Mamhilad Rl. Rd.* (incorporated in 1814), but this was never built.

The Hay Railway ran from Brecon north and connected in 1820 with the Kington Tramway, making the line the longest railway in the world at the time, some 36 miles long (map, *far right*). Its trade included, of course, coal and limestone, but also agricultural produce from the largely rural area through which it ran.

Another long line was the Rumney Railway (also on the map, *previous page*), still a plateway, though not opened till 1826. The engineer was George Overton, who had been the engineer for the Merthyr Tramroad in the adjacent valley twenty-four years before. He also had carried out the surveys for the Stockton & Darlington Railway before getting involved with the Rumney. The Rumney operated as a public railway, with tolls, and connected with the Sirhowy Tramroad, which in turn connected with the Monmouthshire Canal Tramroad to reach Newport.

One unusual long tramway network was used to try to develop a remote area of South Wales. The Brecon Forest Tramroad (also shown on the map, *previous page*) was envisioned by its promoter, John Christie, who had made a fortune in the

Below. This magnificent panoramic painting, *A Plain Representation of the Teams & Trams of Coal, brought down to Pillgwenlly,* was created by John Thomas, an otherwise essentially unknown artist, for Tredegar ironmaster Samuel Homfray in 1821. The original is almost 12 feet long. It shows two teams of four horses, each hauling nine loaded wagons on the plateway approaching Newport from the west on the section of line where the Rumney and Sirhowy tramroads merge to a single line, though double tracked. Pillgwenlly is a short distance due south of Newport and is now part of that city. The painting seems to have been commissioned by Homfray to commemorate the beginning of operation of new rolling stock, which appear to be wagons with bogies, where each set of four wheels pivots on its own axis. The painting gives a good idea of the power and capacity of the horse-drawn tramroads in South Wales.

India trade, as a way to exploit the resources of the Great Forest of Brecon (Fforest Fawr). He had purchased the vast area in 1819 from the government, which was selling off Crown land to raise money in the wake of the Napoleonic Wars, but Christie thought there was coal to be easily mined, which there was not. By 1821 Christie had built a small network of plateways to transport lime to the agricultural areas to the north, including a line to Sennybridge, on River Usk.

But the costs were high and the revenues not enough; by 1827 he was bankrupt, and his assets were taken over by Joseph Claypon, his banker and principal creditor. Claypon extended the line to connect with coal mines and ironworks and concentrated on exporting coal southwards.

In the 1860s much of the route was used by a standard railway, the Neath & Brecon, which ran from Swansea to Brecon.

Above.
Old Tramway marks the route of part of the Hay Railway a short distance east of Brecon (now Aberhonddu) on this 1886 map. The Brecon & Merthyr Railway purchased the Hay Railway in 1860 and used some of its route for its own line but was unable to do so here, as a new tunnel was required. In Brecon all trace of the 1816 line has been erased, first by the Brecon & Merthyr Railway and, after that line was closed in 1962, by new housing.

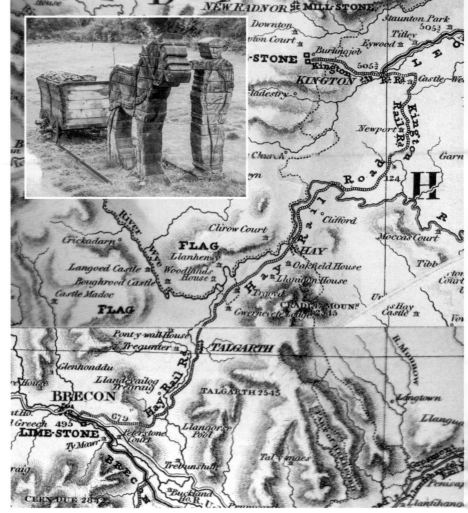

Above.
A northward extension of the large map of South Wales on *pages 66–67*, this part shows the *Hay Rail Road*, completed in 1816, and its extension the *Kington Rail R^d.*, completed in 1820. Together they comprised the longest of the plateway railways, at 36 miles long. At the time it was the longest railway in the world. The line fed into the Brecknock & Abergavenny Canal at Brecon. An interesting monument to the Hay Railway (*inset, top*) was placed on the south side of the canal opposite the Brecon terminus.

Stone Rails — The Haytor Granite Railway

One railway, though constructed on the same principle as other plateways—the flange being on the rail—used a cheaper and more easily available material than iron. Since the railway had been built to transport granite from a quarry on Dartmoor, the obvious local material was granite. And, despite the apparently huge amount of work that would be entailed shaping every piece of rail for a 7-mile-long (9 miles with sidings) line, that is what was used. The Haytor Granite Tramway thus not only transported granite but was made from it!

The 1.7-mile-long Stover Canal, which led down to the estuary of the River Teign, was opened in 1792. It had been built by the Templer family of Devon, major landowners in the region, to facilitate the export of ball clay for use in the Staffordshire Potteries. The original plan had been to extend the canal farther inland, but instead a tramway was built from the end of the canal at Ventiford up onto Dartmoor, to quarries in the vicinity of Haytor. The tramway was completed in 1820.

The reasons for using granite for the railway are not documented, but it seems clear it was simply a cheaper and home-built solution. At least some of the stone used for the second London Bridge, designed by John Rennie and built in 1825–31 (and now at Lake Havasu City, Arizona), came from Haytor and thus passed down this line. The railway lasted until the mid 1850s, when the quarry closed. Parts of the line are still visible, thanks to the long-lasting nature of the material used.

Above and *opposite*.
Photos of the Haytor Granite Tramway as it is today, relatively well preserved owing to the hardness and weight of the granite. The large photo shows that even switches, or points, were made from stone.

Below.
This 1830 map shows both the *Stover Ca*[nal] and the granite railway from it to *Heytor Rocks*.

Below.
By the time the survey for this 1885 map was completed, the Haytor Granite Tramway had been unused for several decades. Branches to a number of quarries near Haytor are still shown, labelled *Tramway (Disused)*. The line led off the moor to the northeast, beyond the *Quarries* in the top right-hand corner of this map, where the disused line is no longer shown.

Inset. Haytor Quarry in 1825.

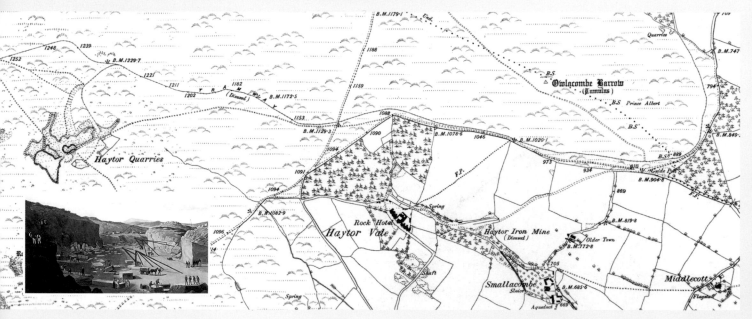

The Iron Edge Railways

Modern rail is edge rail in principle, though the exact profile has evolved substantially over time as the most efficient shape was developed. The rails changed in cross-section, in size and weight, in longitudinal shape and length, and in the material used—originally cast iron, then wrought (malleable) iron, then steel. Here the required guiding flange is on the wheel rather than on the rail. The tractive effort required on an edge rail was about 30 per cent less than on a plate rail, and this was a major reason for the eventual universal adoption of the edge rail.

In South Wales, many of the mines, ironworks, and limestone quarries of the heads of the valleys from Hirwaun to Blaenavon (shown on the map on *pages 66–67*) used bar rails of cast iron during the decade beginning in 1787. They were generally short feeder lines but doubtless totalled a significant distance. And then, after 1796, the L-plate reigned supreme until after 1830. On the waggonways of the northeast coalfield of England, the standalone iron rail followed directly from wooden and iron-strapped rails and by 1814 was in use on George Stephenson's Killingworth line. In 1816 Stephenson partnered with William Losh, a Newcastle iron founder, to patent a new type of cast-iron rail with joints that were an improvement on those then existing. It was this rail that Stephenson used for his Hetton Colliery Railway in 1822 (see page 138).

Above.
The rollers John Birkinshaw patented to roll his new malleable-iron rails in 1820. The T-shapes are formed between the two rollers.

Soon after that, malleable or wrought iron became the material of choice. Wrought iron seems to have been first used on part of the Tindale Fell railway (see page 31) in 1808, but the rails were rectangular in shape and used a lot of iron; hence, they were expensive. In 1820, John Birkinshaw, an agent for the Bedlington Ironworks in Northumberland, patented a 15-foot-long malleable rail with a T-shape able to withstand heavy use but still use a minimum of material. The rollers he patented to roll these rails are shown *above*. These rails revolutionized the railway by at last providing a surface along which heavy pounding steam locomotives could more reliably run. Stephenson would forsake his own patented rails to use malleable iron for most of the Stockton & Darlington Railway in 1825 (see page 148).

This section discusses some of the most significant very early iron edge railways.

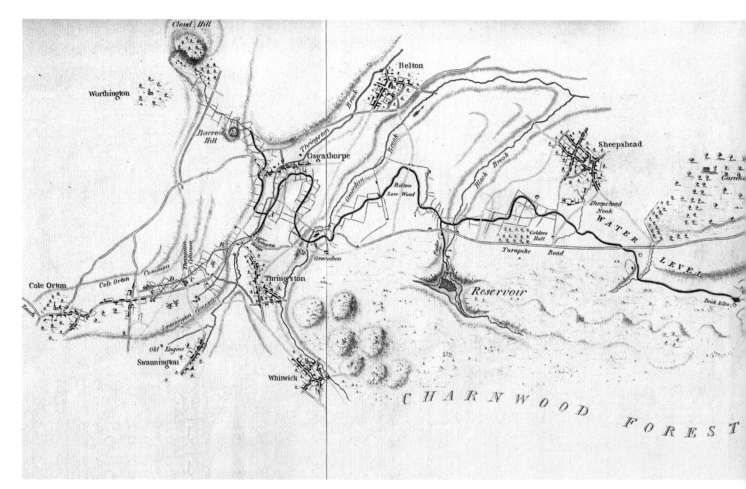

The Leicester Navigation

One of the earliest uses of the iron edge rail is thought to be the so-called Forest Line of the Leicester Navigation, sometimes referred to as the Loughborough & Nanpantan Railway.

The Leicester Navigation Company was created in 1791 to make the River Soar navigable between Loughborough and Leicester, and to make "a communication by Railways, or Stone Roads, and Water Levels, from several places and mines" in the Swannington and Coleorton mining districts to Loughborough, to create a complete route for shipping coal and other merchandise to Leicester. The idea was to make coal from Leicestershire mines available in the city of Leicester cheaper than competing coal from Derbyshire.

The plan was to create a canal from Thringstone to Nanpantan with a railway at either end of the canal to cover the more

difficult terrain there, ending at a wharf in Loughborough (maps *below* and *below, bottom*). William Jessop was appointed as the engineer for the project. For the railway, he used T-shaped iron rails.

After many delays, the canal and railway system finally was able to pass a shipment of coal through it to Loughborough in

Right.
This 1807 map of the wider area shows the *Leicester Navigation* canal (in dark green, almost black) and a *Railway* at each end (in red). With the failure of the Leicester Navigation, the Cloud Hill area was connected first to the *Ashby* [de la Zouch] *Can*[al] by a plateway that also served *Ticknall* (see page 46), and in 1831 the coal mines of Cole Orton and Swannington were connected to *Leicester* via the Leicester & Swannington Railway, an early standard edge railway (see page 201).

Below, across page.
The original survey for the Forest Line of the Leicester Navigation by Christopher Staveley done in 1790 and published the following year. Two short branches of the western end of the canal have rail lines from them to coal mines near *Cole Orton* and *Swannington*, and a limestone quarry at *Cloud Hill*. At the eastern end of the canal, which ends at *Brick Kilns* at Nanpantan, is a rail line to the *Loughborough Canal*, from where a diversion (the thick black line) to the *River Soar* goes south to Leicester.

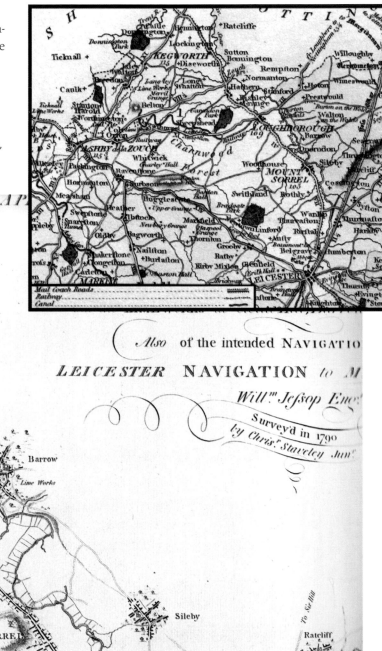

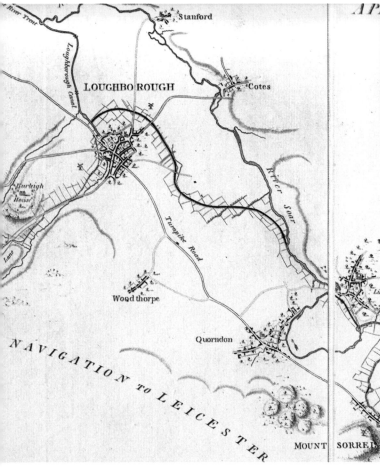

October 1794. The canal seems to have had low-water-level problems right from the start, and the canal company never provided wagons and boats that they had promised, much to the annoyance of the coal mine owners. By July 1795 some 400 tons of coal were stacked at Thringstone Wharf, at the western end of the canal, because of the inability of the canal to transport it. And Derbyshire coal delivered to Leicester was reduced in price so that coal sent along the Forest Line would be non-competitive in any case. Finally, after a winter thaw in 1798, the dam holding back the reservoir that supplied the canal with water burst its banks, destroying earthworks and effectively putting the canal out of commission. The canal was allowed to dry up, and it became overgrown. The Forest Line failed to compete largely because of its mixed railway-canal-railway-canal configuration, a line of communication requiring too many transhipments.

Considerable effort was put into a resurvey as a railway line only in the early 1830s; the idea then was that it could

Above.
By 1883, the date of this map, the line of the canal and railway at the Nanpantan end had virtually disappeared. The blue is where the canal was, with the railway going east from the end by the road, its line undefined.

compete with the newly opened Leicester & Swannington Railway (see page 205), but after much more waste of money, the idea was shelved.

The Lake Lock Rail Road

The Lake Lock Rail Road lays claim to being the first railway line in the world to be built and operated by a company, and also arguably the first public railway in the world, since it opened in 1798.

However, the company was created under a trust deed, a legal way of getting round the provisions of the South Sea Bubble Act of 1720, which had required companies to be authorized by an Act of Parliament (or by a Royal Warrant). Shares in the company were advertised for sale in 1801. The company's trust deed is dated a

few months before the opening of the Surrey Iron Railway in July 1803. It is not clear why the trust deed was not obtained before the company built the line in 1798, but one can certainly see why there is so much confusion as to which was the first public railway.

The Lake Lock Rail Road certainly was a public railway, since it operated by charging tolls to all comers. It ran from a number of branch lines from collieries in the Wakefield, Yorkshire, area, down to the Aire & Calder Navigation (map, *below*). Coal and stone were carried down to the river, and roadstone, shoring timbers for mines, and burnt lime were carried up.

Below.
The line of the Lake Lock Rail Road is shown on this 1854 map in red. The line as built in 1798 followed the dotted red line to the *River Calder.* The route was changed in 1804 to the longer but gentler slope down to the river at *Bottom Boat.* The modern photo, *left,* was taken looking up Lake Lock Road (named on the street sign by the building at left) from the location of the small green arrow on the map and shows the original steep route down to the river, abandoned in 1804.

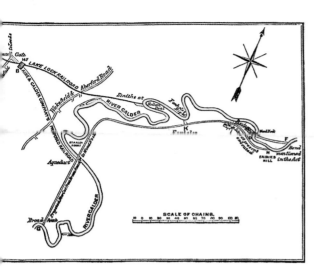

Above.
This little map was included in a legal case argued in 1846 and clearly shows the route of the *Lake Lock Railroad* to *Staithes* at *Bottom Boat* on the *River Calder*.

Right.
This 1830 map shows the *La. Lock RR.* and also the network of private colliery lines that fed into it at the western end. The black dots are collieries. Note also *Brandling's R^l. R^d.* leading into *Leeds* (see pages 20 and 112)

Belvoir Castle

Belvoir Castle railway was a private line constructed by the Duke of Rutland in 1815 to bring coal to his castle from the Grantham Canal. The canal was built to transport coal from Nottingham coalfields to Grantham and opened in 1797. Since the railway ran entirely over the duke's own land, the 1½-mile-long line did not need an Act of Parliament. The rails were laid right into the cellars of the castle, making it arguably the world's first indoor railway! The line is noteworthy because it seems to be the first use of an edge rail that was I-shaped in cross-section.

The duke, unlike most members of the aristocracy at the time, was quite pro-railway and would later allow other rails to be laid across his lands, but this was a horse railway, unlikely to prove objectionable to the castle residents high above, and indeed not even visible from most of the castle. The railway was engineered by the Butterley Company, and the rail seems to have been designed by William Jessop's youngest son, William Jessop (junior), who managed the company after the death of Benjamin Outram in 1805.

Above.
The Belvoir Castle railway: a "train" pauses for a photograph. The I-shaped "fish-belly" rails are clearly displayed, as are the flanged wheels of the wagon. The wood stake at the rear of the wagon was to prevent the wagon from rolling backwards and would have also taken the weight off the horses while standing, such as here.

Above. The shape of the flanged wheel can be seen on this wagon from the railway, now at the National Railway Museum, York.

Left. A clear view of the track at the same location as the photo on the *previous page*; the building at right is the black building on the north side of the *Peacock Inn* on the map, *far left.*

The addition of a bottom flange to the rail added considerably to its strength. The 3-foot-long fishbelly-shaped cast-iron rails were dovetailed at each end to fit into one another and had a flat foot for spiking to a stone block, making a particularly strong and rigid line.

The line lasted a century: the last shipment of coal over the line was in 1916, the line was last used two years later, and most of the track was lifted and taken for the war effort in 1941.

Left.
The line of the Belvoir Castle railway is highlighted in red on this 1884 map. The line ran from *Muston Gorse Wharf* to the cellars of *Belvoir Castle*.

Below.
This is a 3-foot piece of the Belvoir Castle fishbelly I-rail, now on display at the Narrow Gauge Railway Museum at Tywyn, Wales.

The Mansfield & Pinxton Railway

The Mansfield & Pinxton Railway was designed to link Mansfield with the canal system. It would also link a number of collieries. Planning began in 1813, but some collieries near Mansfield, realizing that coal prices would drop in that town, led a concerted attempt to stop the railway, which did not gain enough subscriber support until 1817 to begin building. Even then, the effort to get the required Act of Parliament passed was hindered by these colliery owners, who managed to get a clause inserted in the act, passed in June 1817, to require coal to be sold at no lower than two shillings per ton, the price at which the near-Mansfield owners could still make a profit.

The engineer for the railway was Josias Jessop, William's eldest son, and his recommendation to use edge rails prevailed after some argument. He used the so-called fishbelly rails very similar to those at Belvoir Castle but slightly heavier in cross-section (photo, *below*). They were secured, as was the practice, to stone block.

As late as 1818, one of the line's biggest subscribers, the Duke of Portland, was advocating L-plate rails, or at least a rail that would allow road traffic to run along the line, as he thought this would increase traffic. Jessop had already purchased most of the edge rail and was able to head off the suggestion. The line required a five-arch viaduct to carry it over the River Maun at King's Mill, then just west of Mansfield (*overleaf*).

The first load of coal arrived in Mansfield on 13 April 1819 and was taken to the town square to be ceremonially burned. Over the next few years a number of branch lines were added, mainly to collieries, but also one to the Butterley Company's ironworks at Codnor Park (map, *below*). In 1832 a passenger service—a horse and coach with adapted wheels—began, on Thursdays only, which was market day—from Pinxton to Mansfield. Much of the line was taken over by the newly formed Midland Railway in 1847.

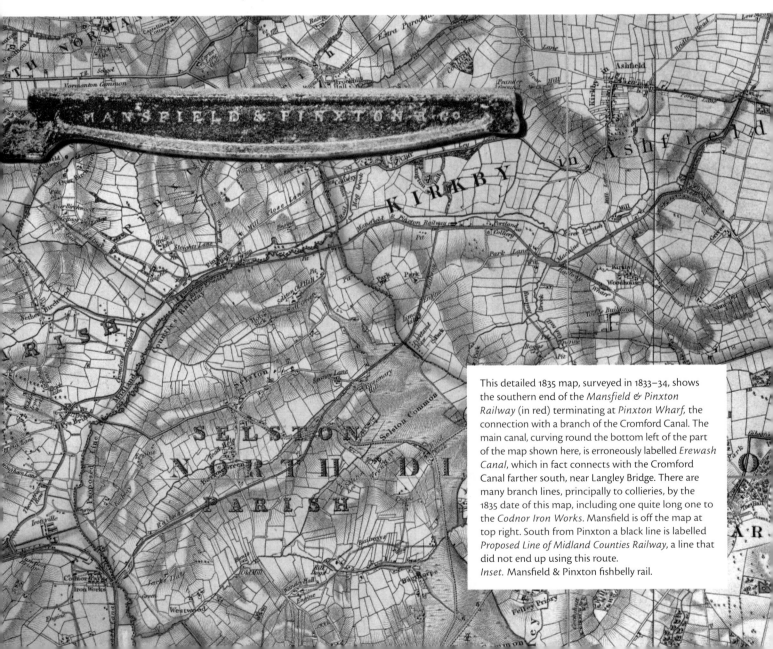

This detailed 1835 map, surveyed in 1833–34, shows the southern end of the *Mansfield & Pinxton Railway* (in red) terminating at *Pinxton Wharf*, the connection with a branch of the Cromford Canal. The main canal, curving round the bottom left of the part of the map shown here, is erroneously labelled *Erewash Canal*, which in fact connects with the Cromford Canal farther south, near Langley Bridge. There are many branch lines, principally to collieries, by the 1835 date of this map, including one quite long one to the *Codnor Iron Works*. Mansfield is off the map at top right. South from Pinxton a black line is labelled *Proposed Line of Midland Counties Railway*, a line that did not end up using this route.
Inset. Mansfield & Pinxton fishbelly rail.

Above.

Another part of the 1835 map shows the Mansfield & Pinxton Railway just south of Mansfield and shows *King's Mill*, where the five-arch viaduct (photo, *right, top*), crosses the *River Maun*. The Kings Mill Viaduct was originally named the Portland Bridge after the Duke of Portland, one of the line's principal investors. The other photo shows how wide the trackbed was; it was double tracked and used from 1848 to 1871 by the Midland Railway, a standard-gauge line. Note also the *Summit* marked on the map. The railway descended in both directions from this point.

The Plymouth & Dartmoor Railway

The second railway to access the remote moorland of Dartmoor, the Plymouth & Dartmoor Railway was a much more conventional affair than its sister, the Haytor Granite Tramway (see page 70), in that it used cast-iron edge rails. Its circuitous route delivered granite to a quay at Plymouth; no canal was involved.

The 25½-mile-long railway was promoted in 1818 by Thomas Tyrwhitt, who had leased land from the Duchy of Cornwall with the aim of converting the moorland into farmland. The line was completed in 1823. Construction costs were kept to a minimum, hence the many twists and turns. But the route did include a 620-yard-long tunnel.

After 1851, supplies for Dartmoor Prison at Princetown, originally opened to house prisoners of war in 1809 but closed from 1815 to 1851, formed the main traffic uphill, and china clay as well as granite were brought down to Plymouth. The Plymouth & Dartmoor Railway's successor line, the Princetown Railway, part of the Great Western Railway and opened in 1883, used some of the original route and was England's highest railway until it closed in 1956.

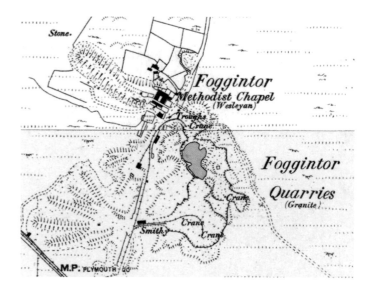

Above.

The railway terminated at the Foggintor Granite Quarry, one of the largest of the quarries on Dartmoor, near Princetown, and the source of the granite used for Nelson's Column in London.

Above.
The winding nature of the *Dartmoor Rail Road* is evident on this 1830 map.
Inset. A typical train consisting of four wagons pulled by two horses.

Right.
This 1854 map shows the *Plymouth* end of the *Plymouth and Dartmoor Railway*. The railway is highlighted in red. It delivered granite to the *Dartmoor Granite Works*, on the part of the *River Plym* estuary known as the Laira, and also to *Sutton Pool* in Plymouth Harbour.

A Wasted Vision

The Stratford & Moreton Railway in Warwickshire and Gloucestershire is a railway with a story. It was the only completed part of a project devised by visionary railway promoter William James, whose schemes seem to have had a habit of not coming to fruition. It was to be part of his Central Junction Railway, designed to connect the canals of the Midlands to London. James, about whom we will hear more later, envisaged his scheme as the first "hundred-mile" railway in the world (see page 146). The section from Stratford to Moreton-in-the-Marsh (now Moreton-in-Marsh) was authorized in 1821 and opened in September 1826.

James wanted his line to be worked by steam locomotives, particularly because he had negotiated a deal with George Stephenson for the rights to his steam engines in the southern half of England and was trying to market them as "Land Agent" engines (see illustration, *page 53*). James was even offered an engine to run on his railway—*Traveller*, the only one ever made by Robert Wilson, owner of an engineering company close to Robert Stephenson in Newcastle—but in 1825, a second Act of Parliament for the railway, required to raise more money, specifically forbade the use of steam locomotives for at least 6 miles south of Stratford. This put an end to James's hopes of using steam traction, and this engine instead went to the Stockton & Darlington Railway (see page 168). Perhaps this was a good thing, for the engine, nicknamed *Chittapratt* then because of the strange noise it made, never performed satisfactorily.

The railway was promoted by James with wrought-iron fishbelly-type edge rails, for he recognized that the greater weight of steam locomotives would put more strain on the rails and that cast-iron rails simply would not work.

James's 1820 map of his plan for the Central Junction Railway that would have connected the Stratford & Moreton line to London is shown on *page 147*.

Right.
The Stratford & Moreton Railway in Stratford-upon-Avon, shown on an 1851 map. The Avon bridge is at lower right. The Stratford-upon-Avon Canal enters the northernmost canal basin at top, under the *Canal Bridge*. This canal, completed in 1816, connected with other canals of the Midlands. The map shows that the railway also ran down the street at left, *Water Side*. The southernmost canal basin has now been filled in, but the canal and northern basin, and the lock entrance to the river, are still in operation.

Far right.
The route of the *Stratford and Moreton Railway*, from *Stratford upon Avon* to *Moreton in the Marsh*, with a *Branch* to *Shipston on Stour*, is delineated on this 1830 map. The bridge across the River Avon (photo, *inset, opposite, top*) still stands and is used as a pedestrian bridge. The other two photos show wagons used on the line; both date from about 1840. The one at *centre* is restored and stands on the wharf at Stratford. The one at *bottom* is in the National Railway Museum.

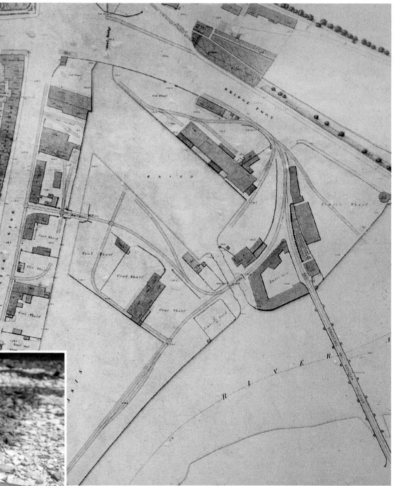

Left.
Detail of the flanged wheel and edge fishbelly rail on stone sleeper block from the wagon on display at the canal basin. The wagon stands right on the line of track just before the first junction north of the bridge, as shown on the map *above*.

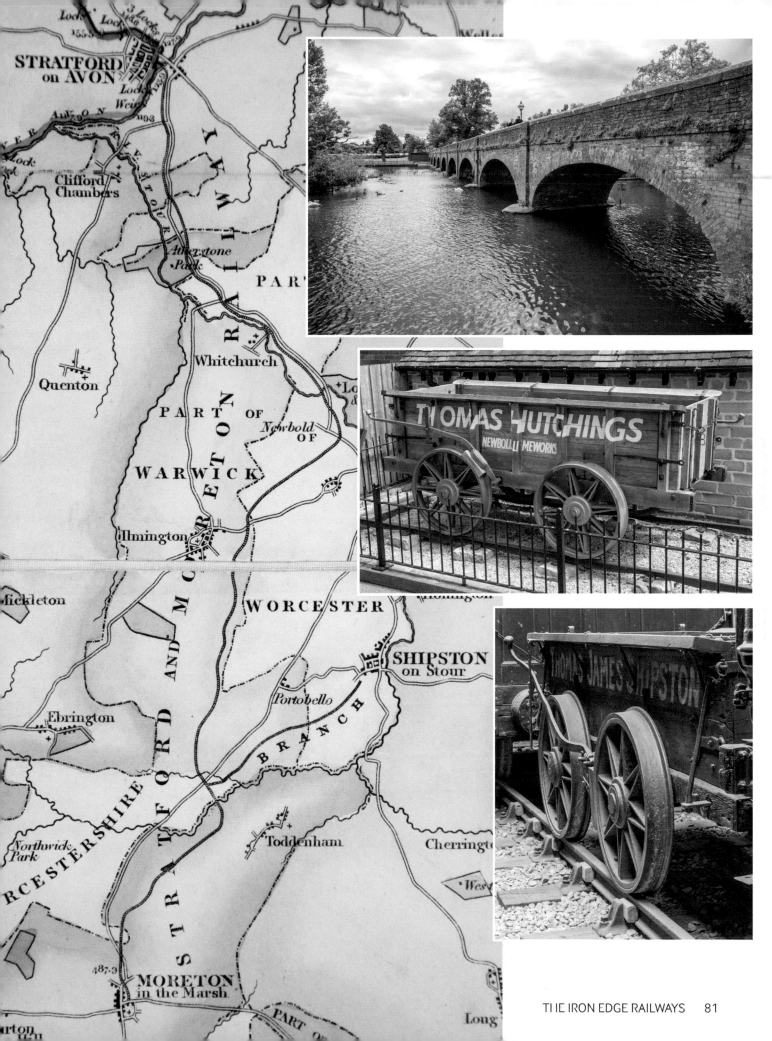

Scotland's Early Railways

Scotland's first iron railway, the Kilmarnock & Troon (see page 63), was a plateway, but after that most lines borrowed the technology of edge rails from northeast England. The first of these was the Monkland & Kirkintilloch Railway, which was completed in 1826 and ran from collieries at Monklands to the Forth & Clyde Canal. The object was to supply coal to Edinburgh, though it could also be sent to Glasgow, Scotland's largest city. The Monkland Canal, fully opened by 1794, had a virtual monopoly on the Glasgow-bound trade, and the new route would break this monopoly, albeit with a longer route. The fact is that coal prices fell in Glasgow once the new route was open. The Union Canal had been completed in 1822 to link the Forth & Clyde Canal with Edinburgh. By carrying coal to the latter canal, the railway company could open up an entire coalfield to a large new market.

The Monkland & Kirkintilloch Railway (and all the railways that connected to it in the next few years) used malleable- or wrought-iron edge rails of the type invented by John Birkinshaw at Bedlington Ironworks in Northumberland and patented in 1820 (see page 72). Although the railway opened using horse traction, it would be ready for locomotives.

In May 1826 authorization was obtained for a direct line from the Monkland coalfield to Glasgow. This was the Garnkirk & Glasgow Railway, and it was really a branch of the Monkland & Kirkintilloch that would enable coal to be sent the whole way to Glasgow without the need for transhipment. Over the objections of the canal companies, which were bound to lose business, the Garnkirk & Glasgow company was authorized to "make the necessary Openings in the Ledges or Flanches" of the Monkland & Kirkintilloch to create a junction. Of course, the same rails were

Left.
The northern end of the *Monkland and Kirkintilloch* Railway on an 1859 map. The railway terminates at two *canal basins* leading to the Forth & Clyde Canal.

Below.
The railways east of *Glasgow* on an 1846 map. The Monkland & Kirkintilloch ran from *Old Monkland* to *Kirkintulloch*; the *Great Canal* is the Forth & Clyde. The Garnkirk & Glasgow is the line into Glasgow; the Ballochney runs from the vicinity of *Airdrie* eastwards, while the southernmost branches are the Wishaw & Coltness Railway, opened between 1833 and 1844.

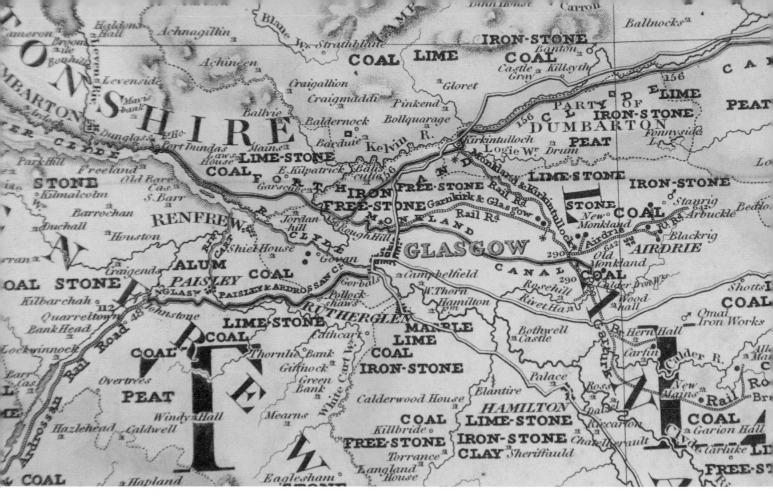

used. Construction began in 1827, and the line opened in 1831. This line is notable as having used steam locomotives from the beginning.

Another branch was the Ballochney Railway, which joined the Monkland & Kirkintilloch at Kipps, between Coatbridge and Airdrie. The purpose was to connect collieries farther east to Glasgow markets. Construction began in 1826, some traffic ran over the line by the following year, and it was completed in 1828. Other lines continued to connect to the Monkland & Kirkintilloch network, which of course also included many short lines serving individual collieries.

The maps on this page demonstrate how a single short "starter" line grew into a much more extensive network that would include the main intercity line in Scotland. (See also the Edinburgh & Dalkeith Railway, page 196.)

Above.
This 1830 map shows the line of the *Monkland & Kirkintullock* (Kirkintilloch), the *Garnkirk & Glasgow Rail Rᵈ.*, the *Airdrie Rˡ. Rᵈ.* (Ballochney Railway), and the *Garturk Rail Road* (the Wishaw & Coltness). The latter line was not in operation until 1833, and then only in parts, but was authorized in 1829 as the Garturk & Garion Railway and thus is on this map. Also on this map is the *Ardrossan Rail Road*, running from the end of the *Glasᵂ. Paisley & Ardrossan Cˡ.* (Canal). This canal had been authorized in 1806, and it was intended to link a sea port at Ardrossan with Glasgow, but the project ran out of money in 1811 and thus terminated at *Johnstone*. The railway shown on the map had been authorized in 1827 to finish the connection built east from Ardrossan but also ran out of money, and the connection was not finally made until a new effort in 1840 by a different company and a line that went straight to Glasgow, ignoring the canal.

Right. Another 1846 map, with the Monkland & Kirkintilloch Railway network grown ever larger. The map now shows the Slamannan Railway, completed in 1840, extending the Ballochney Railway eastwards—it connected with the Union Canal—and the Edinburgh & Glasgow Railway (the northernmost red line on this map), authorized in 1838 and completed in 1842, connecting the two major cities of Scotland. The construction of the latter had been encouraged by the completion of another intercity line, the Liverpool & Manchester (see pages 176–93).

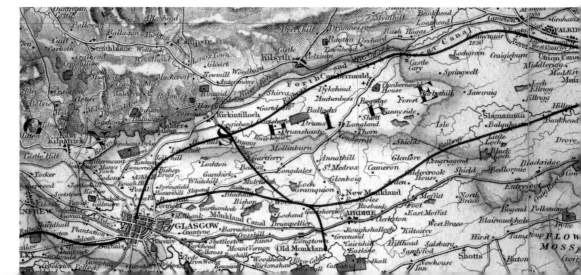

The Slate Railways of North Wales

Slate, a fissile rock used principally for roofing, has been quarried in North Wales for centuries. This heavy rock was quarried from generally remote areas, and thus transportation formed a major portion of its cost.

In 1794 the British government introduced a tax on slate, applied only if it was shipped coastwise, which all North Wales slate had to be (the tax lasted until 1831). The next year a tax on horses used for industrial purposes was imposed. Together, these taxes raised costs and made the North Wales slate quarries less competitive with those in Cumbria and Leicester. The introduction of railways soon after was in major part driven by the need to keep costs down; a horse could pull far more if the load was on rails.

The first line in northwest Wales was not a slate railway, however, but served a grinding mill that ground chert (found in limestone) for use in manufacturing porcelain. This was the mile-long Llandegai Tramway, opened in 1798, which, despite its name, is thought to have been an edge railway, though historians are not quite sure (map, *far right*).

This line was incorporated into a longer railway only three years after it opened—a line that ran from the Penrhyn slate quarry at Bethesda to Port Penrhyn, a shipping quay built at the eastern entrance to the Menai Strait.

A survey for this new line was made by canal and railway engineer Thomas Dadford, who carried out a canal survey in 1799 before determining that it would be impractical. The railway was, perhaps surprisingly, built at a time when the demand for slate was weak, but the quarry owner, Richard Pennant, was worried that his men, 75 per cent of whom were unemployed at the time, would riot. Indeed, in 1800 there were riots in Caernarfon, and this likely prompted haste on a decision later that year to proceed with building the railway. The Penrhyn Railway was opened with great celebration in July 1801.

Dadford had recommended Benjamin Outram's L-plate rail system, but despite this an unusual edge-type rail was used instead (illustration, *right, top*). The rails (photos, *right*) were at first elliptical in cross-section; the wagon wheels were double flanged. This arrangement ran better than a rail on a flat surface owing to reduced friction, but it was later found to cause binding once the wheels wore down a bit. In 1807 a flatter-topped version was introduced, which improved matters somewhat. We know that some elliptical rails were still being used in 1826–27, because visiting German engineers reported on them. The rails were cast iron at first but were replaced with wrought-iron ones. In 1832 the rails were replaced with wrought-iron T-section rails (but with a flat bottom, more I-shaped), and these were found to be much more satisfactory. The initial use of rounded rails is interesting in that they mirrored the ancient use of logs for some of the very first railways (see page 14).

Left.
Fire Queen was one of two identical steam locomotives built for the Padarn Railway, successor to the Dinorwic Railway, and delivered in 1848. The two engines were the only ones built by A. Horlock & Company, of Northfleet, Kent, and were based on a design of Thomas Crampton (see page 262). They worked until the late 1880s, and this locomotive, at the insistence of the quarry owner's daughter, was stored rather than scrapped. *Fire Queen* is now displayed at Penrhyn Castle's Industrial Railway Museum.

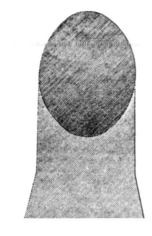

Above.
This plate illustrating the Penrhyn Railway's first type of edge rail and a slate train appeared in a publication called the *Repertory of Arts and Manufactures* in 1803. The elliptical rail was held in a matching chair.

Above and *right.*
Four types of edge rail from the Penrhyn Railway.
From top to bottom: original 1801 elliptical rail, with a simple hand-lifted bar for switching; next is the flattened ellipse, also with switch, developed after it was found that worn wheels were prone to binding; next is the later T- or I-shaped rail, with a flat bottom, with a crossover shown; and at *bottom* is a more portable track with simple iron bars that could be moved around a quarry—this was in use before 1830 but is sometimes attributed to Thomas Hughes, the quarry foreman platelayer, in 1852.

Above.
The route of the 1798 Llandegai Tramway (solid red line) and the 1801 Penrhyn Railway is traced on this 1888 map. The railway used essentially the same route to *Llandegai*, except for the branch at right angles down to *Penrhyn Mill*, a grinding mill, on this map a corn mill, powered from the *Mill Race*. This branch was an inclined plane down to the mill. The railway to the quarry goes off the map at bottom. At the north end of the line is the slate quay at *Port Penrhyn*. Another inclined plane was situated where *Incline Cottage* is marked. The dotted red line for part of the route is where the line was rerouted in 1819 when the road was improved. Most of the area north of Llandegai is part of *Penrhyn Park*, with *Penrhyn Castle*, seat of the Pennant family, owners of the Penrhyn slate quarry. The castle is now a National Trust property and site of the industrial railway museum where *Fire Queen* is displayed.

In 1879 the Penrhyn Railway was superseded by a line with a new route to Port Penrhyn, referred to as the Penrhyn Quarry Railway. This was built to use steam traction, and the different route was to even out the gradients encountered on the 1801 line, which did include an inclined plane but had been entirely horse worked. This line lasted until 1962.

The Penrhyn Quarry was the largest of the North Wales slate quarries. The second-largest, the Dinorwic (now Dinorwig) Quarry, was located on the other side of the mountain to the southwest but accessed via a different valley, close to Llanberis, also known as the terminus for the Snowdon Mountain Railway. The remains of this vast quarrying operation are visible from the main road through Snowdonia (photo, *below, bottom*).

Local legend has it that there was a railway along the shores of Llyn Padarn around 1800, but there is no evidence of this. The first documented railway was opened in 1824 and was built, like the Penrhyn, during a downturn in the cyclical slate business, using otherwise unemployed labour. The railway was operated using horses and ran from the quarry to a location on the Menai Strait that became known as Port Dinorwic. This railway lasted only till 1843, a year after a new line built for steam operation and using a slightly different route to Port Dinorwic, was opened. The new line was also built at a time of a downturn in the slate trade, again using otherwise unemployed labour. This seems to have been a habit in North Wales, but of course it was also the time of lowest possible cost.

The Dinorwic quarries were a group of quarrying operations rather than a single quarry or mountainside, and temporary railways within the quarries were used for internal transport even before 1824. The second railway, the Padarn, closed in 1961.

Below.
A slate wagon from the Dinorwic Quarry at the National Slate Museum in Llanberis, previously the quarry company workshops. The wheels are double flanged.

Far right, top.
Of all the North Wales slate quarry railways, the *Nantlle Rail R^d.* is the only one shown on this 1830 map, as it had been authorized by an Act of Parliament. The line of the 1824 Dinorwic Railway from near *Fachwen* to Port Dinorwic on *Menai Straits* has been added, in red. Its successor from 1842, the Padarn Railway, built for steam operation, is in green. The Penrhyn Railway, from *Penrhyn Quarry* to Port Penrhyn near *Llandegai*, has also been added in red, with the Penrhyn Quarry Railway, its successor steam line (where the route diverged) in green. Minor diversions at the northern end are not shown at this scale. Interestingly, a railway on the Isle of Anglesey called *Penrhyn Mawr Rail R^d.* is shown. This line was authorized in 1812 but never built.

Below.
The massive Dinorwic slate quarry seen from the Llanberis road, across the lake, Llyn Peris. The area visible forms only a small part of the whole, as is evident from the map at *right*. The inclined planes are still visible.

Right, top.
A transporter incline at the Dinorwic Quarry. This one has been restored as part of the National Slate Museum. Note that the right-hand transporter is descending, having wagons full of slate, while the left-hand, empty one ascends. Even steeper inclines were used within the quarry; at least one was nearly vertical, more correctly a lift.

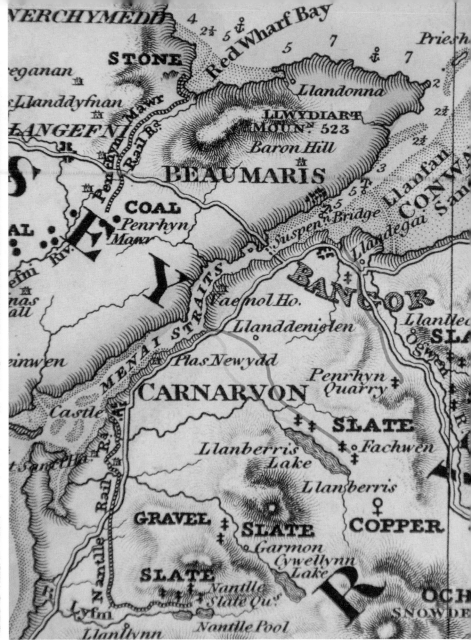

Far left, this page.
Dinorwic Quarry was in full operation when this map was published in 1888. The part bordering *Llyn P*[eris] at bottom is the same as that in the photo, *far left*. Several *Inclined Plane*[s] are marked; at *left* is a photo of the largest. The village of *Dinorwic* (now Dinorwig) is close to the location where the many lines within the quarry came together to form the Dinorwic Railway, through which slate was exported until 1843.

Above.
A Nantlle Railway train pauses for a photograph at the Pen-yr-Orsedd slate quarry about 1900. Three horses are pulling about a dozen loaded wagons.

Below.
This 1888 map shows the Nantlle Railway among a confusion of branch lines running from *Pen-yr-orsedd Slate Quarry* at right past several other slate quarries to the transhipment sidings at *Tal-y-sarn* at bottom left. Before 1866 the line extended north to Caernarfon and was wholly horse drawn.

Inset, below.
A wagon from the Nantlle Railway with double-flanged wheels. The symbol on the side indicates that this wagon belonged to Pen-yr-Orsedd Quarry.

The only one of the slate railways of North Wales to be authorized by an Act of Parliament was the "Nantlle Railway or Tramroad," for which acts were passed in 1825, 1827, and 1828. The additional bills were necessary because the scope and money required had been underestimated. The railway opened in 1828 and ran from several large slate quarries in the Nantlle valley, including the Cilgwyn Quarry, where slate had been obtained since the twelfth century. It was a toll line, with anyone being able to use it on payment of a fee. This line is notable in that the section from Pen-yr-Orsedd Quarry to Tal-y-Sarn was horse worked right up to its closure in 1963.

The line was originally planned as a plateway, but some of the Liverpool investors in the company became displeased with the use of this technology and the pace of progress, and George Stephenson was consulted. Busy with the Liverpool & Manchester Railway (see page 176), he sent his brother, Robert Stephenson, who recommended wrought-iron fishbelly rails, though it remained narrow gauge rather than the Stephenson standard 4 feet, 8 inches that he also recommended.

The railway ran north from the quarries to a quay under the walls of the thirteenth-century Caernarvon Castle (map, *far right*). The quarries that used the Nantlle Railway, in common with the majority of slate railways in the region, had wagons with double-flanged wheels (photo, *left*).

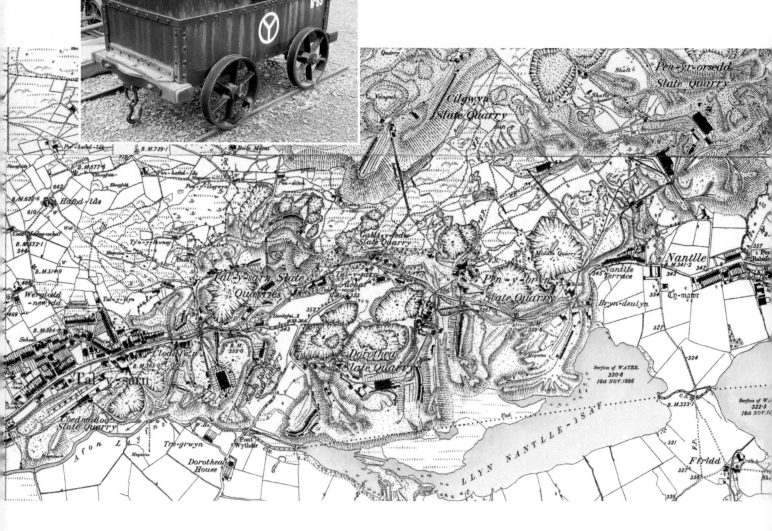

In 1866, the Nantlle Railway between Tal-y-Sarn and Caernarvon was converted to standard gauge and became part of the London & North Western Railway the following year. By then part of British Railways, it was closed in 1964. The part east of Tal-y-Sarn remained horse drawn (and narrow gauge) until its closure the same year. It was the last use of horses by British Railways. The part of the line from Dinas to Caernarfon is now open again—as part of the heritage Welsh Highland Railway; this section opened in 1997.

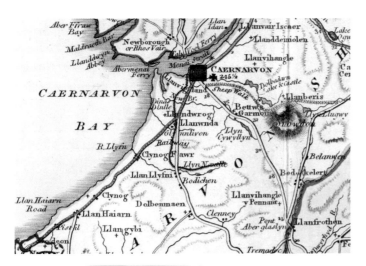

Above, top.
The Nantlle Railway shown on an 1834 map.

Above.
Horses pull a train in a quarry landscape of desolate slates. This photo was taken in 1959, five years before the line was closed.

Right, top.
This 1834 plan of the town of *Caernarvon* (now Caernarfon) shows the Nantlle Railway at its northern terminus—the *Slate Quay* on the River Seiont (Afon Seiont) adjacent to the castle. Note also the *Coal Yards*. The photo, *right, centre*, shows the quay in today's incarnation as a parking lot, though boats are still tied up alongside; heavy chains hint at larger vessels than the sailboats. The preserved heritage Welsh Highland Railway (Rheil-ffordd Eryri) of today terminates at a station along the north side of where these coal yards were located. *Right* is a Welsh Highland Railway train of today arriving at Caernarfon in September 2015, pulled by an articulated Beyer Peacock Garratt locomotive built in 1958. The castle wall is visible in the background. Horse traction has now been superseded by steam!

Incorporated in 1832 and opened in 1836, the Festiniog Railway was the last of the major North Wales slate railways. It ran from slate quarries at Blaenau Ffestiniog some 12½ miles to a quay at Portmadoc (now Porthmadog). The line was carefully graded so that most of the downward journey could be achieved by gravity, though until a tunnel was completed in 1842, there was also an inclined plane involved, designed by Robert Stephenson.

Increasing slate volumes led to the introduction of steam traction—for ascending trains only—in 1863, and the type of locomotive the Festiniog is famous for—the Fairlie Patent—was introduced in 1869. This design was a double-ended articulated engine with driving wheels on bogies that gave greater power while still being able to negotiate the severe bends on the narrow-gauge line (photos, *below*).

In 1896 an extension to the Festiniog Railway north of Blaenau Ffestiniog connected the line to other slate quarries. Slate traffic ceased in 1946. The railway was purchased by enthusiasts in 1954, and the following year the first public passenger train ran. Between 1965 and 1978 part of the line had to be rerouted to accommodate a new reservoir. Today the Ffestiniog Railway (as it calls itself, rather than the single *f* Festiniog as incorporated) or, in Welsh, Rheilffordd Ffestiniog, claims to be the oldest surviving railway *company* in the world (the Middleton Railway—see pages 20 and 114—is the oldest working railway) and is a popular tourist attraction. The line uses the same gauge and is now joined with the Welsh Highland Railway. Passenger workings, first introduced in 1865, are now the line's bread and butter.

Above.
A slate quarry wagon showing the typical double-flanged wheels. This one is preserved at the National Slate Museum at Llanberis.

Right.
Modern-build Fairlie Patent locomotive *David Lloyd George* (with the name in Welsh on the other side) leaves Porthmadog station in September 2015.

Below.
The railway, *Y Cob*, and the Ffestiniog Railway's southern terminus at *Portmadoc* are shown on this 1887 map. As it approaches the town, the line crosses *Y Cob* (the Cob), an embankment that was constructed in 1810 in an attempt to reclaim the estuary lands behind it. The same project created the deep-water harbour at Porthmadog when the diverted river scoured its bottom. *Inset, right, bottom.* Double-ended 1885 Fairlie Patent locomotive, *Livingston Thompson*, at the National Railway Museum, York.

The Northeast Coalfield

As we have seen (pages 20–30), the northeast coalfield of Northumberland and Durham early on had by far the most extensive network of wooden waggonways, developed to transport coal to rivers. It is hardly surprising, then, that this network would eventually convert itself into a system of iron railways. This region almost exclusively converted to edge rails rather than the plates that became the norm in, say, South Wales. The edge principle used on wooden ways was simply transferred to metal. There was only one notable exception, the Wylam Waggonway, where steam traction would be tried in 1813 (see page 120).

Some colliery lines went through an intermediate step of attaching iron strip to the top surface of the wooden rails; others converted directly from wood to iron. The first of the latter appears to have been Lawson's Main Colliery, on the north bank of the Tyne at Walker, in 1797, installed by engineer Thomas Barnes. The rails used for part of this line were T-section cast-iron rails with no bottom widening and were thus relatively weak—it is the I-beam shape that gives the highest strength. This line also had the first-known use of iron chairs, which hold the rail fixed to sleepers—in this case transverse stone.

The advantages of the iron rail—strength, longevity, and lower friction allowing for heavier loads—could be seen by any neighbouring colliery manager, and thus their use spread very quickly. Between about 1810 and 1830 almost all of the major lines of the region were converted, and essentially all new lines were built of iron from their inception.

And it was on these newly installed iron rails that the experiments with steam traction took place; indeed they would not have been able to take place without them—as Wylam's owner had realized in 1805 when he refused delivery of Trevithick's "Gateshead" engine (see page 120). One such waggonway conversion—Killingworth—was to become the scene of George Stephenson's early trials with steam traction. Initially converted to iron strip on top of wooden rails, the track proved inadequate for Stephenson's first locomotives, *My Lord* and *Blucher*, in 1814.

Stephenson (with partner and iron foundry owner William Losh) then developed a cast-iron fishbelly rail with better joints and chairs (illustrated on *page 143*), which were installed by the end of 1818. It is not an exaggeration to say that because of their necessary weight, steam engines would never have succeeded were it not for the simultaneous improvement in the track.

The Newbottle Waggonway, billed as a "waggon rail way," which was completed in 1812 as a brand new edge railway, has been selected as an example of northeast lines, mainly because the superb map (*below* and *overleaf*) has survived. The map was donated to the Sunderland Museum in 2000 and has now been restored. The line was the first to avoid transhipment into keels, barge-like boats on the river that transferred coal to seagoing ships at Sunderland. This handling created much less breakage than transhipment, and larger lumps of coal could be sold for higher prices. The second such line was the Hetton Colliery Railway, completed by George Stephenson in 1822 (see page 138). The latter line was mechanically worked from the beginning, but the Newbottle line was intended for horses. Nevertheless, a steam engine—a very unusual steam engine—was tried out on this line in 1814–15, with disastrous results (see page 126).

The 5¾-mile-long Newbottle railway was intended to serve a number of collieries at its western end, collectively known as the Newbottle Colliery and owned by John Ncsham, descendant of a family that had been mining in the area since 1734. In 1811 he expanded his operations, sinking a new pit, Dorothea, and building the new waggonway. By 1822 he was in financial difficulties and sold his interest to John George Lambton, later the Earl of Durham, who connected his own waggonways to the Newbottle one. In the early 1830s the line was converted to operation by stationary and self-acting engines, and by the 1850s parts of the waggonway were incorporated into locomotive-worked lines.

Above, top. A typical Tyneside chaldron wagon, with iron wheels, possibly on the Willington Waggonway about 1815. Some wagons had wooden rear wheels to better brake by friction; this one, from a more level waggonway, had all-iron wheels. The central path is a walkway for the horse.

Below.
A map of the Newbottle "waggon rail way" dated 1817 but which may have been surveyed earlier (see page 127). Extraordinarily detailed, the map is over 7 feet long and is displayed behind glass, and as such is difficult to reproduce. The image below is a composite of many individual photographs. Details of the map are shown *overleaf*. The tables included on the map showed the lands crossed by the railway, with their acreages, for the calculation of wayleave rents. The map included a view of Wearmouth Bridge (*inset, right*).

All on these pages.

Details of the 1817 map of the Newbottle Railway. *Above* is the ornate title cartouche. *Left* is the westernmost part of the line, ending at *Elizabeth* pit but also showing *Mary* and *Jane* pits. *Below* is a detail of the central part of the line showing passing places, sidings, and [work]*Shops & Stables* for the horses. Note how the "flat" picture of the *Bridge* indicates that the railway passed under the road rather than vice versa.

Below, bottom, is a drawing in the margin of the map showing the usual "Newcastle" type chaldrons of coal being hauled by single horses.

Right is detail of the eastern end of the railway at Sunderland, on the *River Wear*, where the *Staith* was located with spouts (troughs at about 45 degrees with hanging doors to slow the flow of coal) to load the coal into the holds of ships. The waggonway goes through a tunnel to reach some of the other staiths. Beside the waggonway opposite the house is a depot for *landsale*—local sale of coal.

Nicholson Esq

Jews burial Ground

Southwick ferry

Ground

Dock House

Ship Yard

Dock

Black House

Charit

Esq

Gell

Rectory

Dock

Pemberton

Glass House

Bridge

Tho.s Hopper

Charity School

Church

Green

Leighton's Ground

Mr.s Collin's Ground

Hospital

Tany

Steam Mill

Tany

Maling Esq.r Ground

to Sunderland

Rope and Chain — The Inclined Plane

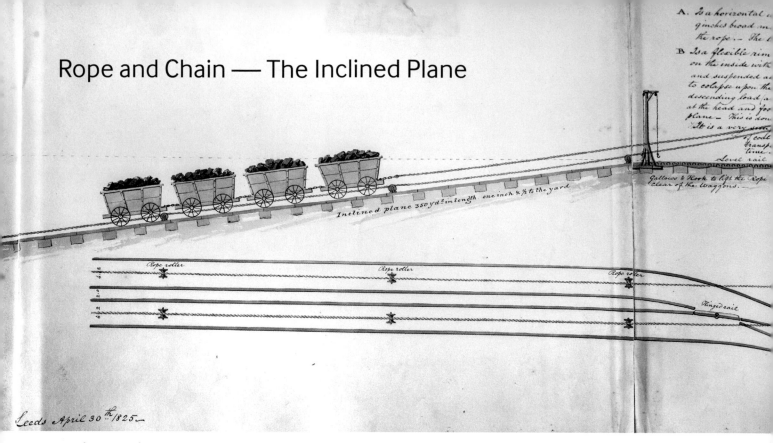

A. *Is a horizontal ... 9 inches broad ... the rope.— The ...*

B. *Is a flexible rim on the inside with ... and suspended ... to collapse upon the descending load ... at the head and foot ... plane.— This is don ... It is a very ... code transp ... time.— Level rail*

Gallows & Hook to lift the rope clear of the waggons.—

Inclined plane 350 yds in length one inch & 2/3 to the yard

Rope roller   *Rope roller*   *Rope roller*

Hinged rail

Leeds April 30th 1825—

Another major form of traction on rails involved inclined planes. They served the same function as flights of locks on a canal by concentrating any change in elevation in one place, where a stationary engine could haul wagons up to the next level. Before that, however, came the balance plane or self-acting plane, where the weight of the descending wagons usually full of coal or stone—counterbalanced the weight of empty wagons being drawn up. All that was necessary in this circumstance was a means of regulating the speed, which was usually achieved by some sort of brake on a drum around which the rope, cable, or chain passed. Rope haulage by this method actually outlasted steam traction in industrial use.

The first self-acting planes are thought to have been in use in Shropshire by 1605, but they were very rare until the end of the eighteenth century. The illustration *below* is an early one showing such a plane; it was published in 1754. They were known in Russia by 1724.

Self-acting inclines, of course, only worked where the heavier load was going downhill. This worked perfectly for collieries and quarries that were sending their coal and stone downhill to a canal or river, as was usually the case. Where there were intervening rises, a source of power was required, and this was provided by the increasing abilities of stationary steam engines, though there is an early example in Russia that used water to power an endless chain to pull hunds (see page 13) up an incline in an iron ore mine. Stationary steam engines working inclined planes first made an appearance in South Wales and Lancashire in 1803, at the London Docks in 1804, and over Black Fell from Birtley in Durham County in 1806. After that they became more widely adopted.

So many early railways incorporated inclines that they are found on lines mentioned throughout the present book. One of the earliest was on the Peak Forest Tramway in Derbyshire (see page 42). They were found on the Stockton & Darlington Railway (see page 148) and planned for the Liverpool & Manchester (see page 176). Even after 1830, lines were being built that included steam-powered inclined planes, notably the Cromford & High Peak Railway, completed in 1831 (see page 203), and the Leicester & Swannington Railway of 1833 (see page 205).

The first application of a self-acting incline in the northeast coalfield of England for which we have details was at Benwell in 1798, though this proved an unusual design. It was single tracked; a counterweight in a deep shaft was pulled up by a loaded descending wagon, and the counterweight then hauled the empty wagon back up the slope. The nature of the topography of the northeast, with many locations being separated from navigable water by interceding hills, ensured that inclined planes became common in the region. The most common location for inclines was for the final descent to staiths on the rivers, which tend to be in steep valleys.

Left.
This early self-acting plane near Broseley was drawn by a Swedish traveller in 1754. Wagons passed on the doubled stretch of track halfway up the incline. The incline used a chain, and a drum at the top had spikes that engaged with it. There was a wooden lever that could be pressed against the drum if the wagons started going down too fast. That was the theory, at any rate; in practice there were many accidents, and later inclines often incorporated catch pits to stop runaway wagons.

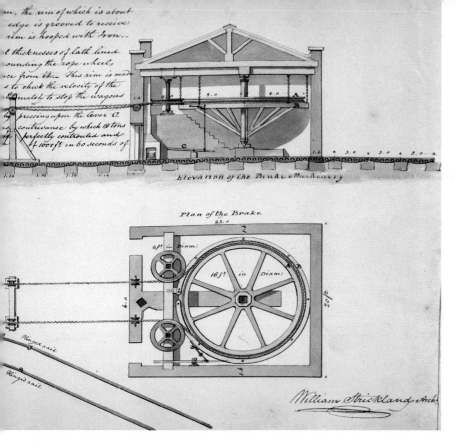

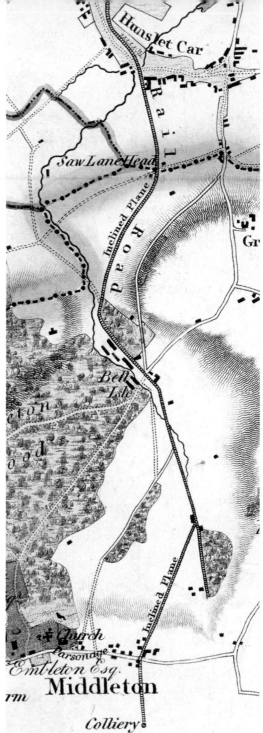

Above.
A superb and detailed plan and elevation of the self-acting incline and braking drum on the Middleton Railway near Leeds, drawn in 1825 by the American engineer William Strickland, who visited Britain to examine technology that could be applied in the United States. There are other drawings by him in this book. The inclined plane at Middleton was known as Todd's Run after the landowner there. Rope ran on rollers placed between the rails and passed around a drum that permitted control of the rope because of its size—it is effectively low geared. The drum (A) was braked by a constricting band (B). Strickland's drawings were published later, but this drawing is from his original notebook, held at Beamish Museum.

Right.
Part of an 1831 map showing the Middleton Railway, with two *Inclined Plane*[s]. The northernmost one is Todd's Run, where the arrangement illustrated by Strickland was located.

By 1822 the 7½-mile-long Newbottle Railway (see pages 91–93) had been reconfigured with three inclines with stationary engines and four self-acting inclines. And some 11 miles of the Stanhope & Tyne Railway, opened as late as 1834, consisted of inclines. This 34-mile-long line was the ultimate in cross-country railways; its route up and down so many hills resulted in the use of multiple inclined planes (see page 207).

The longest line to be worked entirely by inclines and stationary engines was the Brunton & Shields Railway, later called the Seaton Burn Waggonway, which ran to the north bank of the River Tyne; it was 9 miles long and, like several other lines, built to allow coal to be taken directly to deep water, thus avoiding transhipment by keelboats (map, *pages 102–03*).

Rope haulage was first used for passengers on the London & Blackwall Railway (called the Commercial Railway until 1841), a 3¾ mile-long line in east London. It was engineered by Robert Stephenson, using his experience with the Camden incline into Euston Station on the London & Birmingham Railway (see pages 219–20) and opened in 1840.

The only surviving example of a rope-worked railway in Britain is the Bowes Railway, a heritage railway at Springwell, illustrated *overleaf*, also originally built to go directly to deep-water staiths, this time at Jarrow, near the mouth of the River Tyne. That part, which began at Springwell Colliery, was completed in 1826. It was designed by George Stephenson in very similar fashion to his Hetton Colliery Railway opened four years before. The Bowes had eight rope-worked sections. Also known as the Pontop & Jarrow Railway, the line was progressively extended eastwards up to 1855 to serve more and more collieries, eventually reaching a length of 15 miles, though it never reached Pontop Colliery, just beyond the end of the line, as originally planned.

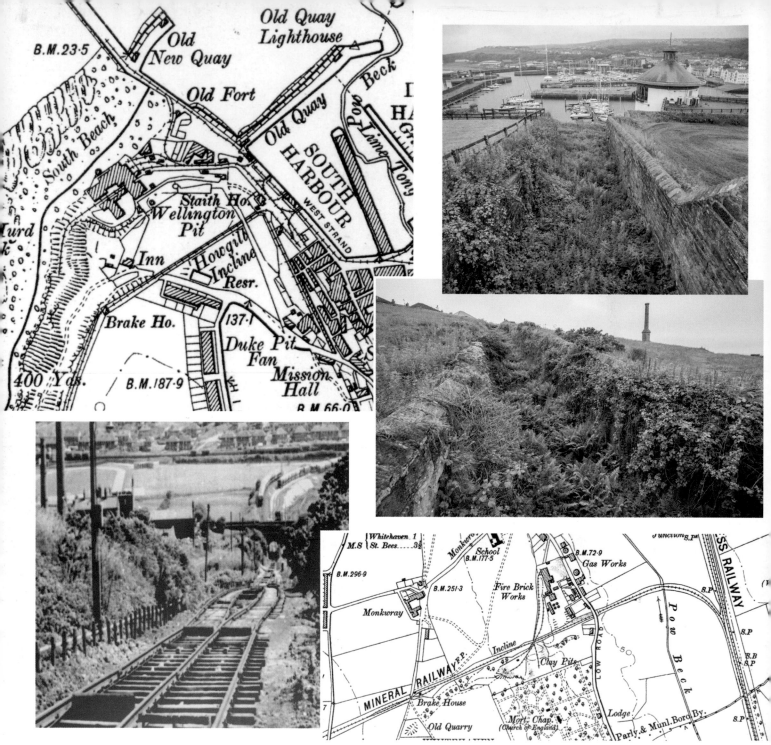

Above, top.
An example of an inclined plane being used to deliver wagons from a higher elevation to a port. This is Whitehaven, on the coast of Cumbria, where coal was mined from the 1600s. There were coal mines along the cliffs north and south of the town. The coalfield extended several miles out to sea. *Howgill Incline*, built in 1813 and shown in the photos, *above, right*, as it is today, allowed coal to reach the staiths, or hurries, along the *West Strand* of the *South Harbour*.

Above, centre right.
This is a much newer *Incline*, also at Whitehaven, the Corkickle Brake Incline, constructed in 1881 by the Earl of Lonsdale's Whitehaven Colliery Company to connect his Croft Pit, up on the cliffs, with the Furness Railway. Note the *Brake House*. Typically of self-acting incline railways, the line splits into two at the halfway point, shown on the photo, *above*, to allow full and empty wagons to pass.

Right. Staith for landsales at Whitehaven. The waggonway ran on top, and coal would be unloaded into carts underneath.

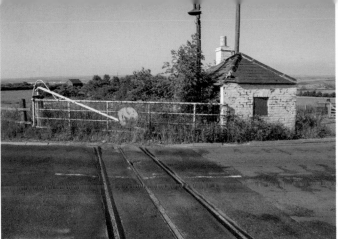

Above, centre.
The Bowes Railway south of Springwell Colliery on an 1857 map. The photo of the track crossing the road (*top*) was taken from the red dot on the map, looking south. Note *Blackimhill Engine*, one of the stationary engines.

Above.
Springwell Colliery, also on the 1857 map. The yard as it is today, with wagons for rope haulage, is shown at *right*. The photo of the track (*top right*), complete with rollers to manage the rope—but no rope—is taken from where the line crosses the road, looking south.

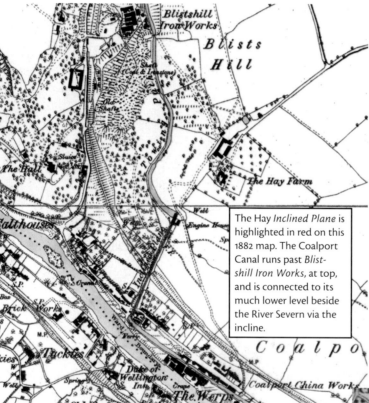

Another use of inclines was to link different levels of canals to avoid having to build locks, which were much more expensive. Inclined planes serving this purpose are relatively numerous throughout Europe. A preserved example is the Hay Inclined Plane in Shropshire, which was used to carry tub boats (small box-like vessels 20 feet long specifically designed to be used on such inclines as well as narrow canals) down to a canal in the Severn Gorge (map, *below, left*). It was opened in 1792–93 and operated until 1894. The 1-in-4 gradient plane was the equivalent of twenty-seven locks and was much faster than they would have been. It was mostly self-acting. A rope would be attached to a cradle at the top, loaded with a full tub boat, and an empty one would be loaded at the bottom. The top cradle would first be drawn out of the water to the top of the incline using a small winding drum, and then a rope around a smaller drum would be attached to control the descent.

The Hay *Inclined Plane* is highlighted in red on this 1882 map. The Coalport Canal runs past *Blistshill Iron Works*, at top, and is connected to its much lower level beside the River Severn via the incline.

Above, right.
The double-tracked Hay Incline. Empty tub boats ascended on one line, hauled up by full tub boats descending on the other.

Right.
An 1832 map shows the Coalport Canal running from the *Shropshire Canal* to a wharf on the River Severn.

Left.
View from the bottom of the incline. The rails went right into the water to enable the tub boats to float off their cradles.

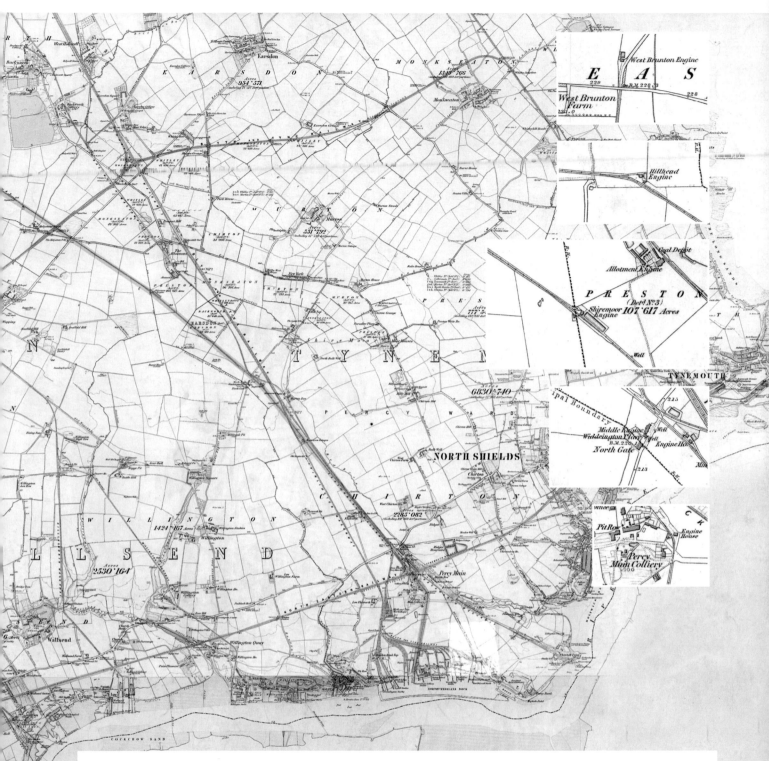

This 1858 map shows the *Seatonburn Waggonway* (highlighted in red), originally the Brunton & Shields Railway. Opened in 1826, this 9-mile-long line was then the longest waggonway operated entirely by stationary engines. It was built to directly transport coal from the *Fawdon* mine to a point on the River Tyne where it could be loaded into ships, thus cutting out the smaller keelboats used previously when the coal was sent south to the river. Note how it is configured, with long, straight sections and engines where the direction changes. One section was worked on the reciprocating basis invented by Benjamin Thompson and patented in 1821. Here a train had a tail rope attached, which became the head rope for the next train in the opposite direction.

As an all-rope line, it was visited in early 1829 by two engineers from the Liverpool & Manchester Railway (James Walker and John Rastrick) to help its directors decide whether to use stationary engines or locomotives on their railway (see page 186). They recommended stationary engines be used on the two inclines, Whiston and Sutton, at either end of the level Rainhill stretch, to gain experience with both stationary and travelling engines before deciding which to use over the whole line. As we know, the final decision was entirely in favour of locomotives.

Insets.
Enlarged details of some of the stationary engines on the Seaton Burn Waggonway. By the time of this survey, 1858, the westernmost part of the line had been closed, and *West Brunton Engine* is shown on the *Fawdon Old Wagonway*.

A Travelling Engine

The revolution that was the railway would come from a marriage of suitable iron track with a reliable source of mechanical power. Up to the end of the eighteenth century, as we have seen (page 32), steam power was in the form of low-pressure, large machines, and the few that were mobile were slow and lumbering. Nicolas Joseph Cugnot's pioneering steam vehicle used higher-pressure steam but was virtually unmanoeuvrable. The fertile mind of genius engineer and inventor Richard Trevithick would change everything.

The answer was what Trevithick called "strong steam"—high-pressure steam coupled with good enough quality of materials and construction to safely contain it. Previous inventors—James Watt pre-eminent among them—had avoided anything much above atmospheric pressure to avoid explosions, and Watt had not helped innovation by weaving an intricate web of patents around his steam engines that

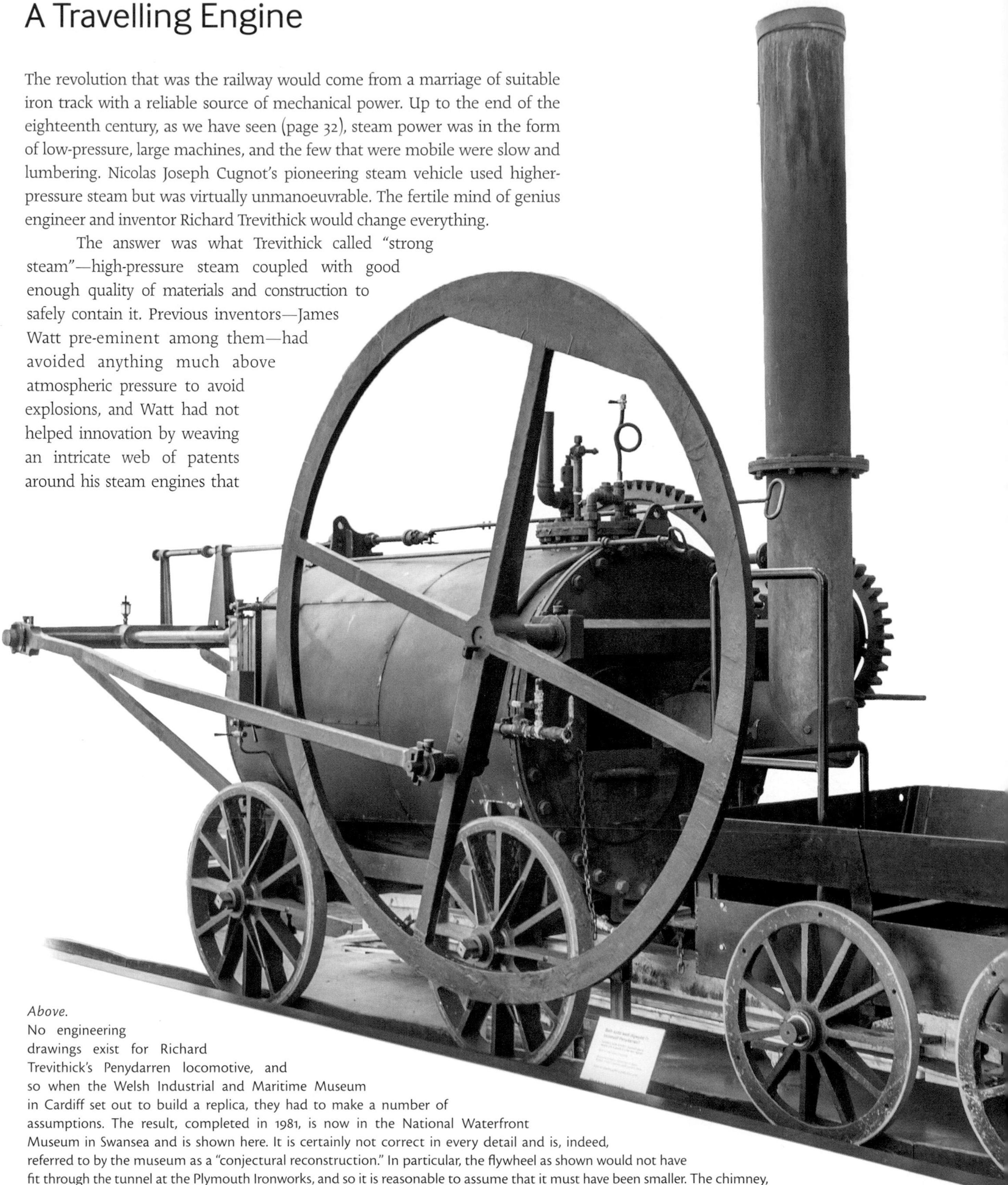

Above.
No engineering drawings exist for Richard Trevithick's Penydarren locomotive, and so when the Welsh Industrial and Maritime Museum in Cardiff set out to build a replica, they had to make a number of assumptions. The result, completed in 1981, is now in the National Waterfront Museum in Swansea and is shown here. It is certainly not correct in every detail and is, indeed, referred to by the museum as a "conjectural reconstruction." In particular, the flywheel as shown would not have fit through the tunnel at the Plymouth Ironworks, and so it is reasonable to assume that it must have been smaller. The chimney, for the same reason, must have been hinged. It does seem likely that the design would have been similar to those that came before and after it—the Coalbrookdale Tram Engine (*page 109, centre*) and the Gateshead engine (*page 109, bottom*)—but its design remains a bit of a conundrum. Note the plateway and non-flanged wheels.

made it difficult for others to build on his work. Trevithick not only improved Watt's engines but also found a way to dispense with the requirement for a separate steam condenser.

The first of Trevithick's high-pressure engines was a stationary machine installed at Cook's Kitchen Mine near Camborne, Cornwall, in 1800. It was reliable, for it was still running seventy years later.

Beginning with models in 1797 (photo, *page 109*), Trevithick by 1801 had produced a full-size locomotive—albeit one that ran on a road rather than rails. This was the famous *Puffing Devil*, which carried Trevithick and his friends up Camborne Hill in Cornwall on 24 December 1801. Four days later, after a minor breakdown, the engine was left outside under some shelter, while Trevithick and his friends repaired to a hostelry for "roast goose and proper drinks"—it was between Christmas and New Year's after all—and the water boiled away, leading to a fire that destroyed the engine and its shelter.

Trevithick didn't give up. His cousin, Andrew Vivian, agreed to a partnership to develop the engine and steered it through the patent process; a patent was granted in March 1802. In 1803 he completed another road vehicle, the London Steam Carriage, which was successfully demonstrated in London—Oxford Street was cleared of horses for the spectacle—yet strangely did not engender enough public enthusiasm to encourage him to continue its development. The idea of a snorting steam engine in among all the horses on a road seemed impractical, and perhaps was.

In August 1802 Trevithick had been in Coalbrookdale, where, it seems, the Coalbrookdale Company, an ironworks, began making stationary engines based on his design. That month Trevithick wrote to a supporter in Cornwall, Davies Giddy, that "the Dale Co have begun a carrage at their own cost for the real-roads and is forceing it with all expedition." This is significant in that it may be the first surviving reference anywhere to the idea of running a steam locomotive on rails.

The possibility of a Coalbrookdale locomotive—which would have been the first in the world—is a bit of an enigma, since there is no direct evidence of one being built beyond Trevithick's letter. We do know that

Above.
Richard Trevithick holding a model of *Catch Me Who Can*. This is a plaster cast of the 1932 statue that stands in the town square at Camborne, Cornwall, scene of his early experiments with steam propulsion.

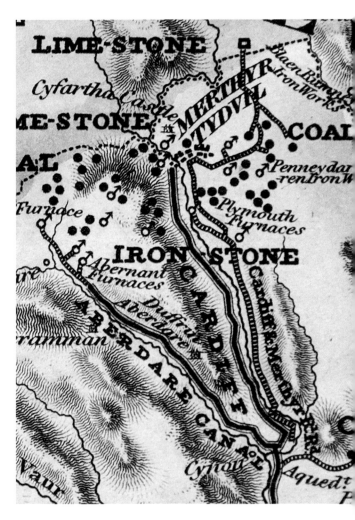

Right.
The Merthyr Tramroad is highlighted in red on this 1830 map. It is labelled the *Cardiff & Merthyr Rl. Rd.* At top right is the *Penneydarren Iron Wks.*

RICHARD TREVITHICK
1771-1833
PIONEER
OF
HIGH PRESSURE STEAM
BUILT THE FIRST STEAM LOCO-
MOTIVE TO RUN ON RAILS. ON
FEBRUARY 21ST 1804 IT TRAVERSED
THE SPOT ON WHICH THIS MONUMENT
STANDS ON ITS WAY TO ABERCYNON

letter. We do know that many years later the nephew of the owner of the Coalbrookdale works wrote that he had been given a wooden model of the Trevithick locomotive—and had broken it up to make something else! The nephew, perhaps not surprisingly with the gift of hindsight, was somewhat contrite.

One possible explanation for the silence is that a Trevithick engine installed at a dockyard in Greenwich exploded in 1803, the result of human error, but nevertheless publicized by James Watt as a manifestation of his warnings about high-pressure steam come true. This might have been the reason the Coalbrookdale engine was not finished or, if it was, not made public. Or it may have been because the ironworks owner, William Reynolds, died that year. In 1884 a visitor to the works was shown a cylinder said to be "cherished as a local artefact," which was supposedly from the Trevithick locomotive. Similar claims had been made in 1871 and 1880. We may never know the truth.

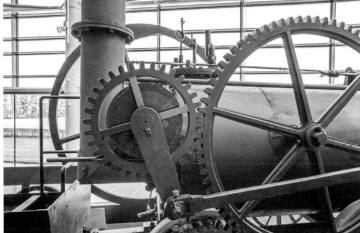

Trevithick's work had caught the eye of Samuel Homfray, owner of the Penydarren Ironworks at Merthyr Tydfil in South Wales, who was sufficiently interested to purchase a share in Trevithick's patent for high-pressure steam engines. Homfray brought Trevithick to Wales to build stationary high-pressure engines for his ironworks. It seems to have been Homfray's idea that the invention could be used to pull wagons on the new Merthyr Tramroad from his works to Navigation (now Abercynon), 9½ miles down the valley. Details of the tramroad, completed in 1802, are on page 64.

Left.
This map, which incorporates surveys from 1868–75 and thus shows many more of the later railways to criss-cross the Merthyr Tydfil area, still indicates the line of the Merthyr Tramroad, engineered by George Overton in 1802, here highlighted in red. This is the line traversed by Trevithick's travelling engine in 1804. The *Pen-y-daren Iron Works* is at top; the Dowlais Ironworks is off the map to the top right corner. At bottom is the Plymouth Ironworks, another of the three initial users of the railway, where the line ran through a tunnel. The green highlighted line is the Penydarren Tramroad to the Glamorganshire Canal. The Trevithick monument (*inset, top,* with a representation of the Coalbrookdale engine), has been placed where the red and green lines diverged. The date of Trevithick's famous run, 21 February 1804, is inscribed on the plinth.
Inset, bottom, is a view down the route of the tramroad today. The monument can be seen at left, and the plateway to Navigation, today Abercynon (the red line on the map), ran down the road and then off to the left between the monument and the light yellow house behind it. The older plateway to the canal at Merthyr, the Penydarren Tramroad (green on the map) ran straight down the side of the road, while another line, the Dowlais Tramroad, mismatched in height, ran down the raised pathway in front of the camera to the right. All three lines are marked on the map.

Right, top, and *right, centre top.*
Two details of the replica Trevithick engine: the plateway wheel and the cog wheels on the opposite side from the flywheel.

Right, centre bottom.
Plate rails and a wagon from the Merthyr Tramroad, on display at the Deutsches Technikmuseum in Berlin.

Right, bottom.
Another view of the Penydarren locomotive at the National Waterfront Museum in Swansea showing the massive cogs and gears driving the wheels. The view is 180 degrees to that shown on the *previous pages.*

Three views of the working replica of the assumed 1803 Coalbrookdale locomotive (the Tram Engine design, shown *right*) at Blists Hill Victorian Town, part of the Iron-bridge Gorge Museums, in Shropshire. It was built in 1989–90 by a local ironworks. It runs up and down on about 30 yards of 3-foot-gauge plateway track.

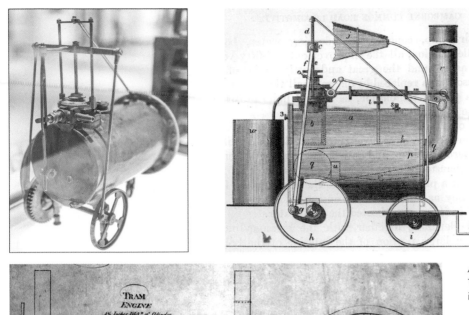

It was Homfray, too, who famously wagered a rival iron-master, Richard Crawshay of the close-by Cyfarthfa Ironworks, 500 guineas—a fortune in those days—that Trevithick could build a "travelling engine" that could haul 10 tons of iron to Abercynon and return with the empties. Richard Hill, the Plymouth Ironworks owner, held the money.

The following February, Trevithick was ready. On 13 February 1804 the engine was first tested on rails—the first documented run by a locomotive in the world—and after a few more test runs, the trip to decide the bet was made on 21 February. Trevithick left his own account of the event, written the next day: "We carry'd ten tons of Iron, five waggons, and 70 Men riding on them the whole of the journey," he wrote. "Its above 9 miles which we perform'd in 4 hours &

5 mints, but we had to cut down some trees and remove some Large rocks out of the road." The latter would have been necessary because the engine, with its flywheel and chimney, was larger than the normal wagons. Unstated is the fact that at least the 11-foot-high chimney would have had to have been removed to pass through the 8-foot-high tunnel at the Plymouth Ironworks.

Trevithick did have to centre some track in the tunnel, and this gave Hill, who it seems was under some sort of recent business obligation to Crawshay, the pretext to refuse to pay out the bet; it is not recorded whether the bet was ultimately paid or not.

Right.
Trevithick's drawings for the Gateshead engine. This was the last of the flywheel designs. It seems likely that the flywheel was incorporated into the design to facilitate stationary working, as Trevithick's engines were intended as all-purpose engines, a useful jack-of-all-trades that would be appealing to colliery owners. The flywheel lessened the likelihood of stalling with a single-cylinder engine. The 1804 Penydarren locomotive is known to have been employed to pump water while it was still being used to haul wagons. Note the wooden track. This illustration comes from Trevithick's biography of 1872, written by his son Francis. See also the engraving on the *contents page.*

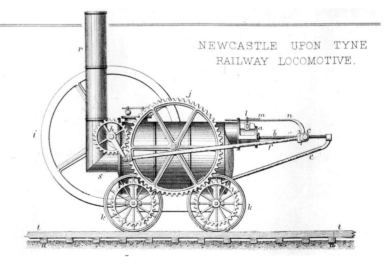

NEWCASTLE UPON TYNE RAILWAY LOCOMOTIVE.

Nevertheless, bet or not, it was clear that Trevithick's travelling engine had performed magnificently; Homfray was delighted. He especially noted that it "goes very easy 4 miles per hour and is as trackable as a horse, will back its load and move it forward as little (and slow) at a time as you please." The engine was used to haul wagons several more times in the following months, but there was increasing damage being done by the 5-ton engine to the cast-iron plate rails, and by July it had been consigned to permanent stationary duties.

Trevithick's engine had proved its worth; it was the track that was the problem, and would remain so until the development of stronger wrought-iron rails a decade or more into the future. The following year Trevithick had a similar engine built at the works of his agent in the northeast, John Whinfield (illustration, *previous page, bottom*). It was offered to Christopher Blackett, owner of Wylam Colliery, for his waggonway, which ran from Wylam to staiths on the River Tyne at Lemington, nearly 5 miles away (map, *page 121*). Blackett's waggonway, however, was at the time made of wood, and he probably quickly realized that such a heavy engine would not work on his much lighter track. In 1808 the waggonway was converted to a cast-iron plateway, unusually for the northeast, and this later allowed the running of pioneering steam locomotives, in 1813 (see page 120). For the moment, though, Trevithick was left without a buyer, and his engine was converted to stationary use powering an iron foundry blower.

Also in 1805, Trevithick completed a locomotive (though possibly for road use) for the West India Docks, in London, for use not only hauling goods to and from ships but also to work as a crane and as a fire engine, by pumping water. However, the engine was refused because its fire was thought too dangerous for a shipyard—rather ironic considering that one of its duties was to extinguish fires!

Above.
As much a view as a map, this well-known illustration is now considered to be a fake in that it was not drawn from the actual event at the time. Nevertheless it likely gives a good impression of Trevithick's demonstration of his locomotive *Catch Me Who Can* in London in 1808. The original illustration appeared in Francis Trevithick's 1872 biography of his father and seems to have been copied some time later for commercial sale.

Right.
This recently completed replica of Trevithick's *Catch Me Who Can* was made by a group of enthusiasts and was photographed in July 2013 on the Severn Valley Railway at Bridgnorth, an appropriate location given that the original was made here in 1808 at Hazeldine & Rastrick's ironworks. Clearly this was a major advance from Trevithick's earlier ungainly flywheel designs and, by comparision, looks positively elegant!

CATCH ME WHO CAN

Trevithick tried one more time to arouse public interest in his invention. In 1808 he arranged for a demonstration circuit of track to be laid down near what is now Euston Station, and a new engine, which, no doubt for marketing reasons, he named *Catch Me Who Can*, was built to his design by Hazeldine & Rastrick, a Bridgnorth ironworks, to give rides to the public—and, he hoped, attract a buyer (illustration, *left*). This was the first purpose-built passenger engine, albeit only for demonstration purposes. The design dispensed with the flywheel and had direct drive to one pair of wheels. Once again it was the track that let Trevithick down; this time wet ground destabilized it and caused the engine to crash.

There survives in the Science Museum in London a Hazeldine & Rastrick–made stationary engine that could be one and the same with *Catch Me Who Can*. Remember that Trevithick's engines were typically built to be multi-purpose and could double as stationary as well as travelling engines. Even if it is not the actual demonstration engine, it certainly is a very similar engine built to Trevithick's design at the same time by the same company (photo, *right*). If it is *Catch Me Who Can*, then it is the oldest surviving railway engine in the world.

Trevithick went on to design a number of other steam engines for various purposes, including, in 1813, a locomotive used in the construction of Plymouth breakwater, but, again, we cannot be sure it was running on rails. In 1816 he went to Peru to design steam pumping engines for mines but was not very successful, finally returning to Britain in 1827 after being financially assisted by none other than Robert Stephenson. He died in 1833, having lived long enough to see the triumph of the steam railway—but at the hands of the two Stephensons. One can only guess at his feelings.

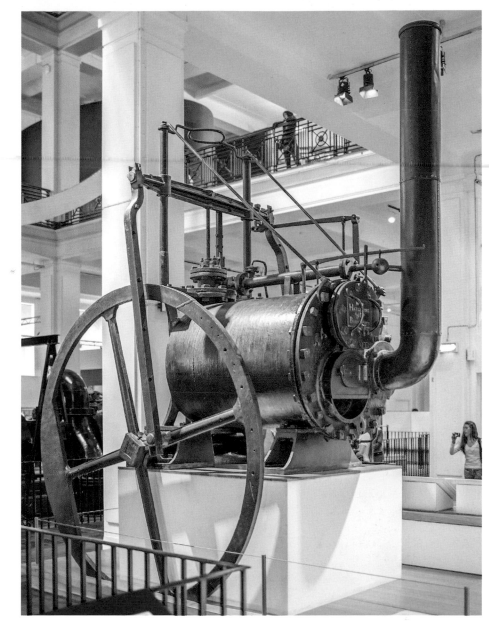

Left.
Another view of the *Catch Me Who Can* replica.

Above.
This plaque is on the wall of one of the buildings of the University of London near where Trevithick demonstrated his London engine.

Above.
Hazeldine & Rastrick's *Engine No. 14* in the Science Museum, London. Could this be *Catch Me Who Can* converted to use as a stationary engine? Even if it is not, it seems almost certain that the same patterns were used to cast some of the parts.

Right.
This watercolour wash by artist J.C. Nattes done in 1808 likely shows *Catch Me Who Can* as it was being installed for the demonstration. Note the similarity of the various openings on the end of the boiler. This would be the earliest image of a steam locomotive other than engineering drawings—the first "artistic" image. The painting is labelled "Part of a machine that was to go by steam without horses 1808 New Road."

The First Working Locomotive

Despite Richard Trevithick's clear demonstration that a locomotive with smooth wheels could pull a heavy load provided it itself was reasonably heavy, many still doubted this, and the Middleton Railway, the first commercially successful line, which opened in 1812, used a cog system much the same as used on rack railways to this day. Invented by colliery viewer (manager) John Blenkinsop, the system worked daily from 1812 to 1835 generally without incident, although the first locomotive, *Salamanca,* exploded in 1818 when overtaxed by its driver. But because it used a rack system, the Middleton Railway has often been overlooked in the history of the railway in favour of smooth rail systems, particularly that of George Stephenson.

William Hedley's son Oswald wrote in his 1858 book *Who Invented the Locomotive Engine?* that "Blenkinsop was taking a decided step in the wrong direction, pregnant with danger to the true principle . . . [by] establishing locomotion by the rack-rail." It is true that the rack rail was not going to be the way forward for regular railways, but his practical engines worked commercially with few problems for many years.

The Middleton Railway in Leeds was originally a wooden waggonway, having been laid down as early as 1758 after being awarded the first railway Act of Parliament, to allow coal from Charles Brandling's coal mines at Middleton to be brought down to the city (see page 20). As early as 1790 records show that John Curr, inventor of the L-shaped cast-iron rail, was involved in laying underground and vertical shaft iron rails at the colliery. By 1807 half of the 4½ miles of waggonway track had been converted to cast iron.

The following year Brandling hired Durham-born John Blenkinsop as his viewer. He knew Blenkinsop from his previous work at collieries near Newcastle and clearly had a great deal of confidence in him, for he was given much of a free hand to implement improvements at Middleton. The waggonway was

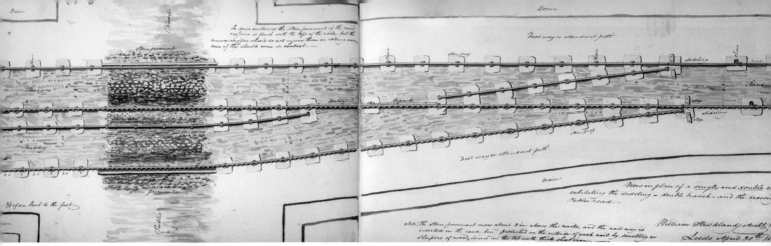

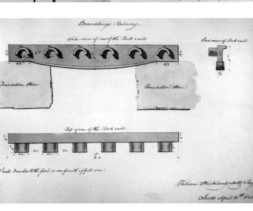

Above. This fine watercolour plan showing how Blenkinsop's engines switched from one track to another was one of several drawn by William Strickland, an eminent American architect and engineer who was sent to England in 1825 by the Pennsylvania Society for the Promotion of Internal Improvements to report on railways. His published report became instrumental in the promotion of early railroads in the United States. Also shown (*left*) is a detail of Blenkinsop's rail, with cogs on a "fishbelly" rail.

The original watercolours drawn for the report are reproduced here and *overleaf*. They are now held at Beamish Museum.

Left and *far left*. A 3-foot section of Blenkinsop's rack rail, and a wheelset, cast in 1870 from an original pattern, on display at the National Railway Museum in York. Cog wheels have mistakenly been attached to both sides of the main axle. Correctly, a cog wheel should have been only on one side.

Left, second from bottom. This display in the heritage Middleton Railway museum has original stone blocks from the trackbed and a section of the rack rail. The 6-foot length of rail has solid cogs to provide extra strength, as it formed part of a switch and hence was moveable. The normal rails were 3-foot lengths in the fishbelly shape typical of early rails, with hollow rack teeth, as shown in the section on the wall and in Strickland's drawing.

Below. This woodcut plate was published in the *Leeds Mercury* on 18 July 1812. It is probably the first newspaper depiction of a steam locomotive.

Right, bottom, and *below.*
A contemporary engraving of a Blenkinsop locomotive and train on the coal staith in Leeds, together with an 1847 map. The church behind the staith is *Christ Chu.,* shown top left on the map.

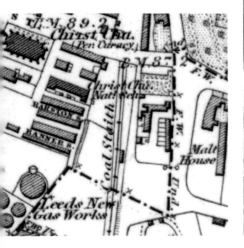

DESCRIPTION OF THE PLATE.

A. Boiler.
B. B. B. Mr. Blenkinsop's Patent Road Rack and Wheel.
C. C. Crank Rods.
D. D. Steam Cylinder.
E. Discharging Pipe.
F. Smoke Chimney.
G. Fire Door.
Scale, 1-eighth of an Inch.

upgraded with stone sleepers, and soon Blenkinsop decided to try locomotive steam engines instead of horses. He likely knew of Trevithick's latest experiment in 1808 with *Catch Me Who Can* but made the bold step of using them commercially rather than, as Trevithick had, in a demonstration. Nonetheless, although he trusted Trevithick's steam engine as a power source, he clearly did not think that steam locomotives could grip a smooth rail enough to haul loaded coal wagons and instead devised his own method of transferring power to the wheels using a rack rail that would engage with a cog on the engine. His patent for the cog-and-rack-rail system was granted on 11 April 1811. After some experimentation with a single-cylinder condensing engine, he found that he needed Trevithick's high-pressure steam engine system and ended up paying a royalty to him for its use.

To build his engines, Blenkinsop turned to Matthew Murray, partner in a local foundry and engineering works, Fenton, Murray & Wood. Murray had experience with building stationary steam engines and even heated his house with a pioneering steam heating system. Murray had patented a portable steam engine as early as 1802 and, in a significant advance, designed the engines for Blenkinsop to have two cylinders, which would prevent stalling if the engine stopped in just the wrong position. This design feature would be followed more or less universally from that point forward.

After a trial on some test track at the foundry, the first engine was steamed on the Middleton waggonway on 24 June 1812. The *Leeds Mercury* recorded that "at four o'clock in the afternoon the machine ran from the Coal-staith to the top of Hunslet Moor, where six, and afterwards eight, waggons of coal, each weighing 3¼ tons, were hooked to the back part. With this immense weight, to which, as it approached the town, was super-added about 50 of the spectators mounted upon the waggons, it set off on its return to the Coal-staith, and performed the journey, a distance of about a mile and a half, principally on a dead level, in 23 minutes, without the slightest accident. The experiment, which was witnessed by thousands of spectators, was crowned with complete success." The paper went on to enthuse that since the invention was applicable to all railroads and that Brandling could dispense with fifty horses in his colliery alone and save corn enough to feed two hundred men, the paper "cannot forbear to hail the invention as of vast public utility, and to rank the inventor amongst the benefactors of his country."

Strong words indeed, and words that have a hollow ring considering the credit given to Blenkinsop and Murray by history, but nevertheless quite true: it was the first application of the steam locomotive to industrial transportation that would be successful on an ongoing basis.

Above. A plate in the 1814 book by George Walker ,*Costume of Yorkshire*, titled *The Collier*. In the background is one of Blenkinsop's locomotives and train, seemingly on the lower part of the Middleton Colliery line. Note that the men operating it are standing on either side. There is no water tender; the train was stopped frequently to be refilled.

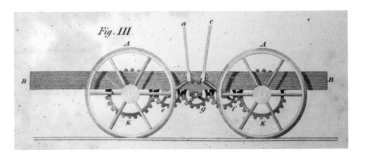

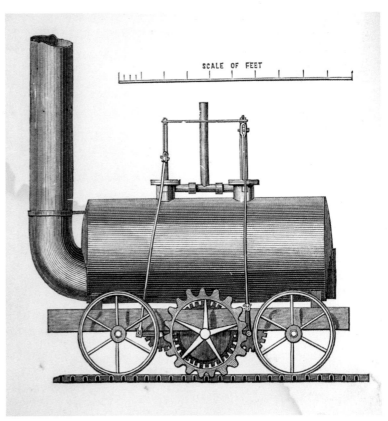

Right. Blenkinsop's rack engine, left-side and right-side wheelset, illustrated in Nicholas Wood's 1825 *Practical Treatise on Rail-Roads*, shows that the rods from the steam engine pistons drove small cog wheels, which engaged with a bigger cog attached to the axle of the main drive cog wheel that in turn connected with the rack rail. It may have been a bit complicated, but it worked!

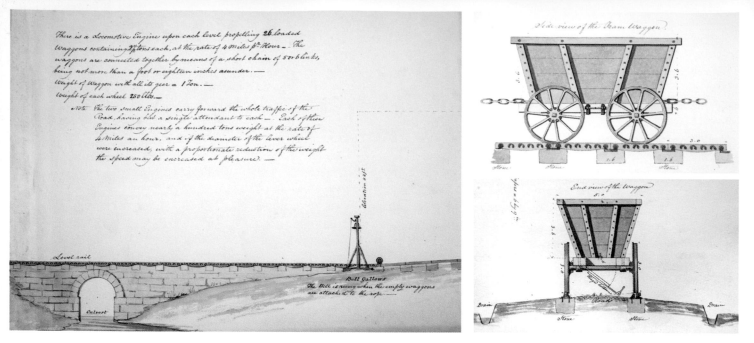

Above. Another of Strickland's watercolour illustrations shows the cog rails of the bottom level stretch of track and the bottom of the Todd's Run incline, where the locomotives were detached and a rope attached to haul the wagons up the incline. It is also one of the first depictions of a railway signal. The top part of the illustration is shown on page 98. At *right*, two views of the wagons used.

Left. The line of the waggon-way from Orrell Colliery is shown on an 1849 map (with selected later updates: the *Lancashire and Yorkshire* Railway crossing the line of the waggonway opened in 1855). The line ends at the Leeds & Liverpool Canal (opened 1774–80). The line crosses the River Douglas just beforehand, across from Crooke, near Wigan in Lancashire. Here Blenkinsop's locomotives worked from 1813 to about 1849. The railway and canal together allowed coal to be delivered to the coast.

Left, bottom. Detail of this 1834 atlas map of Lancashire shows several short rail lines feeding the Leeds & Liverpool Canal, including the one from Orrell, though by that time it seems to have been extended southwards. The line is not particularly accurately depicted on a map of this scale. The canal is the thick black line marked *Canal* to the east of *Wigan*.

Above, right. This 1847 map highlights the waggonway jointly used by the Kenton & Coxlodge and Fawdon collieries. Here Blenkinsop's locomotive worked from 1813 to 1815. The line ran for about 5 miles north of Newcastle to the River Tyne, with the last, steep section to the river worked by a rope incline.

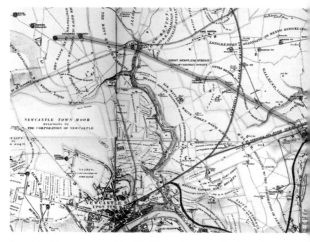

Far right. The route used by Blenkinsop's engines is shown in red on this map from about 1880. The connecting segment (shown in blue) was the location of the rope incline, called Todd's Run after the landowner there. Four engines were normally used, two on the lower rails and two on the higher-level rails. The pits shown, *New Pit* and *Broom Pit*, were more recent additions, both having been sunk in 1868. The grey line bypassing the incline was opened in 1875 and was worked by more powerful locomotives. The preserved Middleton Railway today runs on the grey section south towards the location of Broome Pit, which was the last pit closed, in 1968.

Right. One of the Prussian Blenkinsop-design locomotives with an ornate coach, possibly the one used on a demonstration track in Berlin. The Prussian-built locomotives were smaller than the originals. The print is not dated but presumably is from around 1816, when the locomotives were built.

The replacement of men and horses with machines was not universally popular at the time. At the end of 1812, just after a second locomotive had started working, saboteurs placed large blocks of stone and loose iron rails on the track in two locations and broke up some ancillary machinery. Blenkinsop was so incensed that he offered a reward of fifty guineas for the conviction of the perpetrators, more than a man's annual pay at the time. Nevertheless no one was found.

As might be expected with a successful system, other colliery managers soon became interested. Robert Daglish, manager of the Orrell Colliery, near Wigan, Lancashire, had a slightly enlarged version of a locomotive with Blenkinsop's traction system built in late 1812. It began work at the beginning of 1813, thus becoming the second instance of successful commercial use of steam locomotion. And successful it was. According to Daglish's own account, three Blenkinsop locomotives worked here until 1849, a period of thirty-six years. They seem to have been known to the miners as the *Stalking Horse*, the *Yorkshire Horse*, and the *Walking Horse* on account of the snorting noises they made, and they were powerful: one of the locomotives worked a 1-in-36 incline.

Late in 1813, a Blenkinsop locomotive was sent from Middleton to the Kenton & Coxlodge Colliery on Tyneside, where it worked on a line about 5 miles long, not being used on the final section down to the river, where the grade was too steep. It began work on 2 September 1813 at an opening celebration attended by George Stephenson; after seeing Blenkinsop's locomotive he is said to have remarked scornfully that he could make a better engine, and soon after began work on *My Lord* (see page 132). After some teething troubles the Blenkinsop locomotive worked so well that viewer and part owner John Watson ordered two more locomotives. However, in May 1815, due to a legal dispute and mismanagement of the locomotives, not any inherent fault, their use was discontinued.

Two Blenkinsop-system locomotives were built in Berlin (then in Prussia) in 1816, following the visit to Middleton of two Prussian engineers. These were the first steam locomotives to be built in mainland Europe, and were demonstrated in Berlin. Unfortunately they were badly built. One sent to Gliwice, in Silesia (now in Poland), was found on arrival and reassembly to not fit the gauge of the track. The other locomotive was sent to Saarland, which was Prussian occupied as a result of the defeat of Napoleon. Here the problems were poor construction tolerances leading to loss of pressure coupled with active non-cooperation of government officials. But in neither case was the design at fault.

Blenkinsop was never able to counteract the upcoming influence of better-connected George Stephenson and his locomotives despite mounting a vigorous promotion of his system himself. Blenkinsop died in 1831 at only forty-seven years old. He appears to have had no family and hence no sons to carry on his work and promote his cause, as some later did, notably William Hedley's sons. His system allowed a small locomotive to haul more than twenty times its own weight, and it was not until wrought-iron rails came into use that adhesion locomotives could approach that tractive effort. Most importantly, Blenkinsop—with Matthew Murray—demonstrated to the world that steam locomotives could be successfully and economically useful, and as such he does not deserve the relative obscurity into which he has faded.

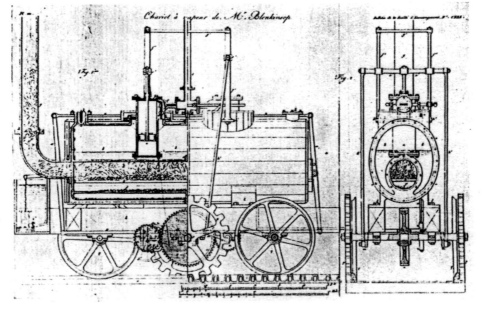

Left. This technical drawing was reproduced in a French scientific magazine, *Bulletin de la Société d'Encouragement pour l'Industrie Nationale*, in 1815. It shows more clearly how the power from the pistons was transferred to the driving cog using Blenkinsop's system. The cross-section also reveals that the boiler was oval rather than round, which likely caused problems with uneven pressure. This was done to permit a boiler with enough power to be used within the confines of the narrow gauge of the track (4 feet, 1 inch).

Wylam Billies and Dillies

When Christopher Blackett, owner of the Wylam Colliery, 10 miles west of Newcastle, was offered Richard Trevithick's locally built travelling engine in 1805, he had refused because he was quite aware that his wooden waggonway was not up to a heavy and erratically moving locomotive (see page 106). In 1808 he rebuilt his waggonway, choosing, uniquely for this area, the L-shaped plateway rails favoured by Benjamin Outram and his disciples.

Blackett believed that economies were to be had by using steam locomotives rather than horses; grain prices were going up because of the war with France. He even tried using oxen, which proved too slow. So he asked Trevithick to build him another engine, but Trevithick, fresh from his debacle with *Catch Me Who Can* that year, had moved on to other ventures and refused. Blackett expanded his operation nonetheless, building coke ovens to supply a new blast furnace at Lemington.

Above. The magnificent working replica of the 1813–14 *Puffing Billy* built by Beamish Museum in 2006.

By 1811 Blackett revisited his ideas about steam locomotives, deciding to have one designed and built by his own employees. As it happened, he had an inventive and skilled team: William Hedley, his colliery viewer; his inventive foreman blacksmith, Timothy Hackworth; and an excellent mechanic, Jonathan Forster.

Blackett was skeptical that that a smooth-wheeled locomotive such as the Trevithick one he had been offered in 1805 would grip his smooth plate rails enough to pull heavy loads. This despite the clear proof, of which he must have been aware, given by Trevithick's very first run in 1804 on the same sort of plate rails.

So Blackett determined to find out whether simple adhesion would work before anything was built. And he went further. He determined, by experimentation, what weight a locomotive had to be to pull a given weight in coal wagons without slipping. Under the direction of Hedley, in late 1812 a "test carriage" was built that allowed a man to operate each of the four wheels with a crank (illustrations, *right*). The experiment was carried out in secret, because Blackett thought that, if he got it right, he could build an

efficient engine that would give him a competitive advantage. First the carriage was tried within the walls of his estate, Wylam Hall, and then moved onto the Wylam Waggonway.

When the result proved that adhesion traction was feasible, Hedley had a steam engine built on the chassis of the test carriage. The boiler was made by Thomas Waters in Gateshead. Waters was familiar with Trevithick's 1805 locomotive and his foundry was close to that of John Whinfield, who had built it; this was the engine Blackett had been offered and turned down. In early 1813, the locomotive was first run on the waggonway, successfully, but only just. It showed, as Hackworth's son would later write, "the spasmodic, intermittent, irregular action so characteristic of these early one-cylindered, fly and

Right and *inset, right.*
William Hedley's "test carriage" for determining the loading on an engine required to pull coal wagons of a given weight without slipping. The line drawing is from Hedley's son's book *Who Invented the Locomotive Engine?*, published in 1858; the photo is of a model.

Above.
Wylam Waggonway is shown as a dotted line on this 1807 map, running from Wylam Colliery (the black dots on *Wylam Moor*) to the staiths at *Lemington* (the southernmost line to the river). This was the highest point on the River Tyne that keels, small barges built to carry coal downriver to waiting ships, could reach. The meander in the river here was cut off in 1876 and began to silt up.

Right.
A modern photo shows all that is left of the Lemington staiths.

spur wheel-driven, cast iron boilered locomotives." It also suffered from a chronic shortage of steam. However, it was clearly the right direction, and Blackett authorized the building of three more locomotives that would incorporate improvements, notably twin cylinders. These were the engines that came to be known as *Puffing Billy, Wylam Dilly,* and *Lady Mary.* The first is thought to have been ready by late 1813 or early 1814, though construction may have stretched into 1815.

But there still remained the issue of the weak rails, so in late 1814 *Puffing Billy* was converted to a bogie design, with eight wheels to spread the load. In this Blackett's crew were following the lead of William Chapman, who was developing an eight-wheeled locomotive of his own close by (see page 128). Indeed, it seems entirely possible that Chapman may have been directly involved with Wylam on this conversion.

These engines worked the Wylam Waggonway for many years, being converted back to four wheels in the late 1820s, this time with flanges, when the track was replaced with stronger edge rails. From 1814 until 1830 they powered the only railway in the world that was completely locomotive hauled. And they were reliable: one engine in 1835 was noted as having travelled 17,000 miles and hauled 64,000 tons of coal that year alone. It is thought that they might have originally been named after Blackett's daughters, Elizabeth and Jane; the name *Puffing Billy* is

a nickname, perhaps from the asthmatic William ("Billy") Hedley, and "Dilly" was simply the local term for a small carriage, hence *Wylam Dilly.*

Wylam Dilly had a brief episode as a marine engine. In 1822 there was a strike by keelmen, the men who propelled the keelboats from the staiths down the river to ships near the mouth, and Hedley quickly had the locomotive installed in a keelboat and converted its motion to operating paddle wheels, in which state, and protected by soldiers, it towed a string of other keelboats laden with coal (illustration, *right*).

Puffing Billy was sold to the Patent Museum, now the Science Museum, in 1862, and *Wylam Dilly* was bought in 1869 by Hedley's sons, intent on preserving the role of their father in early railway history, and in 1882 they loaned it to the National Museum of Scotland, in Edinburgh, where it remains to this day.

Above. Wylam Dilly as a keel-boat in 1822 during the keelmen's strike.

Portrait of *Puffing Billy* in the Science Museum, London.

Above.
Wylam Dilly in the National Museum of Scotland, Edinburgh. The engine is displayed on cast-iron fishbelly edge rail on stone blocks. The driver would have been at the left, while the fireman was beside the chimney, where the firebox is situated.

Right.
Detail of Wylam village, colliery, and ironworks shown on an 1844 map. The *Waggon Way* terminates at two pits. *Wylam Hall*, home of the Blackett family, where the test carriage was first secretly tried, is at top left. This map also shows the line of the Newcastle & Carlisle Railway, opened 1834–38, on the south bank of the river; there was a *Railway Station* at Wylam.

Above, left.
The Wylam Waggonway today. The legacy of the northeast coalfield's waggonways is a network of paths and trails like this.

Above.
George Stephenson was born and grew up in this house, called Street House, adjacent to the Wylam Waggonway; it is marked on the 1828 map at *left* by the r of *High Str.* He moved away in 1789 but kept in touch with developments through his friend Jonathan Forster, who later became chief engine-wright at Wylam Colliery.

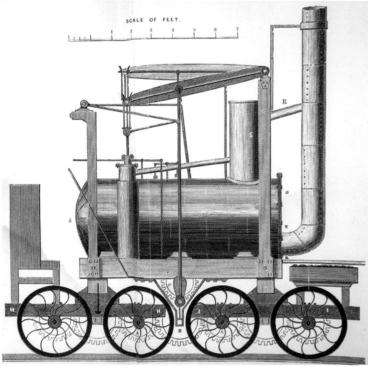

Above.
The plaque attached to Stephenson's house in 1929.

Left.
The eight-wheeled version of *Puffing Billy* and *Wylam Dilly*, shown on plate rail. The extra wheels spread the engine's weight out to make it less likely to break the rails.

Below.
Wylam is justifiably proud of its railway heritage, which includes William Hedley, Timothy Hackworth, Jonathan Forster, and George Stephenson. This sign, complete with *Puffing Billy*, is situated on the approach to the village.

Above.
Detail of the *Lemington Staiths* area on a map surveyed in 1858. The photo, *above, right*, shows the area today. The brick cone was part of a glassworks, shown on the map as a black circle.

Right.
Beamish's *Puffing Billy* replica visiting the National Railway Museum in York.

Below.
The Wylam Waggonway on a map dated 1826. The waggonway is the dotted line from *Wylam* to *Lemington.*

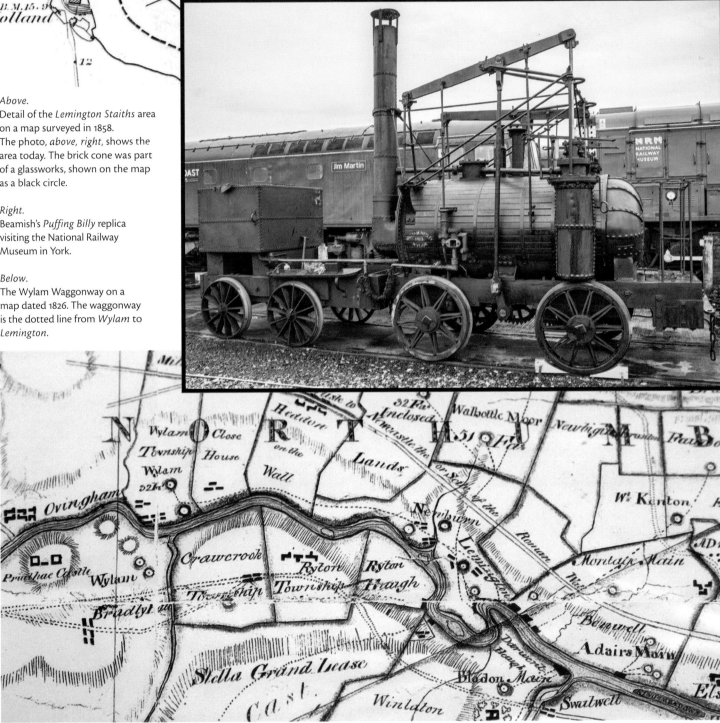

Legs, Chains, and Elephants

In the period from 1812 to 1815 there was a flurry of activity in the steam locomotive invention field. Not only, as we have seen, did Blenkinsop begin operating his rack system in Leeds and Blackett and Hedley the "Billies and Dillies" at Wylam, but others brought forth systems that used locomotives with legs, chains, bogies, eight wheels, and several different designs of steam locomotive, none of which were entirely satisfactory because of one common factor—the failure of the rails to stand up to the heavy pounding of a multi-ton locomotive. Finally, in 1816, one of the engineer-inventors, George Stephenson, would address the rail issue and patent a new kind of rail and joint (see page 143), but it would not be until 1821 that practical longer wrought-iron rails would become available and really begin to solve the problem.

What is viewed today as perhaps the most bizarre of the locomotive inventions was by a Butterley Company engineer, William Brunton, in 1813. He invented a "walking" engine—literally. It had mechanical legs connected to the pistons of the steam engine by a complicated system of levers to convert the straight motion into a walking-type motion. It was so complex that his own patent, issued on 14 July 1813, has been shown not to work as drawn. Yet the locomotive he built did work, and with some initial success.

As a Butterley engineer—though he was building the locomotive on his own account—Brunton looked for a nearby waggonway or railway on which to try out his engine. He found it at the Butterley Gangroad at Crich, a mere few miles from the Butterley works and connected, conveniently, by the Cromford Canal. This was a plateway line that had been completed in 1793 (see page 38).

Brunton tried out his engine sometime in the second half of 1813, and it worked, moving at about 2½ miles per hour and thought to have the pulling power of about four horses. It seems that news of his engine attracted some attention and that someone from John Nesham's Newbottle

Top.
Brunton's locomotive, complete with mechanical "legs." This is a model in the Deutsches Technikmuseum in Berlin.

Left.
The Butterley Gangroad at Crich, Derbyshire. The red line shows the route of the line at the time Brunton was testing his "walking" locomotive. The tunnel at the *Old Quarry* at the northern end had been removed in 1808, however. The base map is from an 1879 survey.

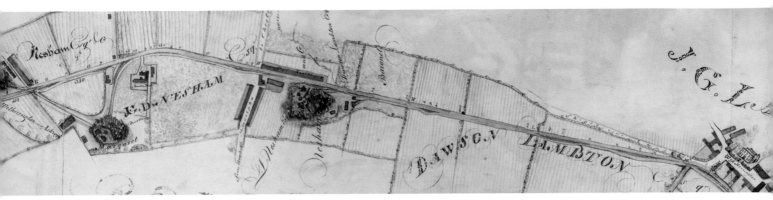

Colliery (which was already a Butterley client) came to see it demonstrated and ordered one for its waggonway (see page 91). Brunton set about building a larger and more powerful version during 1814, and it arrived at Newbottle in pieces on 19 October 1814 with a Butterley employee to supervise its reconstruction. The engine worked successfully through the winter of 1814–15, so much so that Brunton was permitted to increase the boiler size to make it more powerful, as its initial 5-ton weight limit to prevent damage to the track was found unnecessary because the motion tended to lift the engine up as it "walked." In fact, to limit this tendency the first wagon had to be attached higher up than normal to allow the wagon's weight to hold it down.

The new boiler from Butterley was installed, but it led to disaster. On 13 July 1815, probably at the initial demonstration of the new boiler because a crowd of onlookers had gathered around to see it pull 20 wagons, the boiler exploded when the driver held down the saftey valve, killing about 13 people and severely injuring 43 more. Brunton's career as a locomotive inventor instantly evaporated, despite the fact that the explosion was not caused by any fault of Brunton's system of propulsion.

In 1819 and 1822 Brunton did invent something else—mechanical stokers. The 1822 one worked in much the same way as the mechanical legs of his locomotive to move coal. Brunton was remorseful about the Newbottle explosion for the rest of his life.

Above and *below.*
Parts of the magnificent map of the Newbottle Railway, dated 1817. The map shows the line twice, once as it was (*below*) and once straightened to show distances and gradients (*above*). By *Dorothea* Pit on the top map is a building named *Steam Horse*, which appears to be where William Brunton's locomotive was kept. As such it would be the earliest representation of an engine shed. The map is dated 1817, while Brunton's engine blew up in 1815, but this could still be the building that had been used to store it, or, possibly, the survey for the map was done two years before it was finished and dated. The part of the map below shows the portion of the line worked by Brunton's engine in 1814–15, from *Margaret* Pit (at left) to *West Herrington* (at right).

Inset, above.
Brunton's engine at work. The illustration is from J.G. Pangborn's 1894 book *The World's Rail Way*, based on the Baltimore & Ohio Railroad's exhibits at the World's Columbian Exposition in Chicago, for which a replica was made.

The same year John Blenkinsop's rack locomotive began work at Leeds, William Chapman, a canal and civil engineer of some repute, was working on a similar idea for propelling an engine using a chain. The idea was simple: use the locomotive engine to engage with a chain laid along the middle of the track in much the same way as with stationary engines, the difference being that the locomotive would winch itself along the chain, thus obviating the need for an engine every mile or so. The concept was so close to Blenkinsop's rack rail that Blenkinsop called it "mechanical larceny."

William Chapman's patent was granted to him and his brother Edward on 30 December 1812, for "a method or methods of facilitating the means, and reducing the expense, of carriage on railways and other roads." An addendum to the patent pointed out that the advantage of their system was that (since the engine would not gain traction from the rails) "no alteration is required in the waggon-ways, whether of wood or iron, already constructed; because if strong enough to sustain the coal-waggons, which they necessarily must be, they will be amply capable of supporting the loco-motive engine, when placed on six or eight wheels, accordingly as its weight may require."

Chapman realized early on that spreading the weight of the engine would be necessary to stand any chance of the rails of the day supporting it. To this end the Chapman's patent also covered an invention that would become very widespread on railways all over the world—the bogie, or wheel truck. To spread the weight and still accommodate tight curves on the track, he had the idea of putting at least one set of four wheels on a pivot so that it could swivel independently.

In 1813, at the same time Blenkinsop's rails were being laid on the Kenton & Coxlodge Waggonway (see page 119),

Chapman's chains were being prepared at the nearby Heaton Colliery waggonway (map, *below*), assisted by the colliery viewer, John Buddle. Buddle was an innovative viewer or consultant viewer for a number of collieries and was so dominant in the northeast for a generation he was known as the "King of the Coal Trade." He foresaw that the future lay in mechanization and was prepared to experiment to find the best solutions.

Buddle had even paid for Chapman's patent, and it was he who conducted the trials of Chapman's chain engine at Heaton in October 1813. Friction caused the chain to fail prematurely. Modifications were tried, including using rollers to hold the chain up so that it engaged more readily with the on-board winch gears, to no avail. The wooden track of the waggonway added to the engine's problems. Then, in May 1815, the colliery flooded, and production was halted. Chapman's engine was quickly converted to help pump out the mine.

Buddle could see that the engine had potential and in 1814 ordered a new engine for another colliery for which he was viewer, at Lambton (map, *overleaf*). The new engine was built by the local engineering shop of Phineas Crowther, inventor of the vertical winding engines widely used in northeast coalfield pits. It had eight wheels and used Chapman's bogie system but only used chains on the steeper sections of the waggonway; otherwise it ran by adhesion, possible because, after several delays, the Lambton waggonway was upgraded from wood to iron that year. This was apparently a more successful solution, and according to a newspaper report, on 21 December 1814 the "locomotive engine . . . drew after it eighteen loaded coal waggons (weight about 54 tons) up a gentle ascent . . . and went nearly at the rate of four miles an hour."

Chapman was by then working on a new design that was simpler, with no bogies and no chains. It had six wheels, still to spread the weight. John Buddle was also viewer at Wallsend Colliery (map, *below*, and *overleaf, centre right*), and it was here that Chapman would try the new locomotive. Dubbed the *Steam Elephant* (a name applied to many of the early steam engines at the time but which came to be reserved for this design of Chapman's), the design somehow dropped from railway history until 1931, when a librarian came across a picture of such a locomotive decorating a hand-drawn coalfield map (illustration, *overleaf, top*). There were a few other places where an image of the engine turned up, but it was not until Beamish Museum discovered an oil painting of it in 1995 (illustration, *left*) that research on this hitherto unknown engine progressed. It is now accepted as a William Chapman design from 1815. In 2001 Beamish completed a replica of the *Steam Elephant* (photo, *overleaf*) after working out the engineering drawings from the painting and four other representations that had been found.

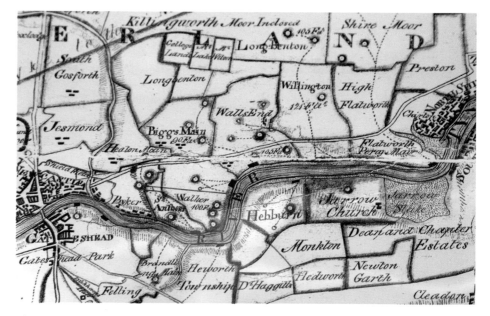

Above.
A map from 1826 showing the north bank of the River Tyne east of Newcastle. *Heaton Main* and *Walls End* collieries are shown, with waggonways as dashed lines leading to the river.

Left. Beamish's stunning oil painting of the *Steam Elephant* at work on the Wallsend line. The location was painstakingly worked out based on all the other landmarks included in the picture. The artist is, unfortunately, unknown.

The *Steam Elephant* was not particularly successful at its trials on the Wallsend waggonway, largely owing, once again, to the track, which was still wooden. "The wood ways obstruct it much," wrote Matthias Dunn, another colliery viewer. It was also tried on the Washington colliery line the following year, again on wooden track, and again, not very successfully. Another steam elephant–type engine was tried on a line at Whitehaven collieries in Cumbria, where John Buddle was a consultant viewer. The parts seem to have been made by Phineas Crowther and shipped to Whitehaven, where they were assembled by a brilliant but dissolute colliery engineer, Taylor Swainson. Local people then came to believe he had made the locomotive, which gave rise to a misleading train of research for many years. Again, however, this engine was once again not very successful, this time being run on poor cast-iron rails, which broke under the locomotive's weight. It was converted to a stationary engine in 1818.

In 1820 the rails at Wallsend were converted to iron, and the *Steam Elephant* tried once more. This time it was successful and pulled heavy coal trains for a number of years. Another similar design seems to have been run on the Rainton (also known as Old Ducks) colliery line, down to the River Wear, from 1822, and another at Heaton Colliery. The latter appears to have been a rebuild of the Lambton engine. It is thought to have been the first engine to have solid springs (rather than Stephenson's steam springs). The evidence for the running of all these locomotives remains remarkably sparse, given they were significant events, and is likely partly the result of such records being deemed of low importance at a time when George Stephenson was being glorified as the father of railways. The *Steam Elephant* notably did not appear in Nicholas Wood's seminal *Practical Treatise on Rail-roads* published in several editions between 1822 and 1831, but Wood, an enormously influential mining engineer, was an associate and friend of Stephenson.

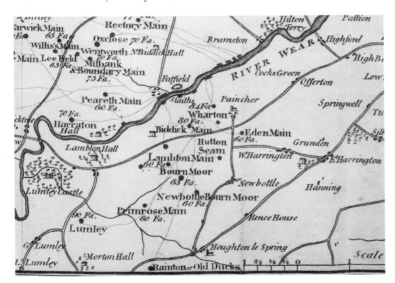

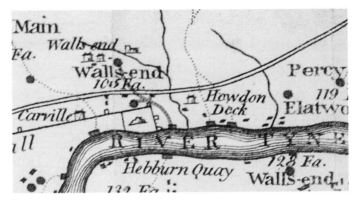

Above, top.
The *Steam Elephant* depicted as part of a cartouche on a coalfield map discovered in 1931.

Left.
A map published in 1807 shows the *Lambton Main* and *Rainton or Old Ducks* collieries and their waggonways running north to the *River Wear.*

Above.
Another part of the same map shows the Wallsend line on which the *Steam Elephant* ran in 1815 and 1820. The line is highlighted in red. At left is *Carville* Hall, which has been identified as the house in the distance on the oil painting on the *previous page.*

Left.
A typical colliery scene, this one set in 1913 but with chaldron-type wagons similar in design to the early ones lined up at the pithead. This is a reconstruction at Beamish Museum.

The 2001 replica *Steam Elephant* and its driver pose for a portrait at Beamish in 2013. It is likely that the original engine was a lot less clean than this beautifully maintained replica!

Stephenson and Killingworth

George Stephenson has often overshadowed his contemporaries in the era of early railway development, to some extent because he gathered around him powerful friends who were more than ready to advance his cause over others. Although the role of Stephenson has been overemphasized in the past, this should not in any way belittle his achievements, which were highly significant in the early development of the railway. Stephenson did not invent things—and specifically, did not invent the steam locomotive—so much as put together both his and others' accomplishments to create something of wider importance.

Stephenson was born in 1781 in a cottage adjacent to the Wylam Waggonway (see page 116), where he lived till the age of eight. He never had a formal education. His family moved several times thereafter, his father following jobs at collieries wherever they could be found. George exhibited mechanical skills from an early age, and by seventeen he was in charge of a steam water-pumping engine at Water Row, a colliery also close to the Wylam Waggonway, just west of Newburn (on map, *page 117*). He married in 1802, and by 1803 Stephenson was in charge of a steam winding engine on the incline at Willington Quay, where he began to repair and clean clocks as a sort of sideline. It was here that his son, Robert Stephenson, was born. George did not stay long, and in July 1804 he became

Above.
The George Stephenson memorial at Newcastle, unveiled in 1862.

brakeman at West Moor Pit and moved to Killingworth (illustrations, *overleaf*); his wife died a few months later. After a brief sojourn in Scotland as superintendent of a Watt steam engine in a mill, he was back at Killingworth. In 1812 he managed to fix a new colliery engine that no one else could, including the colliery engine-wright, and this achievement brought him to the attention of the colliery's owners, the powerful group known as the Grand Allies. When the engine-wright was killed shortly thereafter, Stephenson was given the job—and, importantly, support for his emerging ideas on steam traction on the waggonways.

The extent to which Stephenson had actually seen other travelling engines at work is unclear, but he soon came up with his own design. In 1813 he began work on his first locomotive, called *My Lord*, which was completed in July 1814. Another, called *Blucher* (named after a Prussian general, an ally of Britain in the war against Napoleon) swiftly followed later in the year. It was capable of pulling 30 tons up a grade at 4 miles per hour.

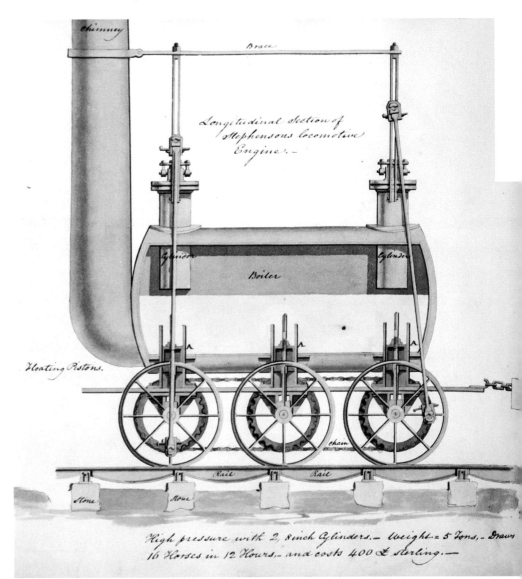

Above, across page.
American architect and engineer William Strickland visited Britain in 1825 and made extensive notes and drawings, which he took back to his sponsor, the Pennsylvania Society for the Promotion of Internal Improvements. They were published in a book in 1826, but this is his superb watercolour of Stephenson's 1816 engine from his original

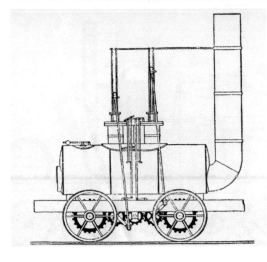

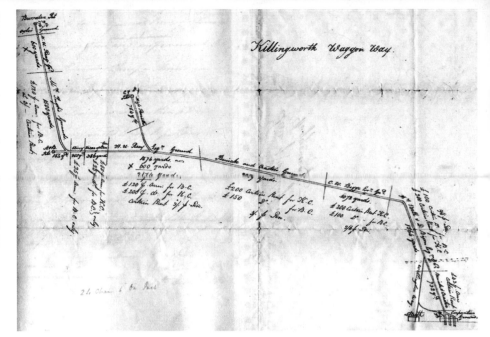

Above.
Stephenson's first locomotive design, on which *My Lord* and *Blucher* were based. The wheels are gear-coupled to the piston shafts, and the engine bears a considerable resemblance to that of Blenkinsop and Murray in 1812 (see page 114). Nicholas Wood contributed to the design, with eccentrics to actuate valve gear. There is no doubt that Stephenson built on the ideas of others, but he continued the development of concepts well beyond their inception.

Above. An undated sketch of part of the Killingworth Waggonway, on which Stephenson's early locomotives ran. It shows the land ownership along the line, together with the wayleave payments (or rents) due to each owner.

His first patent, for a new steam engine design, followed in early 1815. This new design replaced the gear train that seems to have been derived from John Blenkinsop's designs (illustration *above, left*) with a chain linking the axles, similar to that of William Chapman (see page 124).

Later that year the inventive Stephenson also devised a safety lamp for use in the mines—where naked flame often caused explosions—and became engaged in a battle with Humphry Davy, who maintained that he had invented it first, a claim that many scientists supported at the time because they

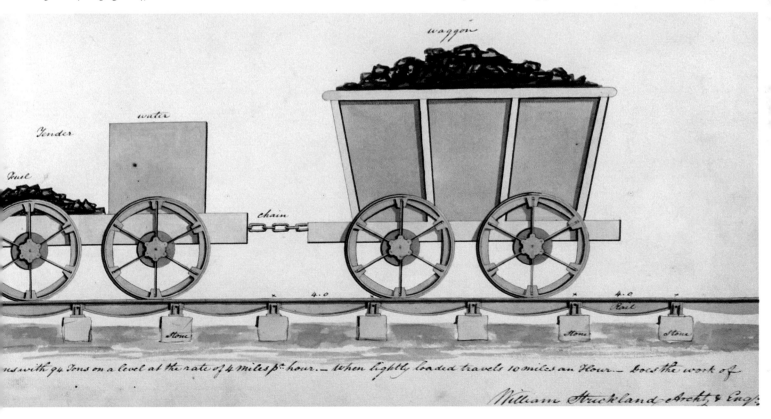

notebook, now held at Beamish. The locomotive had direct drive to the wheels, chain coupling, and steam springs (labelled *A*) and is depicted on his patented (with William Losh) fishbelly cast-iron rail with an improved overlap joint (see page 147).

West Moor Colliery.

Above.
A contemporary engraving of West Moor Pit, part of Killingworth Colliery.

Below.
Shown in several depictions with different shaped chimneys, this view of Stephenson's "standard" locomotive in its 1816 form is particularly spectacular, all the better to impress potential clients, since this is clearly an advertising piece of some kind.

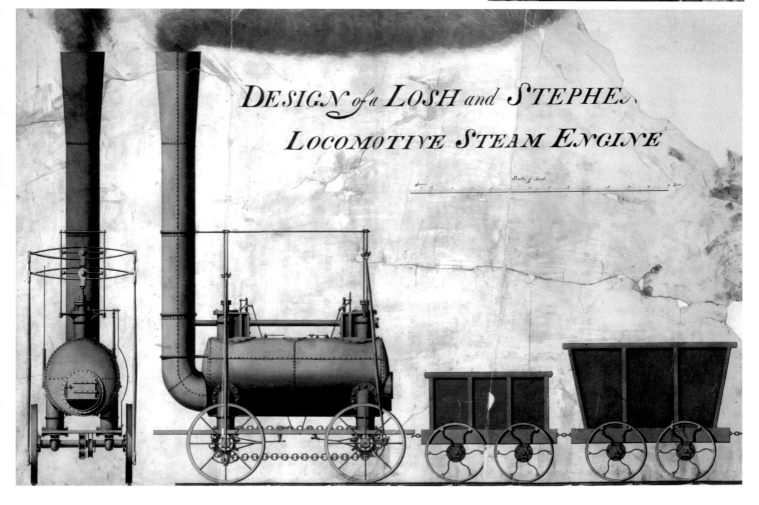

DESIGN of a LOSH and STEPHE...
LOCOMOTIVE STEAM ENGINE

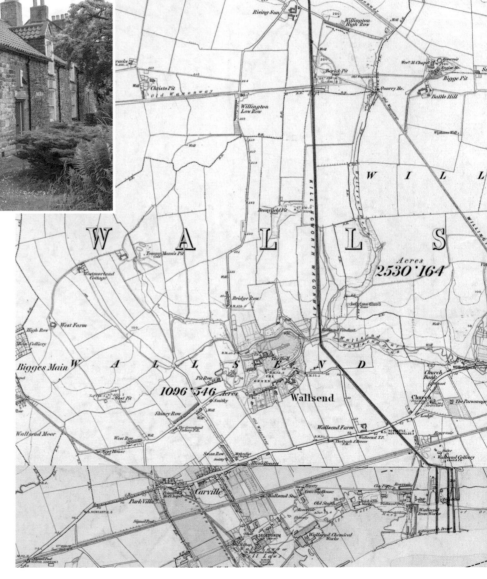

Right.

The *Killingworth Wagonway*, shown on an 1858 map. The line is highlighted in red, with sections shown in the modern photos (*top, left*) in yellow; (*top, inset centre*) in blue; and (*top, inset right*) in green, the latter two views being taken from the same place in opposite directions. Linear green spaces like the one shown are common in this area, now built up with suburban housing. In Stephenson's day these were open fields. *Killingworth Colliery West Moor Pit* is at the northern end of the waggonway. Nearby, where the waggonway crosses the road (Great Lime Road) is *Paradise Row*, the cottages pictured *above*. This is Dial Cottage, and was George Stephenson's home during his Killingworth days. The waggonway was conveniently located in his backyard! Today the house stands forlorn and unlived-in, surrounded by cookie-cutter modern housing. Above the door of the cottage is the sundial (*left, centre*) that was made by Robert with George's assistance in 1816, reflecting, perhaps, George's early interest in clocks. Note, however, that the later inscription refers to Stephenson as the "Inventor of the Locomotive Engine," a totally untrue notion that still exists in popular literature. It also refers to his first locomotive as *Blucher*. This is now thought to have been his second engine, after *My Lord*.

thought that Stephenson could not have invented such a thing without having had a formal education. The reality is that both invented it at the same time, but independently. This controversy did, however, bring Stephenson's name to the notice of a wider technical audience.

Further patents for steam engines were granted in 1816, and Stephenson continued to refine his ideas, helped by the Killingworth viewer, Nicholas Wood, who had a strong technical knowledge that supported Stephenson's more intuitive approach. In 1816, with William Losh, a Newcastle iron founder, he patented a new type of cast-iron rail with better joints than existing ones (illustration, *page 139*).

By 1821 Stephenson had developed a locomotive capable of hauling twenty loaded coal wagons up a 1-in-288 gradient with what the *Newcastle Chronicle* called "an amazing degree of rapidity which beggars description."

Stephenson during this period developed a wide-ranging business advising on steam engines and railway or waggonway layout. In 1816 he built and supplied a locomotive, a six-wheeler, to the Kilmarnock & Troon Railway (see page 63); this was the first locomotive in Scotland. Another engine was built for a railway at Llansamlet in South Wales in 1819. By the time he began work on his first major railway, the Hetton Colliery Railway, in 1821 (see page 134), Stephenson had built at least six locomotives.

In April 1825, Stephenson famously stated that he had built sixteen locomotives. Since that time researchers have been trying to identify them all, but records were not kept (until the creation of the locomotive-building firm of Robert Stephenson & Company in 1823), and their task is quite difficult; not all have been positively identified even now. It may be, of course, that Stephenson was exaggerating—he was known to do such things—and the line between new-build and re-build (using parts again when a design did not work out) is not particularly clear. The locomotive photographed on these pages, *Billy*, may have been included in the total despite having been completed in 1826, because it had been ordered and may have been under construction when Stephenson spoke. At the time, he was testifying for the use of locomotives for the Stockton & Darlington Railway and would have wanted to demonstrate that they were common rather than an untested idea.

Left and *right*.
Stephenson's 1826 steam engine *Billy*, on display at the Stephenson Railway Museum in North Shields. The locomotive may be considered the last of the Killingworth type. It was in use on the Springwell and Jarrow line (the Bowes Railway; see pages 99 and 101) from 1826 until about 1880. Unfortunately, it was heavily modified during those years and there are no records, so it is difficult to tell whether some parts are original. Nevertheless, the engine's overall appearance is likely similar to the original.

Stephenson's *Billy* was still working in 1862, the date this photo is thought to have been taken. The engine was donated to the City of Newcastle in 1881.

An All-Mechanical Line

In 1822 the Hetton Colliery Railway opened to service a colliery also opened that year at Hetton le Hole, Durham County. The Hetton Colliery was developed once it became practical to mine deep beneath the covering limestone strata that become thicker closer to the North Sea, and it soon became the largest colliery in Britain.

Wanting to service the lucrative London market, the mine owners determined to load their coal into coastal colliers directly, avoiding the common transhipment via keelboats. This necessitated a nearly 8-mile-long railway from the pithead to staiths at Sunderland where there was deep water at the entrance to the River Wear (map, *overleaf*).

In July 1820 the mine owners invited local engineers to submit their proposals to build such a line, and George Stephenson's design was the one accepted. His design included three self-acting inclines with the intermediate, more level sections, worked either by horses or by his locomotives. It seems likely that the cost savings expected by using locomotives are what resulted in their being chosen, and when the railway opened on 18 November 1822 there were three Stephenson "patent travelling engines" working the line.

All locomotive working up to this time had been on previously existing horse-powered waggonways, and Hetton was the first to be purpose-built to use no horses at all. The project was enormously influential and was visited by engineers from all over the world. It demonstrated clearly that locomotives were a viable power option, despite the fact that one section of locomotive-worked line later reverted to rope haulage because of unreliability of the travelling engines. Nevertheless, it was being able to actually see the successful operation of locomotives on the Hetton line that persuaded the owners of the Stockton & Darlington Railway, opened three years later, and also engineered by Stephenson, that they should likewise use steam locomotives.

The mine's output was recorded in 1826 at an astonishing 79,000 Newcastle chaldrons (see page 30) of coal per year, most of which left the pit via the railway. Clearly it was a very busy line.

Just over half of the route was worked by locomotives, 1½ miles from the pithead (4 on the "map-view," *below*), and 2½ miles on the level section before the incline to the staiths. Both sections are marked with little locomotives on the map. The other five sections

A Description of the HETTON RAIL ROAD, in England,
BY WILLIAM STRICKLAND, ESQ., CIVIL ENGINEER.

The Hetton Rail Road extends from the town of Sunderland, on the River Wier, to Hetton Collieries. Its length, from the pit to the staith, is seven miles five furlongs—it has an ascent of two hundred and sixtysix feet, and a series of descents, equal to five hundred and forty-six feet: making in the whole 812 feet of elevation and depression, overcome by a series of levels and inclined planes. The first portion of the road, from the pit to the foot of the ascending plain, is one mile seven and a half furlongs in length, and its general descent is one ninth of an inch to the yard, (with a portion of it five-sixteenths,) which is equally favourable for loaded and light carriages. A single locomotive engine, with twenty-four wagons in train, has drawn six hundred tons per day, going nine gaits, equal to thirty-five miles forward, and returning.

On another portion of the way, in length two and a half miles and sixty yards, with a descent, for the greater part, between four and five sixteenths of an inch to the yard, on which the loaded wagons tend to move of themselves, and consequently produce less stress on the light train, two locomotive engines, in use at the same time, have conveyed the quantity above mentioned.

Stationary reciprocating engines are placed at the summits of the inclined planes. These engines draw loaded and light wagons, alternately, each way, and each successive station performs its operation in the same time, the relative speed of the wagons being according to the distance between the engines, so that their respective journies may be completed in similar times, and maintain a uniform succession of carriages each way, by means of ropes, alternately winding and unwinding upon drum wheels eight feet in diameter.

On one of the inclined planes, the ropes are upwards of two miles in length, being supported by light cast iron concave rollers, fixed at a distance of forty or fifty feet apart, in the centre of the way, between the rails; and as the ropes are wound on and off the drum, the small rollers revolve, and keep them from coming in contact with the soil of the road.

Where the road-way deviates from a straight line, in plan, or where the plane winds to the right or left, the axes of the rollers are placed in nearly a vertical direction, in order to keep the line of draught midway between the rails.

It will be perceived by the engraved view, that this road is formed over an undulating or hilly country, and that the transportation of all the articles from the Collieries and its neighbourhood is made to surmount a series of very considerable ascents, by means of fixed engines, placed on their summits; and the motion given by the machines to the wagons, reciprocally, is equal to nine miles an hour.

The rails are made of cast-iron, four feet in length, are known generally by the denomination of the edge, or round top rail, of Losh and Stephenson.

The locomotive engines are made of thick sheet-iron, and are obviously of the high-pressure kind—they are only made to ply upon level lines of road; for the engine itself, in any material ascent, consumes a great portion of its power in the movement of its own weight, and that of its fuel, and any sudden rise would annihilate its object and use.

GENERAL VIEW OF THE HETTON RAIL WAY, LEADING FROM THE COAL MINES TO THE TOWN OF SUNDERLAND.

1. Staith — 2. Fixed Engine — 8. Fixed Engine — 4. Pit — Whole length of the ro

The first Hetton locomotives were of the standard Stephenson "improved Killingworth" design. The illustration is taken from the original commemorative lithograph issued for the line's opening in 1822. The engine has the chain-linked design shown on *page 134*. The locomotive in this image displays a plaque with the words "G. Stephenson Patent Locomotive Steam Engine" and another bearing the royal coat of arms of George IV.

Below, across page.
In November 1822, when the Hetton Colliery Railway opened, a commemorative lithograph was issued depicting the route as a sort of map-view showing the route from the colliery (4) to the staiths (1). It is a measure of the international interest in the project that this slightly modified reproduction found its way into a Boston, Massachusetts, newspaper as long after as 1829, when interest in railways in the United States was beginning to heat up. The explanation (*left*) and illustration of a train (*overleaf*) formed part of the same plate.

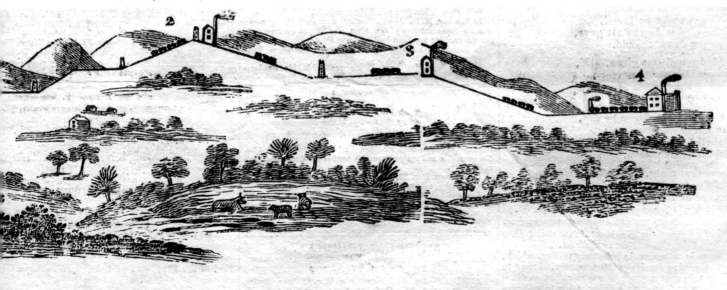

and 5 Furlongs. The elevation and depression overcome, 812 feet.

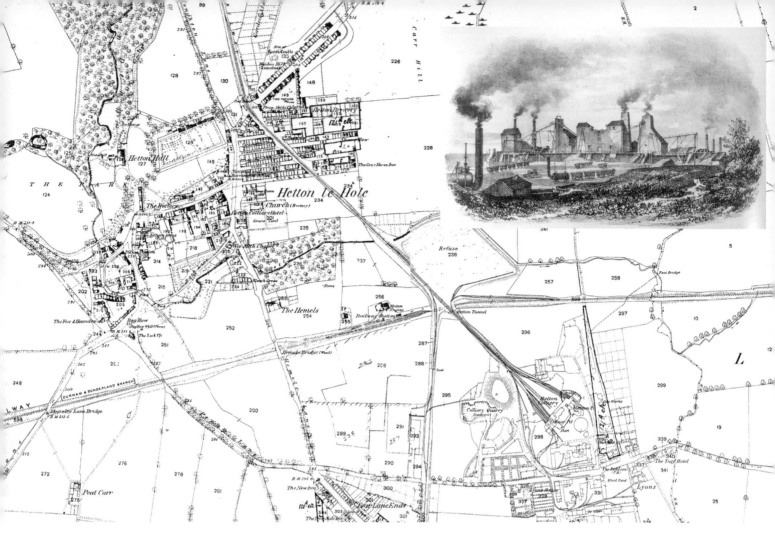

Above.
This 1856 map shows the southern end of the Hetton line ending at *Hetton Colliery*, just to the south of the mining village of *Hetton le Hole*. By this time a branch of the North Eastern Railway, created in 1854 by the merger of four smaller railway companies, runs west to east. This line was completed in 1846. It also originally used stationary engines; *Hetton Engine* is at the *Railway Station*. Soon after this map was published, the North Eastern Railway began using locomotives on this line.

Inset is a view of Hetton Colliery about 1825 by artist James Duffield Harding. Two locomotives are in evidence, though one appears to be off the rails. This may simply be an artistic inaccuracy; illustrators were not at that time used to vehicles running on rails.

were all inclines. Three were worked on a self-acting basis, where, as the full chaldrons were let down the slope, the empties were pulled back up (see page 94), and two used engines (as can be seen on the map-diagram, *previous page*).

Despite being advised by Stephenson and also Robert Stevenson (the Scottish railway engineer) to use malleable- or wrought-iron rails, the Hetton Colliery Railway used patented Stephenson & Losh cast-iron edge rails, each 3 feet, 9 inches

long and laid on stone and wooden blocks (illustration, *overleaf*). They gave the company a lot of trouble; it is on record that the colliery foundry replaced almost an astonishing 21 tons of broken rails in a twelve-month period in 1823–24. It seems likely that this was one of the reasons why Stephenson would recommend wrought-iron rails for the Stockton & Darlington, despite its very much not being in his immediate best financial interest (see page 157).

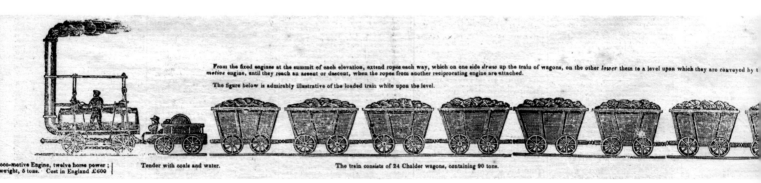

Right; below, top; and *below, bottom.*
The history of the surviving Hetton locomotive is somewhat enigmatic. Long thought to have been one of the original engines built by George Stephenson for the Hetton Colliery line, it is now known to have been built about 1852 and extensively rebuilt about 1874. It was named *Lyon*. There seems little doubt that its design was based on an earlier model, and for this reason some experts think it might actually be the world's first *replica* locomotive. This view is supported by the fact that the colliery owner at the time was Lindsay Wood, the son of Stephenson's close friend Nicholas Wood. Whether built regressively like this, complete with upright cylinders, deliberately to appear old or for other reasons is not known. Certainly the locomotive had a long life. *Below*, a postcard view, shows it working in 1901 with an elaborate side shelter for the driver and touted as "the oldest working locomotive in the world." Finally retired in 1912, it was preserved for many years at the colliery and eventually passed to the National Railway Museum. The modern photo shows the locomotive at Beamish Museum.

Right.
An 1826 map shows the northern end of the Hetton Colliery line ending at *Hetton Staiths* on the River Wear at Sunderland. Note that the *Hetton Rail Road* crosses the *Newbottle Rail Road* on its way to the *Lambtons Drops.*

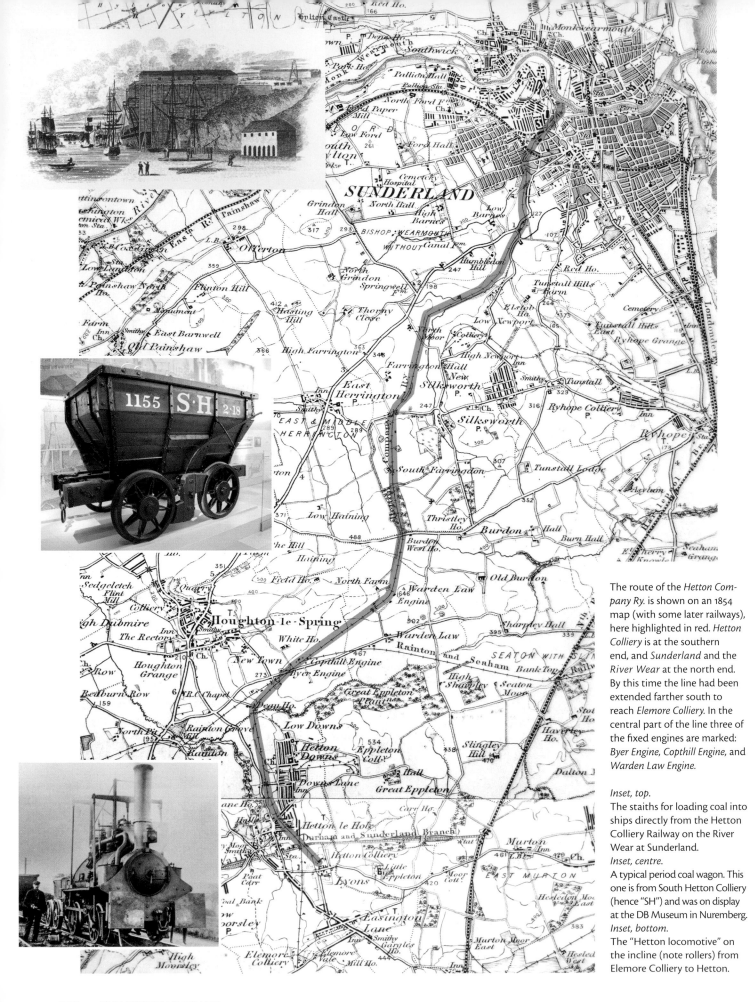

The route of the *Hetton Company Ry.* is shown on an 1854 map (with some later railways), here highlighted in red. *Hetton Colliery* is at the southern end, and *Sunderland* and the *River Wear* at the north end. By this time the line had been extended farther south to reach *Elemore Colliery*. In the central part of the line three of the fixed engines are marked: *Byer Engine*, *Copthill Engine*, and *Warden Law Engine*.

Inset, top.
The staiths for loading coal into ships directly from the Hetton Colliery Railway on the River Wear at Sunderland.
Inset, centre.
A typical period coal wagon. This one is from South Hetton Colliery (hence "SH") and was on display at the DB Museum in Nuremberg.
Inset, bottom.
The "Hetton locomotive" on the incline (note rollers) from Elemore Colliery to Hetton.

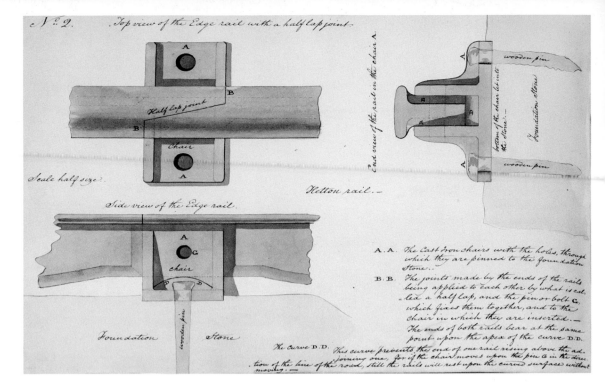

Right.

Perhaps the most artistic of any illustration of a rail, this is American engineer William Strickland's drawing of the patented Stephenson–Losh cast-iron rail, which had a new type of joint that was an improvement over previous designs. Despite the improvement, these rails gave the Hetton Colliery Railway trouble with frequent breakage that was almost certainly the major factor in persuading George Stephenson to use malleable-iron rails for future projects.

Another problem for the company was the staith (illustration, *left, top, inset*), which was at the bottom of a virtual cliff at the river's edge. The staiths needed much modification to avoid damaging the coal as it was loaded into ships. However, despite considerable ongoing modifications and improvements over various sections of the line, including the reduction of locomotive-worked sections to just one in 1827,

the railway proved conclusively the value of the locomotive engine and provided valuable experience for Stephenson that he would apply in his next major project, the game-changing Stockton & Darlington Railway.

The Hetton Colliery Railway lasted for well over a century: the last section closed only in 1972, the result of the decline of the coal industry rather than issues with the railway.

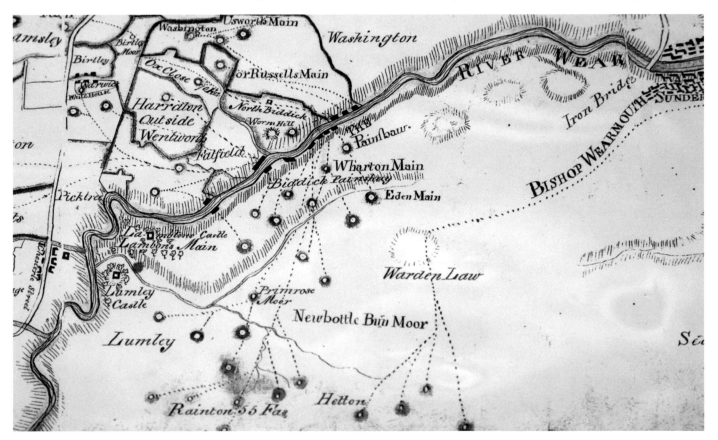

Above. The depiction of the Hetton Railway on this hand-drawn 1826 map is a little different from the accurate 1854 map opposite. It also is selective with the waggonways it shows; the Rainton Waggonway is shown, while the newer Newbottle Waggonway is omitted (see page 91).

The Visionaries

Almost all the earliest railways reviewed in this book are relatively short lines that ran from a source of materials—such as a coal mine or a quarry—to a navigable water—a river or a canal (to which they were feeders)—possibly via a processing facility of some kind, such as a smelter or a kiln (for limestone, used as a flux in ironmaking).

Long before railways were a practical proposition for long-distance travel, a few men (they all seem to be men, but that might just be those recorded—the traditional bias of history) came up with suggestions and even proposals for such lines—long-distance intercity lines, horse or steam locomotive drawn. And—what a revolutionary idea—they would carry passengers and general cargo. By connecting cities, they would break the mould of all railways built before 1825. These days this seems like an obvious concept, but it certainly was not two hundred years ago.

Surprisingly, perhaps, there were pioneers in related fields that never let their vision extend to railways. James Watt developed the stationary condensing steam engine (see page 33) and even a portable (but not self-propelling) engine. He also surveyed a number of feeder waggonways or railways to feed canals and recommended them sometimes (though only for horse traction) but never contemplated using steam power to run them, even if it

was possible. Indeed, Watt put every barrier he could construct in the way of other steam power pioneers, even serving an injunction for patent infringement on Richard Trevithick.

Benjamin Outram, that pioneer railway maker and champion of the plate rail, let his views be known through a paper nominally authored by his father-in-law, J. Anderson, in 1801. He thought that railways could be used for general transportation—for example, to link the London docks with what he called "commodious" parts of the city—and worked out a system of what were essentially containers that could move from rail wagon to road wagon very easily; this was a similar idea to the one employed at his Little Eaton Gangway and Peak Forest Tramway constructed a few years before. He proposed double-tracked intercity railways, from "London to Bath, and every other part of the country." Such railways were to be used solely for heavy goods, thus leaving the easily damaged roads for coaches and light carriages. He costed out double-track intercity lines at £2,000 per mile and £3,000 near London. Hence the price of the carriage of goods was to be reduced to an "amazing extent." Notably, his railways were all to be in public ownership, so as to prevent their misuse.

In 1802 Richard Lovell Edgeworth, an Anglo-Irish politician and inventor of an optical telegraph system, among other things,

wrote a paper titled *On the Practicability and Advantage of a General System of Rail-roads*, advocating a national railway network similar to that of Outram and Anderson, as did Richard Phillips in 1813 and Richard Preston, a Member of Parliament, in 1816. Phillips, a teacher and author, was inspired by the Surrey Iron Railway. "Yet a heavy sigh escaped me," he wrote, "as I thought of the inconceivable millions of money which have been spent about Malta, four or five of which might have been the means of extending double lines of iron railway from London to Edinburgh, Glasgow, Holyhead, Milford, Falmouth, Yarmouth, Dover, and Portsmouth." He continued: "we might, ere this, have witnessed our mail coaches running at the rate of ten miles an hour, drawn by a single horse, or impelled fifteen miles an hour by Blenkinsop's steam-engine!" The "Malta" issue he was referring to was the fortification of that island, taken from the French in 1800 and made a British colony in 1813. How many others have thought government money would be better spent on non-military endeavours!

Of course, it was relatively easy to write about what might be. Thomas Telford, on behalf of a group of Edinburgh investors, actually surveyed the entire route of a 125-mile proposed double-track railway line from Glasgow to Berwick in 1809–10. His report, dated 12 March 1810, first weighed the pros and cons of canals versus railways and then made some interesting statements. After noting inconveniences with canals such as freezing in winter, he conceded that "by constructing (rail) roads of very easy inclination with cast iron rails, most of the before-mentioned inconveniences are avoided and that for facility and cheapness, it nearly rivals a canal." Telford, the great surveyor of canals, could hardly allow railways to be better than a canal! "The utility of railways has, by the experience of many years, upon a great scale, been fully established in sundry parts of England and Wales," he wrote—in *1810*, remember. Then he recommended a railway rather than a canal. His survey was detailed, with costings for every section of line, bridges, road crossings, embankments, fencing, walls, cuttings, and land acquisition. He arrived at a total cost of £365,700.0s.9d. It appears that Telford did draw a plan of the route, because William Jessop is on record as having examined it and concurring that the cost is "probably right," but whether it survives is unknown.

Above and *below*.
Thomas Gray's 1822 third edition of *Observations on a General Iron Rail-way* contained these engravings showing intercity steam locomotive traction for first-class passengers (*top*) and two kinds of goods transport (*below*). Note the locomotives: they are Blenkinsop rack-system engines, not adhesion engines. The words are from the engraving.

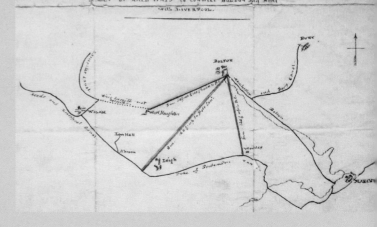

In 1812 John Stevens, engineer, inventor, and steam pioneer in the United States (see page 232), published a book titled *Documents Tending to Prove the Superior Advantages of Railways and Steam Carriages over Canal Navigation*. This was the first book written anywhere in the world on the subject of railways. Stevens wrote of trains travelling at an amazing 100 miles per hour! Scottish civil engineer Robert Stevenson surveyed hundreds of miles of railway in Scotland in the period from 1815 to 1826 (map, *below, far right*). Stevenson is mainly remembered for his construction of lighthouses around Scotland's coasts but was also involved in canals and railway surveys, believing that railways "would ultimately be the general highways of the world." He surveyed what is essentially an intercity system of railway lines in Scotland. All of his lines were surveyed with horse-drawn traction in mind and tended to follow the contours of the land to minimize grades. He was also an early supporter of the use of wrought-iron (malleable) rails, and it seems that it was a report of his that initially gave George Stephenson the idea of using them.

Then there was William James, a workaholic polymath, a visionary before his time, whose list of projects, schemes, ideas, and dreams would fill an entire book. Notably, he arguably has greater claim to the title of "father of the railways" than George Stephenson, to whom the moniker is often popularly attached. As early as 1802 he produced a map of possible railway lines from Bolton, Lancashire, to connect the town with Manchester and Liverpool, albeit with some routes also using canals (map, *above*). By 1822 he was carrying out an "ocular (eyeball) survey" of the route from Liverpool to Manchester, the earliest of the surveys for the 1830 railway (see page 173). In 1808 he advanced the idea of a General Railroad Company to build a network of railways across Britain. His Stratford & Moreton Railway (see page 80) was intended as only the first part of an extensive network of railways connecting existing canals and extending all the way to London. For this purpose James created the Central Junction Railway in 1820, which he envisaged as the first "hundred-mile railway" in the world (map, *right*). James's son,

William Henry James, in 1825 patented a multiple-wheel-drive system for trains in an attempt to make adhesion running more foolproof. It was similar to a road train developed in 1903 by Charles Renard of France, and the same idea as today's multiple-unit trains (EMUs and DMUs).

In 1821 Edward Pease, of the Stockton & Darlington Railway then being promulgated, saw George Stephenson's steam locomotives working at Killingworth and wrote to a friend that he saw "no difficulty [in] laying a railroad from London to Edinburgh on which waggons would travel and take the mail at the rate of 20 miles per hour."

Thomas Gray's 1820 book, *Observations on a General Iron Rail-way,* was the first to advocate in detail a railway network covering all of the British Isles (maps, *below*). Gray's main thesis was that the construction of such a system could be used for poor relief, by creating massive employment during its construction. Unemployment and attendant unrest had risen in Britain following the end of the Napoleonic Wars. He worked out many of the details, including the composition of trains (illustrations, *previous pages*) using Blenkinsop locomotives. "An iron rail-way," he wrote, "from London to Edinburgh," with many branches, "would be productive of incalculable advantage to the country at large." He suggested beginning with a line between Manchester and Liverpool "which would employ many thousands of the distressed population of the county."

The very concept of the railway, and especially one powered by steam engines, was exciting to many a dreamer, but within a few decades it was to become commonplace, such was their utility to a previously geographically hidebound population. The effects of speed and the resultant lower costs would be overwhelming.

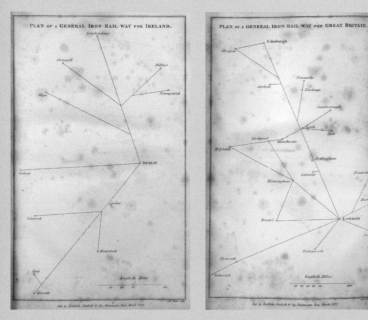

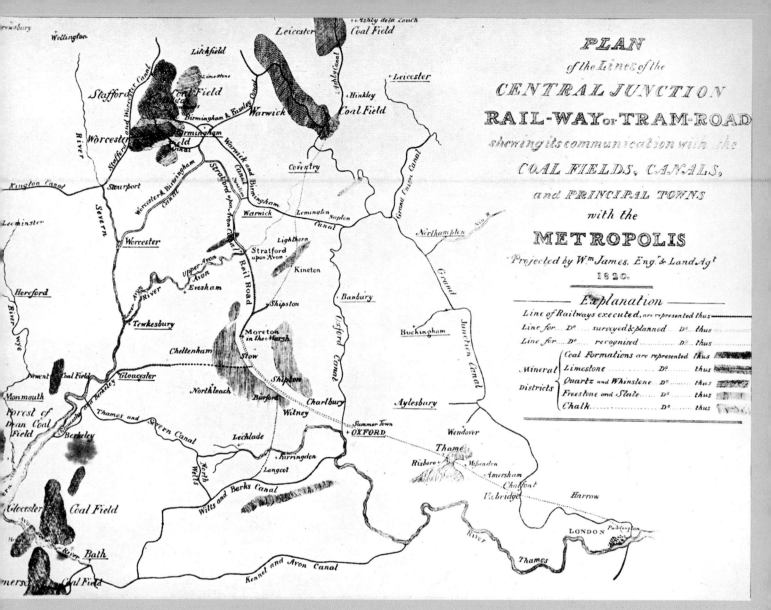

Plan of the Lines of the CENTRAL JUNCTION RAIL-WAY or TRAM-ROAD shewing its communication with the COAL FIELDS, CANALS, and PRINCIPAL TOWNS with the METROPOLIS

Projected by W.m James, Eng.r & Land Ag.t 1820.

Explanation

Line of Railways executed, are represented thus
Line for D.o surveyed & planned D.o thus
Line for D.o recognised D.o thus

Mineral Districts	Coal Formations are represented thus
	Limestone D.o thus
	Quartz and Whinstone D.o thus
	Freestone and Slate D.o thus
	Chalk D.o thus

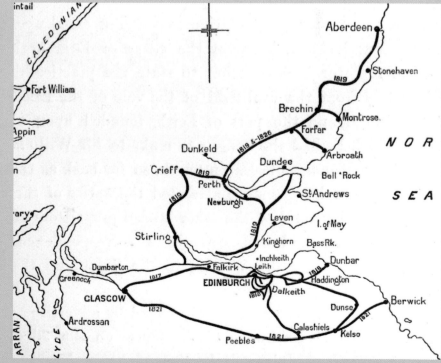

Above.

William James's 1820 map of his Central Junction Railway, also called the Central Union Railway. This is a copy from his daughter Ellen Paine's 1861 book, but in it she states that "the lithographed plan . . . is still in the possession of the family," so there is every reason to think it is the same map. The railway was to connect with the Stratford-upon-Avon Canal, completed in 1816, and go all the way to Paddington, London. Only the section from Stratford to Moreton was completed, as the Stratford & Moreton Railway in 1826 (see page 80).

Right.

This map shows the early railway lines projected by Robert Stevenson, the Scottish engineer well known for his construction of lighthouses. The map comes from a biography written by his son David and published in 1878. As can be seen, Stevenson was remarkably active, for he surveyed all these lines and made reports to various supporting groups. There is even a line from Glasgow to Berwick, as surveyed by Thomas Telford in 1810 (though on a different route). Stevenson tried to avoid inclines on his rail lines in much the same way as he tried to avoid locks on his canals. Thus, his surveys generally followed the contours of the land rather than taking the most direct route. The Berwick-to-Kelso line shown here got as far as an Act of Parliament but was not built.

The Stockton & Darlington Railway

The Stockton & Darlington Railway, which opened in 1825, is the beginning of the railway era in many people's minds, yet, as we have shown, there were hundreds of miles of railway in operation before that. The Stockton & Darlington, however, began the process of putting the elements of the modern railway together, operating both goods and passenger services over a line of unprecedented length—some 25 miles. But it still included horse traction and inclined planes, and was usable by all vehicles on payment of a toll—all features not included in the modern railway. Indeed, it would not be until the opening of the Liverpool & Manchester Railway five years later that these features would be excluded from a railway.

The Stockton & Darlington Railway is considered here in some detail because of its relevance and importance in railway history. The

Above.
George Stephenson's famous engine *Locomotion* stands at the Head of Steam railway museum at North Road Station, Darlington, on the route of the Stockton & Darlington Railway. Modern-day trains still call at the other side of the station building. The engine is similar to his Killingworth design (see page 132), but used coupling rods between the wheels.

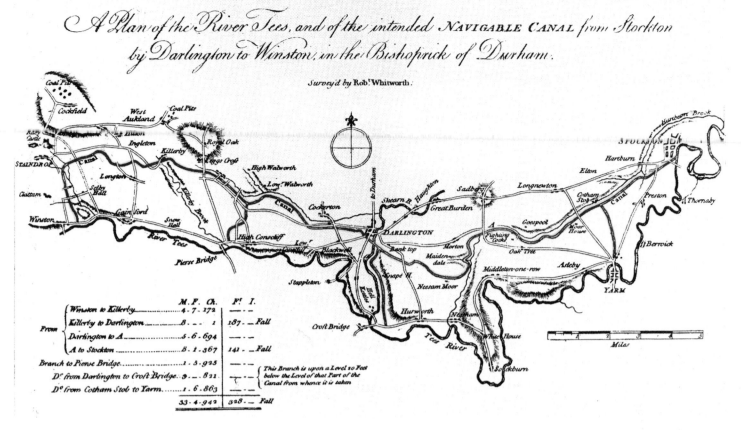

A Plan of the River Tees, and of the intended NAVIGABLE CANAL from Stockton by Darlington to Winston, in the Bishoprick of Durham.

Survey'd by Rob.t Whitworth.

		M.F. Ch.	F.t I.	
From	Winston to Killerby	4 . 7 . 172		
	Killerby to Darlington	8 . — . 1	187 . — .	Fall
	Darlington to A	5 . 6 . 694		
	A to Stockton	8 . 1 . 367	141 . — .	Fall
	Branch to Pierse Bridge	1 . 5 . 925		
	D.o from Darlington to Croft Bridge	9 . — . 821		
	D.o from Cotham Stob to Yarm	1 . 6 . 863		
		33 . 4 . 942	328 . — .	Fall

This Branch is upon a Level 10 Feet below the Level of that Part of the Canal from whence it is taken

railway originated in the usual way—the need to transport coal to a navigable waterway. Here the collieries concerned were a long way from navigable water, but the case for a railway or canal was helped by the desire of the residents of several towns to ensure that the commerce of their hinterland funnelled through them rather than rivals. The towns, of course, were Stockton, on the River Tees near its mouth; Darlington, a market town on the River Skerne, a tributary of the Tees; and Yarm, a small town at the head of navigation on the Tees.

And the schemes came together, again not unusually, after several schemes for canals or combinations of canals and railways had been shown to be impractical or too expensive. The route for the railway, at first seemingly constrained by a need to follow a similar route to the proposed canal, was revised a number of times and was only finalized when George Stephenson came on the scene and persuaded the protagonists that a route allowing for steam locomotion was their best bet.

Another important factor was at play here, too. The businessmen, bankers, and investors involved were mainly Quakers, with a reputation for extreme honesty. As such they had access to a financial network of other Quakers in other parts of Britain that enabled them to come up with the required financing—which was a large amount by the standards of the day.

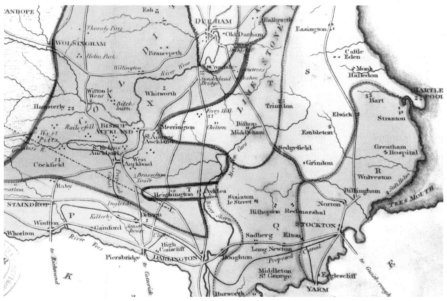

Above, top.
James Brindley and Robert Whitworth's canal proposal, surveyed in 1768–69. This summary map was published in *The Gentleman's Magazine* in August 1772. *Winston* is at far left, *Stockton* at right. The canal has been highlighted in blue. The distance from Stockton to Winston as the crow flies is about 20 miles; the canal would have been about 27 miles long without the branches.

Above.
This 1810 map shows the canal and branch canal proposals, each labelled *Proposed Canal*. The branch is not connected to the main canal; this gap was proposed to be filled by a self-acting plane rather than the alternative, a much more expensive flight of locks. The *Coal District* is the area coloured red.

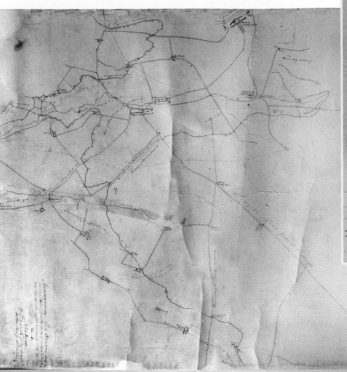

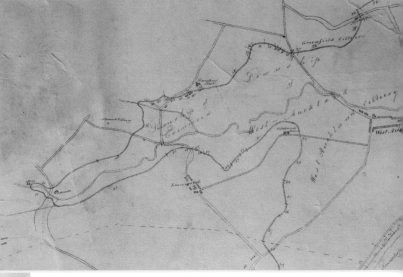

Whole map, left—and enlarged details.
This is the hurried plan produced by George Overton for his first survey in 1818, deposited on 30 September, now suffering from cracking with age from being stored rolled up. The tramroad route was inked over in red before deposit, and black ink additions were made to add better geographical context. The map was drawn on two sheets, which are shown together at left. They did not include the area east of Darlington. The latter part, in the form of a section showing only gradients, was allowed to be deposited the following March. Owing to "illness of one of the surveyors," it had not been deposited at the proper time.

Below. The route crosses the River Skerne not at Darlington but at Croft, near the confluence with the Tees, and then takes a southerly route to the collieries of west Durham not far removed from the route originally proposed by Brindley for his canal. The western part of the route (*above* and *bottom left*) is very circuitous, following the contours of the land. Overton was doubtless following his practice of surveying a route requiring the least cost to the colliery owner.

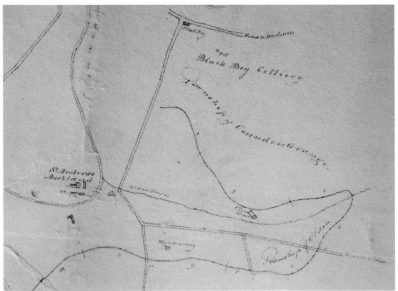

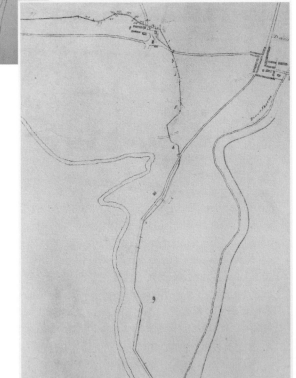

In 1767 the residents of Darlington engaged one of the principal canal builders of the time, James Brindley, to survey a route for a canal from the Durham coalfields to navigable water, via, of course, their town. The following year Brindley's assistant Robert Whitworth carried out the survey and recommended a canal from Winston, on the River Tees 9 miles west of Darlington, to Stockton, conveniently passing through Darlington and with a branch to Yarm (map, *page 145, top*). Brindley himself checked it the next year and produced a report that was considered at a meeting of potential subscribers in Darlington in July 1769.

At the meeting it was suggested that a higher-level branch canal be built to bring the canal nearer some collieries at West Auckland and area, connecting to the main canal via a self-acting plane, and a survey for this was made (map, *page 149, bottom*). Here, then, are the essential elements of the route of the later railway. However, subscriptions to build the canal were not forthcoming because of doubts about its profitability, and the scheme languished.

In 1808 the Tees Navigation Company was created to improve the access to Stockton. In 1810 it was celebrating its first success, the completion of the short Mandale Cut, which sliced off a large meander in the river just downstream of the town. (It would complete another cut, the Portrack Cut, in 1831; see map, *page 167, top*.) At the celebration Leonard Raisbeck, a town official, moved that a committee be appointed to "inquire into the practicability and advantage of a railway or canal from Stockton, by Darlington and Winston, for the more easy and expeditious carriage of coals, lead, etc." This is the first record of a proposal for a railway.

The committee reported back two years later that "a canal or railway" would be "productive of considerable advantage to the country in general but would likewise afford an ample return to the subscribers." Engineer John Rennie (the elder) was asked to advise on a route and reported in August 1813 that he preferred a canal and that the route of Brindley and Whitworth's canal was as good as any. When Rennie's report was finally considered at a meeting in 1815, the cost was considered too high, and the project did not proceed. Rennie warned that subscribers would not receive an adequate return on their investments. The end of the war with France had resulted in a business recession and a local bank failure that affected many businesses in Durham.

Interest in linking the coalfields with the coast did not subside, however. In 1816 a new suggestion was made to use both railway and canal, with a canal between Stockton and Darlington, and a railway, now not to Winston but directly to a point in the coalfields near West Auckland. In 1818 Christopher Tennant, a Stockton merchant, at his own expense engaged canal engineer George Leather to survey a direct line from Stockton to "the present working coalfield." His report recommended the Stockton & Auckland Canal (see the green line on the map on *pages 150–51*), which was received with enthusiasm in Stockton.

Such enthusiasm was not shared by the residents of Darlington or Yarm. Darlington resident Jonathan Backhouse led the charge against the canal proposal, claiming that coal export from Stockton would be "hopeless, at least for a century to come," and that landsales would form the major source of profits. He was still in favour of a canal, though on the original Winston alignment.

In 1818 events occurred that would change things forever. As one early railway historian, William Tomlinson, wrote, it was "that curious element of chance which plays so mysterious a part in human affairs." A resident of Yarm, Jeremiah Cairns, was related by marriage to the Welsh railway engineer and promoter of the plateway, George Overton. Cairns wrote to Overton, who replied citing the "superior advantages" of a tramroad. The letter was shown to Richard Miles, a local merchant, who realized that a railway along the lines advocated by Overton was the answer to Yarm's (and Darlington's) problems. On 17 August 1818 a meeting of Darlington and Yarm businesspeople was held, with the result that Miles invited Overton to come to Durham and carry out a survey for a tramroad. Overton hastened north and began his work on 3 September.

Many in the two towns were still unsure whether a railway might be superior to a canal. Backhouse addressed this question in a letter to Rennie, who replied that a canal was preferable if the trade in each direction was about the same but that a railway was preferable if the downhill traffic exceeded that of the uphill. Rennie's letter, received on 12 September, tipped the balance of opinion. Overton finished his survey on 20 September, recommending the Winston route if a canal was still an option but his roughly surveyed line if a tramroad or railway was to be used. Galvanized into action by the fact that if they wanted to proceed with the application for a necessary Act of Parliament that year, the plans had to be lodged with the Durham County clerk before the end of the month, Overton's first survey was handed to the clerk on 30 September 1818 (map, *left*). Overton also produced a cost estimate for his surveyed line amounting to £124,000, which, critically, was some 40 per cent less than the estimates for Tennant's canal.

Overton's survey map, as can be seen, reflects its hurried origins. The plan was on two sheets and did not cover the area east of Darlington, except in a section showing gradients that was filed a few months later. The route in the coalfield is somewhat convoluted, so as to create as gentle and continuous a gradient as possible, which necessitated following the contours of the ground. Interestingly, the line of the railway does not reach into Darlington but instead makes a long detour to Croft-on-Tees, crossing the River Skerne near its confluence with the Tees (*enlarged detail, left, bottom*). It seems that the map, *overleaf*, is an undated neater copy of Overton's first survey that eliminates the "Darlington detour" but shows the same route otherwise, though the route east of Darlington has now been added, as have the land ownership parcels for the whole line. The authorship of some of these early surveys for the Stockton & Darlington Railway—the name first being applied to the project on 21 September 1818—is not as clear as might be wished for, but we can see that the latter map is dated as being deposited with the Durham clerk on 3 April 1819.

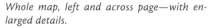

Whole map, left and across page—with enlarged details.

This is the unsigned 7-foot-long map deposited with the clerk at Durham on 3 April 1819. It appears to be a copy of George Overton's first survey redrawn in a more professional way with the addition of land ownership parcels, the route east of Darlington, and the elimination of both the "Darlington detour" to Croft-on-Tees and the branch to the Tees at Piercebridge. The committee agreed to remove these branches on 12 February 1819 in the hope of lessening some of the opposition. The title of the map has been changed from the "Intended Rail or Tram Road" of Overton's survey to "Intended Railway." Notably, the route in the vicinity of Lord Eldon's estate (*detail, bottom right*) has not changed despite the problems that would ensue.

Plan
OF THE
INTENDED RAILWAY
FROM
STOCKTON
to the Collieries in the Neighbourhood
OF
West-Auckland.

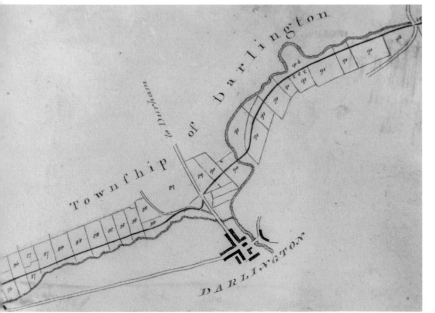

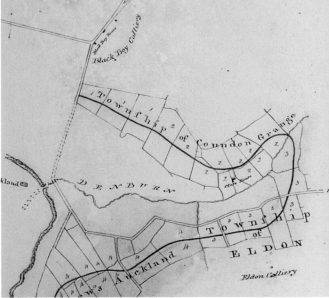

Letters were being exchanged in the local papers at this time extolling the merits of railways over canals, in particular the fact that branches of a railway could go right into a colliery and thus minimize the need for transhipments that necessarily broke coal into smaller, less valuable, pieces, the precise reason that direct-to-staith waggonways such as the Hetton Colliery Railway (see page 138) and the Newbottle Waggonway (see page 91) had proved such a success. Overton was able to add the fact that the Sirhowy Tramroad (see page 64), a line of 23 miles and therefore similar to the Stockton & Darlington in length, paid its subscribers an 18 per cent return, while the parallel canal paid only 8 per cent—facts of overriding interest to potential investors! Those opposed to the railway were able to point to the relative failure of the Surrey Iron Railway, which had been built by none other than George Leather, but that line did not run from a heavy user source like a coalfield.

As we know, the railway won the day. It did so primarily on economic grounds. Because it was cheaper to build than a canal, it was likely to produce a better return. At a meeting of potential subscribers on 13 November 1818, a respected Darlington merchant, Quaker Edward Pease—destined to play a major role in the creation of the railway—produced detailed figures derived from existing coal traffic on the turnpike that proved to his satisfaction that the railway was "assured" a "certain" return of 5 per cent. Some, he said, might calculate the return at "6 or 8 or 10 or 12 per cent" but that he was satisfied with 5 per

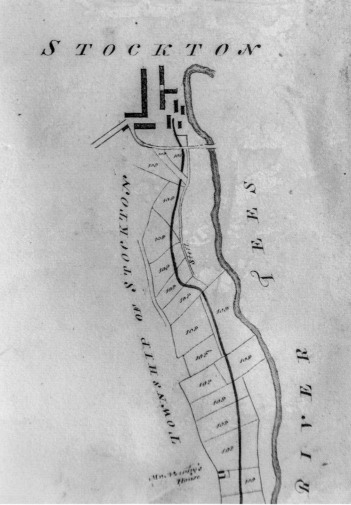

cent. Despite all the other arguments, it was Pease's universally respected opinion about his safe 5 per cent that carried the day with other investors. The meeting approved a motion to apply to Parliament for "an Act to make a tramway on the plan and estimates given by Mr. Overton" and also authorized surveys to be made of possible extensions southwards into the North Riding of Yorkshire.

There seems to have been an overall feeling of resolution at this point, for six weeks later the subscription lists were full. Nevertheless there were hurdles to overcome. For one, Overton's route was found to pass through estates of Lord Eldon, then Lord Chancellor of England, and Lord Darlington, the latter obsessed with preserving his fox coverts for hunting.

It seems, too, that some members of the committee created to guide the project did not have much confidence in the abilities of George Overton and in December 1818 decided to invite both John Rennie and another engineer with railway experience, Robert Stevenson, to review his survey. Rennie would not work with another engineer and refused to help, but Stevenson accepted.

Robert Stevenson is today more famous for the lighthouses he built around the coast of Scotland, including the Bell Rock

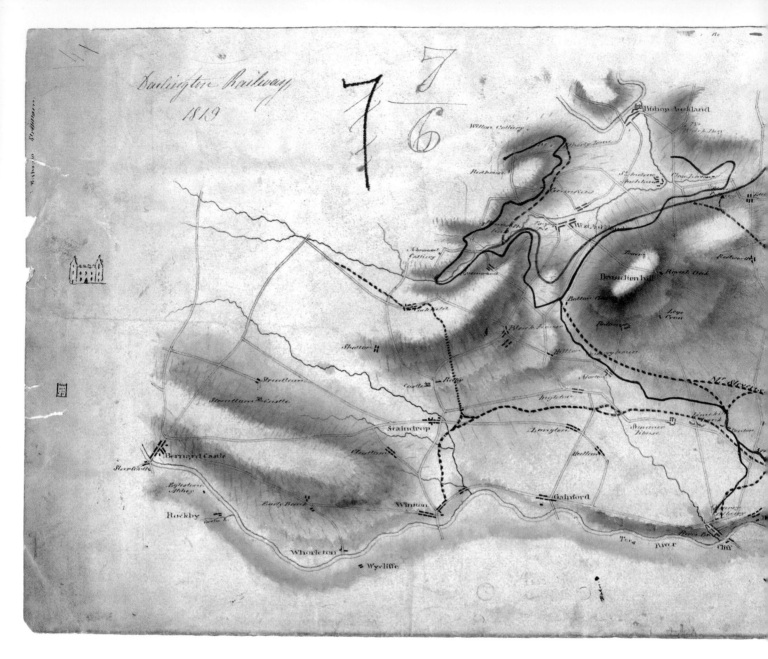

Lighthouse, but at the time had surveyed a number of routes for railways in Scotland (see page 147). As his son, David Stevenson, wrote in 1878 in a biography of his father, he "had made a great advance in bringing the subject [railways] before the public." His fame led to his survey for the Stockton & Darlington in 1819. Unfortunately, because of the similarity of his name, he is often confused with George Stephenson or Stephenson's son or brother, both named Robert.

Stevenson's report was not received by the committee until after the first bill had been defeated. On 5 April 1819, at the second reading of the bill, it was lost by a vote of 106 to 93, a narrow margin. The defeat might have been averted but for the lobbying efforts of Lord Darlington. Determined to protect his foxes, he had "posted" (that is, travelled by fast mail coach) to London the previous night and set about lobbying all who would listen. And he was influential.

The Quaker investors saw this as merely a setback rather than a defeat. Although Stevenson had only been requested

to examine Overton's route and comment upon it, he went much further, recommending many alterations to Overton's line, "indeed new lines from Darlington to the coalfield" altogether. The map, *above*, is thought to show the new routes he recommended.

The committee might have retained Stevenson as their surveyor after this, but Overton, perhaps sensing the competition, offered to carry out a new survey that would avoid Lord Darlington's foxes for a fee of £120, on the understanding that should a new bill based on it fail because of any defect in the plan, he would refund the money. This appears to have done the trick, because his offer was accepted on 9 July 1819.

In the meantime, Christopher Tennant's canal proposal had changed and was now for a railway, referred to as the Northern Railway. This was much more of a problem to the promoters of the Stockton & Darlington; the railway would also run from the coalfields to the coast, a location downstream of

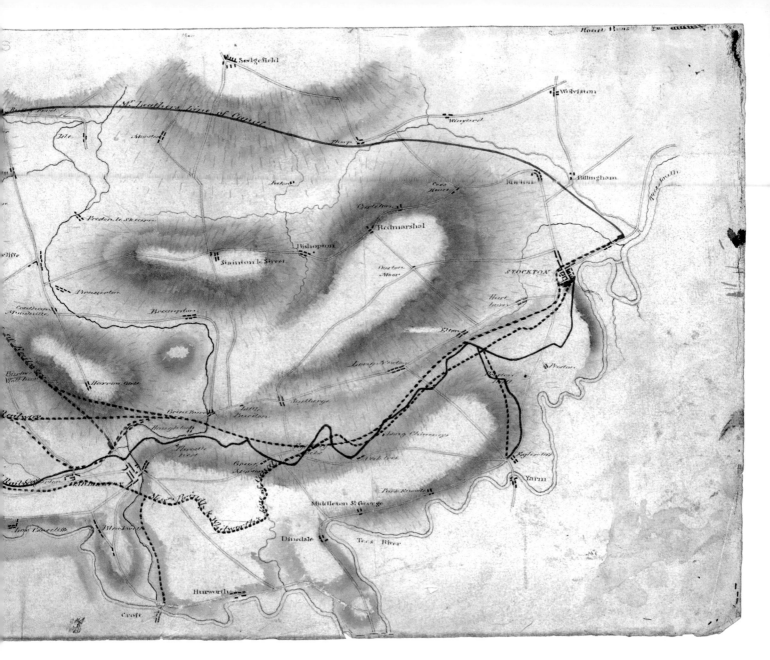

Stockton, just by a different route—one that would avoid all their towns. This situation was solved by agreeing on the tolls that would be charged on the Stockton & Darlington, thus assuring the northern route subscribers that they would get the cheapest means of transporting their coal.

Overton completed his second survey in September 1819, and the plans were duly registered with the county clerk by the end of that month. This time Overton's route was quite different from his first, following a more northerly route closely aligned to one suggested by Stevenson (and much the same as on the third survey (map, *pages 158–59*, less some extensions noted in the caption for that map). It now avoided Lord Darlington's lands altogether—and Lord Eldon had been satisfied with compensation—so the way now looked clear for the introduction of a new bill. Unfortunately the line now crossed the lands of a different aristocrat, Lord Barrington, who was to give them further trouble. As Tomlinson so aptly put it: "whichever way they went there was a noble lord to be propitiated."

Above.

This map, which comes from Robert Stevenson's papers, is thought to show the new railway routes he considered superior to those of Overton's first survey. The map is dated 1819 but not signed. It may be a summary map prepared by someone else in Stevenson's office, or elsewhere for him, but it seems clear that his own proposals are those shown on it. The map also shows the two proposed lines for canals. The first is that of *Messrs Brindly & Whitworth* (James Brindley and Robert Whitworth), surveyed in 1768–69, the dashed blue line, and includes the proposed branch to the coalfield north of Winston, here shown connected to the main canal. The second is George Leather's canal proposal for Christopher Tennant in 1818, the solid green line labelled *Mr. Leather's Line of Canal. Mr. Overton's Line of Railway*—his first survey—is shown as a solid red line. Added to these routes are the ones Robert Stevenson was suggesting in 1819, one as a dashed red line connecting Overton's lines in the coalfield with a straighter and more direct line from Stockton, and a branch to Yarm that evens out the bends in Overton's line. Stevenson seems to be suggesting a simpler system than Overton, though doubtless the avoidance of bends would have resulted in higher construction costs. In addition, there is another Stevenson line—the dashed green one—that cuts across to seemingly join Leather's canal, but, interestingly, it is a route much closer to the one that would ultimately be followed.

The promoters were determined to quickly try again for an Act of Parliament but were stymied by the death of King George III on 20 January. In those days this meant a new Parliament had to be elected and hence all pending private legislation would be cancelled. A new application would have to be made.

At some point around this time Robert Stevenson was again involved, in that he drew up (or had someone do it for him) a map that compared Overton's second survey with one of the lines he had suggested the previous year (map, *pages 150–51*), now extended into the coalfield itself in the form of sweeping curves ending at Etherley, near Witton Park Colliery, the same place as one of Overton's branches (map, *right*).

Also during 1820 Overton was asked to resurvey the line in an attempt to avoid the estates of lords. The plan was very similar to the 1819 one and was lodged with the county clerk as required, on 30 September 1820. This plan, Overton's third survey, is shown *overleaf, pages 154–55*.

The committee geared up for a new submission to Parliament in 1821, issuing a new prospectus, complete with a map (*page 160*). "Local circumstances peculiarly entitle this undertaking to the support of the public," it stated. "The Line passes through a populous district, in which an extensive Trade already exists . . . General Merchandise will be carried from [the] Coast *upwards*, and Coal, Lime, Lead, Blue Stone for the repair of roads, and agricultural [produce], from the interior of the County *downwards* . . . By the facilities thus given to the conveyance, the carriage will be reduced nearly *one-half* the present charge."

The prospectus also pointed out that the "Line of Road does not (as is frequently the case with similar undertakings) interfere with the residence of any gentleman, in any part of it." It was finally able to state this truthfully because Lord Barrington, the last holdout, had been financially appeased to the extent that his name now appeared on the bill as a proprietor!

Right.
It is thought that this map was drawn by someone in Robert Stevenson's office in 1820, or for him, before Overton produced his third survey, for the line shown as *Mr Overton's Line of Railway* is his second survey, done in 1819 (the green line). Also plotted (in red) is one of Stevenson's route recommendations (*Mr Stevenson's Line of Railway*), now extended right into the South Durham coalfield in two canal-like wide curves following the contours. Stevenson and Overton were both thinking of horse traction when they did their surveys. It was not until George Stephenson became involved in 1823 that survey lines were altered to suit steam traction. This map is now with the Stevenson papers at the National Library of Scotland. This map has been mistaken in the past for one showing George Stephenson's survey compared with Overton's, but this cannot be, for Overton's line is the second, not the third, survey, and Stephenson was not involved with the Stockton & Darlington Railway in 1820.

Plan and Section
of the Intended
RAILWAY or TRAMROAD
from
STOCKTON *by* DARLINGTON
to the
COLLIERIES
near
WEST AUCKLAND
with several intended
Branches of Railway or Tram Road
in the County of
DURHAM
1820
From the Line marked out by George Overton Engineer.
D. Davies, Surveyor.

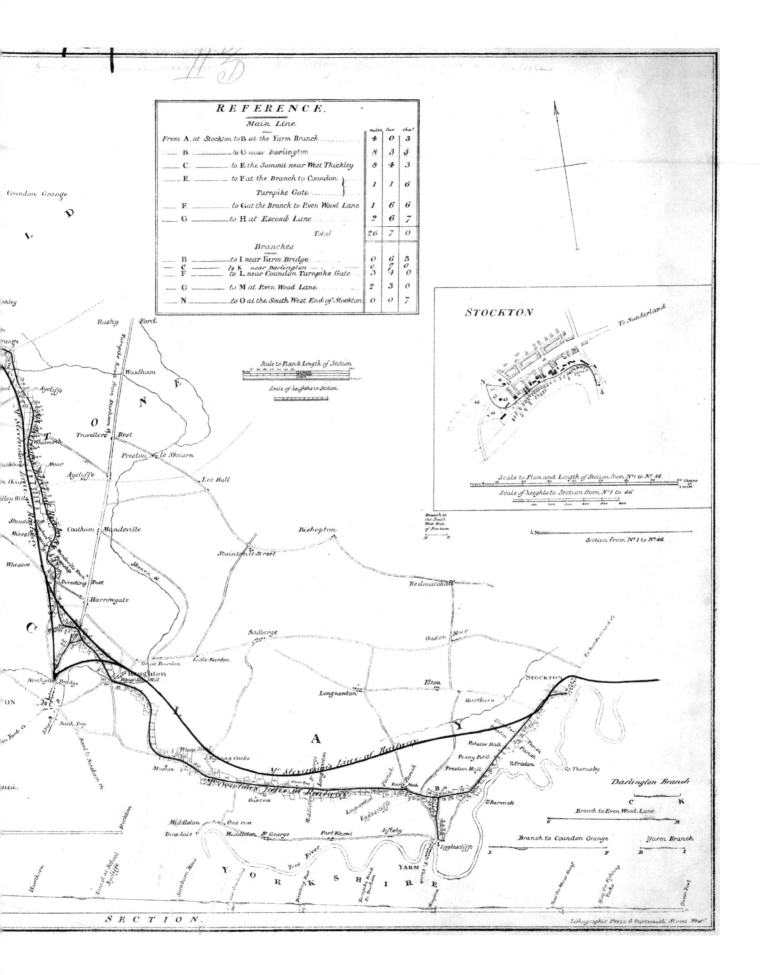

REFERENCE.

Main Line

		miles	fur	cha[s]
From A at Stockton to B at the Yarm Branch		4	0	3
B _____ to C near Darlington		8	3	5
C _____ to E the Summit near West Thickley		8	4	3
E _____ to F at the Branch to Coundon		1	1	6
Turnpike Gate				
F _____ to G at the Branch to Even Wood Lane		1	6	6
G _____ to H at Escomb Lane		2	6	7
Total		26	7	0

Branches

B _____ to I near Yarm Bridge		0	6	3
C _____ to K near Darlington		0	7	0
F _____ to L near Coundon Turnpike Gate		3	4	0
G _____ to M at Even Wood Lane		2	3	0
N _____ to O at the South West End of Stockton		0	0	7

STOCKTON

Scale to Plan & Length of Section

Scale of heights to Section

Scale to Plan and Length of Section from N.º 1 to N.º 46

Scale of heights to Section from N.º 1 to 46

Branch to the South West End of Stockton

Section from N.º 1 to N.º 46

Coundon Grange

Rushy Ford

Woodham

Travellers Rest

Preston le Skearn

Lee Hall

Aycliffe

Whitworth

Coatham Mundeville

Bishopton

Staintonle Street

Redmarshall

Ouston Moor

Wheatley Hills

Standalone

Miersfield

Wheasoe

Directing Post

Harrowgate

Sadberge

Little Burdon

Great Burdon

Elton

Longnewton

Hartburn

STOCKTON

Northgate Bridge

Houghton Mill

Bank Top

Mr Stephenson's Line of Railway

Potato Hall

Peany Pot G.

Preston Hall

Thornaby

Darlington Branch

Wheat Sheaf

Fighting Cocks

Morton

Oaktree

Egglescliffe

Berwick

Branch to Even Wood Lane

Middleton

One row

Dinsdale

Middleton St. George

Part Knowl

Aislaby

Egglescliffe

Branch to Coundon Grange

Yarm Branch

Tunnel at School Aycliffe

Tees River

YARM

Y O R K S H I R E

S E C T I O N.

Lithographic Press 6 Dartmouth Street West.

To Sunderland

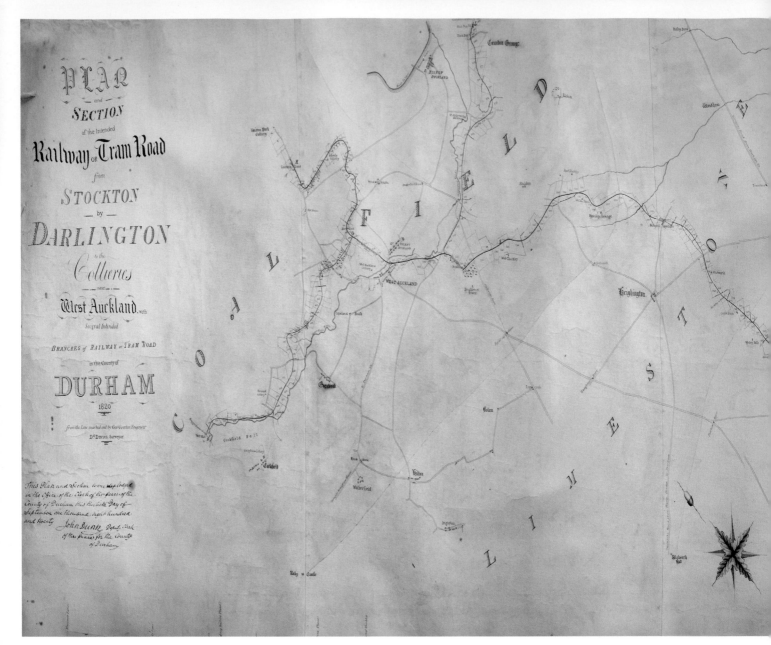

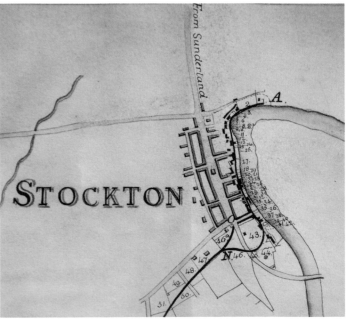

Above and *detail, right.*
George Overton's third survey for the Stockton & Darlington Railway, completed in September 1820. It was actually surveyed and drawn by Overton's assistant, David Davies. As can be seen from the reference table at right, the length of the main line (from *Stockton* (labelled *A*) to *Escomb Lane* (labelled *H*)) was now nearly 27 miles, with another 9 miles of branches, for a total of almost 37 miles. This is more like Overton's normal work, since it was relatively unhurried in its making compared with his first survey. The map is huge and consequently difficult to reproduce, being about 10 feet long. The Stockton detail (*right*) shows one of the minor changes from the second survey, with the line now extending to all the wharves.

Overton's second survey, done in 1819 (not reproduced in this book), plotted the same route as this one, except the branch to *Hagger Leases Lane* (at far left on the main map) was shorter, the *Coundon Grange* branch (top left) was also shorter, and the line within Stockton did not go to all the wharves. The route of the second survey is shown on the map on the *previous page.*

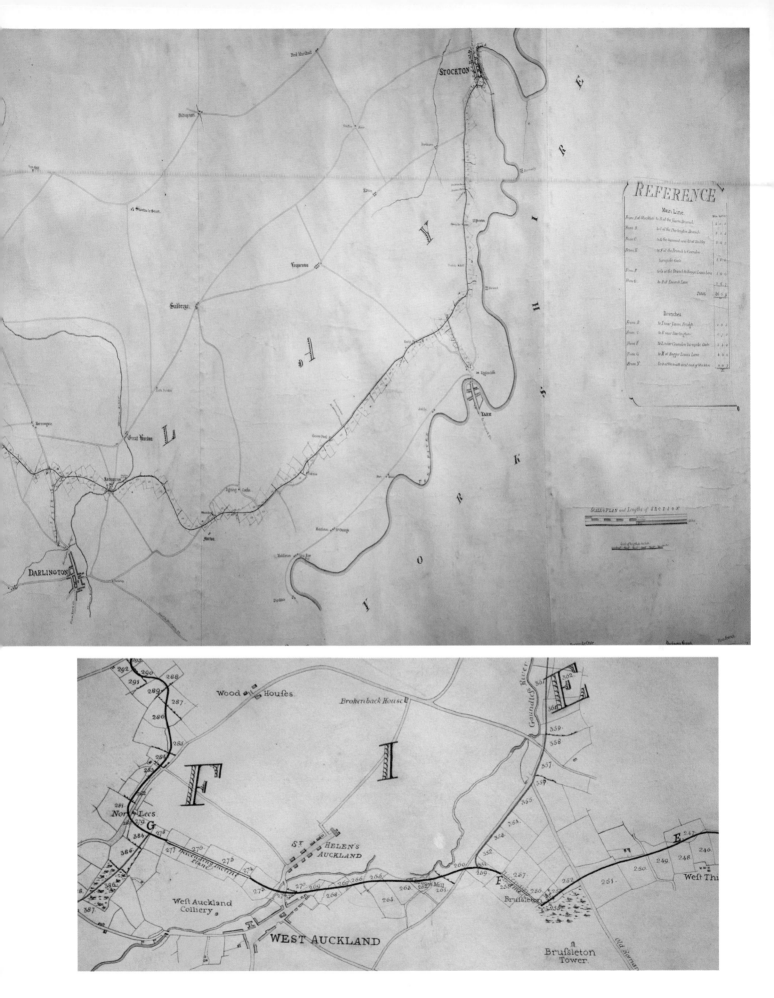

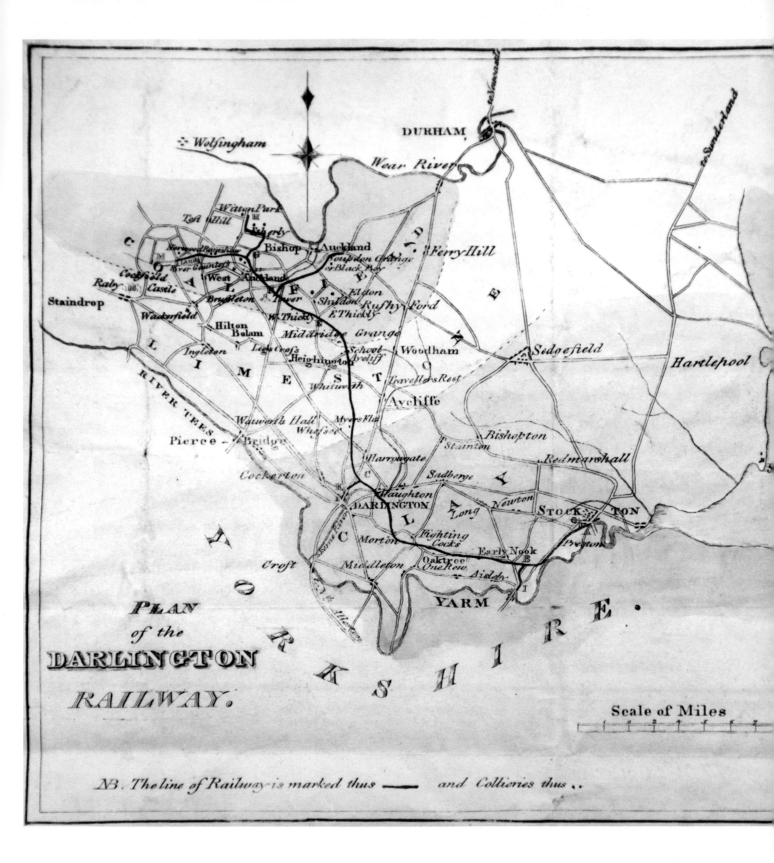

Above.

This map was part of the prospectus published in late 1820 or early 1821 and shows George Overton's third survey, the basis upon which the first Stockton & Darlington Railway Act was granted (but not the route that was actually built; that would await the arrival of George Stephenson). The coalfield, limestone area, and clay area are distinguished with coloured washes.

Above.
Stockton & Darlington Railway's malleable-iron rails, on display at the Head of Steam railway museum in Darlington. They are of the fishbelly type, thicker between the supports, and are fastened to stone blocks with cast-iron chairs. Oak blocks (made from old ship timber) were used instead of stone on the eastern part of the line. A length of rail is much longer than the 3 feet, 9 inches of the Stephenson–Losh patented cast-iron rails.

Overton's third survey plan accompanied the bill, and it was approved on that basis, receiving Royal Assent on 19 April 1821. This was after Edward Pease had personally subscribed another £7,000 at the last minute; the rule was that four-fifths of the share capital had to be subscribed before the bill went into committee, and the committee's solicitor, Francis Mewburn, had unexpectedly and belatedly found them short that amount.

The 1821 act creating the Stockton & Darlington Railway Company was the twenty-first railway act and was modelled on the one granted the Berwick & Kelso Railway (which was not built) in 1811. It was to operate a toll line, with the railway being open to anyone who paid the toll.

The company would now have to make a decision as to what kind of line should be built—plate or edge. And while the line as surveyed already included some inclined planes, there was also the question of the motive power for the rest of the line—horses, travelling engines, or stationary engines, though steam had not been considered an option before in that its authorization was not in the act just passed.

Edward Pease from this juncture assumed the leading role in guiding the railway through to completion, and he soon became convinced of the utility of steam power. Pease had heard of the successes George Stephenson was having on his own Killingworth Waggonway, and his construction, then under way, of the Hetton Colliery Railway (see page 134). While the company's act was being considered by Parliament, Pease invited Stephenson to visit him, which he did, coincidentally, on 19 April, the same day the company received its act. Stephenson, unsurprisingly, rapidly convinced Pease that steam power was the way to go. After once more consulting Robert Stevenson and reviewing a letter from William James—who described the edge rail as "infinitely preferable" based on his survey of most of the existing railways in the country—the directors made a decision, heavily influenced by Pease: they would use edge rails—building a "railway" rather than a "tramroad." James also expounded on the virtues of the travelling steam engines that Stephenson had built at Killingworth, and, intrigued, the directors also decided to engage George Stephenson to make yet another survey of Overton's line with a view to assessing its suitability for steam. Overton, who had expected to be appointed engineer for the line, was understandably upset and refused to attend any more meetings. The line as authorized allowed for some deviation from it—100 yards on either side—but if these limits were exceeded, a new act would have to be sought. Stephenson began his survey in October 1821, helped by his eighteen-year-old son, Robert.

At this time, iron prices were lower than normal, and the directors wanted to place an order to secure these lower prices, but while they had decided on edge rails, they had not decided whether to use cast iron or malleable (wrought) iron—the latter being better but more expensive. Stephenson heartily recommended malleable rails, and James was also ardently in favour of wrought-iron rails. Stephenson wrote that "although it would put £500 in my pocket to specify my own patent rails, I cannot do so after the experience I have had." In a letter to William James he explained that the railway company advertised for cast-iron rails for about one-third of the line in order to satisfy a few of its subscribers who had been "bought over" by cast-iron founders. The main line, at least, was to be of malleable iron. Stephenson's patent co-holder William Losh was furious, suggesting in a letter to Pease that Stephenson was receiving a kickback from Michael Longridge, who was to supply the malleable rails.

Stephenson completed his survey in December, bringing to bear what seems to have been a natural talent for selecting the best line for a railway. He recommended a course much straighter than that of Overton, which reduced the length of the line by 3 miles while reducing gradients so that a horse would be able to pull a 30 per cent heavier load. It was also suitable for steam locomotives. Stephenson wrote to James in December 1821 that "we fully expect to get the engines introduced on the Darlington Railway." The new route is shown on the map *overleaf*.

The directors were, as might be expected, very pleased with Stephenson's survey work, for it held out the promise of lower costs and thus higher profits, and on 22 January 1822 he was appointed engineer for the railway. Construction was to begin on those parts of the railway unaltered by the new survey while another application to Parliament was made for the parts beyond the first authorized route.

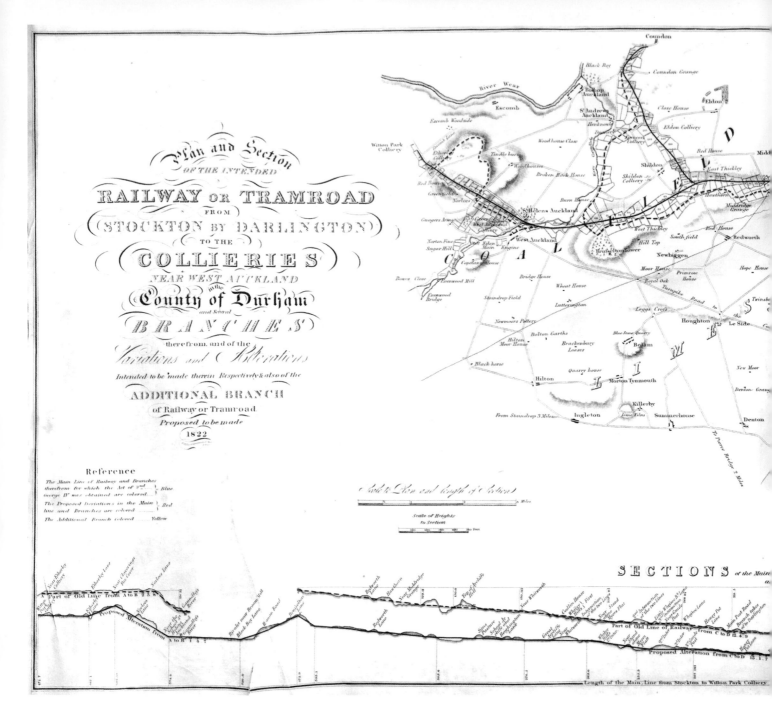

Contracts had already been signed with Michael Longridge's Bedlington Iron Company for 1,200 tons of malleable-iron rail, and with the Neath Abbey Iron Company in South Wales for 306 tons of cast-iron rails and 304 tons of cast-iron chairs. Stephenson staked out part of the eastern part of the line and the Yarm branch before going to London to purchase oak blocks, on which the eastern part of the railways would be laid, and then to South Wales to inspect the cast rails being made there. On 23 May 1822 a celebration was held as the first rails—malleable ones—were laid in Stockton, the first part of what would eventually be an interconnected network covering the entire country. And they were laid at Stephenson's favourite gauge—4 feet, 8 inches apart—a gauge that would ultimately be replicated over much of the world (½ inch was added for play). Stephenson had retained the gauge of the Killingworth Waggonway, the earliest part of which dates to 1762.

Later that year Stephenson completed his Hetton Colliery Railway, enabling the Stockton & Darlington directors to visit and see for themselves what they were building. They now had to make a decision as to motive power. A battle of newspaper letters was raging at the time between a proponent of stationary engines and self-acting planes, an engineer named Benjamin Thompson (see page 99), and Nicholas Wood, viewer at Killingworth and Stephenson's friend. Luckily the directors had faith in their engineer, for otherwise they might have plumped for a stationary engine system (as the Liverpool & Manchester nearly did, seven years later).

The bill to authorize the revised route, with the addition of a branch to Croft, importantly also included a clause allowing the company to use "locomotive or moveable engines for the purpose of facilitating the transport, conveyance and carriage of

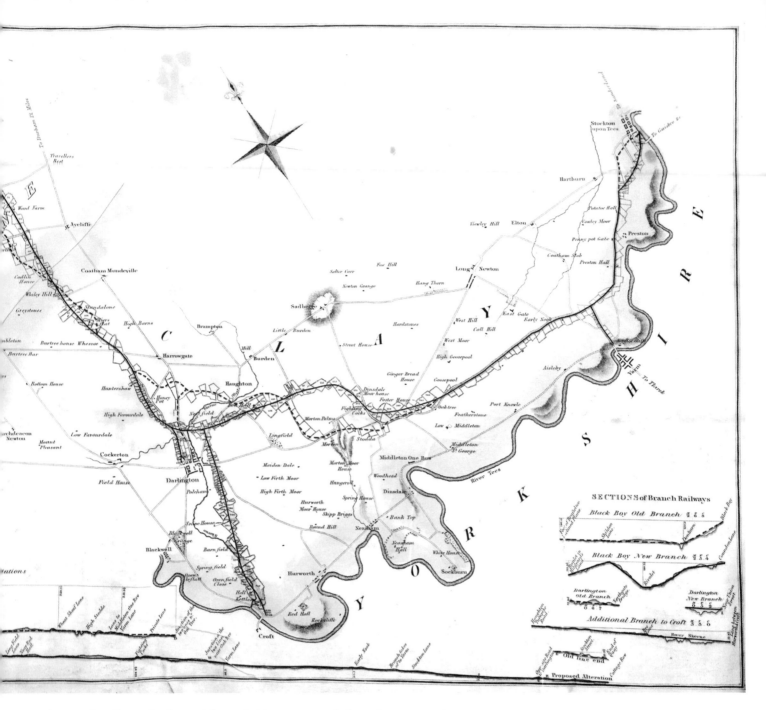

Above.

This map, with accompanying sections to show gradients, was drawn in 1822 to illustrate George Stephenson's new route (the solid line) for the Stockton & Darlington Railway as compared with George Overton's third survey (the dashed line). The map was printed (in Edinburgh) and then added to by hand. The "additional branch" referred to in the title is the one to Croft (bottom right). The map was not drawn *by* Stephenson; he would never have given it a title that included the word "tramroad" as an option! While some of Stephenson's route is the same as Overton's, there are significant variations on much of the line, consistently straightening it out, and, not coincidentally, making it more suitable for working by steam locomotives.

goods, merchandise and other articles and things upon and along the same roads, and for the conveyance of passengers upon and along the same roads." Locomotives and passengers in one clause! This, the second Stockton & Darlington Railway Act, received Royal Assent on 23 May 1823, exactly one year from the day the first rails had been laid. George Stephenson had spent eight weeks in London along with some of the directors and their solicitors prior to the bill's passing, thus gaining his first direct experience of the parliamentary process.

Yet another addition to the route was to come. To satisfy colliery owners, a new branch was to be added, to Hagger Leases Lane at the extreme western end of the line. This was a branch that, on a different alignment, had been on George Overton's third survey (map, *pages 154–55*). The branch required yet another act—the third—which was obtained on 17 May 1824. George's son Robert was appointed engineer for the branch and given the task of surveying this branch in late 1823; his map (*overleaf, page 160*) accompanied the application for the bill. This was the first railway survey for which Robert Stephenson was responsible on his own.

Above. Part of the opening day train on the Stockton & Darlington Railway, from a contemporary engraving.

Above.

The River Gaunless was spanned in 1823 using this wrought-iron girder bridge designed by George Stephenson. It was one of the first railway bridges to be built of iron and was the first to use lenticular iron trusses. It was removed in 1901 because it was unable to support the increasing weight of coal wagons. The bridge has been in a museum display since 1927 and is now on display outside the National Railway Museum in York, where it was placed in 1975.

Work progressed on the construction of the railway under George Stephenson's watchful eye. At Myers Flat, about 3 miles north of Darlington (and shown on the map, *previous pages*) his contractors encountered a swampy area that required the dumping of hundreds of tons of rock, though to this day it is not stable. A few years later he would come across a similar problem at Chat Moss, while building the Liverpool & Manchester Railway, but solve it better.

On 16 September 1824 the railway confirmed an order for two steam locomotive engines with Robert Stephenson & Company, set up in 1823 by George Stephenson specifically to manufacture locomotives. The other partners in the business were Robert Stephenson, Michael Longridge, and Edward Pease. The first one to arrive was what we know today as *Locomotion No. 1*, delivered to the railway by a team of horses pulling a wagon on 16 September 1825. Two stationary engines, one for Etherley Hill and one for the Brusselton Incline above Shildon, were ordered from Robert Stephenson & Company also, and the last of these was ready, at Etherley, the same day *Locomotion* was placed on the rails.

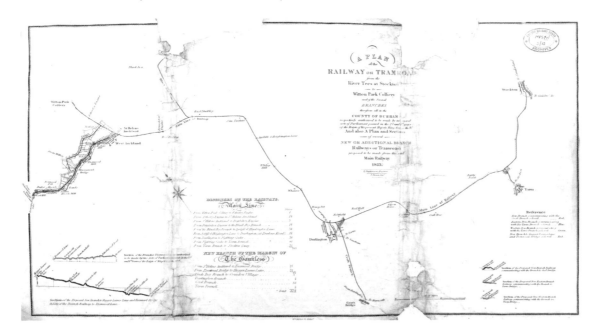

Left.

The survey of the Hagger Leases branch carried out by Robert Stephenson as engineer, with John Dixon as his surveyor, towards the end of 1823. It was submitted to Parliament with the application for a third act in 1824. The branch is at extreme left, shown in red. The parallel branch to its north is the Evenwood branch, which was relinquished and the Hagger Leases branch authorized in its stead.

The main line was completed and ready for operation in September 1825, and the official opening of the railway was set for 27 September. The opening, a rightly famous event, is well known. Thousands of people from miles around converged on the Stockton & Darlington to witness the inaugural train, pulled from the base of the Brusselton Incline to Stockton by *Locomotion*, driven by George Stephenson himself. The train was a long one and amply demonstrated the new power of steam. It had twelve wagons filled with coal that had made the complete journey from Etherley Colliery over the inclines, a wagon filled with sacks of flour, a specially built coach for the directors (but without Edward Pease, whose son had died that morning), a wagon for the engineers and surveyors, twenty wagons filled with workmen and others, plus the engine and its tender. And on top of the coal wagons were more passengers—one estimate put the total number of people aboard at 553. Among the passengers were representatives of several nascent railway companies—the Liverpool & Manchester, the Leeds & Hull, and the Birmingham & Liverpool, offspring of a boom in the creation of railway companies from the year before.

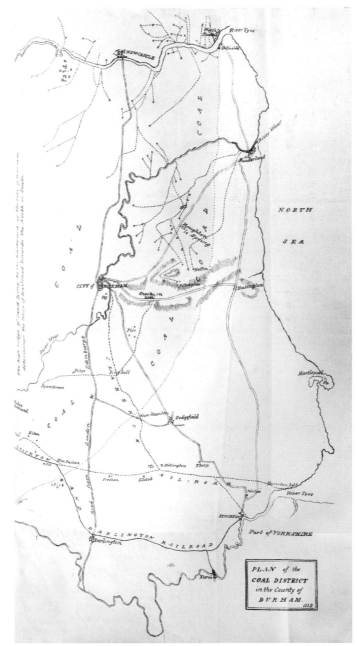

Above.
The opening day train crosses the River Skerne at Darlington, as shown in a contemporary engraving.

Right.
This 1829 sketch map places the *Stockton and Darlington Railroad* in the context of the other rail lines of the northeast coalfield. Also shown is the then-projected *Clarence Rail-Road* (see page 206). The terms railroad and railway were interchangable at this time.

Above, top.
The Brusselton Incline shown on a map from an 1858 survey. The *Haggerleases Branch* is the incline, with the *Brusselton Engine Ho.* at the top. Locomotives or horses took over at the bottom of the incline, at *New Shildon*, where Timothy Hackworth set up his *Soho Works* when he was appointed locomotive superintendent for the railway in 1825. Today that is the location of the National Railway Museum's Shildon branch.

Inset, left, top.
The incline shown in a rather exaggerated view in an engraving from 1826.

Left and *above, left and right.*
Views down and up the Brusselton Incline as it is today, with restored stone blocks that held the track in place. The bridge, the remains of which are in the photo *above*, is shown on the map running through the first *E* of *Haggerleases Branch*.
Above, right, the remains of the Brusselton engine house can be seen on the left through the trees. The set of stone blocks is the same set as shown at *left*.

After some tense financial moments in the first year or two, the Stockton & Darlington Railway proved to be an immense success, both technologically and financially, returning its investors 8 per cent a year by 1832.

The four early locomotives the railway possessed by May 1826 did not work as well as required, tending to never have enough steam, and the possibility of using only horse haulage was discussed several times. Until 1832, passengers were carried by horse in any case, with the *Union* running from 1826; this was essentially a mail coach with adapted wheels (model, *right*). On the recommendation of George Stephenson, in May 1825 the company hired Timothy Hackworth as its locomotive superintendent. He had helped build *Puffing Billy* and *Wylam Dilly* at Wylam in 1813–14 and was then working at Robert Stephenson & Company's locomotive works in Newcastle. He ran the Soho Works, a repair and maintenance shop at New Shildon (the first of many railway-created towns), where he displayed considerable ingenuity in keeping the locomotives running and improving their performance, This culminated in 1827 with a new locomotive design, the *Royal George*, the first six-wheeled coupled locomotive, with better steaming characteristics than any before, which saved the day for the railway. It used parts from another engine, Robert Wilson's less-than-perfect *Chittapratt* (see page 80). The engine proved to be the first of a number of heavier engines built for the railway. Hackworth would build an entry, *Sans Pareil*, for the Rainhill Trials in 1829 (see page 182).

The Stockton & Darlington Railway became an example to industrialists, investors, and promoters everywhere, and the country was soon alive with proposals for railways. Within a few years a network of lines would criss-cross Britain (see page 210). In 1828 a direct competitor was sanctioned by Parliament—the Clarence Railway, which would connect with the Stockton & Darlington and end farther downstream than Stockton (see page 206).

In 1829, Edward Pease's son Joseph, seeing an opportunity, purchased 527 acres of farmland called the Middlesbrough Estate downstream of Stockton using his extensive Quaker connections for financing and set about transforming it into an iron-manufacturing powerhouse, starting with new docks for the railway at a place named Port Darlington. The railway was extended there in 1830, and another branch in 1842 linked a new and extensive dock system to the railway (map, *page 167, top*). The Stockton & Darlington Railway essentially created the city of Middlesbrough. Another cut through the meanders of the River Tees in 1831, the Portrack Cut, made access to Stockton easier for larger ships. The railway had begun a process of industrialization and urbanization in the lower Tees valley from which there would be no return. The railways are said to have facilitated the late industrial revolution, and nowhere is that more evident than here.

Above.
Regular passenger service between Stockton, Yarm, and Darlington began in 1826 with coaches like the *Union*, run by a private contractor who paid tolls to the railway. It was by no means the first railway passenger service; the Oystermouth Railway had begun passenger rail service in 1807 (see page 54).

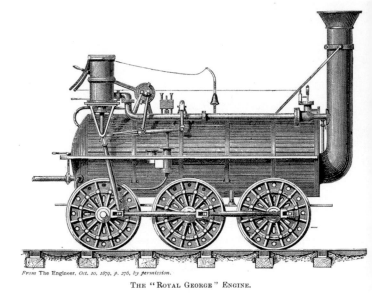

From The Engineer, Oct. 10, 1879, p. 276, by permission.

THE "ROYAL GEORGE" ENGINE.

Above.
The *Royal George*, built in 1827 by Timothy Hackworth for the Stockton & Darlington in his role as locomotive superintendent, finally solving the perennial problem of not enough power. Many more locomotives were built to this basic design, firmly establishing Hackworth's reputation.

Right.
This locomotive was long thought to be *Bradyll*, the oldest surviving six-coupled engine, built by Timothy Hackworth at his Soho Works in Shildon before 1840. It is now thought to be a different locomotive, built about 1845, named *Nelson*. It is stored in the Soho Works building, now part of the National Railway Museum.

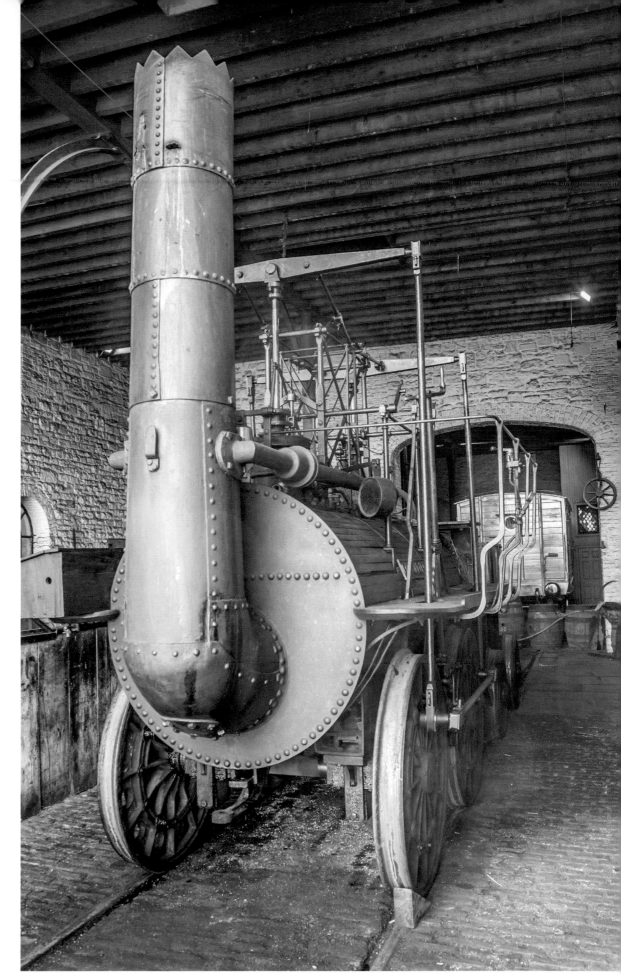

Right.
The superb working replica of *Locomotion* at Beamish Museum, which has now worked for longer than the original. This probably gives a fairer view of what the original locomotive looked like when it first began pulling coal wagons on the Stockton & Darlington Railway, because the original had many replacement parts fitted over its working life. This started in 1828 with the boiler, which had exploded when the driver fastened down the safety valve in an effort to gain more power.

Above. A modern diesel multiple unit pauses at Shildon station.

Right. A map of the Stockton & Darlington in relation to modern lines and roads. The map is on a platform at Darlington station, and the station is reflected in the glass.

Below, bottom.
An 1830 map now showing the *Clarence Rail Road* (see page 210) connecting to the Stockton & Darlington at *Sim Pasture*. The Clarence was not completed until 1833.

Right, centre.
The modern map of the line may be functional, but it is not as interesting as the earlier versions!

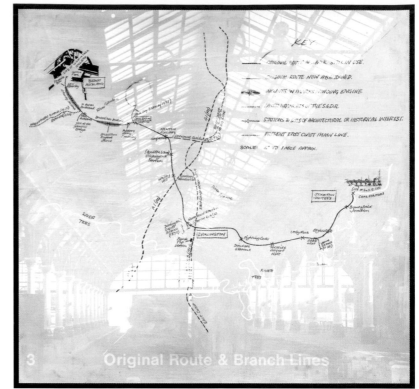

Original Route & Branch Lines

bishop line

Bishop Auckland   Shildon   Newton Aycliffe   Heighington   North Rodd   Darlington

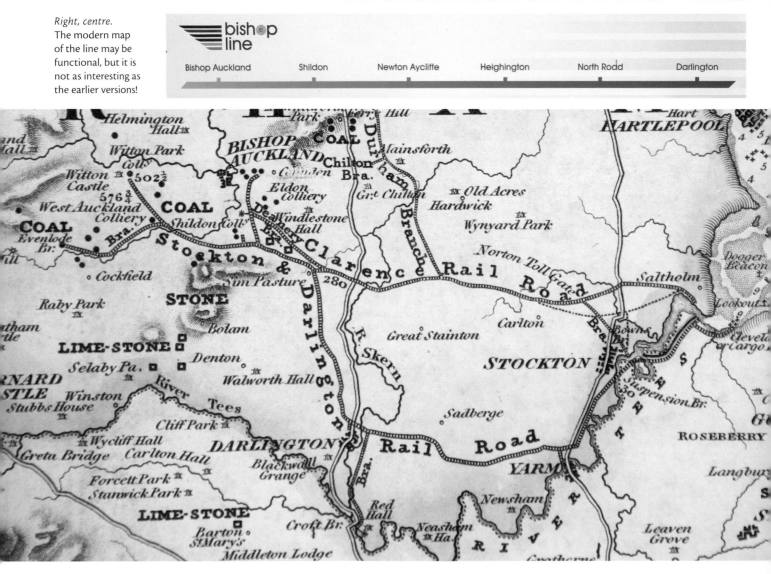

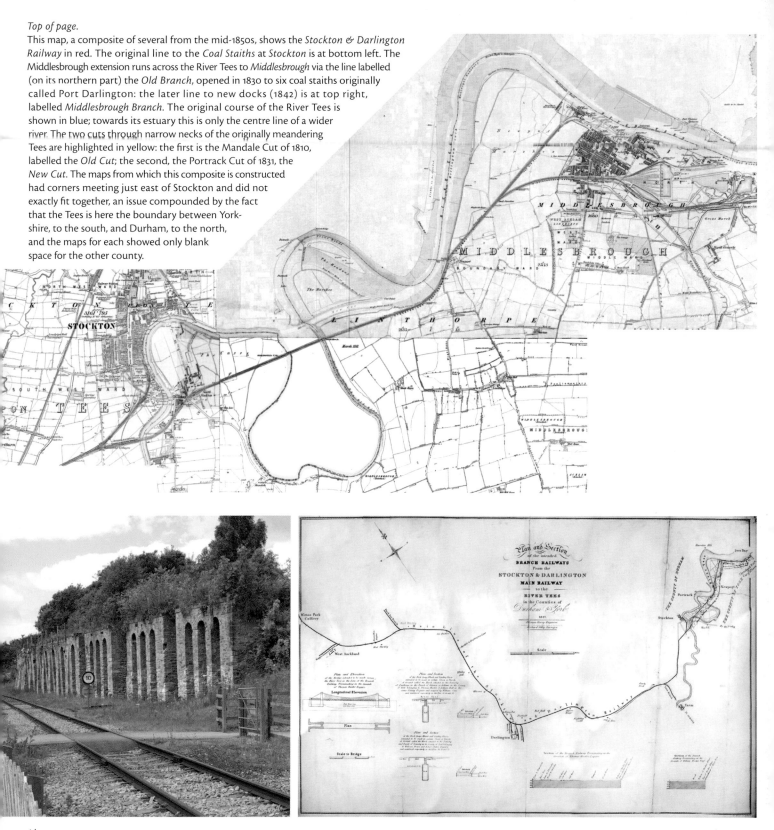

Top of page.
This map, a composite of several from the mid-1850s, shows the *Stockton & Darlington Railway* in red. The original line to the *Coal Staiths* at *Stockton* is at bottom left. The Middlesbrough extension runs across the River Tees to *Middlesbrough* via the line labelled (on its northern part) the *Old Branch*, opened in 1830 to six coal staiths originally called Port Darlington: the later line to new docks (1842) is at top right, labelled *Middlesbrough Branch*. The original course of the River Tees is shown in blue; towards its estuary this is only the centre line of a wider river. The two cuts through narrow necks of the originally meandering Tees are highlighted in yellow: the first is the Mandale Cut of 1810, labelled the *Old Cut*; the second, the Portrack Cut of 1831, the *New Cut*. The maps from which this composite is constructed had corners meeting just east of Stockton and did not exactly fit together, an issue compounded by the fact that the Tees is here the boundary between Yorkshire, to the south, and Durham, to the north, and the maps for each showed only blank space for the other county.

Above.
An 1827 map showing the plans to extend the Stockton & Darlington Railway farther north towards the mouth of the Tees, to new docks built at a place that would be named Port Darlington.

Left.
Coal staiths (called land staiths) at New Shildon close to the locomotive works as they are today. A railway line ran up a slope to the top of the staiths, where all the vegetation is now, and coal was dropped through the bottoms of wagons via chutes into the tenders of locomotives beneath. No one had to touch the coal. This was in contrast to most later coal staiths, which required much physical shovelling.

A Southern Enterprise

A few months before the Stockton & Darlington Railway opened in 1825, two other railways gained their Acts of Parliament—the Cromford & High Peak Railway (on 2 May) and the Canterbury & Whitstable Railway (on 10 June). These railways were planned somewhat as the Stockton & Darlington had been, with stationary engines and inclines on the steeper parts of the route but then only steam locomotives on the flatter sections; horse traction was not used as it was in the beginning years of the Stockton & Darlington.

Both lines began operating in 1830, just before the much more famous Liverpool & Manchester Railway, which opened in September 1830. The Canterbury & Whitstable opened on 3 May 1830, while the first part of the Cromford & High Peak opened on 29 May. The latter was not completed, however, until a year later, and thus will be discussed later (see page 199). The Canterbury & Whitstable thus became the first railway in the world to regularly convey both passengers and goods by mechanical means.

The citizens of Canterbury had long wished to improve the transport of coal and merchandise from the coast to the city; the only method available used a turnpike road. The River Stour had been used in times past but had silted up. In 1825 an Act of Parliament was obtained for the Canterbury Navigation, really just a dredging and straightening of the river (map, *right, top*). It was not long before someone, in a letter to the newspaper, pointed out the absurdity of a 70-mile-long route when the city was only 6 miles from the coast to the north.

However, the visionary William James (see page 146) was ahead of them, having come to this conclusion two years before. Holder of an agreement with George Stephenson to market his engines in the south of England, he was looking for opportunities. In October 1824 he surveyed a line for a railway north from Canterbury to the sea at Whitstable, a small fishing town. James had little trouble attracting support for his scheme, and he was appointed engineer to the group of Canterbury residents intent on building the railway; his plans were used to apply for the necessary Act of Parliament. The cost was found to be much underestimated, and the group asked George Stephenson for advice; the cost estimate was then increased. After the act was granted on 10 June 1825, the directors of the new railway company appointed Stephenson, rather than James, as the engineer. The perennially unfortunate James faded from the picture at this point, plagued by his debts and his profusion of other schemes.

Costs were still found to be higher than anticipated, and, partly because of a change of James's route at the Canterbury end by Stephenson, surveyed in 1826 by John Dixon, there were further Acts of Parliament in 1827 and 1828 to authorize raising more capital. The company had actually stopped work in the summer of 1827 owing to lack of money. The route was modified to include a tunnel through Tyler Hill, above Canterbury.

The line was built in the typical Stephenson fashion, with inclined planes as well as a flatter section where trains could be horse or steam-locomotive hauled. The route can be followed with both plan and (exaggerated) section of the map, *below*. A train from Canterbury on the initial route up to and through Tyler Hill Tunnel was pulled up by a stationary engine (the *Tyler Hill Engine*), then up to the summit of the line by the *Clowes Wood Engine*, let down again to a relatively flat section where the locomotive engine took over.

In 1829 the directors placed an order with Robert Stephenson & Company for a steam locomotive to work the flattest section of the line on the Whitstable end. The engine was shipped by sea from Newcastle to Whitstable. It was named *Invicta* after the motto on the flag of Kent, meaning "undefeated." It turned out to be unfortunately named, for it was indeed defeated by being perennially underpowered even though modified; the railway stopped using the locomotive in 1839 in favour of another stationary engine that had been installed in 1832. However, no buyer for *Invicta* could be found, and the locomotive was stored, which ultimately led to the engine being preserved rather than scrapped.

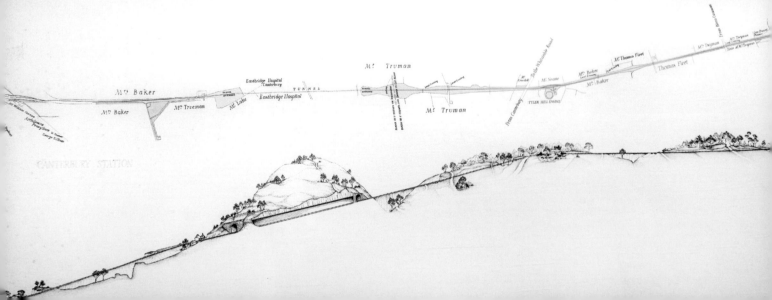

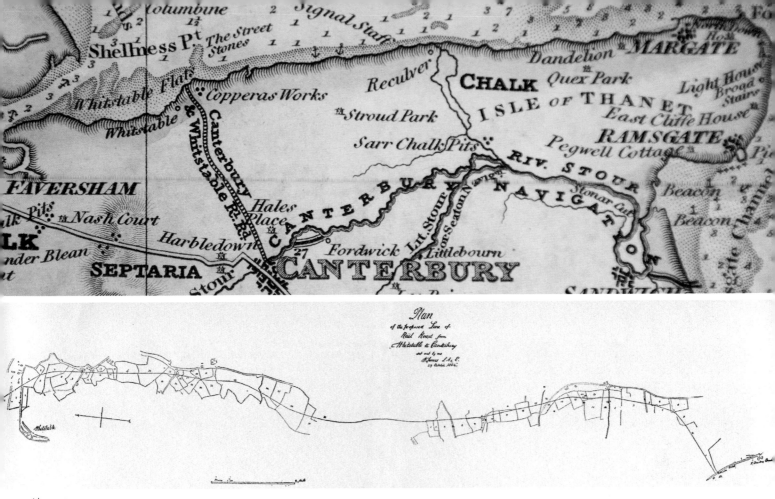

Above, top.

The 1830 map shows the route of the *Canterbury & Whitstable R^{l.} R^{d.}* and also the proposed *Canterbury Navigation*, approved in 1825 as an improvement of the *Riv. Stour* that was passed over in favour of the railway.

Above.

William James's original survey of the line of the Canterbury & Whitstable Railway, done in October 1824. The route was altered at the Canterbury end (at right) to go straight into the town rather than to the *Turnpike Road* that required a tunnel, but is otherwise as built.

Below.

This large, detailed map of the line of the Canterbury & Whitstable with an accompanying section was created in the 1970s as part of the celebration of the 150th anniversary of *Invicta* in 1980 and hangs in the Canterbury Heritage Museum. It was compiled from original deeds and abstracts, many of which were only descriptions, from the museum and from Canterbury Cathedral Archives. The museum has, unfortunately, lost the creator's name, and the map has suffered some water damage from a leaking roof. It is displayed in the museum alongside *Invicta*. On the map, Canterbury is at left, Whitstable at right. Tyler Hill *Tunnel* is clearly shown. The locomotive ran on the relatively short section of the line near Whitstable where a train is depicted. The rest of the line was operated by stationary engines shown as *Engine* at intervals along the line, which correspond to the tops of inclines. Land ownership through which the line passes is also noted in detail.

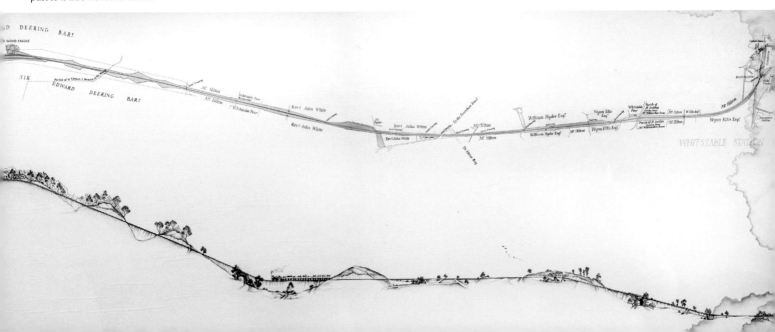

This page.
The *Canterbury & Whitstable Railway* shown on a map published in 1833. Several engines are named, and several inclined planes. The location of the *Tunnel* is also marked. The straightness of the route made it ideal for stationary engine working.

Inset, above, right.
Invicta pulls the first train out of Whitstable on 3 May 1830. It is interesting to note the differences between the engine shown here and the preserved one in the Canterbury Heritage Museum. The latter has all four wheels of equal size, as is shown in the locomotive's engineering drawings. The engine's tender did not survive.

Inset, below.
The first train is hauled up the incline from Canterbury. The rope attached to the front is from the Tyler Hill Engine (incorrectly *Tile Hill Engine* on the map) at the top of the incline on the other side of the tunnel.

On 2 May 1830 Robert Stephenson made some trial runs of *Invicta* to ascertain what it was capable of pulling, and the following day, the official opening of the railway took place, with cheering crowds and a train taking dignitaries to lunch at Whitstable and back to Canterbury for a celebratory dinner at a local tavern.

Two years later, a new harbour at Whitstable was opened to allow direct unloading onto a railway quay. Southern England's first steam-powered railway, which had beaten even the Liverpool & Manchester out of the gate, later became entirely locomotive worked, but required specially built cut-down locomotives to pass through Tyler Hill Tunnel. The line was finally closed in 1953 and is now a footpath and cycle trail, the Crab & Winkle Way, named after the railway's nickname.

Above.
A Canterbury & Whitstable train approaches a rather exaggerated incline in this 1830s engraving.

Right and *below.*
Invicta on display in cramped quarters at the Canterbury Heritage Museum, complete with a mannequin for a driver! The engine is believed to have been considerably modified from its original state.

Below, right.
The entry in the ledger of Robert Stephenson & Company, the engine's manufacturer, shows it cost £635 in 1830.

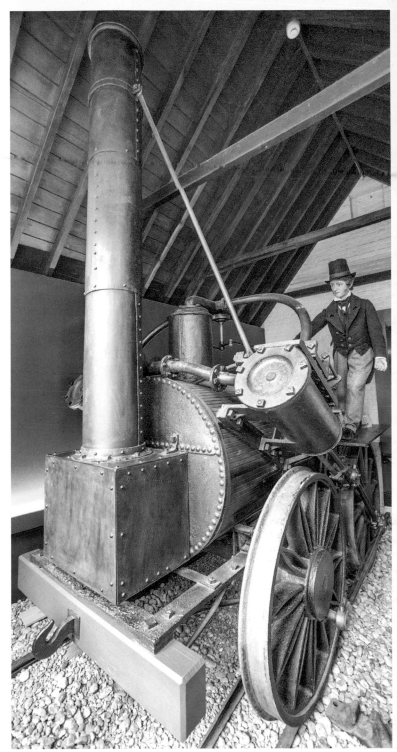

The First Modern Railway

The Liverpool & Manchester Railway, undoubtedly the most famous of all the early railways, was an idea in the right place at the right time. While not the first railway, of course, it was the first to bring together many elements of the modern railway. Finally technology had reached the point where materials to make such items as boilers were strong enough to withstand high pressures, locomotives were reasonably reliable and could be employed on a continuing basis, and rails could stand the high load and constant pounding without breaking. This technology, advanced by a few talented promoters and engineers, found a place for itself in the heavy traffic corridor between Liverpool and Manchester, which provided the economic viability that is also a requirement for a railway. Manchester was at the time emerging as the leading manufacturing centre in Britain, largely owing to its cotton mills, and Liverpool had overtaken Bristol as the second port in the country, after London, importing raw cotton and other goods from the ascendant British Empire to feed its hinterland.

The first promoter of a railway between the two cities was none other than William James, engaged in another of his visionary schemes. The difference here was that when he failed to follow through, he had sufficiently inspired others that they took over the project from him. Finally one of his schemes would come to full fruition—but, sadly, without him.

Both railway pioneers William Jessop and Benjamin Outram, about whom we have heard much before, are said to have proposed railways between Liverpool and Manchester as early as 1797—Jessop an edge railway, Outram a plateway—but there seems to be no hard evidence for this. In any case they would have been horse operated.

By 1821, there were already three canals along which goods could be sent between Manchester and Liverpool: the Mersey & Irwell Navigation Act of 1720 had given powers to a so-called Board of Undertakers to dredge, cut, widen, and straighten a river route;

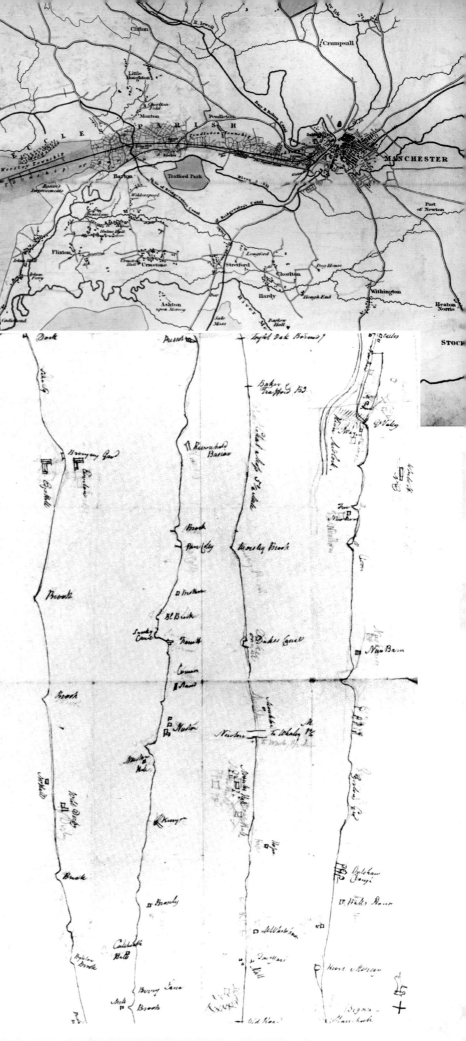

Above.
The famous *Rocket* with its train (the National Railway Museum's replica) is superimposed on the Liverpool & Manchester Railway resurvey done in 1825 by surveyor Charles Vignoles on the instructions of George and John Rennie (the younger). This was the route approved by Parliament in May 1826.

Right.
William James's "ocular survey"—that is, done by eyeball—in 1821. It was intended to demonstrate the feasibility of a route to help Joseph Sandars gain support for the nascent project.

the Duke of Bridgewater's Canal, completed in 1776; and the Leeds & Liverpool Canal, which completed an extension that made a connection between Liverpool and Manchester in 1821. The canal owners and managers had a virtual monopoly on traffic and charged accordingly, and although in theory the canal was open to all comers on payment of tolls, difficulties were routinely put in the way of barges belonging to others, with the result that the transit from one city to the other could take days. And the Bridgewater Canal, in particular, owned so much of the available land along the banks of the canal that there was nowhere left for others to build the warehouses necessary for them to ply their trade. The circumstances constantly frustrated businessmen in both cities whose livelihood and profit depended on moving their products to their customers.

James had visited Lancashire in 1802 and at that time had drawn a map suggesting rail connections from Bolton to several canals (map, *page 142*). In 1821, when he became aware of the transportation difficulties in the region, he saw an opportunity. He talked to Manchester businessmen, one of whom introduced him to Joseph Sandars, a corn merchant and underwriter—and a Quaker—in Liverpool, who not only was very well connected with other businessmen but had been leading attacks on the canal companies. Sandars was very keen on James's proposals and gathered a group of like-minded individuals as a provisional committee to investigate the feasibility of a railway. In Manchester, others responded to Sandars's invitation, including wealthy cotton manufacturer John Kennedy, a mechanical expert and supporter of steam railways.

With the committee's support, James hired several surveyors, including Paul Padley, his brother-in-law, and Robert Stephenson, each to cover a part of the route. Broken instruments stopped them from finishing very quickly, and it soon became apparent that James was not going to deliver the survey in time to be lodged with the county clerk by the end of September 1822, as would be required for an application for an authorizing act in 1823. The survey does seem to have been completed by October, as James sent a copy to George Stephenson for advice on the practicability of the line for stationary engines and steam locomotives to work the line, but it seems not to have survived. The unfortunate James found himself in debtors' prison in November and stayed there until February, which clearly did not help with his promotional activities. In fact James was in

prison over his financial difficulties three times over the next two years and was at the same time planning the route south from the Surrey Iron Railway (see page 53); as was usual for him, he was spread too thin. He had initiated the interest and the process but was unable to follow through. The Liverpool and Manchester groups meanwhile had combined themselves into a single committee and generally left the planning of the line to James, but it was rapidly becoming apparent after multiple delays and excuses that he was not reliable.

At the beginning of May 1824 Sandars and other members of the provisional committee, Kennedy, Henry Booth and Lister Ellis, visited the northeast, saw the Stockton & Darlington Railway, nearing completion, and visited George Stephenson's Hetton Colliery Railway, where not only could they see the locomotives and stationary engines working, but they actually rode on a locomotive. That must have been a defining moment for them, for at a committee meeting on 20 May they resolved to do two important things: to form a joint stock company to raise the requisite capital to build the line, creating the Liverpool & Manchester Railway Company; and to invite George Stephenson to be their engineer, dispensing with the services of James, who at that precise moment had once again found himself back in debtors' prison.

Stephenson was at that point the obvious choice for the job. He had far more experience with actual railway building and locomotive engineering than anyone else. His son Robert, however, had decided a few months before that he did not want to work with him. Whether they had a falling out as such is unknown, but Robert was James's friend (and after his death paid him the tribute of the epithet "father of the railways," much to the annoyance of George). At any rate Robert sailed from Liverpool bound for South America in June; he would be gone for three years, and his absence would prove critical for his father.

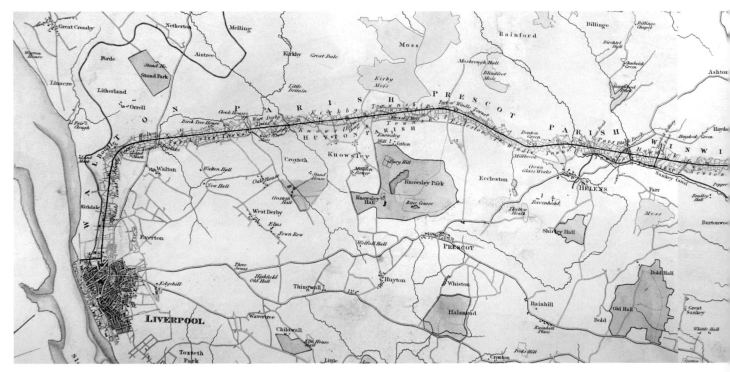

George Stephenson left his work with the Stockton & Darlington to his assistants and arrived in Liverpool, immediately hiring Padley as his surveyor, thus enraging James even more. "He knows my plans of which he and Stephenson will now avail themselves," he wrote. In fact James's surveyed route was more similar to the route that would finally be adopted than to the route Stephenson would recommend (map, *below*). Sandars, probably feeling some responsibility towards James, offered him several positions with the railway, all of which James turned down. He either wanted to do the entire job himself—which would have taken him forever—or he did not want to be involved at all.

Stephenson, just like James, was spread thin, with a number of other projects or consultations under way, including the Stockton & Darlington and a new position with the proposed Newcastle & Carlisle Railway (see page 213). He was away enough that the committee became concerned whether he would do his job properly. They did not want a repeat of their experience with James!

For the surveyors, their job was often not easy at all, and the difficulties are well known. "Sad work," Stephenson termed it. Some landowners, adamantly opposed to the idea that a railway might impinge on their lands, denied them entry to any of the canal company's property. Lord Sefton and Lord Derby, in particular, and, Robert Bradshaw, trustee of the Bridgewater Canal, denied them entry to their properties and blockaded them as much as possible. Some even instructed their gamekeepers to shoot at them. Instruments were damaged. At least once the surveyors showed fake letters of permission to Sefton's tenants, hurriedly doing their survey before the ruse was discovered. Some of the surveying was done at night to try to avoid confrontations, but one owner even arranged for random shooting to take place at night to discourage trespass. Surveyors sometimes arranged for guns to be fired at some other spot to distract those assigned to keep them away. It was hardly surprising, then, that estimation was substituted for actual survey in a number of cases.

History would repeat itself many times, though often opposition was ameliorated once the benefits of railways became widely realized. Even today, landowners are often against railways near or through their properties when no benefit is directly derived. The proposed £50 billion high-speed line from London to Manchester (HS2) was similarly opposed in the area of the Chiltern Hills, and this has resulted in additional costs for extra tunnelling.

On 29 October 1824 the company issued its first prospectus. It was a long statement of the value of implementing the railway scheme. A few words, capitalized, stood out: "PUBLIC GOOD" and "IT IS COMPETITION THAT IS WANTED," which, by themselves pretty much summed up the railway's case. One other word was capitalized—"COALS"—in a paragraph aimed at the colliery owners, many of whose collieries were not directly served by the canals.

The Mersey & Irwell Navigation Company set up an experiment where a barge was towed, by horses, from Manchester to Liverpool, loaded, and returned, a process that took just under twenty-four hours. The speed was nothing like what was achieved in everyday practice but nevertheless was used in evidence against the railway's bill. Not to be outdone, the committee arranged for trials of locomotives at Killingworth that demonstrated speeds up to 7 miles per hour with trains of 32 to 59 tons, again for evidence.

Below.
George Stephenson's survey for the Liverpool & Manchester Railway as presented to Parliament in February 1825. The railway approached Liverpool from the north but did not enter the city.

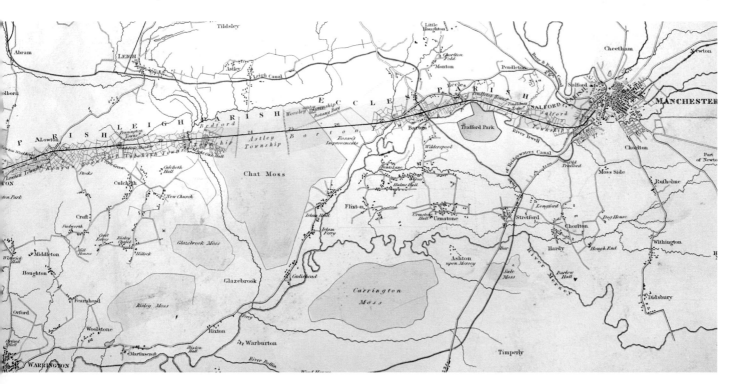

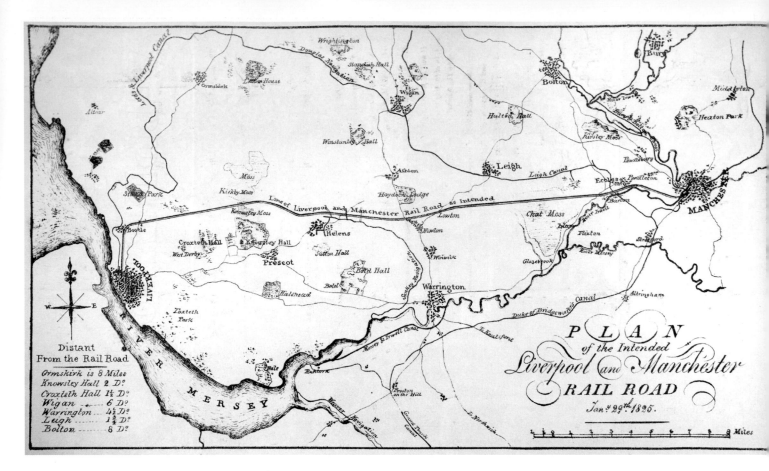

Above. In early 1825 the committee issued a pamphlet called *A Short Statement of the Advantages Offered to the Public by the Proposed Rail Road between Liverpool and Manchester* in support of their application to Parliament for an enabling act. The document was signed by Charles Lawrence in his capacity as chairman of the railway committee and is shown at *right.* Contained in the document was this map showing the route as surveyed by Stephenson in relation to the existing canals and roads. The intention was to show that the route of the railway was much more direct.

Below. A composite map of the routes proposed for the Liverpool & Manchester Railway. The black line on the base map is the line as submitted to Parliament for the second time and is essentially as it was built. The green line is the route surveyed by and for William James in 1821 and 1822, which, apart from his first "ocular" survey (*page 173*) appears to have been lost. The red line, with a considerably different route for the western half, is Stephenson's surveyed line, incorporated in the first bill in 1825, which failed (as shown on the map on the *previous page*).

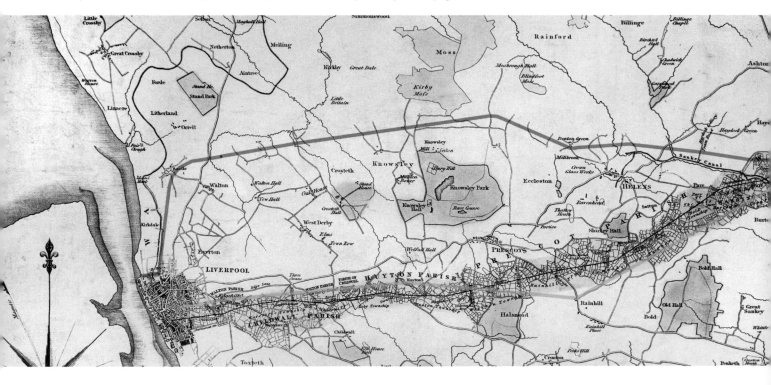

The trials were carried out in the presence of Stephenson and several other prominent engineers, including William Cubitt, Nicholas Wood, and William Brunton, the latter of walking engine fame (see page 122). Sandars's own company, which shipped corn, kept a record from October 1824, which was used in evidence for the railway bill. It showed that the Duke of Bridgewater's Canal had never shipped a cargo on the day it was sent to them. Both sides, then, were busily collecting evidence that favoured their case.

The council of the City of Liverpool was divided on whether to allow steam locomotives into the city, despite the obvious advantages. They voted in early 1825 to exclude them from the streets of the city, and a clause to that effect was inserted in the bill being prepared for Parliament.

Plans of the railway's proposed route had been lodged with the county clerk in November 1824, as was then required, and the bill was sent to London, where it had its first and second readings in February 1825. The president of the Board of Trade, a cabinet minister, and one of the members of Parliament for Liverpool, William Huskisson, made a major speech in favour of the railway.

Arrayed against the bill were an assortment of solicitors and others principally representing landowners and the turnpike and canal interests. An inflammatory leaflet titled *Public Reasons against Railways and Loco-motive Engines* was circulated among members of Parliament, many of whom apparently believed its unfounded claims. However, disturbingly, Cubitt had checked parts of Stephenson's survey and found the levels and cost estimates for the section across Knowsley Moss (shown on the map, *left, top*) to be inaccurate to the tune of £100,000. Further hurried checking revealed Stephenson's levels to be out by anything from 10 to 50 feet over the entire line. The stage was set for a debacle. At the end of April, Stephenson was called for cross-examination and at first performed splendidly,

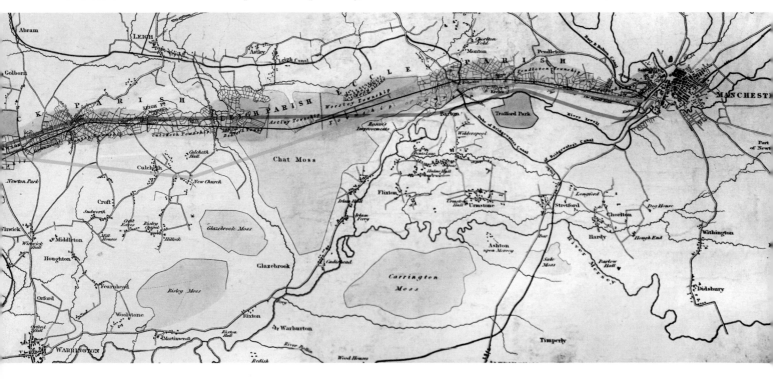

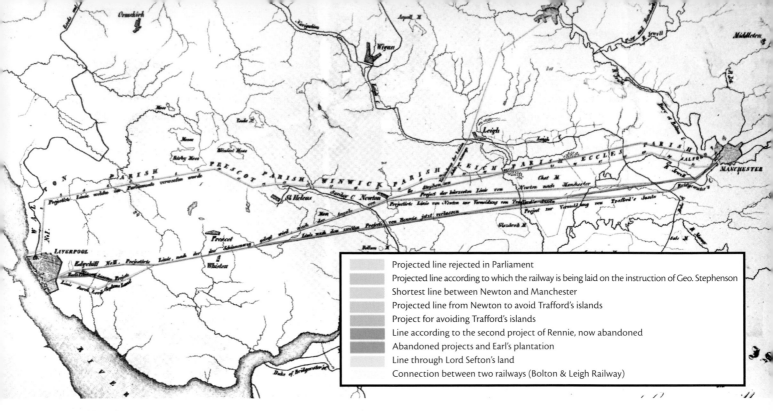

Key:

Projected line rejected in Parliament
Projected line according to which the railway is being laid on the instruction of Geo. Stephenson
Shortest line between Newton and Manchester
Projected line from Newton to avoid Trafford's islands
Project for avoiding Trafford's islands
Line according to the second project of Rennie, now abandoned
Abandoned projects and Earl's plantation
Line through Lord Sefton's land
Connection between two railways (Bolton & Leigh Railway)

Above.
This is a somewhat schematic map of the planning for the Liverpool & Manchester Railway from the report of German engineers Karl von Oeynhausen and Heinrich von Dechen after their visit in 1826–27 and shows their interpretation of the various projected routes and variations for the line from Liverpool to Manchester. The routes have been coloured for clarity. The brown line is Stephenson's original line, as shown on the map, *pages 174–75.* The green line is the route more or less as built, as shown on the map on the *previous page.* Most of the other lines represent attempts to avoid the estates of the landowners opposed to the railway. The key text is translated from the original German.

answering questions about general railway construction and operation with which he had much experience, impressing with promised performances of 8 miles per hour with 20-ton loads and 4 miles per hour with 40 tons. Once the hearing turned to the survey, however, it soon became evident to all that he knew little about either specific levels or costs; he frequently admitted mistakes or claimed he could not remember. When Stephenson was asked about a bridge over the River Irwell, it was quickly demonstrated that he knew neither the width of the river there nor how many arches the bridge would have to have to cross it. It seems that Stephenson, being involved in too many projects, had left the surveyors to do their jobs but that some of them had made many errors. Although Stephenson had inspected all the levels, he had not checked them carefully enough, and since he was ultimately responsible, it was deemed to be his fault. If his surveyors had done their survey accurately, Stephenson would not have found himself in the predicament that he did. It is tempting to suggest that had Robert remained with him, the job might have been done properly in the first place, thus avoiding all the grief.

Interestingly, another attack on Stephenson's survey involved his plan to "float" the line across Chat Moss, the largest of the bogs between Liverpool and Manchester, rather than go around it. This was attacked by the one opposition solicitor as "ignorance almost inconceivable" and "perfect madness." Another, Francis Giles, an engineer who had worked with Rennie, stated flatly that "no engineer in his senses would go through Chat Moss." Stephenson would demonstrate that it was his detractors who did not know what they were doing!

While other evidence was being gathered, the committee asked Cubitt to quickly resurvey the line, which he did, it seems in little over a week. But the new survey was too late. On 1 June a vote was taken on the clauses in the bill enabling a railway to be built and to take land along its route; it failed. There was nothing left to do but withdraw the bill and try again.

And this the company did, immediately planning for a second application to Parliament the following year. The committee believed that if they presented a new and accurate survey, prepared this time by an engineer with impeccable credentials, they would have a good chance of success. To mute opposition, they would also downplay the planned use of steam locomotives. Stephenson was fired, despite protests from Sandars and Booth, and John Rennie (the younger) was offered the position of engineer, which he accepted with his brother, George, on the condition that they would not be bound by any decisions that had previously been made by Stephenson. With the agreement of the railway committee they appointed Charles Blacker Vignoles as their surveyor. Vignoles had recently been employed by the Rennies on the survey of a projected line from London to Brighton.

Vignoles was given the task of resurveying a route from Liverpool to Manchester, avoiding as much as possible the estates of landowners and the canal interests. In July 1825 he first went over the Stephenson route and then worked out one he felt was better, which he discussed with John Rennie, convincing him that it would work. Rennie concurred, and Vignoles began a survey, assisted by George Rennie, which on 12 August he was able to present to the committee for approval. The committee approved his route, and he was instructed to carry out a detailed survey and draw up the plans and section required for the application to Parliament (the base map of the map on *pages 176–77*, and the map, *pages 172–73*, with *Rocket* superimposed).

Vignoles's survey met with similar opposition to that of Stephenson, and much of it had to be done at night. His route was close to Stephenson's east of Newton, about halfway along the line, though all of it carefully avoided influential landowners' properties as much as was feasible. In particular the estate of Lord Sefton was avoided completely, and that of Lord Derby was encroached upon only in a few detached fields. West of Newton, the route ran much more directly than Stephenson's to Liverpool. The latter's route had approached Liverpool from the north to reach the docks without crossing many city streets, whereas Vignoles's route approached directly from the east. To avoid running through the city, he proposed a tunnel under it, enclosing an inclined plane directly to the docks, an ingenious solution to a difficult problem. At the Manchester end, the route was terminated at Salford so as not to cross the Mersey & Irwell Navigation's channel, thus avoiding that company's opposition to it. An early railway historian, John Francis, writing in 1851, put it succinctly: "every sacrifice, save that of honour, was made to further the great scheme."

As well-thought-out as Vignoles's route was, it had one major drawback—cost. The previous estimate for constructing the railway had been £400,000; now it was increased to £500,000, an enormous sum at that time. This was a result of several new engineering works that would have to be done: the tunnel in Liverpool; a 2-mile-long deep cut through solid rock at Olive Mount, at the eastern entrance to the tunnel; and inclined planes at Whiston and Sutton, either side of elevated ground on which the village of Rainhill sat. The committee thought that the advantages of the new route made the increased costs worthwhile and so accepted it.

The canal companies, meanwhile, were busy expanding their warehousing facilities, adding locks and wharves, and creating cuts to shorten their distances, all with a view to undercutting the railway's case when it was sent for parliamentary approval.

The railway company then managed a rather clever end run around Robert Bradshaw, the Duke of Bridgewater's Canal trustee and major railway opponent. Although Bradshaw was in charge of the canal's affairs, it was actually owned by the Marquess of Stafford, and Charles Lawrence and others approached him with a view to getting him to invest in the railway, offering him, conveniently, the £100,000 of stock the company now additionally required for the new route. The Marquess agreed to purchase the stock, seeing it, correctly, as a good investment opportunity. For this he would receive the right to appoint three members of the railway's board. He had apparently not been much in agreement with what he saw as Bradshaw's lack of foresight or his autocratic methods. Now Bradshaw would find it much harder to oppose the railway, as would the other canal interests.

On 26 December 1825 the company issued its second prospectus. It now not only described the projects but went to great lengths to show that the major objections that had applied before had been dealt with and that the company had "engaged the professional services of the most eminent engineers." And, of course, it made much of Stafford's investment.

At a meeting of Liverpool City Council on 4 January 1826, Lawrence, who was still a member of the council as well as being chairman of the railway, managed to get the council to approve of the new railway scheme, with its tunnel under the city, though by a narrow margin and not without a fight. It is perhaps surprising in retrospect that the council of a city that stood to benefit so much from the railway could have ever been against it, but the council was made up of a diverse set of gentlemen with all the usual vested interests, including shares in canal companies, and a mechanically worked railway was still seen by many as an untried experiment that did nothing but produce a great deal of noise and dirt.

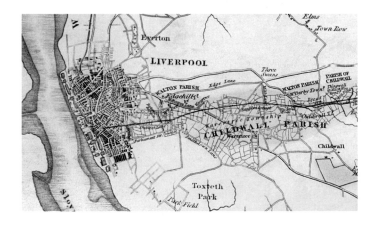

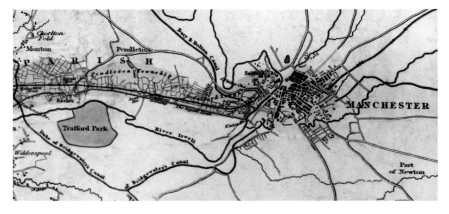

Right.
Two details from the Rennies' 1826 survey: the *Liverpool* end of the line, showing the line that would be taken by a tunnel through the city to avoid locomotives on the streets, as demanded by Liverpool Council, and the *Manchester* end, showing the railway ending across the River Irwell in Salford. The act would be amended in 1829 to extend the railway across the river into Manchester.

On 7 February 1826 a petition for a new bill was submitted to Parliament, and leave was granted to bring in an enabling bill for the railway two days later. During March and April the cases for and against the railway were argued, and on 6 April the railway's bill looked as though it was going to fail—by being referred for reconsideration six months from that date—when it was saved by a forceful speech by William Huskisson and passed by the House of Commons that day.

The bill then moved on to a committee of the House of Lords, where it ran into the determined opposition of Lord Derby. However, during the committee grilling of witnesses such as had destroyed George Stephenson the year before, Vignoles spoke confidently and with authority and knowledge. The opposition solicitors were unable to shake him. Josias Jessop (at the time building the Cromford & High Peak Railway; see page 199) was called as a witness and stated that he saw no reason that building the railway would not be practicable and in particular supported the decision to cross Chat Moss, citing the Kilmarnock & Troon Railway, where a similar bog had been successfully overcome (see page 63). George Rennie was next, and he gave a similar sterling performance and also emphasized the railway's intention to work the line with horses rather than steam engines. Other engineers were called as witnesses, including Alexander Nimmo, an Irish engineer, who claimed that crossing "mosses" was not a problem, though he recommended cuts and embankments.

The opposition in turn brought forth witnesses that claimed the railway was unnecessary, that the canals were providing as good a service as was required, and that land values would be destroyed, but their case was losing its impact. On 1 May the Lords' committee passed the bill on to the full house, and the following day it passed the House of Lords, receiving Royal Assent on 5 May 1826.

The lengthy, two-hundred-section act authorized a "Railway or Tramroad." It gave the railway company powers to build and operate a double line of track between Liverpool and Manchester, taking land up to 22 yards wide, and 150 yards where there were turnouts, embankments, and cuttings, and a little more at the terminals. The railway was authorized to use stationary or locomotive engines except within the boundaries of Liverpool, where only stationary engines were to be employed. As all the public railways before, the railway was open to all on payment of a toll, though the railway was empowered to regulate them. Before the railway opened there would be three more amending acts, which would allow borrowing, alter the line slightly between Rainhill and Chat Moss when a better alignment was found, and, most importantly, in May 1829, allow the railway access across the River Irwell and into Manchester.

A letter was sent to George and John Rennie asking the terms on which they would act as engineers for the railway, and Charles Vignoles was requested to begin the detailed survey for construction, which he did. The Rennies, however, demanded sole control over the building of the line and specifically stated that while they would be prepared to work with Josias Jessop or Thomas Telford, they would not work with George Stephenson. Many of the directors, including Sandars and Booth, still had high regard for Stephenson and felt he had more *practical* experience building railways than anyone else, including the Rennies, and wanted him involved. To this end, letters of recommendation were obtained from Joseph Pease of the Stockton & Darlington Railway and Michael Longridge of Bedlington Ironworks (manufacturer of malleable-iron rails). George Stephenson was appointed principal engineer on 3 July 1826. Vignoles by this time was at work, as surveyor, staking out the line and letting contracts for cutting ditches as drains through Chat Moss, and he continued with this work for a while. However, as might be expected, he had many disagreements with Stephenson and on 2 February 1827 he resigned, leaving Stephenson in complete control.

Stephenson now hired capable men as resident engineers. Joseph Locke, who had been apprenticed to Stephenson and stayed as his assistant, and who would go on to engineer a number of the major railways in Britain, was made responsible for the Liverpool tunnel and the western end of the line. John Dixon, who had worked with Stephenson on the Stockton & Darlington and the Canterbury & Whitstable, would look after the eastern end of the line, including the difficult section over Chat Moss. And William Allcard, another Stephenson apprentice, was made responsible for the middle section of line. In turn, others were appointed as superintendents at specific places such as the tunnel, the Olive Mount cutting, and an inclined plane at Whiston. The drawings needed for the work were drawn by another up-and-coming engineer and Stephenson apprentice, Thomas Gooch. It became very much a Stephenson affair.

The Liverpool tunnel, called the Wapping or Edge Hill Tunnel, was to be 2,250 yards long, and the line there on a 1-in-48 gradient, too steep for the locomotives of the day; it was to be operated as an incline, with stationary engines hidden inside an ornate structure at the top end. Shafts were dug at several points along the line of the tunnel and then excavations laterally in both directions with pickaxes and shovels wielded by some three hundred workmen working by the light of candles. Much care, of course, had to be taken to ensure the various sections aligned. By June 1827 the first two sections had been joined, and the entire tunnel was completed by June 1828. Costs were driven up by water seeping into the tunnel, requiring waterproof cement and brick lining. In August 1828 the public was allowed to inspect the tunnel, now outfitted with gas lighting. Thousands flocked to see it.

The other major natural feature needing to be overcome was Chat Moss, a large peat bog, which the railway would have to cross for about 4 miles. Stephenson relied on drainage and filling, a relatively novel method (excavating and refilling was the normal method), though one that had been used elsewhere with success. Four parallel drains 4 miles long and 48 feet apart were cut to drain the land between them and allow the land to harden. Some of the drains filled in as soon as they were cut; here Stephenson used old barrels preserved with tar. Dried peat and brushwood hurdles were then used to create an embankment, on top of which earth, sand, gravel, and cinders were applied. A lot of fill material went into the bog before any apparent effect was noticed, and the railway committee became worried enough to send a deputation to inspect the works themselves. But Stephenson was sure it would work, and his persistence paid off. Trains run across Chat Moss on Stephenson's base to this day. At the parliamentary hearing one "expert" witness, engineer Francis Giles, had estimated the cost of the line over Chat Moss at £270,000; Stephenson actually achieved it for only £28,000.

Another major engineering work was the Sankey Viaduct, a nine-arch structure to carry the railway over the Sankey Canal, also called the St. Helens Canal, which had been completed in 1757 to connect the Lancashire coalfield at St. Helens to the River Mersey. The arches of the viaduct had to be 70 feet high to allow clearance for sailing vessels to pass underneath. The viaduct was completed in early 1830.

Stephenson intended to use the wrought-iron rails that had proved themselves on the Stockton & Darlington. Some 160 tons had been purchased for use while the railway was being built, and 2,000 tons were purchased for the rest of the line. The specifications were exact, and the rails had to undergo testing with a weighted carriage before being accepted. One hundred tons a month were delivered. There never seems to have been any discussion as to gauge; the company minutes simply record that "the width of the Waggon Way between the Rails be the same as the Darlington Road, namely 4' 8" clear, inside the rails." Stephenson's so-called standard gauge was becoming established.

Stephenson seems to have kept to an agreement to spend nine months of the year with the Liverpool & Manchester project, but some of the directors were unhappy about even this, wanting him to spend all year on it. But he was at the same time working on the Canterbury & Whitstable (see pages 168–71), the Bolton & Leigh (see page 206), and the Nantlle (see page 88).

By mid-1828 the directors had come to the conclusion that the railway ought to terminate in Manchester at its eastern end, rather than on the other side of the River Irwell as authorized. It took some long and hard bargaining to persuade the two canal companies involved (the Old Quay Company of the Mersey & Irwell Navigation, and Robert Bradshaw, of the Duke of Bridgewater's Canal) to sell the necessary land, but with concessions such as granting railway frontage for warehousing, they were persuaded.

Since the railway had been authorized by Parliament and was obviously going to be completed, the canal interests likely saw that they would be forced to sell the land required, so they might as well get some quid pro quo for it. The inevitability of the coming of the railway also seems to have muted opposition to the extension. The requisite legislation was passed in May 1829.

In early 1828 the directors began to consider what motive power ought to be used on their railway. Opinion was beginning to swing in favour of steam locomotion. Director Henry Booth had been working on a method of producing steam without smoke and, together with Stephenson, the pair told the board that for £550 they could build such a locomotive that would weigh about 6 tons and haul 20 tons of goods and 50 passengers. The board authorized them to build the locomotive. This was the *Lancashire Witch*, originally called the *Liverpool Travelling Engine*, and it incorporated a number of advanced design features, primarily having the cylinders at an angle instead of vertical, and wood wheels rimmed with wrought iron instead of cast iron, which tended to break. This engine was very much a prototype for an even more improved engine that would emerge from the Stephenson firm very soon—the *Rocket*. As it happened, the directors authorized the order to be transferred to the Bolton & Leigh Railway, since it was near opening, where it became that line's first locomotive. It seems that the directors expected the Bolton & Leigh to be a sort of testing ground for locomotives. The next year the directors ordered another locomotive to assist with construction and excavation work at Olive Mount. Also manufactured by Robert Stephenson, the locomotive, named *Twin Sisters*, had two boilers and two chimneys. It arrived in July 1829 and began work a week later, and was said to be "superseding thirty horses." It attracted a lot of attention and favourable comment because it not only had been designed to consume its own smoke (by using coke) but had a number of safety valves to minimize the possibility of boiler explosion. Perhaps here was a practical solution to the question of motive power?

Steam locomotives were by no means the unanimous choice of the railway's board. Some thought that a system of stationary

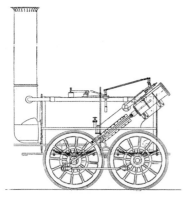

Left.
Engineering drawings of *Lancashire Witch* survive. The visual similarity to *Rocket* is immediately apparent. The engine had a boiler with two flue tubes; the *Rocket* would have twenty-five.

Right.
The Stephenson-built locomotive *Twin Sisters*, with its unusual double boilers and chimneys, was used in the construction of the Liverpool & Manchester Railway.

engines—perhaps one every mile—would prove to be more reliable, and yet others still preferred horses as the tried-and-tested method. Henry Booth, the treasurer, who later wrote a history of the railway, wrote that "communications were received from all classes of persons, each recommending an improved power, or an improved carriage; from professors of philosophy, down to the humblest mechanic." Everything conceivable was proposed, right up to perpetual motion machines!

In September 1828 the board chose two of its number, Booth and James Cropper, the latter a stationary steam supporter, to visit the Stockton & Darlington Railway and report on the best motive power used there. This achieved nothing, for Cropper still recommended stationary engines and Booth locomotives. Further consultations took place with such figures as Nicholas Wood, a locomotive (and Stephenson) supporter, and Benjamin Thompson of the Brunton & Shields Railway, the longest of the stationary engine lines (see page 99). Then the directors decided to engage two prominent engineers, John Urpeth Rastrick and James Walker, to investigate the issue and provide a recommendation.

The pair spent January 1829 travelling all over northern England viewing railways and finally submitted their reports on 9 March. They came down in favour of stationary reciprocating (that is, self-acting) engines but also suggested that if the directors wished to "proceed by degrees," as they put it, then stationary engines could be used on the Sutton and Whiston planes at either end of a level stretch at Rainhill, and locomotives on the rest of the line, until experience showed which system worked best. This indecisiveness was not what the directors wanted to hear, and any use of stationary engines was certainly not what Stephenson wanted to hear.

Robert Stephenson and Joseph Locke, guided by George Stephenson, then collected yet more information about the performance of locomotives, gathering reports on existing working ones such as on the Stockton & Darlington, where Timothy Hackworth, maker of *Royal George*, stated flatly, "I am verily convinced that a swift engine, upon a well-conditioned railway, will combine profit and simplicity, and will afford such facility as has not hitherto been known." That *was* what Stephenson wanted to hear!

Despite further discussion demanded by the stationary engine supporters on the board, it seems to have been recognized that the steam locomotive was likely to improve rapidly, and the majority of the board did not want to box themselves in with technology that might soon be outdated. James Walker had suggested that a premium be offered to inventors for the development of a locomotive that would be suitable for the railway, and at a board meeting on 20 April it was decided that "a Premium of £500 be advertised for a Locomotive Engine which shall be a decided improvement on those now in use." Thus the idea was born for the now-famous Rainhill Trials.

The following month the horse supporters must have had second thoughts, because the offer was clarified as "an improved moving Power"—it did not need to be a steam engine. The conditions for the contest were published, and they stipulated that the engine be lighter than 6 tons, be able to pull 20 tons on the level (or a proportionate amount if the engine was lighter), must "consume its own smoke," have two safety valves, have springs, be no higher than 15 feet, have a pressure gauge, be delivered for trial by 1 October 1829, and cost no more than £550.

Five entries met the deadline. Robert Stephenson's *Rocket* arrived first. It had been taken by road from Newcastle to Carlisle, by barge to Bowness, on Solway Firth, then shipped on a steamer to Liverpool. Then came Timothy Burstall, from Scotland, and his engine *Perseverance*, and *Novelty*, built in seven weeks by John Braithwaite and John Ericsson of London to a design similar to a road engine they had patented. Timothy Hackworth, of the Stockton & Darlington Railway, entered *Sans Pareil*, which he had designed as a lighter version of *Royal George*. Because he did not have appropriate facilities at his works at Shildon, the boiler and cylinders had been made elsewhere—the boiler at Bedlington and the cylinders by Robert Stephenson in Newcastle. The latter would lead to some finger pointing when Hackworth lost out to the Stephensons' engine. Finally, there was the non-steam engine the directors had allowed—Thomas Brandreth's *Cycloped*, essentially a moving horse treadmill. It was more an experiment than

Left.
Timothy Hackworth's entry to the Rainhill Trials, *Sans Pareil*, displayed at the National Railway Museum at Shildon. Like *Royal George*, but unlike *Rocket*, it had vertical cylinders.

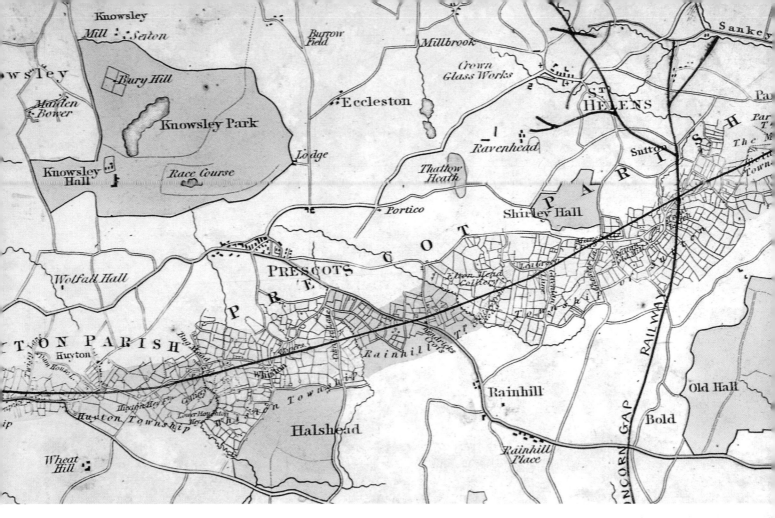

Above.
The directors picked a stretch of track that was more or less straight and level for the Rainhill Trials in October 1829. The level stretch was bounded by steeper gradients, potential stationary engine–worked inclined planes, at either end, at *Whiston* and *Sutton*.

a entrant, even a deliberate plant, for Brandreth was a close friend of George Stephenson.

Three judges were appointed—Nicholas Wood of Killingworth Colliery; John Urpeth Rastrick of Stourbridge, a locomotive builder in his own right who made the first steam locomotive to run in the United States (see page 232); and John Kennedy, the Manchester cotton magnate.

Whole books have been written on the Rainhill Trials; a brief summary will suffice here. The village of Rainhill is about 12 miles east of Liverpool. Here, on the morning of 6 October 1829, over 10,000 people gathered along the line to witness

Right.
Rocket, somewhat altered from its original state, is now preserved in the Science Museum in London. Note the wooden wheels rimmed in wrought iron, an idea first used on Stephenson's *Lancashire Witch* of 1828.

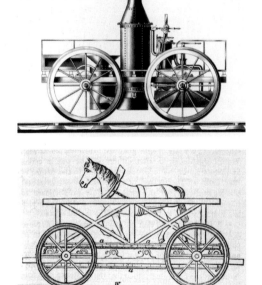

the coming spectacle. Notably, among the spectators were Horatio Allen of the Delaware & Hudson Canal Company, who would become the first to drive a steam locomotive in the United States (see page 232), and E.L. Miller, one of the promoters of the South Carolina Railroad (see page 234). The innovative technology being developed in Britain was being noticed elsewhere in the world.

The trial demanded that each locomotive run 1¾ miles in each direction ten times, including some distance at the beginning for getting up speed, so that the total distance covered would be 32½ miles, the equivalent of a journey between Liverpool and Manchester. The test would then be repeated, to simulate a return journey. A load would be pulled equivalent to three times the weight of the engine.

Perseverance was judged to have insufficient power—and in any case was damaged before it arrived—and did not compete, though it did manage a demonstration, when it achieved 6 miles per hour. *Cycloped* was judged to be of insufficient power and also did not compete.

The first day was a sort of free-for-all, with the several engines darting back and forth to please the crowd. Without a load, *Rocket* achieved a speed of 24½ miles per hour; *Novelty* did even better at 30 miles per hour. The following day, with more preliminaries, *Novelty* burst one of its cylinder bellows after achieving 25 miles per hour. The next day *Rocket* ran the prescribed distance with the load at an average speed of 11 miles per hour. When *Novelty* tried, it burst a pipe and had to be taken away for repairs. On 13 October *Sans Pareil*, which was overweight according to the rules of the contest but allowed to compete anyway, attempted the trial, but after about two hours the pumps supplying water from its tender broke, and it had to be taken for repairs. The following day *Novelty* was once again ready but had been disassembled and rebuilt in the intervening time since its first failure and now had many untested joints. After two round trips attaining speeds of 24 miles per hour, the joint of a boiler pipe failed. It would have taken days to fix, and so *Novelty* was withdrawn from the contest. Stephenson took advantage of the available time to demonstrate the power of his engine by drawing a full load up the 1-in-96 Rainhill inclined plane, achieving 12 miles per hour in the process.

The judges had little difficulty declaring the *Rocket* the winner and awarded the premium to Stephenson. The question of what motive power to use on the railway had finally been settled—and indeed was settled then for generations of railways to come. As the directors of an organization called the Internal Improvements of the State of Massachusetts put it the following year, "this invention promises to produce a new era in the business and arrangements of society." They were right.

Robert Stephenson's *Rocket* had a number of innovative design features that enabled it to be relatively strong and efficient. The first was the multi-tubed boiler, which allowed for more efficient transfer of heat from fire to water and hence better steaming. Henry Booth first suggested it, though Marc Seguin in France had patented this idea the year before (see page 248). Regardless, it was this feature that revolutionized steam locomotives of the day. *Rocket*'s cylinders were at an angle and also transferred the power from the pistons to the wheel via an iron bar that connected the hub to the rim, thus applying power more directly to the rim, where it was required. *Rocket* also used a blastpipe to draw air through the fire, though this was not a new feature of such engines.

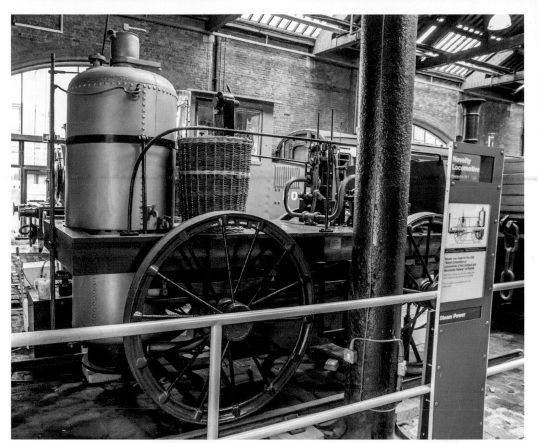

Right.
Crammed in with a selection of other engines and wagons at the Manchester Museum of Science & Industry is the replica of John Braithwaite and John Ericsson's Rainhill entry, *Novelty*. The early favourite, it was untested and too lightly built to maintain the pace required. It was built in seven weeks to a design Braithwaite and Ericsson were using for fire road vehicles, and it might even have been a converted fire engine. This replica was built in 1979–80 at Springwell Workshop on the Bowes Railway (see page 101) for the celebration of the 150-year anniversary of the Rainhill Trials.

Below.
A replica of *Sans Pareil* at the National Railway Museum at Shildon. This is how the engine might have looked when competing at Rainhill. The vertical cylinders are quite distinctive.

Right, bottom.
Another view of the original *Rocket*.

Robert Stephenson conducted further tests after the Rainhill Trials to determine the limits of his engine. On the level, *Rocket* pulled 42 tons at 14 miles per hour. More tests showed that reasonable loads could be managed even on the inclined planes—an important finding, since locomotives could now be used over the entire length of the line, considerably speeding things up. The next year fifteen more locomotives were ordered, twelve from Robert Stephenson & Company, and most of these improved on the capabilities of *Rocket* even more.

By June 1830, the railway was complete enough for the directors to travel over the entire line, hauled by the second Stephenson engine, *Arrow*, and after more trials the official opening day was set for 15 September. As would be fitting, it was planned to be a huge celebration. Even the prime minister, Lord Wellington,

Above.

The *Liverpool and Manchester Railway*, complete, on an 1833 map. Canals are also shown, variously in green (the *Duke of Bridgewater's Canal*), red (the *Sankey Canal*, the *Worsley Branch* of the Leeds & Liverpool Canal, and the *Bury & Bolton Canal*), and blue (the *Mersey and Irwell Canal*). Several branch lines to the

Liverpool & Manchester Railway are shown, only one of which, the *Bolton & Leigh Railway*, was open in 1830, and then only between *Bolton* and *Leigh*. The rest would open in the two years after 1830 (see page 206).

known to be ambivalent about railways, accepted an invitation to attend, and a special ornamental carriage—wider than normal—was constructed for him, together with some of his aristocratic friends and other people of importance. Every dignitary in the county attended, including Member of Parliament for Liverpool, William Huskisson. Eight trains were made up to run from Liverpool to Manchester, where a dinner was planned, and back again. Some 772 people were assigned to the trains, organized by coloured flags corresponding to the guests' ticket colour. Thousands of spectators lined the tracks.

The prime minister's train, first in the procession, was hauled by a new engine, *Northumbrian*, which had an improved firebox and cylinders at a lower angle than *Rocket* to give smoother running. The train included a wagon with a band and the directors' carriage. George Stephenson himself was the driver. The next train was hauled by a locomotive named *Phoenix,* driven by Robert Stephenson; other drivers included George's brother, Robert Stephenson Sr.; Joseph Locke; Thomas Gooch; and William Allcard.

Wellington's train used the southernmost of the double tracks; all the others used the northern one. This arrangement allowed the duke's train to speed up or slow down as required. At Parkside station the trains stopped so that the engines could take on water. Guests had specifically been warned not to leave their carriages, but Huskisson, along with many others, left their carriage to stretch their legs and talk to others. Huskisson wanted to greet Wellington and was just shaking his hand when the train pulled by *Rocket* approached on the other line. Everyone scrambled to safety—except poor Huskisson, who fell on the

track and was run over by *Rocket*—which, like all the engines, had no brakes. He was carried aboard the duke's carriage, and Stephenson, driving *Northumbrian* as fast as he could, rushed him to Eccles, where he was taken to a vicar's house, to which doctors had been summoned. Nothing, however, could be done for him, and he died that evening.

Stephenson had built the line using four equally spaced rails; he envisaged that this would allow the line to operate as a double tracked railway line under normal circumstances but that in the event of a locomotive needing to haul a particularly wide load or if one of the outside rails broke, a locomotive could use the central pair of rails. The rails being close together would also reduce the amount of land required the railway. But on this day the specially built duke's carriage was wider than normal and so left no space between it and another train, and this is why Huskisson was unable to escape the onrushing train.

The duke continued to Manchester but by now a restless crowd greeted the prime minister, who was at that time worried—indeed paranoid—about the possibility of revolution, so he remained in his train, protected by an army regiment. As a result of all the confusion, some trains did not arrive back in Liverpool until after 10 o'clock that evening, though the duke left his train to visit friends at Childwall, then just outside Liverpool. Opening day had been marred by tragedy and the death of one of the railway's most ardent supporters.

Nonetheless, the railway began operations right away. A full-time regular schedule was put into effect two days later, on 17 September 1830, and the age of the railway, as we know it today, had well and truly begun.

Above.
The classic illustration of the Liverpool & Manchester Railway: a first-class passenger train (*top*) and second-class train. These illustrations were published in 1831, prompted by great public interest in the new society-changing railway.

Right, top.
A contemporary hand-coloured pamphlet issued to celebrate the opening of the Liverpool & Manchester Railway. At top is a representation of the Duke of Wellington's train, with his specially built wide ornamental carriage and a band in the first wagon behind the engine. The middle train is pulled by the locomotive *William the Fourth*, one of two built for the railway by Braithwaite and Ericsson, who had entered *Novelty* in the Rainhill Trials.

Right.
Another map of the Liverpool & Manchester Railway in 1830, here called the *Manchester and Liverpool Rail Road*, with the *Bolton & Leigh Rl. Rd.*, completed in 1828–29, shown connected to the Liverpool & Manchester by the *Kenyon & West Leigh R. Road* (the Kenyon & Leigh Junction Railway), completed in 1831.

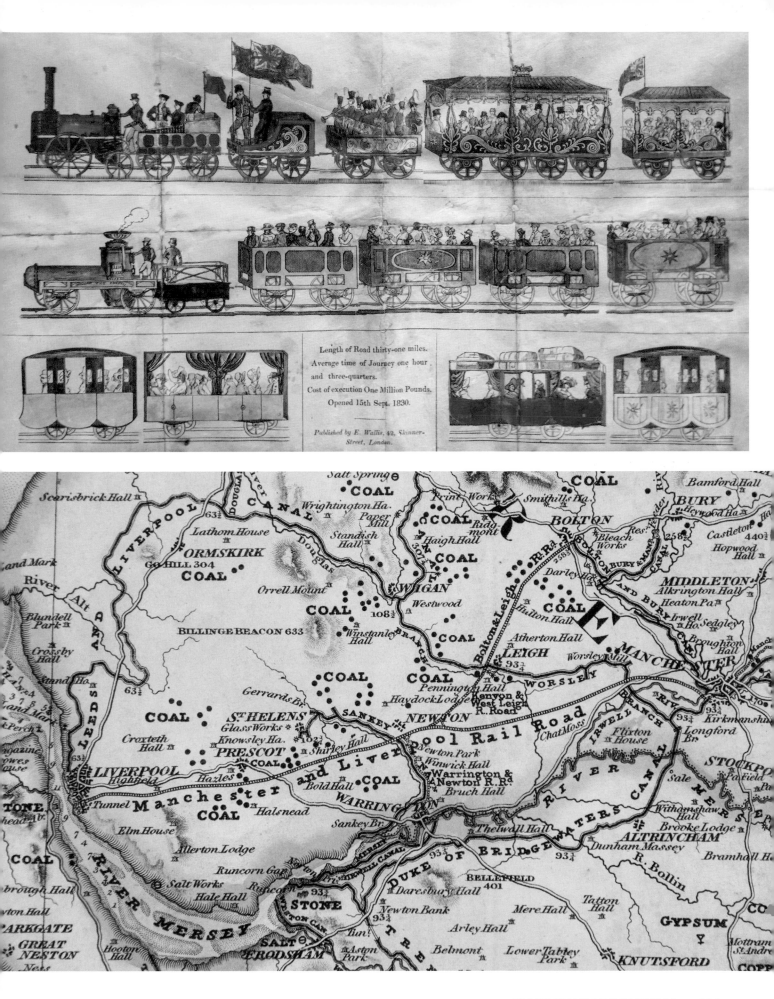

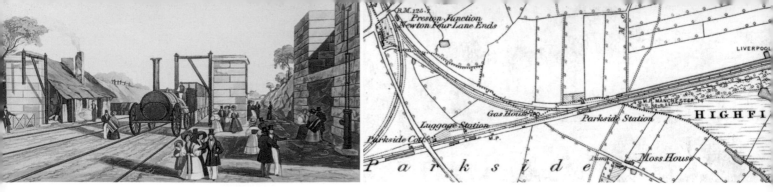

Above, right.
Parkside Station is shown on a map surveyed in 1847 as *Luggage Station. Parkside Station* on this map was created in 1839 to allow it to be used with the Wigan Branch Railway (the line to the north), by then part of the North Union Railway. The illustration, *above, left,* is of Parkside Station. Note the equally spaced rails, which contributed to the demise of William Huskisson on opening day.

The railway proved enormously popular, so much more comfortable, less expensive, and faster it was than the alternatives. So heavy was the passenger traffic that goods traffic could not begin until December, by which time additional locomotives had been acquired. The new engine *Planet*, with an improved design, hauled the first goods train on 4 December. Some 51 tons were delivered to Manchester in just under three hours. Subsequent journeys with new engines over the next year or so yielded even better results in speed and weight carried; the superiority of the railway over canal was established without question.

The following year the company allowed the use of the railway by others on payment of a toll, but few had the requisite locomotives, and so the railway company maintained an effective monopoly, just as it would be with railway operation over much of the world in the future. It was one thing to allow private users on a slow-moving canal and quite another on an increasingly fast-paced railway. The quick and obvious success of the Liverpool & Manchester unleashed a flood of applications for other railways, leading to the first "railway mania" of 1836 (see page 222). It also spurred others in continental Europe and North America to propose and build railways, safe in the knowledge that such an enterprise, done properly, was entirely viable.

The Liverpool & Manchester Railway established many of the conventions and rules that govern railway operation to this day. It cemented the use of the 4-foot, 8-inch (later with ½ inch added for play) Stephenson or "standard" gauge. And the line is still in use over essentially the same route as the one laid out by Stephenson.

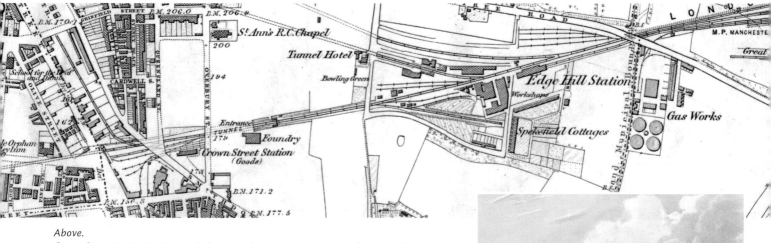

Above.
Crown Street Station in Liverpool, the original passenger terminus, is shown on this map surveyed in 1849. It also shows *Edge Hill Station* and lines leading to two other, later tunnels: the one leading to Liverpool's current main-line station, Lime Street Station, opened in 1832 (the tunnel) and 1836 (the station)—the tunnel entrance is at the *Tunnel Hotel*; and the Victoria Tunnel, which, together with its extension, the Waterloo Tunnel, leads to Waterloo Dock. It was opened in 1849.

Right. Liverpool Crown Street Station looking east in 1831. The layout of the station is clearly shown. To the left a train can be seen standing at the departure platform, adjacent to the main building and all of the station's facilities. The train has no locomotive, as trains worked to Edge Hill by gravity via the Crown Street Tunnel in the distance. The cable can be seen in the centre of the middle line. The arrival platform is to the right, and passengers can be seen making their way from it to waiting omnibuses that would transport them to the city centre.

Above.
The railway across Chat Moss, shown on an 1849 map.
Inset, right, is the 1831 illustration by artist Thomas Bury.

Below, bottom.
Additions to an 1829 map show the line of the *Wapping Tunnel*, the *Lime St Tunnel*, opened in 1832, and the *Victoria Tunnel*, opened in 1849.

Below. Bury's illustration of the Wapping Tunnel. His first illustration of the tunnel showed a locomotive in it and had to be revised to depict the correct rope working. The Wapping Tunnel was the first tunnel ever built under a city.

Right. The western entrance of the Wapping Tunnel, and an interior view (*inset*), as it is today, somewhat less grand than Bury's illustration.

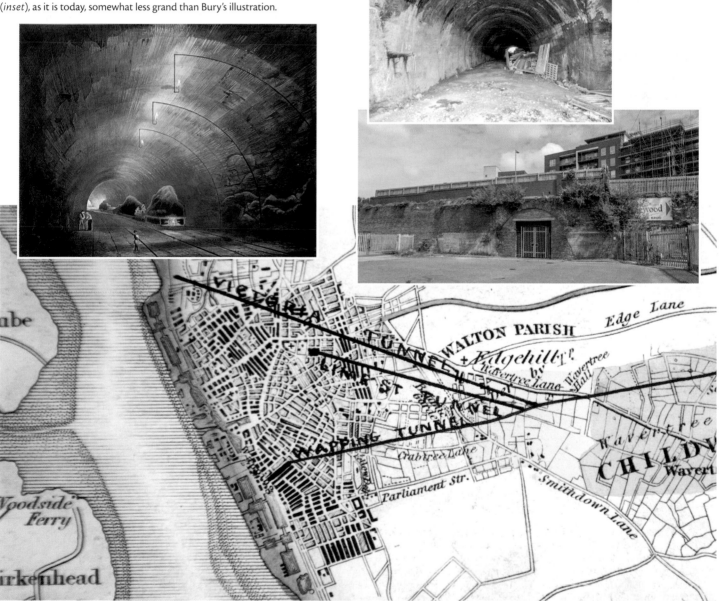

Above, left.
The railway's entrance into Manchester, across a bridge over the River Irwell, is shown on this map from an 1845 survey. *Inset, above,* is a view of the station buildings today; on the map they are immediately above the *L* of *Liverpool* Road. *Inset, left,* are warehouse buildings behind the station, also shown on the map.

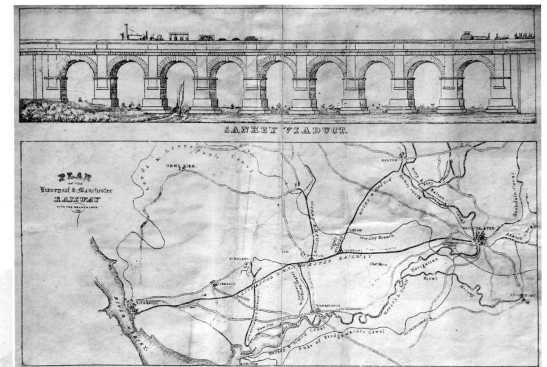

Above.
The Sankey Viaduct, which carried the railway across Sankey Brook and the Sankey Canal, takes pride of place on this map published in the early 1830s. The arches of the viaduct had to be high enough to allow the sailing barges such the one shown *left* to pass underneath. This illustration was another of Thomas Bury's famous views of the railway. He was commissioned by the railway's directors to create these views to publicize the railway and encourage investment in it, though the near-immediate success of the line and its handsome returns would surely have been enough to attract investors.

Above, top left, and *above, top right.*
Two types of early carriage used by the Liverpool & Manchester Railway. *Left* is the earliest, essentially sort of three stagecoach bodies sewn together. This is a replica in the National Railway Museum. *Right*, a slightly later design, for second-class passengers, who were at first in open trucks (see illustration, *page 192*). This is a replica at the Museum of Science & Industry, Manchester. Liverpool Road Station is in the background.

Above and *centre left.*
Two views of *Planet*, a locomotive built by Robert Stephenson for the Liverpool & Manchester Railway in 1831. Locomotive design evolved very rapidly once there was an everyday experience of using them. This was the railway's ninth locomotive and a change in design from the *Rocket* and *Northumbrian*, an intermediate step. *Planet* had inside cylinders, which was a way of conserving heat and thus making the engine more efficient. The locomotive shown is a replica built in 1992 by the Friends of the Museum of Science & Industry in Manchester. It is displayed, like the *Novelty* replica (see *page 185*), tightly packed with other engines and wagons, and thus difficult to photograph.

Left.
Satirists and cartoonists had a field day with early railways, typically illustrating explosions and the like. This well-known lithograph imagines what the rise of the railway would do to horses. It was published about 1831. Between Liverpool and Manchester, 26 stagecoaches had been reduced to 12 before the end of 1830.

Railways, Railways

Agenoria's Railway

Although the opening of the Liverpool & Manchester Railway can be said to have marked the beginning of the modern railway, there were many other projects under way at the time that would be completed in the several years following 1830. And some of these would maintain the features of the earlier railways, such as inclined planes and even horse working. While their historical significance is thus diminished, they are interesting and worth mentioning.

Plenty of colliery railways would remain, with their use of steam locomotives increasing as the years went by. One of the earliest of these happens to have its locomotive preserved and displayed in pride of place at the National Railway Museum in York: *Agenoria*, named after a minor Roman god converted to female form. Built in Stourbridge, just west of Birmingham, by the new locomotive-building firm of Foster Rastrick (one partner being John Urpeth Rastrick, the Rainhill judge) in 1829, this locomotive is of particular interest because it was one of four

Above.
Agenoria is superimposed on an 1885 map on which the route from Shutt End Colliery (not named, at right) to Ashwood Basin on the Staffordshire & Worcestershire Canal (at left) has been highlighted in red.

built at the same time; the other three went to the United States, where one—dubbed the *Stourbridge Lion*—became the first steam locomotive to run in North America (see page 230). That locomotive has not survived complete, whereas *Agenoria* has. It is vertically cylindered and is at about the same technological level as Stephenson's *Lancashire Witch*, built the year before.

Agenoria worked at Corbyn's Hall Colliery at Shutt End, Kingswinford, about 3 miles north of Stourbridge, until 1864. It hauled coal wagons down from the colliery to barges waiting in the

Ashwood Basin of the Staffordshire & Worcestershire Canal. The capacity of the purpose-built canal basin was sixty barges, which gives some idea of the intended scale of operations. The railway had steep inclined planes at either end that were worked on the self-acting principle, since the loaded, heavier wagons were going downhill, and the locomotive hauled the wagons on the flatter section in the middle. The railway was of the edge type, which from then on would be used by all serious railways, and was mounted on stone blocks. And it was of "standard" gauge—4 feet, 8 inches.

The colliery railway opened on 2 June 1829 with *Agenoria* carrying eight wagons loaded with 360 people in addition to twelve filled with coal. It covered the 3¾ miles in 30 minutes, at a speed of 7½ miles per hour. Clearly the locomotive was a powerful one. The railway later became incorporated into a larger 40-mile-long system of colliery railways called the Pensnett or Earl of Dudley's Railway. *Agenoria* was preserved in 1884 and is now considered by some to be the most original of all the surviving early steam locomotives.

Above.
This 12-piece collage of details of *Agenoria*, on display at the very centre of the National Railway Museum's Great Hall, in York, reveals some of the complexity of the moving machine that was the locomotive engine. Most of it is original, though the balance weight cover plates on the rear wheels (one at bottom left) were likely added later, and shows its makers—Foster, Rastrick & Company—the place of birth—Stourbridge—and the date—1829.

The Edinburgh & Dalkeith

Plans to link the Midlothian coalfield with Edinburgh and Leith had been advanced as early as 1800, but it was not until 1817 that several of the colliery owners got together and asked Robert Stevenson to survey a route. His survey was done in 1818, but avoiding landed estates became such an issue that the route ended up favouring some collieries at the expense of others, and the resultant quarrels meant nothing was built. One of the colliery owners, John Wauchope of Edmonston (or Edmonstone), decided to take matters into his own hands and that same year had Stevenson build the Edmonston Waggonway for him, which delivered coal not to Edinburgh but to the main road leading to that city (map, *below*).

The opening of the Union Canal in 1822 threatened Midlothian collieries by making coal from western coalfields available more cheaply, and by 1824 enough support had been gathered for an application to Parliament. Once again landowners gave the railway many problems in refusing to allow the line to cross their lands. The engineer for the line was John Grieve, manager of one of the collieries, not Robert Stevenson. However, Grieve seemed to know what he was doing, planning for the use of steam locomotives as well as horses, stationary engines, and self-acting planes, but subsequently abandoning horses for more locomotives "of the type used in Newcastle." The shareholders then obtained a report on the proposed line from William Chapman (see page 128) who, surprisingly perhaps, given his record of locomotive building, recommended the use of horses to allay the fears of the estate owners whose land the line had to cross.

Below.
The terminus of the Edinburgh & Dalkeith in Edinburgh is shown on this 1832 map. A *Tunnel* was necessary to gain access to the desired location for a *Coal Yard* at St. Leonards, where coal was transhipped into carts.

Despite Chapman's recommendation, the first application to Parliament, based on a survey by Grieve, failed in May 1825 largely owing to landowner opposition. It took another survey, this by a more eminent engineer, James Jardine, before the required act was obtained, on 26 May 1826. The line was as shown on the map at *left*. This pattern of events may seem by now familiar to the reader.

The line was under construction for many years, and two further applications authorizing extensions and branches were made. The first act had authorized the line from Edinburgh to Dalhousie Mains (as shown on the map, *below*) and branches to

Above.
The *Edinburgh & Dalkeith Railway* is shown on this 1828 map highlighted in red, running north from the colliery at *Dalhousie Mains*. Stevenson's 1818 *Edmonstone Railway*, which at first terminated at the main road into Edinburgh, is shown in green.

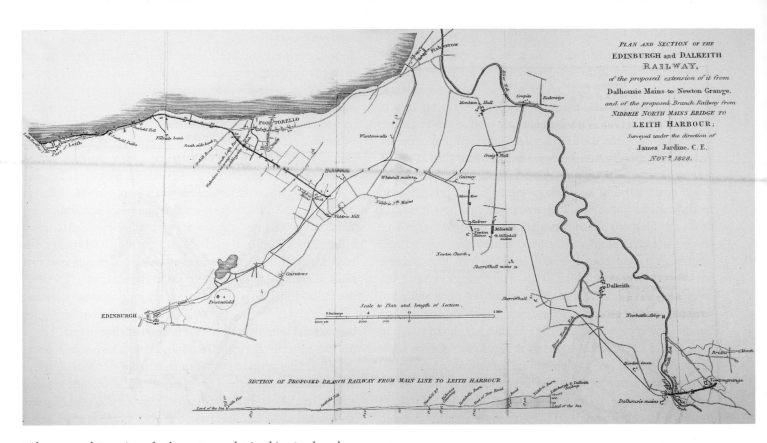

Above.
James Jardine's 1828 survey for the branch to the *Port of Leith* and main-line extension to *Newtongrange*.

Fisherrow and Cowpits; a further act was obtained in 1829 based on an 1828 survey by Jardine (map, *above*), which allowed the branch to Leith—important because it is Edinburgh's port—and an extension of the main line to Newtongrange. A third act in 1834 authorized a branch to Dalkeith and an extension to Leith Harbour. Colliery owners wanted their collieries to be linked to the railway. The Newtongrange extension was paid for by the owners of the collieries it connected. The Edinburgh & Dalkeith Railway was, however, more just an enlarged colliery-to-market scheme like the Stockton & Darlington, rather than an intercity railway like the Liverpool & Manchester. And it still used horses and stationary engines. Most of the line opened in 1831.

The Dundee & Newtyle

Farther north, another early Scottish railway, the Dundee & Newtyle, also opened in 1831. The intention here was to link Dundee, on the east coast of Scotland, with a fertile valley some miles inland, Strathmore. In 1817 Robert Stevenson had proposed a canal from Strathmore to Arbroath, on the coast a few miles north of Dundee. However, the intervening high land, the Sidlaw Hills, made a canal too expensive.

Dundee business interests were behind the idea of the railway, since they wanted to ensure that the produce of Strathmore was funnelled though their town rather than Arbroath or somewhere else. An act was

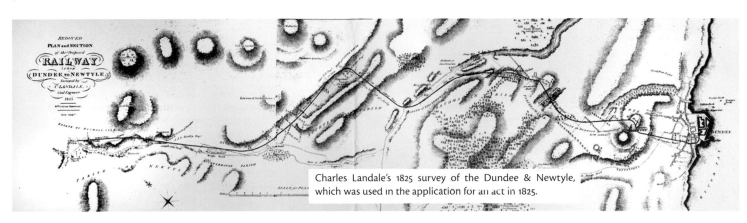

Charles Landale's 1825 survey of the Dundee & Newtyle, which was used in the application for an act in 1825.

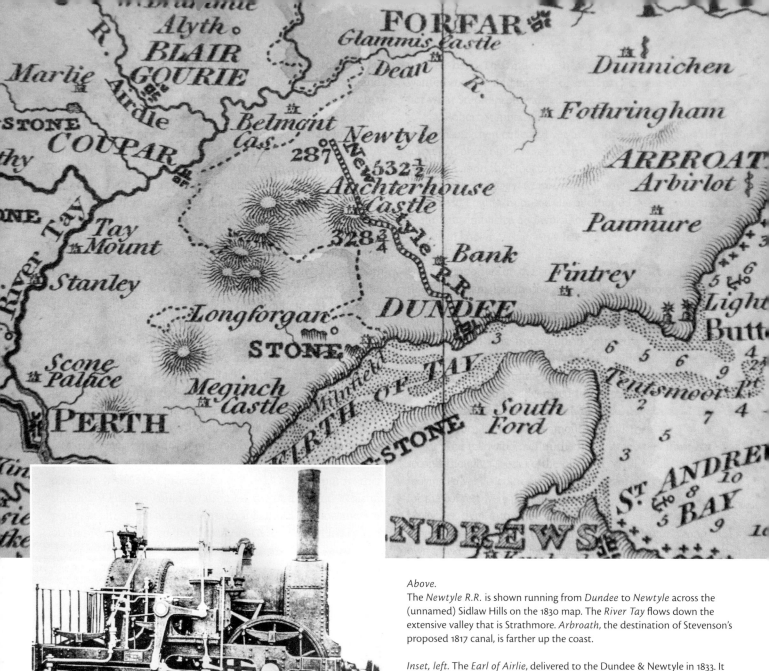

Above.
The *Newtyle R.R.* is shown running from *Dundee* to *Newtyle* across the (unnamed) Sidlaw Hills on the 1830 map. The *River Tay* flows down the extensive valley that is Strathmore. *Arbroath*, the destination of Stevenson's proposed 1817 canal, is farther up the coast.

Inset, left. The *Earl of Airlie*, delivered to the Dundee & Newtyle in 1833. It appears that the engine's owners were cognizant enough of its historical value to clean it up and take its photo—which dates from the engine's retirement in 1846—but not to preserve it.

obtained on 26 May 1826—the same day the Edinburgh & Dalkeith was approved—on the basis of a survey by local engineer Charles Landale (map, *previous page*). The railway crossed the Sidlaw Hills using three inclined planes, ending abruptly at Newtyle, then almost literally in the middle of nowhere—the little settlement grew up around the terminus during the 1830s, largely the result of a development scheme sponsored by the railway company. The line served no towns beyond Dundee, and little population. A later attempt to make the line work saw two other railways, actually branches, extend up and down Strathmore in 1837–38 to connect with the railhead at Newtyle.

The railway was at first horse operated. In 1832 Nicholas Wood was asked to review the method of traction but concluded that horses were best until the line's traffic became heavier. The railway company, however, determined to use steam locomotives and commissioned two, *Earl of Airlie* (photo, *above, left*) and *Lord Wharncliffe* (both named after investors in the company), from local engineering company J & C Carmichael, and they were delivered in September 1833 and put into service on the line between the inclined planes. Two more locomotives were subsequently delivered, and the use of heavy engines then revealed deficiencies in the engineering of the line.

Much of the route of the railway survived into the 1960s, though merged many times and nationalized and altered in many details.

The Cromford & High Peak

Coincident in time with the Liverpool & Manchester Railway, and almost exactly the same length, the Cromford & High Peak Railway makes an interesting comparison, for here the directors decided to use horses, stationary engines, and inclined planes rather than steam locomotives, which would quickly prove to be the superior choice.

The Cromford & High Peak received its act in 1825, after an easy passage through Parliament because it did not cross the lands of influential objectors. It was engineered by Josias Jessop but not built under his direction since he died the following year. The line was 33 miles long and linked Whaley Bridge to the Cromford Canal, just south of its termination at Cromford, over the Peak District of Derbyshire, the southern end of the Pennine chain that divides northern England. Whaley Bridge was connected to Manchester via the Peak Forest Canal. At the time the only other way to ship goods from Lancashire to Derby and Nottingham was via the more roundabout Trent & Mersey Canal. So in theory it was a desired link in a transportation network. It was designed in accordance with the advice of many engineers of the day, with four inclined planes at either end and one at Hurdlow, in the middle.

The railway was completed and opened in two sections: the southern part from the Cromford Canal to the bottom of the Hurdlow Inclined Plane on 29 May 1830—three months before the Liverpool & Manchester—and the northern part of the line to Whaley Bridge

on 6 July 1831. Horses were used initially between the inclines, though from 1833 steam locomotives began taking over; the first was named *Peak* and was purchased from Robert Stephenson & Company. It seems that the following year the railway company tried a smaller locomotive built locally at Cromford.

Several attempts were made to join the Cromford & High Peak to the Liverpool & Manchester, with the connection in Manchester, but these were foiled by opposition from the canal companies who would have had much to lose by being bypassed. In any case the differences in engineering between the two lines would have made a connection difficult for through-running. The Cromford was a line of many tight curves, and trains capable of negotiating them needed to be short. The many inclines could have

Below.
Cromford & High Peak rails, 4 feet long and made of cast iron in the fishbelly shape, supported on stone blocks.

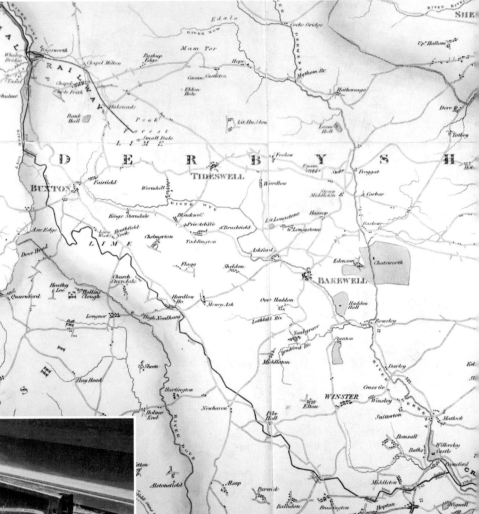

Above.
This 1833 map shows the line of the Cromford & High Peak Railway as a black line from *Whaley Bridge* (at top left) to near *Cromford* (at bottom right). The middle incline is at *Hurdlow Ho.* The other *Railway* shown at top is the Peak Forest Tramway of 1796 (see page 42).

Left.
A distinctive locomotive on the Cromford & High Peak, a "Crewe Goods" at the top of Hurdlow Incline deviation, about 1890. Water is stored in tenders above it.

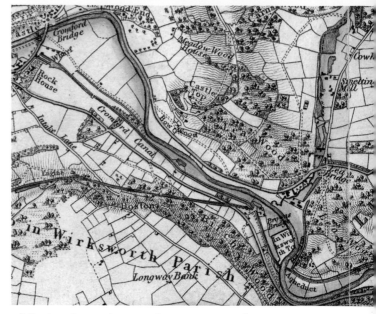

Right.
The Cromford & High Peak Railway is the red line ending at the *Cromford Canal* on this map published four years after the complete length of the line was open. An *Engine* is marked at the top of the incline up from High Peak Junction—Cromford and Sheep Pasture inclines, two inclines worked as one. The view, *below*, is looking up from the bottom of this incline today. The line was double tracked here.

been avoided by the construction of detour lines if more investment had been possible, but investors were not very interested in the railway, as right from the beginning it did not carry the traffic projected for it, in stark contrast to the Liverpool & Manchester, which exceeded all traffic forecasts in its early years.

The middle incline, the Hurdlow Incline, was in fact by-passed in 1869 to allow through-running by locomotives for the 24 miles between the multiple inclines at either end of the line.

The Cromford & High Peak connected two canals, which were soon in decline in step with the general rise of the railway, while the Liverpool & Manchester connected two major cities—sources of traffic for both passengers and goods that could withstand all competition. The Cromford & High Peak always seemed to remain stuck in the past: horse shunting was still in use in the 1950s. Locomotives did eventually use some of the inclines, but needed to have light loads and to take a run at it! One of the light loads often hauled consisted of tenders full of water, for there was little water available on the higher ground. The last section of the line finally closed in 1967.

The Leicester & Swannington

When the early plateway and canal system that was the Forest Line of the Leicester Navigation failed (see page 73), collieries and lime quarries of northeastern Leicestershire were left with inadequate means of getting their products to market in Leicester. The Leicester & Swannington Railway was essentially a substitute for the earlier route, one that became one of the critical early edge railways. It was engineered by Robert Stephenson with advice from his father, George. It was a 16-mile-long single-track railway.

West Leicestershire colliery owner William Stenson, who could not compete in Leicester with Nottingham collieries owing to their cheaper water transportation, had visited the Stockton & Darlington Railway in 1828 and realized that a railway could solve his problem. The two Stephensons were induced to come to Leicestershire and look at a proposed route. On 12 February 1829 Stenson called a meeting of like-minded owners and investors at the Bell Hotel in Leicester. A provisional committee they set up engaged Robert Stephenson as engineer, and it was he, assisted by a surveyor, Thomas Miles of Leicester, who refined the route. It ran from West Bridge, Leicester, on the River Soar, to Swannington, via some other collieries. To achieve this, a mile-long tunnel was required at Glenfield (map, *overleaf, bottom*), as well as two inclined planes, one at Bagworth and one at Swannington.

An act was obtained on 29 May 1830, and construction began. Using contractors, as was the general practice at this time, Stephenson soon had his hands full as problem after problem surfaced: one contractor abandoned his contract, and one fell down a tunnel air shaft and was killed. Half of Glenfield Tunnel's length encountered sand, which required that the tunnel be lined with bricks, but the brickwork was not done properly, causing more problems. The tunnel turned out to be an attraction; gates had to be erected at its entrances to keep out sightseers on Sundays, the only day work was not being carried out.

Despite all the difficulties, the line was completed as far as the Bagworth Incline and a grand opening held on 17 July 1832, with the requisite train, one carriage and wagons converted with seating, pulled by a locomotive, *Comet*, recently arrived from Robert Stephenson & Company. The engine's tall chimney struck the tunnel roof at one point, causing a minor delay. A fine dinner was then held at the Bell Hotel. Passengers were carried from the beginning, with the company's one second-class carriage being attached to coal trains as demand warranted. The Bagworth Inclined Plane and the section of track north to Bardon Hill were completed on 1 February 1833, and the entire line, to the top of Swannington Incline, opened on 25 November 1833.

The Coleorton Railway, which was really just an extension of the Leicester & Swannington, was incorporated that year and completed a line in 1835 that connected Leicester to more collieries, some previously served by the Ticknall Tramway (see page 46), including Cloud Hill Lime Works. It was only horse worked.

Glenfield Tunnel continued to be a problem all its life. The brick lining had made it narrow, and so the windows of passenger carriages were barred, and doors had to be locked before

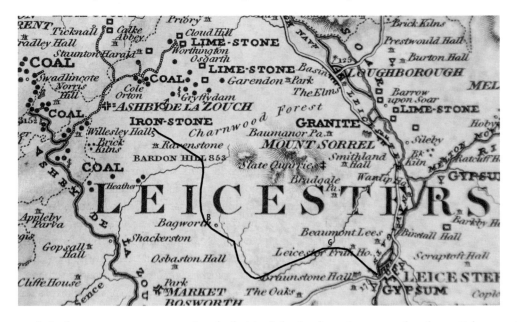

Left.
The Leicester & Swannington Railway. *G* is the location of Glenfield Tunnel; *B* is Bagworth Incline; and *S* is the Swannington Inclined Plane. The earlier plateway is the Ticknall Tramway (see page 46). The Coleorton Railway would be opened in 1835 as an extension of the Leicester & Swannington to connect with *Cole Orton* and the *Cloud Hill* limestone quarry, essentially widening the catchment area funnelled through Leicester.

Below. A length of fishbelly rail thought to be from the Leicester & Swannington, on display at the National Tramway Museum at Crich, Derbyshire. The museum is located in a limestone quarry once leased by George Stephenson.

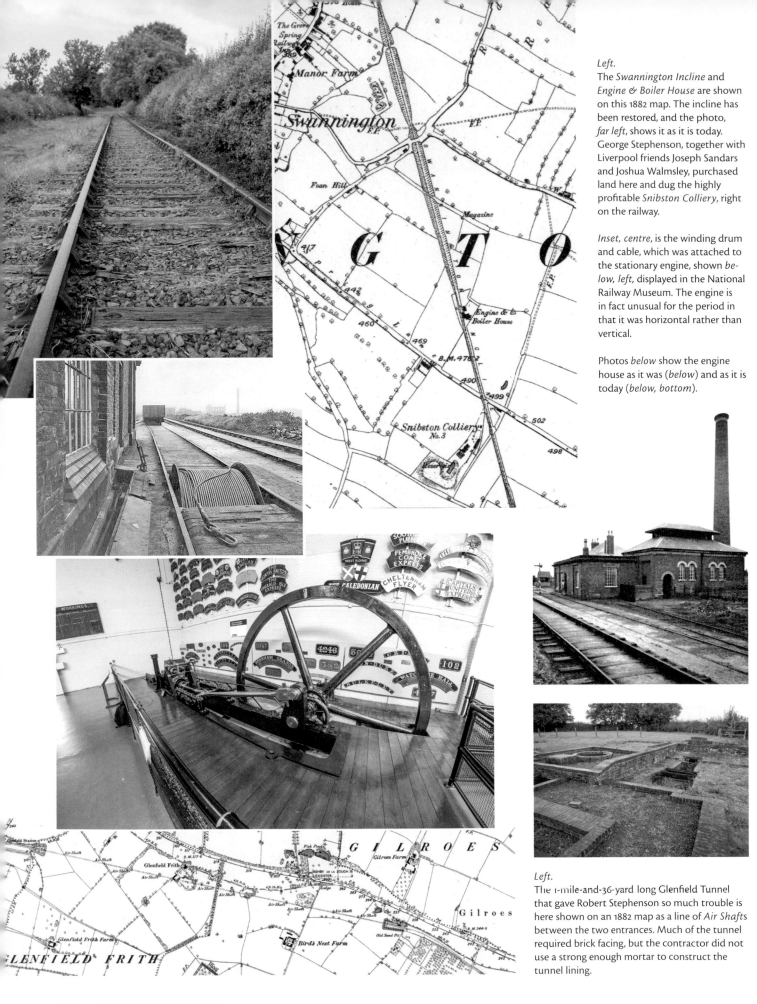

Left.
The *Swannington Incline* and *Engine & Boiler House* are shown on this 1882 map. The incline has been restored, and the photo, *far left*, shows it as it is today. George Stephenson, together with Liverpool friends Joseph Sandars and Joshua Walmsley, purchased land here and dug the highly profitable *Snibston Colliery*, right on the railway.

Inset, centre, is the winding drum and cable, which was attached to the stationary engine, shown *below, left*, displayed in the National Railway Museum. The engine is in fact unusual for the period in that it was horizontal rather than vertical.

Photos *below* show the engine house as it was (*below*) and as it is today (*below, bottom*).

Left.
The 1-mile-and-36-yard long Glenfield Tunnel that gave Robert Stephenson so much trouble is here shown on an 1882 map as a line of *Air Shafts* between the two entrances. Much of the tunnel required brick facing, but the contractor did not use a strong enough mortar to construct the tunnel lining.

before going through the tunnel. The guard had a special inward-opening door for use in emergencies, though quite how he was supposed to get out if the tunnel was so narrow is unclear!

The line was intended to use locomotives between the inclined planes and was engineered for this. The company's first steam locomotive, *Comet*, and three more, *Phoenix, Samson* and *Goliath*, came from Robert Stephenson & Company, but not before competitive tenders had been requested from two other companies: Rothwell, Hick & Rothwell, of Bolton; and Fenton, Murray & Wood, of Leeds. In the early 1830s a number of new locomotive-manufacturing companies were founded, and existing companies turned their hands to locomotive manufacture; it was to become a growing business.

The stationary engine at Swannington would have a long life: the incline officially closed in 1948, and in 1952 it was moved to the former North Eastern Railway Museum at York, where it is still exhibited in its successor, the National Railway Museum.

The Stanhope & Tyne

The Stanhope & Tyne Railway, opened in 1834, is the most egregious example of a railway built not only to the old standards which were increasingly outdated, but over the most physically and economically barren landscape—a railway that should never have been built. It did, however, provide a lesson.

The original intention of its promoters was to bring limestone quarried at Stanhope to the River Tyne for shipment. The promoters hoped to save money on land acquisition by adopting the tried-and-tested wayleave system, with which landowners in the coalfield area were very familiar. But some eastern landowners saw it as a way to make more money and charged usurious rents. This created an impossible ongoing requirement for rents to be continually paid, even if (as happened) a section was abandoned. And the agreements were only for twenty-one years, with no right of renewal, which, of course, limited the ability to borrow.

The 33¾-mile-long route involved a moorland summit at 1,445 feet, and a 150-foot-deep and 800-foot-wide ravine. It combined all forms of motive power, all mixed up into a horrendously slow transportation cocktail: horses for 10½ miles, locomotives for 9¼ miles, 3 miles of self-acting inclined planes, and 11 miles worked by nine separate stationary engines. At Hownes Gill Ravine were two impossible inclines worked by one engine at the summit; they had gradients of 1 in 3 and 1 in 2½, and required special incline wagons on which regular wagons travelled sideways! This arrangement created a major bottleneck, limiting throughput to a mere twelve wagons per hour. The surprising thing about all this is that it was engineered by none other than Robert Stephenson.

Stephenson made the mistake of accepting payment in the form of shares in the enterprise, which turned out to be a huge liability when the railway became insolvent, for it was not a limited liability company but a group of proprietors—hence the wayleaves, which did not require a parliamentary act—and thus Stephenson, with the other proprietors, could be called on to pay the railway's debts. And Stephenson, known by then to be making a lot of money, was the first person creditors came to. When the line became bankrupt in 1841, it nearly ruined him, and he was only saved by a scheme to use a section of the eastern part of the line as a connector in his father's—and "railway king," promoter George Hudson's—plans for an east coast connection from London to Newcastle. Hudson's last link, his Newcastle & Darlington Junction Railway, in 1844 connected the Durham Junction Railway, opened in 1838, to the Stanhope & Tyne across the River Wear via a new Victoria Bridge, and finally made entrance into Gateshead, opposite Newcastle, via the Brandling Junction Railway, which had been completed in 1839 (map, *below*).

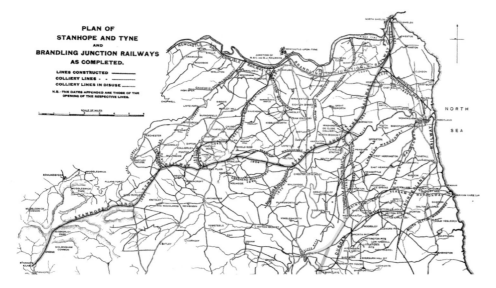

Left.
The Stanhope & Tyne Railway as completed in 1834 traversed over 33 miles of hilly country to get from Stanhope (at left) to the Tyne at South Shields (top right). It is shown here highlighted in red. George Hudson's connections in 1844 included new track, north from Darlington (blue) to the Durham Junction Railway (green), and the Brandling Junction Railway (yellow). By that time the eastern part of the Stanhope & Tyne had become part of a line called the Pontop & South Shields Railway.

Below.
In 1846 the short section of line across the *Victoria Bridge*, spanning the River Wear just below Chester-le-Street, connected George Hudson's Newcastle & Darlington Junction Railway to Gateshead using the Durham Junction Railway (south of the river) and the *Pontop and South Shields Railway*, built in 1834 as part of the Stanhope & Tyne, which in turn connected to the Brandling Junction Railway (see map, *previous page*). It was now possible to travel by train from London to Gateshead. A section of an economically unviable railway that should never have been built was turned into part of a major main line, albeit one that was soon diverted to a more straightforward route.

Above, top.
The other stationary engine that is preserved at the National Railway Museum is the Weatherhill Engine from the highest part of the Stanhope & Tyne Railway. A traditional vertical engine, it hauled wagons up the Weatherhill Incline, over a mile long with a gradient of 1 in 13, at an elevation of over 1,400 feet. The rather bleak-looking incline is shown in the photo, *above.*

And a Few More . . .

In much the same way as the Leicester & Swannington had been designed to transport coal from the West Leicestershire coalfield to the market in Leicester, so the Bristol & Gloucestershire Railway was intended to bring coal from a coalfield to the north of that city. Authorized in 1828, it was completed in 1835. A branch, the Avon & Gloucestershire Railway, authorized at the same time, was completed in 1832 to bring the same coal to the Kennet & Avon Canal system, by which it could be taken to London. The Somerset Coal Canal Railway had already tried the same thing thirty years before (see page 62).

The Whitby & Pickering Railway, authorized in 1833 and completed in 1836, was an attempt to stem the decline in trade suffered by the port of Whitby by opening up its hinterland and, specifically, connecting with the fertile Vale of Pickering. This line is preserved today as a heritage steam railway—the North Yorkshire Moors Railway.

And finally the Bodmin & Wadebridge Railway, opened in 1834, should be mentioned. This line was intended to bring sea sand inland from the head of navigation at Wadebridge to improve agricultural land; it also served quarries at Wenfordbridge. A unique set of original passenger carriages, first plus second, second only, and third class, are preserved at the National Railway Museum in York. The railway was unconnected with others until 1887.

Right, top.
Both the Bristol & Gloucestershire and Avon & Gloucestershire railways are shown on this 1830 map reflecting lines authorized. Bristol is at bottom left.

Right, centre.
The route of the Whitby & Pickering Railway (the black line) is more winding than the turnpike road, shown in red, since it follows the river valleys. This is now the route of the popular heritage North Yorkshire Moors Railway.

Right, centre bottom.
The route of the isolated Bodmin & Wadebridge Railway at its opening in 1834.

Below, bottom.
The ceremonial opening train of the Bodmin & Wadebridge Railway, 30 September 1834. It carried some three hundred guests and was hauled by a locomotive named *Camel*.

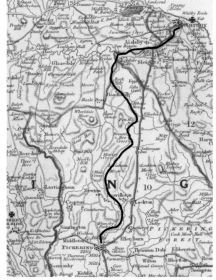

Left.
Interior of a second-class compartment in a combined first- and second-class carriage on the Bodmin & Wadebridge, and an all-second-class carriage (*far left*).

Beginnings of a Network

It was only natural that once investors and promoters saw the success that was the Liverpool & Manchester Railway, they would come up with their own ideas for similar ventures. Indeed, long before that, in the applications for a parliamentary act in 1825—the first railway "mania"—a large number of schemes were advanced, and the *Monthly Repository of Theology and General Literature,* hardly on theme, felt the need to list them along with the warning that the majority were "chimerical." There were 251 in total, 48 of them for railways. Others included 9 ship canals, 41 gas companies, waterworks, mining companies, agricultural improvement companies, and insurance companies all vying for the same investors to raise money. Then, in 1825, the economy faltered. In this environment the wonder is that any got off the ground, but some did, and they included some we have already reviewed, such as the Stockton & Darlington (but the third bill was 1824 and a fourth 1828), the Cromford & High Peak, and the Canterbury & Whitstable.

Another was the Bolton & Leigh, the first of the lines that would form branches to the Liverpool & Manchester itself (map, *right*). This line, originally named the Bolton & West Leigh and on which the Stephenson locomotive *Lancashire Witch* ran, was completed in 1828, even before the Liverpool & Manchester, and another line, the 2½-mile Kenyon & Leigh Junction Railway, connected it to the main line. The first through passenger train, engine *Union* with coaches *Elephant* and *Castle,* arrived in Liverpool on 13 June 1831. It was the first connection of railways, the precursor of a vast network. The other branches to the Liverpool & Manchester are shown on the map (*right*) and are listed in the caption.

(Continued on page 210.)

Right.
Although dated 1829, this base map of the Liverpool & Manchester has had later branches added to it. From Bolton is the Bolton & Leigh and its connector Kenyon & Leigh Junction, engineered by Robert Stephenson. He was also responsible for the Warrington & Newton Railway, from Warrington and beyond, southwards; it was completed in 1831 and was destined to become part of the *Grand Junction Railway,* as labelled here. The *St. Helens and Runcorn Gap Railway* was completed in 1833, and the *North Union Railway,* to Wigan, was a railway created in 1834 by the merger of two before it: the Wigan Branch of 1830 and the incomplete Wigan & Preston Junction Railway; it was the first railway company to be created as a result of a merger, and the full line opened in 1838. There would be many more mergers in the years to come. The *Manchester Bolton and Bury Railway* was built in 1838 as the Manchester & Bolton Railway by the Manchester, Bolton & Bury Canal Navigation & Railway Company. The line was built following the arms of a canal. The *Clifton Branch Railway* was conceived by the Liverpool & Manchester in 1845 as a spoiler to a rival proposal for a line from Liverpool to Bury. But both gained parliamentary approval. The Clifton Branch was completed in 1850. Most of the railways here, including the Liverpool & Manchester itself, were amalgamated in 1846 as the London & North Western Railway, the first railway behemoth of its day.

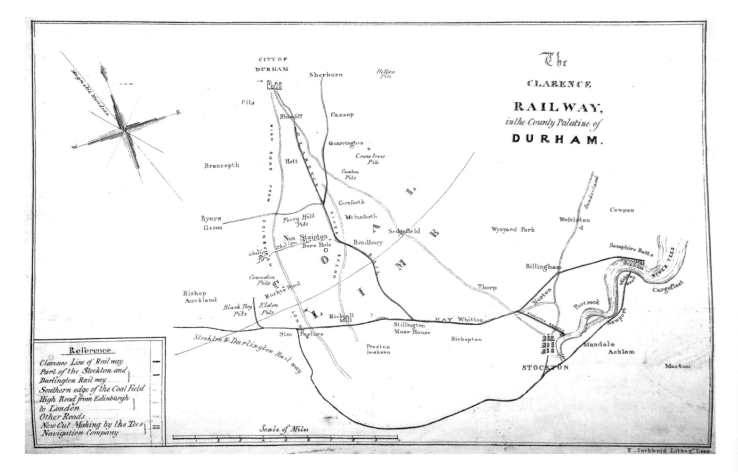

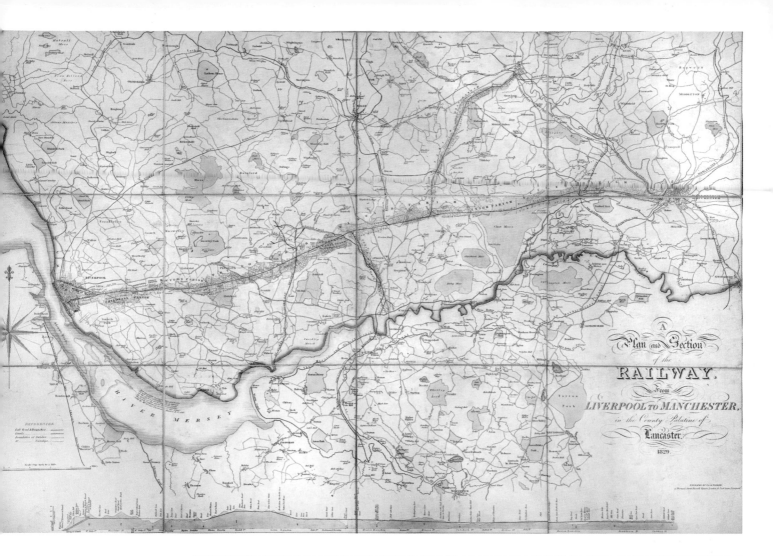

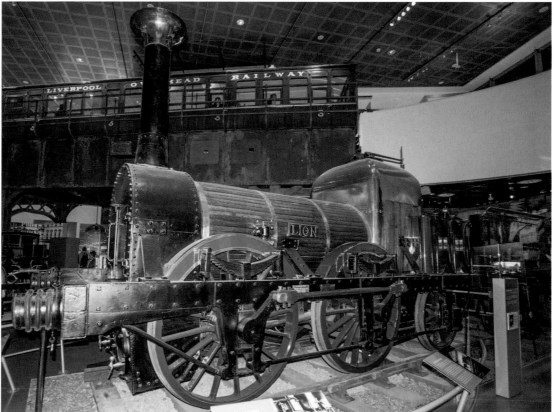

Left.
The Stockton & Darlington had a competitor early in its existence—the Clarence Railway, promoted by Christopher Tennant, who in 1817 had a survey done for a canal that would have competed with the railway (see page 151). The Clarence Railway connected with the Stockton & Darlington at *Sim Pasture* and from there provided an alternative to a shipping point on the River Tees downstream of *Stockton*, which was one of the reasons the Stockton & Darlington extended its line to what would become Middlesbrough in 1830 (see page 167). Those bypassed always wanted to be connected, which is why rail networks were born.

Right. The Liverpool & Manchester 1837 locomotive *Lion* in the Museum of Liverpool. Note the Liverpool Overhead Railway above, an early multiple-unit electric train.

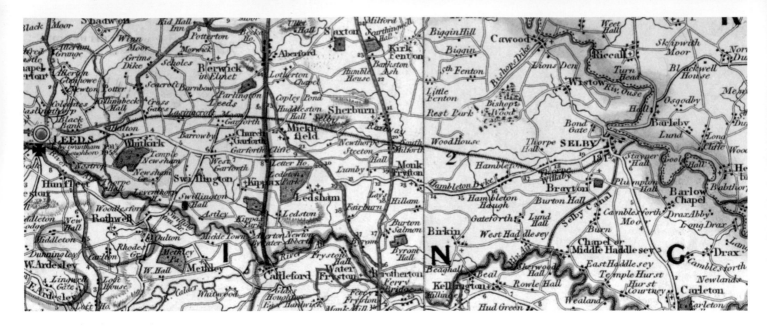

Above.

Reliable communication with the North Sea had long been desired by the merchants of the industrial city of Leeds. In 1814 there was a suggestion, in the *Leeds Mercury* newspaper, for a railway along the lines of John Blenkinsop's rack "Patent Steam Carriage" railway, which had been successfully operating in the city for two years (see page 114). The Leeds & Selby Railway was an early long-distance line authorized in 1830 and completed in 1834. The Leeds & Hull Railroad Company had been formed in 1824—representatives had been present at the opening of the Stockton & Darlington—and had appointed George Stephenson engineer; the line had been surveyed by his assistant, Joseph Locke. It was to be a double-tracked line, more or less level except for three inclined planes at *Leeds*. Like many projected railways at that time, the project was shelved, but revived in 1829 as a line just as far as *Selby*, which was linked by the *Selby Canal* to navigable water on the *River Ouse*. The canal had been completed in 1778 to avoid the difficult lower reaches of the *River Air* (Aire). Scottish engineer James Walker was appointed to resurvey the route, and the line received an enabling act the following year. There was little opposition because most of the route followed land owned by shareholders in the venture. Walker's plan removed the inclined planes, replacing them with cuttings and a tunnel through Richmond Hill in Leeds, shown on the map, *right, top*. The tunnel had a reputation for nearly asphyxiating passengers. Interestingly, when the inaugural train left Leeds early in the morning of 22 September 1834, a train of ten carriages slipped approaching the tunnel—where one of Stephenson's recommended inclines was to have originally been—and was reduced to walking pace. An extension of the line to Hull was completed in 1840, and the line continued to be joined to others, becoming an important link in the railway network right up to the present time.

Right, top.

This 1831 map shows the approved entrance of the Leeds & Selby Railway into Leeds, via a *Tunnel* through *Richmond Hill*. The notoriously smoky tunnel was converted to a cutting in 1893. The station location is shown in red. Today the line continues west to the main Leeds Station.

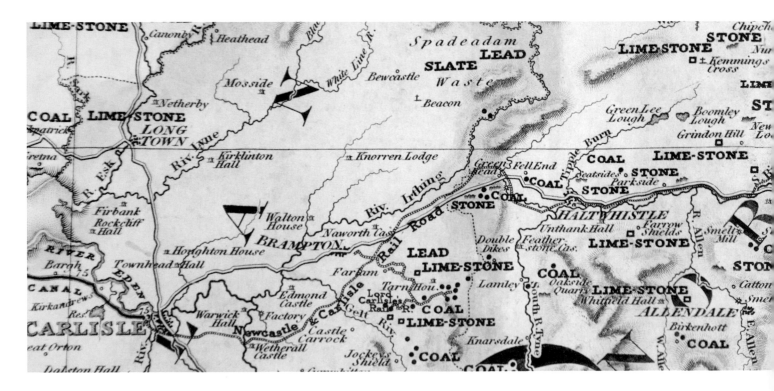

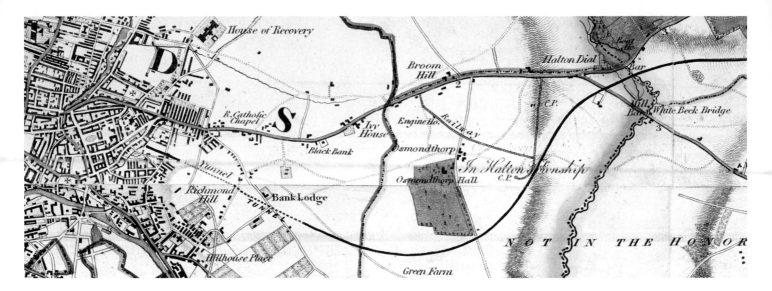

Below.

A transportation outlet to the Irish Sea, across England, was a long-held dream of many Newcastle businessmen. In 1797 a proposal for a canal prepared by William Chapman, the engineer who would later design steam locomotives (see page 124), had got as far as a third reading in Parliament before being turned down. A plateway following the planned canal alignment was discussed in 1805. Like the canal, it was opposed by landowners. In 1823 a canal from the Solway Firth to Carlisle was completed, and Chapman prepared an estimate of extending it to Newcastle, finding that a canal would cost nearly four times as much as a railway. In 1825 Chapman surveyed a route for a railway, to be used for an application for an enabling act, which was checked by Josias Jessop, who had recently completed the survey for the similar Cromford & High Peak Railway (see page 203). The route was also reviewed with Benjamin Thompson, advocate and patentee of a reciprocating stationary-engine system, and engineer of the longest rope-worked line, the Brunton & Shields Railway (see page 103). George Stephenson, who had Joseph Locke surveying an alternative route on the north bank of the Tyne (it is unclear why), found many errors in the survey. The final plan, deposited in November 1825, bore only Thompson's signature. It hardly mattered, as the bill was withdrawn in February 1826 after the defects became known. A complete revision and resurvey followed, in which the requirements for both stationary engines (and locomotives) were removed

in favour of a horse-drawn line, seemingly to placate irate landowners, whose estates had been assiduously avoided as much as possible in any case. The new survey was used in a presentation to Parliament in May 1829, and, despite Stephenson's continuing claim of a cheaper route, the Newcastle & Carlisle Railway received its act. Thompson's survey, however, had been questioned on many points, and the company turned to another engineer, Francis Giles, to report and improve upon Thompson's survey, and he was then appointed chief engineer. Giles was thorough but very slow and was supervised by two separate company committees, one for each end of the line, and the first part of the line was not opened until March 1835. The company had, however, rethought its decision about using horses and ordered three locomotives—no doubt encouraged by their successful use elsewhere—and two were used to pull an inaugural train over the completed section from Blaydon to Hexham on 9 March 1835. A local landowner, Charles Bacon Grey, was upset at the use of locomotives and applied for an injunction against them, which was granted. It took another application to Parliament for an act allowing steam locomotive use, which was granted on 17 June 1835, before the locomotives could be used again. Construction continued on the rest of the line, and the first train from Newcastle through to Carlisle ran on 15 June 1838. The map shows the *Newcastle & Carlisle Railroad.*

From then on, railways would be thought of more as a means of long-distance travel rather than just connecting a mine and a market; the dozens of railways already with authorizing acts or merely still in promoters' minds came rushing forth after Stephenson's locomotives had shown what they could do at the Rainhill Trials. Wrought-iron rails had proved up to the task. The lesson of the magnificently successful Liverpool & Manchester showed how the power of the new steam locomotive could be used to produce a fine return on investment, not to mention a huge boost for the towns and economies connected, now in minutes rather than days or weeks. The technological and social environment had together reached the point that railways as we know them were truly viable. Ever longer lines were projected, with the ultimate goal of connecting northern towns with the capital now being within reach.

And the new situation required a new breed of railway engineer. In 1823, when the firm of Robert Stephenson & Company was created by the Stephensons, Michael Longridge, and Edward Pease to build locomotives in the absence of anyone else to do it, another company, George Stephenson & Company, had also been set up to provide the know-how to build railways. George had gathered around him apprentices and trainees who had quickly become experts in railway building—arguably more so than George himself, given his poor performance in support of the application to Parliament for the Liverpool & Manchester. Now, engineers from that breeding ground, such as Joseph Locke, John Dixon, William Allcard, Thomas Gooch and, indeed, Robert Stephenson, were ready to become railway engineers on their own accounts. They had worked on the Stockton & Darlington, the Canterbury & Whitstable, and the Liverpool & Manchester and had built up their expertise to the point where they could engineer a line on their own. George Stephenson, predictably, did not like this and fought to retain control. This came to a head in 1833, when Joseph Locke, his best engineer, became directly in competition with George for the position of chief engineer for the Grand Junction Railway.

All of Stephenson's protégés continued to use the "standard" gauge that he had established—it made sense to build to the same gauge lines that would likely be connected, after all. One engineer was to flout that standard, however. Not from the Stephenson stable at all, this was Isambard Kingdom Brunel, who would prefer a much wider gauge for stability at higher speeds and would build the long Great Western Railway from London to Bristol and beyond using it. It would not be until 1892 that the necessity for standardization would result in all of Brunel's lines being converted to Stephenson's gauge.

Nascent railways in the 1830s wanted George Stephenson's name to be associated with their project, despite his known engineering deficiencies, because of one thing—it attracted investment. He was now famous for the successful Liverpool & Manchester, despite the fact that it had not used his surveyed route.

Rough surveys had been made for railways connecting London to Birmingham and Liverpool in 1825, but investment was not forthcoming at that time. The Warrington & Newton Railway, completed in 1831, ran south from the Liverpool & Manchester and was intended to be extended farther south. Robert Stephenson had been requested to survey a route from Warrington to Sandbach, in Cheshire, 18 miles to the south, in 1829, but that route upset the Marquess of Stafford (now a major Liverpool & Manchester shareholder) and was not used. Joseph Locke, still under George Stephenson's direction, surveyed an alternative route south that went west of Sandbach and was acceptable. This route passed Crewe, where the railway would set up its major works later in the decade.

There were rival schemes directly from Liverpool, but they were deemed too expensive, and it was Locke's route that was submitted to Parliament, and an enabling act for the 78-mile-long Grand Junction Railway was obtained on 6 May 1833—an act that, interestingly, but for unknown reasons, forbade a parson from sitting on the company's board!

Locke now hoped to be appointed chief engineer to the Grand Junction Railway, for his contract with George Stephenson & Company had expired. Stephenson opposed this to the extent that Locke withdrew, but the board wanted both him and Stephenson to be involved, so they offered the northern section of the line to Locke and the southern part to Stephenson. Both accepted, though Stephenson only reluctantly. Locke, realizing that this could make or break his reputation, determined to do an excellent job and produced detailed cost estimates that were all let out—in 10 mile sections—at almost exactly what he had calculated. Locke had finished this job, while Stephenson, seemingly making the same mistakes he had originally with the Liverpool & Manchester—using untrained or incompetent assistants—had only let one contract; potential contractors found his specifications difficult to understand. The railway's board suggested that perhaps both Locke and Stephenson could work together, but this clearly would not work, and Stephenson withdrew; in August 1835 Joseph Locke became chief engineer for the entire line.

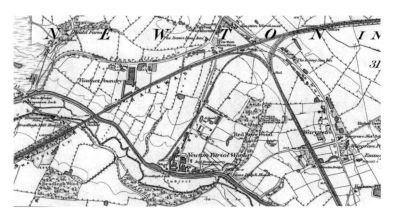

Left.
This map, surveyed in 1847, shows the Liverpool & Manchester Railway with the Grand Junction Railway's junction at *Newton*. The Warrington & Newton Railway, as the branch was first built, was absorbed by the Grand Junction in 1835.

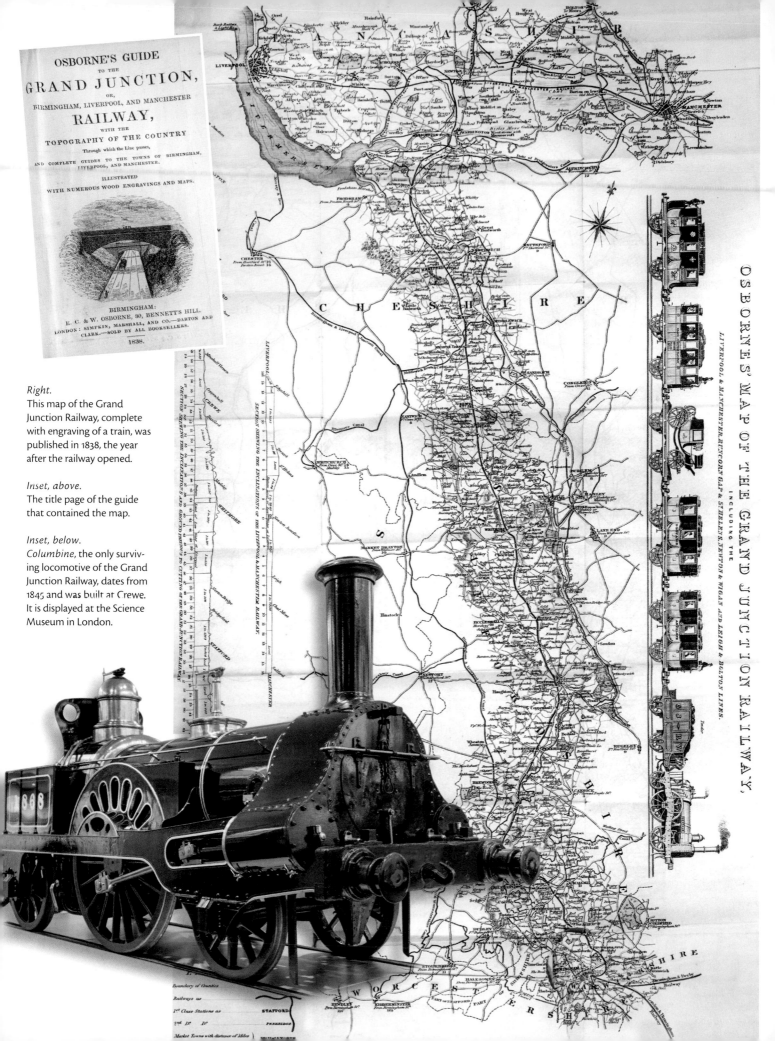

Right.
This map of the Grand Junction Railway, complete with engraving of a train, was published in 1838, the year after the railway opened.

Inset, above.
The title page of the guide that contained the map.

Inset, below.
Columbine, the only surviving locomotive of the Grand Junction Railway, dates from 1845 and was built at Crewe. It is displayed at the Science Museum in London.

OSBORNE'S MAP OF THE GRAND JUNCTION RAILWAY,
INCLUDING THE
LIVERPOOL & MANCHESTER, RUNCORN GAP & ST HELENS, NEWTON & WIGAN AND LEIGH & BOLTON LINES.

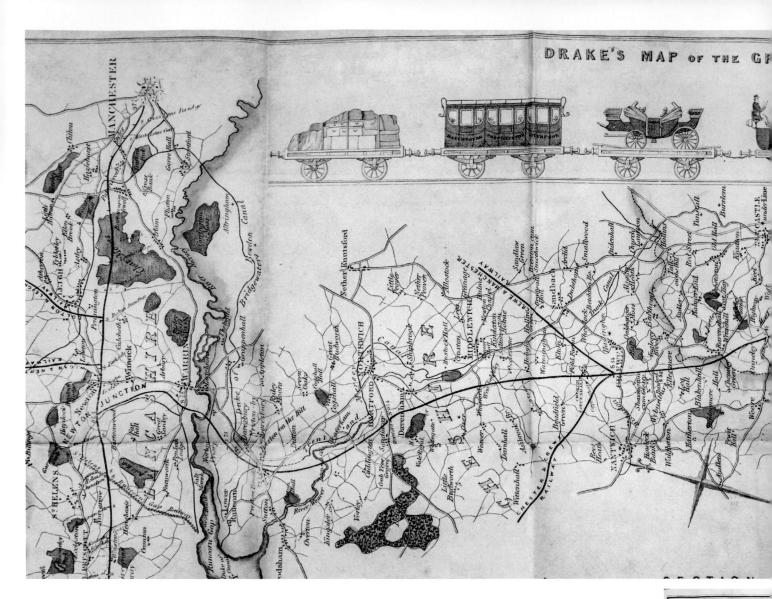

DRAKE'S MAP of THE GR

Above.
An even more artistic view of the Grand Junction Railway was this map, published by a Birmingham printer, James Drake, in March 1839. It came with a guide to the railway, including a timetable and schedule of fares.

Right.
A map of the London & Birmingham Railway prepared by Robert Stephenson and dated 1835. The *Birmingham & Derby* [Junction] *Railway* and the *Birmingham & Gloucester Railway* are also shown; both were authorized in 1836 and completed in 1839 and 1840, respectively.

The engineering, as it turned out, was not that difficult, and the railway speedily took shape. For one viaduct, the Penkridge Viaduct over the River Penk, the contract was won by a Cheshire land agent and surveyor named Thomas Brassey. He would go on to become the greatest of the railway contractors, often in concert with Locke, building nearly 4,500 miles of railway in all parts of the world, including 1,700 miles in Britain. He would prove to have unique skill in managing large labour forces and was able to inspire loyalty from tough gangs of navvies, as the railway builders would become known.

The Grand Junction was completed in 1837, and the first train, led by the locomotive *Wildfire*—not built by Stephenson—drew into Birmingham on 4 July. It pulled a train with coaches from both Liverpool and Manchester, which had been put together at Newton Junction.

The continuation to London, the London & Birmingham Railway, which had received parliamentary approval at the same time as the Grand Junction, was then still under construction, for here the required engineering was of a higher order and the length of the line, at 112 miles, somewhat longer.

Preliminary surveys of possible routes had been made by both John Rennie and Francis Giles when the idea had first been broached, and groups of investors formed in 1824–25. Rennie's route out of London followed the one eventually used by the Great Western Railway and then north via Oxford and Banbury, whereas Giles's alignment

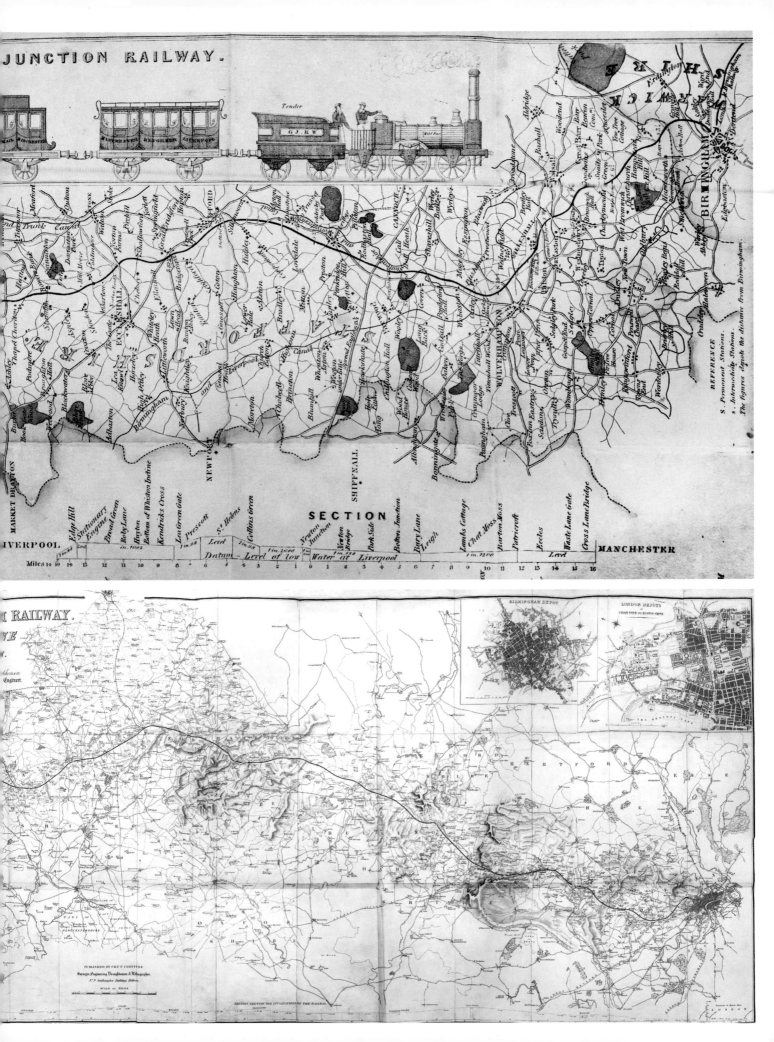

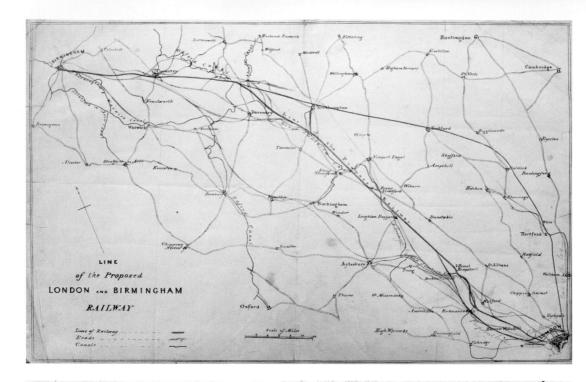

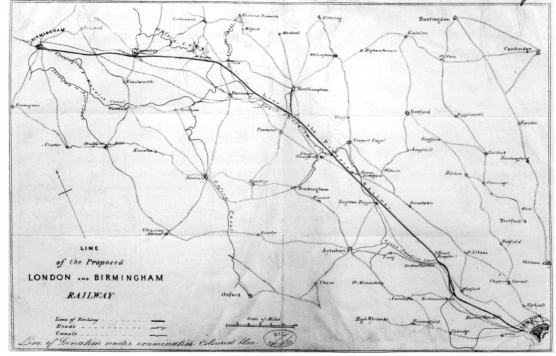

Left and *left, below.* These two maps originally from the British Transport Commission Archives of the proposed line of the London & Birmingham Railway have no date and no other information but appear to have been produced quite early on in the planning process. They do not show earlier surveys for the route by John Rennie (through *Banbury* and *Oxford*) or Francis Giles (though his general routing through *Coventry* and *Rugby* was adopted). Confusingly, the blue lines are not canals but alternative possible routes for the railway. The red lines, marked *Line of the Proposed Railway,* follow the general route of the railway as built but are only approximations of the final line. One notable deviation the final line took was to follow the *Grand Junction Canal* between *Hemel Hempstead* and *Leighton Buzzard,* the alternative blue line on the lower map. At a few places the projected line on both maps follows what was built, such as through Rugby. The *top,* presumed first, map has a veritable spider's web of possible alternative routes into London, some from totally different directions to the one built. The *bottom* map shows (one of the lines in blue) approximately the route that was ultimately followed into *London* at Euston Square.

was through Coventry and Rugby. In 1830 "George Stephenson & Son" obtained the contract for a new survey of the route—the Stephenson name would attract investment—but it was actually carried out by Robert Stephenson, assisted by Thomas Gooch. Unable to complete the survey in time for the 1831 session of Parliament, a second survey was carried out in 1831; it was similar to Giles's route in the north but different in the south. Nearer London, Stephenson and Gooch ran into the same sort of opposition from landowners as had interfered with the surveying of the Liverpool & Manchester, and some clandestine work was required, such as surveying through the lands of a hostile parson on a Sunday morning while he was preaching to his flock.

Nevertheless, the survey was completed, and an application for an enabling act was presented to Parliament in February 1832.

In Parliament opposition was stiff; here was a long-distance railway that would put hundreds of businesses out of a job, from flyboat operators (who carried perishables and travelled faster than larger barges) on the Grand Junction Canal to the entire coaching business from London to the North. Robert Stephenson displayed great competence, in stark contrast to his father's earlier performance with the Liverpool & Manchester. Famously, when challenged that the angles of slope in a cutting through the chalk of the Chiltern Hills was too steep, he and Gooch made an overnight visit to a similar cutting made by Thomas Telford on the Holyhead Road, and, finding the angle identical, returned the next day with the irrefutable evidence.

The bill was passed by the Commons in June 1832, but despite all Stephenson's herculean efforts, it was rejected by the House of Lords the next month. Sir Astley Cooper, one of the landowners through whose land the line was to pass, was outraged: "if this sort of thing be permitted to go on," he said, "you will in a very few years destroy the *Noblesse!*" Nonetheless, Stephenson had made such a good impression that a committee meeting a few days after resolved to look favourably on a new application in the next session of Parliament.

And so it was. The railway company found that it could buy off the opposition by grossly overpaying for land. As Tom Rolt, Stephenson's biographer, wrote, "if the landowners were shown blank cheques the impending destruction of the *noblesse* miraculously ceased to be a matter of concern to them." Some changes to the route were also made to accommodate the opposition. The act was finally granted on 6 May 1833. And Robert Stephenson, alone, was appointed chief engineer on 20 September. George Stephenson's company was gone. At the age of thirty Robert Stephenson was in sole charge of the most ambitious engineering project the world had yet seen.

Contracts were let for each 6-mile length of the line, plus separate contracts for major works such as viaducts and the Kilsby Tunnel, twenty-nine in total. The line was staked out in bad winter weather in November 1833 to February 1834; Stephenson, who very much had a hands-on approach, was out in all weathers. Work began on all the contract sections as they were let.

The 1833 act had stipulated that the London terminus should be short of land owned by Lord Southampton, who had been resolutely opposed to the railway, but Stephenson learned that he had changed his mind based on the success of the Liverpool & Manchester and managed to get the railway extended farther into London, to "a vacant piece of ground in a place called Euston Square." Here, at the foot of a rope-worked inclined plane down from Camden Town, the company had Thomas and William Cubitt build an imposing edifice (map and illustrations, *overleaf*). In fact the inclined plane was later found to be usable by locomotives.

Several tunnels and viaducts were required, and many cuttings in which Stephenson tried to maintain as level a grade as possible. The greatest of these was at Tring, in Hertfordshire, where the railway crossed the Chiltern Hills (map, *above, right*). It was a cutting 2½ miles long and an average of 39 feet deep, and it required the excavation of some 1.4 million cubic yards of material.

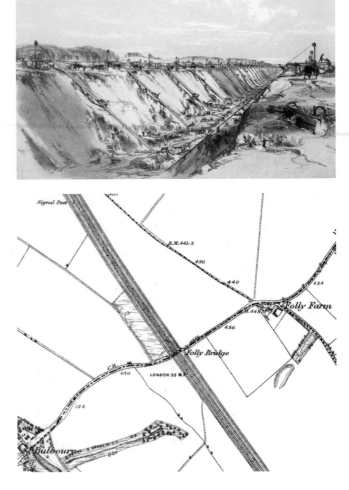

Above.
Tring Cutting, one of the major engineering works on the London & Birmingham. Some 2½ miles long and an average of 39 feet deep, it was excavated by means of horses pulling up wheelbarrows attached to ropes, guided by a navvy, as seen in the engraving by J.C. Bourne (*top*). The map is from 1878 and depicts the cutting with hachures.

Below.
The London & Birmingham Railway from a guide to the line published in 1839 by London mapmaker James Wyld.

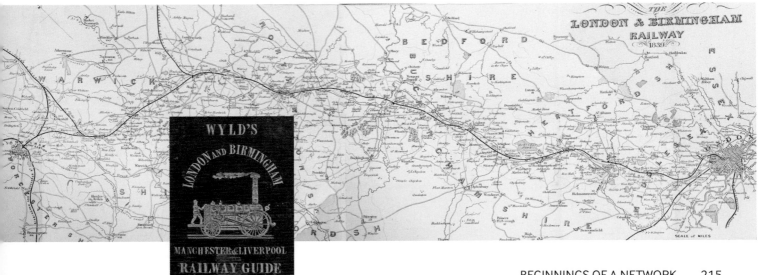

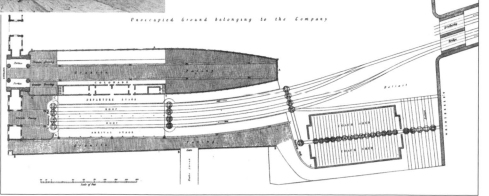

Left.
An enlargement of the detailed inset of the London end of the railway from the 1835 map on *pages 212–13, bottom,* shows the *Railway Comp^ys. Depot* at Euston Square and the line of the railway past the *Railway Comp^ys. Depot* at Camden Town (at top). The lithograph (*above*) by artist John C. Bourne shows a Bury locomotive leaving the depot. The line crosses the *Regents Canal* here. *New Road* is today's Euston Road. The Doric arch at Euston Station (*inset, left*), designed by architect Philip Hardwick, formed a symbolic great gateway to the north and is illustrated here, but is not yet shown on the map.

Below.
A detailed 1838 plan of Euston Station, which does show the Doric arch, marked *Portico* at the *Entrance.* Of interest are the numerous turntables for manhandling coaches between the *Coach Shed* and the station. Although locomotives could pull trains up to Camden Town, the original act stipulated that a stationary engine should be used, and this was the method of operation until 1844.

Left, bottom. A statue of Robert Stephenson presides over the entrance to Euston Station today.

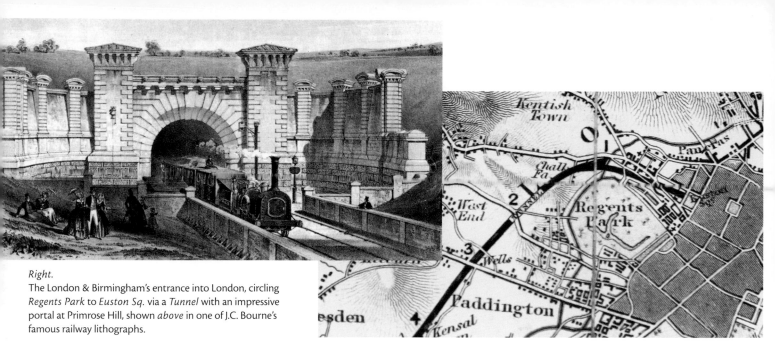

Right.
The London & Birmingham's entrance into London, circling *Regents Park* to *Euston Sq.* via a *Tunnel* with an impressive portal at Primrose Hill, shown *above* in one of J.C. Bourne's famous railway lithographs.

The track was laid—to the Stephenson standard gauge of 4 feet, 8½ inches, of course—using diagonally laid stone blocks, a holdover from earlier practice. By 1837 the line was complete except for the 2,432-yard-long Kilsby Tunnel, in Northamptonshire, and trains were run on the sections on either side of the tunnel, with a coach connection. In the tunnel subterranean quicksand had been encountered. The treacherous conditions had defeated the contractor, and Stephenson took over the work personally. A force of 1,250 navvies and 200 horses working with a battery of thirteen pumping engines, working day and night for nineteen months, drained the ground sufficiently to complete the tunnel, bringing mayhem to the nearby little village of Kilsby. It was not until 21 June 1838 that the tunnel was completed, and with it the entire line of railway from London to Liverpool. On 24 June a train in each direction ran between Birmingham and London; the line was opened for regular scheduled service on 17 September 1838, the official opening date. The railway had cost £5.5 million to build, compared with the originally estimated amount of £2.4 million.

To aid in the construction work, the company had ordered a locomotive from Robert Stephenson & Company, but the appearance of monopoly, highlighted by some of Stephenson's opponents, led the company to appoint someone else, Edward Bury, as locomotive superintendent, and he built most of the locomotives supplied at his own works. He was a believer in small engines, and often several had to be coupled together to pull a train, possible only because Stephenson had managed to make the line so level.

Even before the London & Birmingham was complete, other railways had connected with it. What became the longest section of line rapidly turned into the backbone of a network. In 1846 the railway merged with the Grand Junction Railway (which the year before had merged with the Liverpool & Manchester) and the Manchester & Birmingham Railway (which connected Manchester to a junction at Crewe and opened in 1840) to form the London & North Western Railway (LNWR), the first of the large corporate railway businesses.

Below. The *Tunnel* at *Kilsby* penetrates the *Kilsby Ridge* on this 1835 map. The tunnel was still under construction at that time. One of J.C. Bourne's lithographs (*right*) illustrates a working shaft; workers are being lowered in a basket.

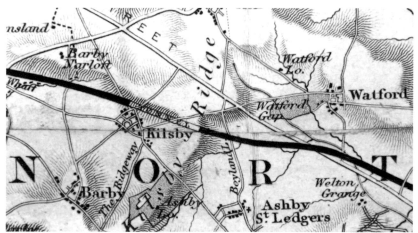

Above.

An 1839 map produced by commercial mapmaker James Wyld shows the length of the Great Western Railway from *London* to *Bristol*, though one could not actual travel the distance by train until 30 June 1841, following the completion of Box Tunnel, between *Chippenham* and *Bath*. The locomotive (*right*) is *North Star*, which pulled the opening train to Maidenhead on 1 June 1838. This engine, a replica containing some parts of the original, is on display at Steam, the Museum of the Great Western Railway, in Swindon.

Left.

A prospectus map from 1833 showing that the line of approach to *London* could be from either the north or south bank of the River Thames. The line from London to Bristol is in red, with the proposed branches to *Glocester* [*sic*] and *Oxford* in yellow. Note also the *Proposed Southampton Railway*, the London & Southampton, which opposed the Great Western's application because its directors also wished to build a branch to Bristol.

Right.

A revised prospectus map from 1835 showing now a single line of approach to *London*, on the north bank of the Thames, and joining with the line of the *Birmingham & London Railway* into the city at Euston, an idea that fell apart because of the difference in the gauges used by the two companies. On both maps the line is shown as eventually reaching Plymouth.

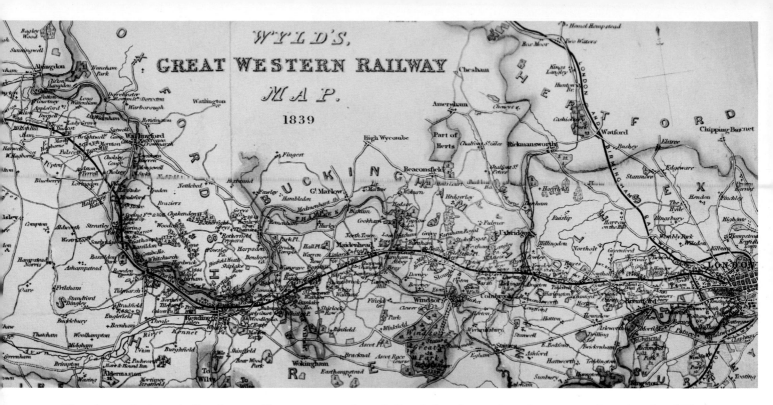

The other major intercity line that would spawn a network of branches was the Great Western Railway. A route for a London & Bristol Railroad Company had been surveyed in 1824 by John Loudon McAdam, better known for his road surfaces, but like many others at that time, its plans were shelved. In 1832 a group of Bristol businessmen drew up plans for a Bristol & London, then the London & Bristol railway. In 1833 they were searching for an engineer, when 27-year-old Isambard Kingdom Brunel applied for the job, insisting that they should build only an excellent railway, not necessarily the cheapest. The group was impressed, and he got the job. Brunel surveyed the route in nine months, initially with William Townshend, builder of the horse-drawn Bristol & Gloucestershire Railway (see page 62), who had also applied for the job but lost out to Brunel.

The application for an act was passed by the House of Commons in March 1834 but then, like the London & Birmingham, thrown out by the House of Lords because of objecting landowners and rival interests who also wanted to build a railway. It took another application and a revised survey of a new, not-quite-as-straight route for the railway to receive its act in August 1835. A prospectus had been issued with the new route in September 1835 (map, *right*), and investment had been forthcoming. The route Brunel chose was north of the Marlborough Downs, rather than a similar route to the Kennet & Avon Canal, to provide easy branches both to Oxford and to Gloucester. And, of course, the line was designed using the 7-foot-wide gauge that was to become his trademark and the first serious challenge to the Stephenson "standard." He

believed that the resultant low centre of gravity, the ability to use larger boilers, and thus more powerful engines, coupled with engineering the line to be as level as possible, would make for the fastest and smoothest of railway rides.

Brunel's level line was not without its problems. A bridge over the Thames at Maidenhead had to be designed to be wide and flat—each arch was 128 feet wide but only 24 feet high—so the directors, believing it incapable of bearing the weight of trains, ordered the wooden formwork left in place. Brunel did leave it but lowered it a few inches so that it was not actually touching the bridge itself. The bridge stands to this day, carrying the main line to Bristol over the river.

Initially the London terminus of the railway was intended to be shared with the London & Birmingham at Euston, but the difference in gauges made this difficult to achieve, and a new

Great Western Railway
Between
BRISTOL AND LONDON
I.K Brunel F.R.S. Engineer

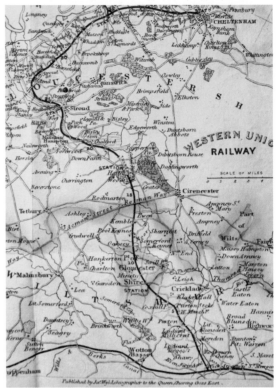

Above.
James Wyld's map of the Cheltenham & Great Western Union Railway, completed in 1841. From its opening it was leased to the Great Western and was amalgamated with it two years later.

Right, top.
Wyld's map of the Bristol & Exeter Railway, authorized in 1836 but not completed as far as Exeter until 1844.

Left.
The broad-gauge locomotive *Firefly* at the Didcot Railway Centre in Oxfordshire, a former Great Western Railway engine stabling point. This locomotive is a beautifully made replica, built in 2005, and runs on a specially constructed mixed-gauge line, seen outside the shed, complete with a broad-gauge passenger coach.

and a new terminus was selected in a vacant field at a place called Paddington. When the present station was built in 1854, the old station became the goods depot and is so marked on the map, *right, centre*.

The first section of the railway, from Paddington to Maidenhead, opened on 4 June 1838, and other sections opened over the next three years as they were completed, notably between Bristol and Bath, on 31 August 1840. The last section to be completed was the one through Box Hill, where a 3,212-yard-long tunnel was required. Work began in September 1836 with the sinking of shafts, from which the tunnel could be dug in either direction. Large numbers of navvies were employed, rising from about 1,500 at the beginning to 4,000 towards the end, as the urgency to complete the line reached a crescendo. As with Kilsby, the nearly villages of Box and Corsham experienced much in the way of drunken melees; one workman is known to have died from drinking too much beer. When the sections of the tunnel finally joined up in the spring of 1841, Brunel's calculations were

found to have been so accurate that the tunnelways were out only an inch and a half. The tunnel, which had a 25-foot-diameter bore to accommodate the wide-gauge trains, was adorned with a fine portico on the western end, where it could be seen. One track was ready on 30 June 1841, and on that day a directors' train made the journey from Paddington to Bristol in four hours.

In 1841 Swindon was selected as the location for a locomotive works, ironically partly because it was on the Wiltshire & Berkshire Canal, which gave it direct access to the Somerset Coalfield. For more than a hundred years locomotives were manufactured, serviced, and scrapped here.

By this date trains could not only run from London to Bristol but also onward as far as Bridgwater, on the Bristol & Exeter Railway, authorized in 1836; it would reach Exeter in 1844. Brunel was also its engineer. A number of other lines soon connected with the Great Western, which absorbed many of them later. But the gauge was always an issue. Gloucester featured in cartoons lampooning the free-for-all that sometimes accompanied the

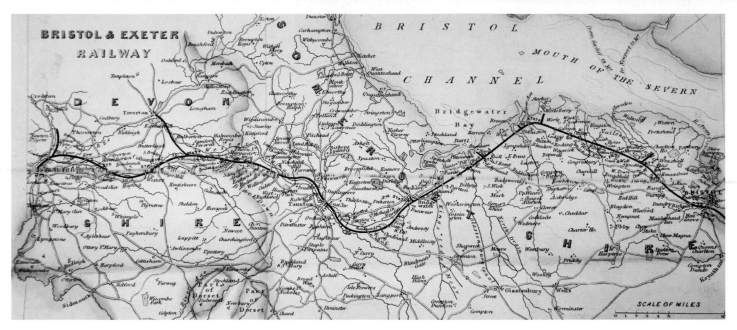

changing of trains there. In 1846 a Parliamentary enquiry determined that although the wide gauge was probably superior to the Stephenson standard, more miles of standard-gauge track had by that time been laid and so mandated that no more broad-gauge lines could be built. The Great Western's broad gauge lasted until 1892, when, over a well-coordinated weekend, all the track was changed over to the standard

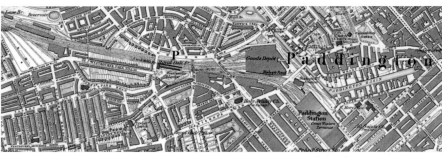

gauge. In the process hundreds of otherwise perfectly serviceable locomotives went to the cutter's torch, as did large numbers of coaches. Stephenson no doubt would have smiled had he lived to see it.

Above, right, centre.
The Great Western Railway's Paddington Station, shown on an 1866 map. The original station, opened in 1838, is the building marked *Goods Depot*.

Right, centre.
The western portal of the Box Tunnel, nearly 2 miles long through Box Hill, an outlier of the Cotswold Hills. Note the early Great Western Railway signal and railway policeman controlling access to the tunnel. This is a lithograph by J.C. Bourne.

Right.
Replica of the broad-gauge locomotive *Iron Duke*, at the National Railway Museum, York. It is a working locomotive, made in 1985 for the 150th anniversary of the Great Western Railway. The Iron Duke class was built between 1846 and 1855 for express passenger use and could achieve speeds of 80 miles per hour. This "Flying Dutchman" service was for several decades the world's fastest train. Save one, a small dock shunting locomotive named *Tiny*, no original broad-gauge locomotives survived, probably because of the lack of rails to run them on. *Tiny* survived because it was a small vertical-boilered engine and was used to power machinery after its railway use ended.

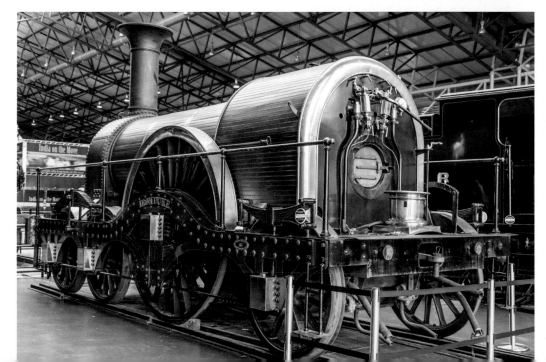

As the enthusiasm for railway gathered steam, so to speak, many schemes were put forward, ranging from the legitimate to the downright fraudulent. Two "manias" occurred, when applications for railway acts got somewhat out of hand. The first, a relatively minor one, was in 1836–37, when fifty new lines totalling about 1,600 miles obtained enabling acts. Potential shareholders were only required to put up a deposit of 5 per cent. With the second railway mania, from 1844 to 1846, things really went off the rails; in 1846 alone some 4,540 miles of new lines received authorization. The satirical magazine *Punch* in 1845 published a prospectus for a "Great North Pole Railway. Capital, two hundred millions, Deposit, threepence." But this was a bubble.

Above, left.
A cartoonist depicts the 1836 railway mania with all manner of maps of legitimate proposals, such as the competing Rennies' and Robert Stephenson's London-to-Brighton lines, being presented to John Bull, along with absurd proposals such as "tunnel to the East Indies direct" and "steam communication with the moon."

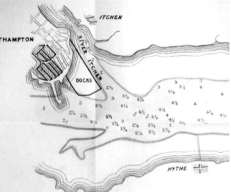

Left and *above.*
The London & Southampton Railway was the first realization of William James's ideas for a railway from London to the South Coast. It was authorized in 1833 and completed in 1840. The company's directors opposed the Great Western's proposals because they wished to build a branch to Bristol themselves. The railways would transform countless towns and cities. One was Southampton, where the London & South Western Railway (previously the London & Southampton Railway) would serve docks for ocean liners. Both of these maps come from an 1839 companion to the railway. The blue line is a "short cut," as built.

Many lines that would never be viable had been authorized. The bubble burst, as they always do. Railway shares halved in value between 1846 and 1849, and by 1849 only 17 miles received acts.

Nevertheless, there were by then enough good projects to create a formidable network. By 1850 most of the country had been covered, though the railway network would not reach its peak mileage until about 1920. In the meantime, railways had completely changed the social fabric of the country, bringing such things as fresh milk and eggs from the countryside into the big cities, or allowing those living inland to taste fresh fish for the first time, and introducing the concept of commuting (see page 226). The maps on the next two pages show the whole railway network of Britain at two dates in the 1840s.

Above.
Railways entering London are shown on this 1840 map. The first, from the northwest, was the London & Birmingham. From the northeast, with two lines forming a junction at *Stratford*, is the Eastern Counties Railway, opened in 1839. From the west is the Great Western; the Paddington-to-Maidenhead section opened in 1838. The *Southampton Rʸ* (London & Southampton) leaves from a terminus at Nine Elms, near the Vauxhall Bridge; this section opened in 1838. The *Brighton Railway* (the London & Croydon, completed in 1839) is shown going southwards from a junction with the London & Greenwich Railway, London's first commuter line.

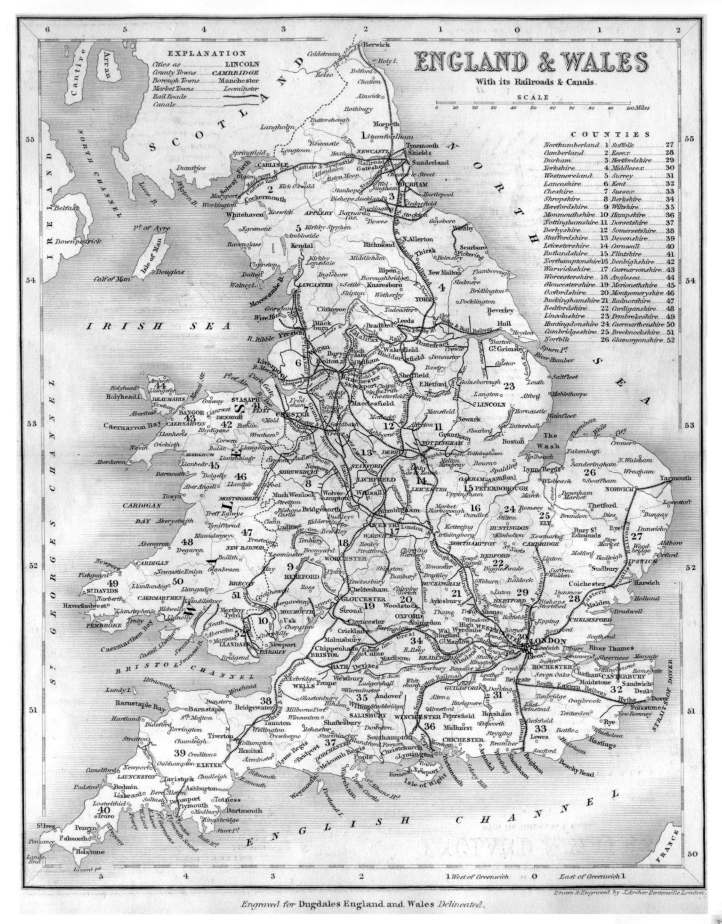

Above.

This is the British railway network at about 1844, just before the second railway mania. It is interesting to compare it with the network in 1847, just three years later, shown on the map at *right.*

Below.

This map was published in 1847. The lines authorized at the height of the second railway mania in 1846 are shown as red lines. Black lines are completed railways, dashed lines under construction (at the beginning of 1847). Particularly dense railway networks now occupy the Midlands and the smaller area around *Durham*, while in the South, where the main traffic would be passengers, the railway network is still much lighter. The South Eastern Railway reaches *Dover*, albeit by a rather roundabout route that would soon be challenged by a competitor, the London, Chatham & Dover Railway. The *London & Brighton Railway* reached *Brighton* in 1841 and with four other companies became part of the larger London, Brighton & South Coast Railway (LBSCR) in 1846. The London & Southampton has been renamed the [London &] *South Western Railway*, and as such would expand westwards, challenging the *Great Western*. The London & North Western Railway is not yet shown despite being created in 1846 as a merger of the *London & Birmingham, Grand Junction*, and *Manchester & Birmingham* (which had already absorbed the *Liverpool & Manchester* the year before).

The First Commuter Railway

The first railways having been used exclusively for freight, it took a while for the idea of transporting passengers, by a method many considered dangerous, to catch on. Once the Liverpool & Manchester Railway had demonstrated the demand for faster travel—and its safety—many schemes were advanced for passenger railways. One, which became London's first railway and the world's first commuter railway, was the London & Greenwich.

A railway connecting the capital to the English Channel and boats for France had been promoted in 1824 as the Kentish Railway, and employed the great canal engineer Thomas Telford at first, but this was not enough to attract the required capital, and in 1825 Telford was discovered to have been advising canal proprietors how to counteract the threat of the railways and had withdrawn from the Kentish Railway scheme. In late 1825 he was succeeded as engineer to the Kentish Railway by none other than Henry Palmer, better known for his invention of an early monorail. The grand plan nevertheless died in 1826 for want of financial backers.

It was in reference to the Kentish Railway scheme that an anonymous anti-railway writer in the *Quarterly Review* for March 1825 penned oft-quoted lines "we should as soon expect the people of Woolwich to suffer themselves to be fired off upon one of Congreve's richochet rockets [the same of "the rocket's red glare" in the American national anthem] as to trust themselves to the mercy of such a machine [a steam locomotive] going at such a rate . . ." It is this quote that is said to have led Robert Stephenson to name his 1829 locomotive *Rocket*.

The notion of a line from London to the South Coast made sense, and the London & Greenwich Railway was conceived as the first section of such a line. This time it was the brainchild of a retired military engineer, George Landmann, who had built fortifications in Canada, Gibraltar and Spain and early in his career had travelled by canoe on the Great Lakes with the explorer Alexander Mackenzie. Landmann had established himself as an independent civil engineer, and in 1831, hot on the heels of the success of the Liverpool & Manchester, he interested several other businessmen in his railway scheme, and a company was created.

Below.
The map of the London & Greenwich line issued with the prospectus for potential investors in 1832. *Corbets Lane,* the location of the later junction with the London & Croydon Railway, is shown at midpoint.

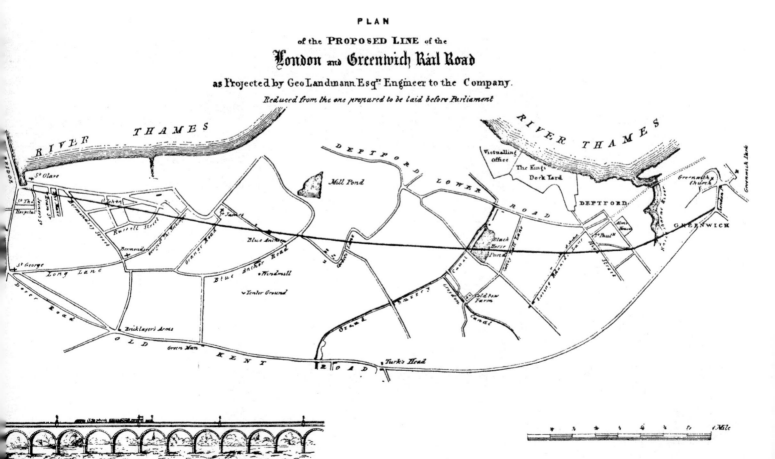

GREENWICH RAILWAY.

Above.
An engraving dated 1837 shows the London & Greenwich Railway in operation, with the view towards London. The locomotives were not turned, running forwards towards London and reversed away, as shown here. One feels the illustrator here had not seen many loco-motives, given his rather strange depiction of the engine's wheels.

Below.
A map from 1836, showing the line of the *London & Greenwich Railway* together with a copycat *Westminster & Deptford Railway*. The latter also proposed an elevated railway and intended to make the interiors of its arches into a shopping arcade, with stores on either side. The London and Croydon and Dover railways leave the line near *Corbetts Lane*. The London & Greenwich Railway is shown extended westwards to *Westminster Bridge*.

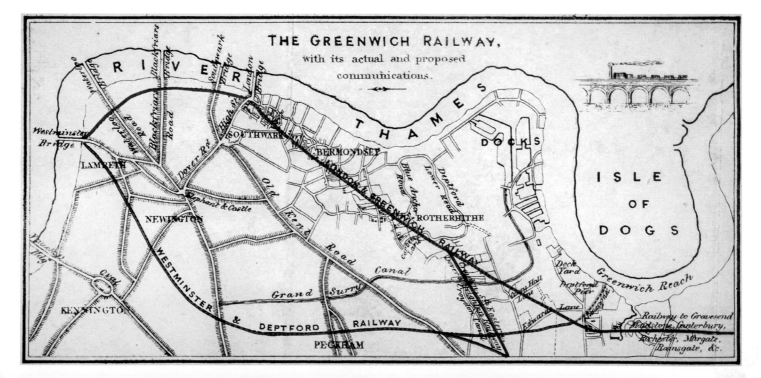

John Rennie's new London Bridge had been opened in August 1831, and Landmann's plan was to begin his railway at that location, proceed straight to Deptford, with its naval yard, and then curve slightly to terminate in Greenwich. Both Deptford and Greenwich were totally separate from London at the time, with a combined population of about 45,000. However, it was intended from the beginning to extend the line both deeper into London (as shown on the map, *previous page*) and extend it beyond Greenwich.

It was easier to plan the line on paper, however, than on the ground, for the first part of the line from London Bridge was a densely populated area of squalor, with tightly packed old buildings, little in the way of sanitation, and frequent outbreaks of cholera. Building the railway was to be an exercise in slum clearance, one that many other railways originating in London would follow. The line of the railway crossed many streets, and for this reason Landmann planned to build the railway on a long viaduct, essentially a continuous bridge across all the roads. The line would descend to ground level via an inclined plane just before reaching Deptford.

The construction of the viaduct was a massive project for its day. It was 3½ miles long and consisted of 878 arches, all about 22 feet high, and the structure contains about 60 million bricks. The original intention was to rent the arches for use as dwellings as another source of revenue, but it was soon discovered that the brickwork leaked and the arches proved suitable only for storage, a use that continues to this day.

The railway received its charter in 1833 and was opened between Deptford and a temporary station at Spa Road in February 1836 (a bridge in Bermondsey still being unfinished), and for its full length in December that year. London's first railway was conceived and built to carry passengers only and was the first such railway to be planned this way. Small platforms on the carriages intended for small freight items soon gave way to more space for passengers. Although only 4 miles long, it dramatically demonstrated how a railway was more efficient as a people mover than the crowded turnpike, which ran on a parallel route. In the railway's first year of operation it carried nearly 1.5 million passengers, not including season ticket holders, and could handle 25,000 passengers in a single day.

Extension of the line was not long in coming, with other railways joining farther out of London to use the London & Greenwich viaduct through the more densely populated area. The London & Croydon Railway was authorized in 1835 and opened in 1839 from Corbett's Lane Junction to Croydon. The London & Brighton Railway, with a sharing agreement from the London & Dover Railway, later the South Eastern Railway, was

Below. A modern view of the London & Greenwich viaduct shows the arches used by businesses and for storage, just as it has been almost since it was built. This is the view looking towards London, with the ultra-modern landmark of the ninety-five-storey Shard, opened in 2013, towering above London Bridge Station.

Right.
This painting, created in 1836, the year the railway opened, shows the viaduct crossing the Grand Surrey Canal. The horses seem to be taking a rest after towing the barge under the viaduct. The view gives a good idea of the fact that the viaduct was a major piece of engineering work.

Right, centre top.
This map, published in 1836 by the Society for the Diffusion of Useful Knowledge, shows the pioneering *Greenwich Rail Road* as initially built, in its opening year, with no connections.

Right, centre bottom.
A map of the *Greenwich Terminus* in 1867. The line was not extended directly beyond Greenwich until 1877, as extensions to the South Coast branched off the line farther north.

Right, bottom.
This engraving, titled *Bird's Eye View of the London and Greenwich Railway*, appeared in a newspaper called the *Mirror of Literature, Amusement, and Instruction* in December 1836, a few days after the railway had opened along its entire length. Considerable artistic licence has been taken, since the viaduct is straight, not curved as depicted.

authorized to build south from a junction with the London & Croydon at Norwood in 1837, reaching Dover in 1844. The South Eastern Railway took over the London & Greenwich in 1845 as part of this line to the South Coast, much the same as the route initially intended by Landmann. The London & Brighton line became part of the London, Brighton & South Coast Railway (LBSCR) in 1846.

Other than the viaduct, which was widened several times as other railways joined the London & Greenwich line for the last stretch into London, not much remains. None of the railway's locomotives were preserved as such, but there is an interesting sequel to this story. In 1845, when Sir John Franklin's ill-fated Arctic expedition was being fitted out, his two ships, *Erebus* and *Terror*, had small steam engines installed, to turn a propeller as a supplement to the main sails. The engine for the *Erebus* came from London & Greenwich No. 4 *Twells* (named in 1836 after board member John Twells); the one for *Terror* came from a London & Birmingham locomotive. In 2013 *Erebus* was rediscovered beneath the Arctic ice of Victoria Strait in what is now Canada (and *Terror* was discovered in 2016). So it seems likely that a part, at least, of a London & Greenwich locomotive still exists!

Transfer of Technology

Railways came together as a viable new and exciting technology in the late 1820s in England, but it was not only English engineers and investors who immediately saw the opportunities it brought with it. The railway—or the railroad, as it would be called in North America—was, after all, a revolutionary concept for its time and promised to open up the world. The opening of the Stockton & Darlington in 1825 had acted like a pre-announcement of the great event, and engineers from other European countries and the United States came to look at it, but at the same time the Liverpool & Manchester was struggling through the parliamentary approval process and was again watched around the globe.

Thus we have the arrival in 1825 of William Strickland (whose detailed and artistic drawings are shown elsewhere in this book—see *pages 94–95, 112, 114,* and *128–29*), sent by the Pennsylvania Society for the Promotion of Internal Improvements, whose instructions told him that he would arrive "at a peculiarly fortunate era in the construction and employment of railways." That same year the German engineers Karl von Oeynhausen and Heinrich von Dechen began documenting many English lines, both steam and horse worked (see page 178). In 1828 the newly created Baltimore & Ohio Rail Road Company sent three of their engineers to Britain "for the purpose of gaining information relative to the most approved construction of Rail-roads . . . and the application of a moving power upon them." And a number of foreign engineers attended the Rainhill Trials in 1829. Britain would teach the world about its new invention.

The United States

A halting and far less universal start had already been made with railways in the United States. The first recorded use of a rail way (as it was called) of any sort was in 1762–64 by John Montresor, a British army captain and engineer, who built an inclined plane for military purposes at the Niagara Portage at what later became Lewiston, New York.

The first commercial rail line was opened in 1810—Thomas Leiper's railroad, in Delaware County, Pennsylvania, in what are now the suburbs of Philadelphia (1 on outline map, *left*). This horse-drawn line transported stone from his quarry to Ridley Creek, which gave access to the Delaware River.

The first chartered and completed railway was known as the Granite Railway (2 on outline map), another horse-powered line completed in 1826 to transport slabs of granite from a quarry at Quincy, a few miles south of Boston, to the Neponset River, where they could be shipped to Boston; there they were first used to construct the Bunker Hill Monument. This railway was built by Gridley Bryant, a self-

Below.
The survey for Thomas Leiper's railroad, drawn by engineer John Thomson and dated 1 October 1809. *Ridley Creek Landing* is at right, the quarry at left. The map was given to the Delaware County Institute of Science in 1873 by Thomson's son, J. Edgar Thomson, then president of the Pennsylvania Railroad, to prove that Leiper's railroad was the first in North America.

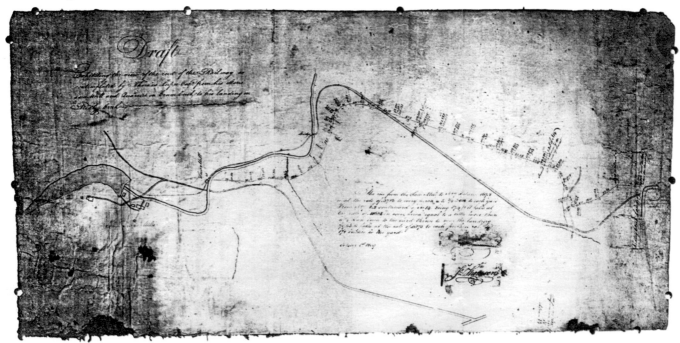

educated engineer who had been to Britain and seen the railways there. He introduced several innovations: he was the first in North America to use track switches (points) to allow a train to change tracks, the first to use a turntable, and the first to use swivelling trucks (bogies) on his wagons to allow them to be used on tighter curves.

The Granite Railway at first used two-piece oak rails. When these proved unsatisfactory, granite top strips were tried; they in turn were superseded by iron strips and, later still, iron rails. The railway was taken over by the Old Colony & Newport Railway in 1871. That company upgraded the line and began using steam locomotives, taking the granite directly to Boston, doing away with the intermediate waterborne step.

Above.
A rare view of the horse-drawn Granite Railway in the 1840s or 1850s.

Right.
The Granite Railway on an 1826 map, here labelled the *Quincy Railway*, runs from Bunker Hill Quarry to the *Neponset R.*, where granite could be shipped to *Boston*, a few miles north.

Below.
This map shows the Granite Railway in greater detail. It is of unknown date; this reproduction comes from a booklet produced to mark the centenary of the railway in 1926.

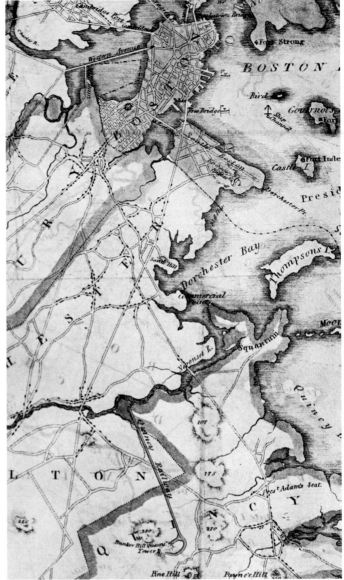

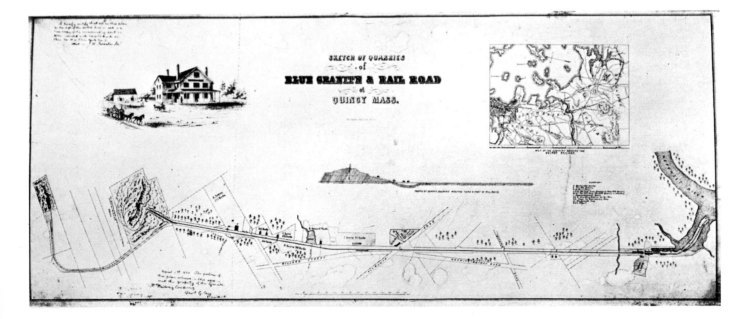

In 1812, the visionary Colonel John Stevens published the world's first book on railways. Four years before, Stevens and his son Robert had completed a steamboat he intended to operate as a ferry across the Hudson River from New York to New Jersey, but had been defeated by a New York State monopoly obtained by Robert Fulton and Robert Livingston. In 1809 Stevens steamed the boat, named *Phoenix*, out into the Atlantic and along the coast to the Delaware River, where it went into service between Philadelphia and Trenton. *Phoenix* had thus become the first steamboat to sail in the open ocean.

The first railroad charter in the United States was obtained by Stevens in 1815 for a service to connect New York and Philadelphia, but it was before its time and did not attract the required investors, who were too focused on canals at the time. The railroad would be built, but not until 1831. In 1825 Stevens built the first steam locomotive in North America. It followed the ideas of John Blenkinsop's system (see page 110), being driven by a large cog engaged to a rack rail laid in the middle of the track (photo, *right*). This "steam wagon," as he called it, was demonstrated on a half-mile-long circular track on Stevens's estate in Hoboken, New Jersey—shades of Richard Trevithick here!

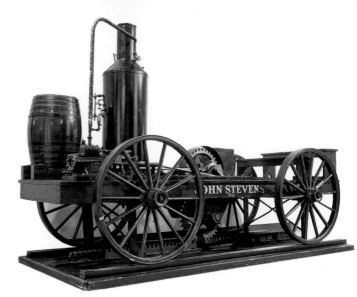

Above.
John Stevens's original steam wagon, built in 1825, did not survive, but there are two replicas. This one was constructed for the Pennsylvania Railroad in 1928 and exhibited at the 1933–34 Century of Progress world's fair in Chicago. Since that time it was in the Museum of Science & Industry in that city, but was recently sold—for US $66,000—along with some other replicas and one original locomotive, the *Mississippi* (see page 260), to make space for other exhibits.

The Delaware & Hudson Railroad

Most of the early railways of North America were portage railways, connecting two navigable waters, or, as in Britain, a resource with navigable water. The first to use a steam locomotive was an extension of a canal, the Delaware & Hudson Canal. It was completed in 1828 from Rondout Creek, which flows into the Hudson River, to Honesdale, on the Lackawaxen River, to transport anthracite from the coalfields of northeastern Pennsylvania to New York. The company's mines, however, were at Carbondale, 16 miles farther inland and much higher than the canal. So the anthracite was to be brought to the canal by a railway that would include inclined planes, each worked by a stationary steam engine.

In 1828 Horatio Allen, the company's assistant engineer, was sent to Britain to learn about railway practice and purchase strap iron for rails and four locomotives. Three of the locomotives were obtained

Below.
This 1835 map shows the location of the Delaware & Hudson Canal (dark blue) and the Delaware & Hudson Gravity Railroad (in red) that extended it westwards to Carbondale.

Below.
The 1829 *Stourbridge Lion*, a replica. The engine was very similar to *Agenoria* (see page 194), made at the same time by Foster, Rastrick & Company, and undoubtedly used many of the same moulds for castings.

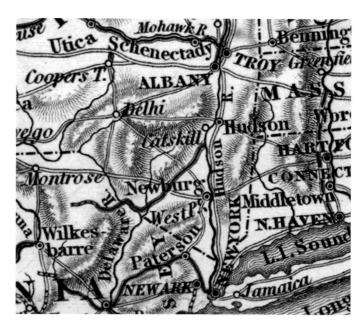

from Foster, Rastrick & Company, of Stourbridge, and a fourth from Robert Stephenson & Company, of Newcastle. Two were destroyed by a fire shortly after they arrived in New York. The Delaware & Hudson Gravity Railroad was completed in 1829 and consisted of 15 miles of 4-foot, 3-inch–gauge wooden track with iron strapping nailed on top. The line included eight inclined planes connected by nearly level sections, slightly graded to allow wagons to roll easily in the direction of Honesdale and the canal. The intention was to use the locomotives on some of these level sections between the planes.

One of the Foster & Rastrick engines, dubbed the *Stourbridge Lion*, was assembled by Allen and on 8 August 1829 ran on a section of track between Honesdale and Seelyville, about 1½ miles west of Honesdale. This was the first locomotive to run on a commercial line in North America. However, the iron-strapped track was not up to the strains imposed by a 7-ton locomotive and was nearly destroyed in the process. The *Stourbridge Lion* was quickly converted to a stationary engine and used on one of the inclines, and the company reverted to using horses on the level sections. This brief but ambitious experiment had failed, but once again, as in many British cases, only because the track had been laid to standards inconsistent with heavy steam locomotive working.

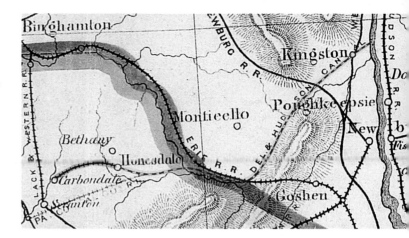

Above.
Although drawn much later, in 1854, this map shows more clearly the purpose of the Delaware & Hudson Gravity Railroad, in red, between *Honesdale* and *Carbondale*, and the *Del. & Hudson Can.* The Hudson River is at right. Later lines are also shown, including the *Erie R.R.*, chartered in 1832, which connected New York with Lake Erie and which briefly ran in the Lackawaxen valley alongside the Delaware & Hudson Gravity Railroad.

Above and *above, centre right.*
Two views of Honesdale about 1898. Barges are waiting in the canal to be loaded with anthracite delivered by the railroad. A new line along the south bank of the Lackawaxen was built in the 1840s, and this included the inclined plane shown in the photo *above*. The map (*above*) shows Honesdale in 1872, and the location of the two photos can be seen at far right, where the bridge crosses the canal. By this time there were a number of new lines, divided into loaded lines, for full wagons coming to the canal, and *Light Track*, for empty wagons going back to the mines. The 1829 line left Honesdale going north, parallel to the canal; by the time of this map it was used as a loaded track and is so labelled outside the extract shown here. The *Union Loaded Plane*, which crosses the Delaware & Hudson inclined plane (also shown in the photo) accessed a huge "piling ground," a coal dump above the canal.

The South Carolina Railroad

Horatio Allen had seen the potential for steam locomotion in England, so when the Delaware & Hudson decided to stick with stationary engines and horses, he went looking for another job. He was soon hired by the South Carolina Canal & Railroad Company in Charleston, South Carolina. The merchants of that city wanted to divert some of the lucrative cotton trade to their city from Savannah, farther south down the coast. In 1830, cotton bales from the interior were mainly shipped from Augusta, Georgia, down the river—to Savannah. The Charleston merchants came up with the idea of building a 136-mile-long railway from Augusta to their city as an alternative route.

Allen lost no time in persuading the company's directors that steam locomotives were the way to go, that horse power was known and would not change, whereas steam engines had an unlimited future potential. A vertical-boilered steam locomotive was built at West Point Foundry in Cold Spring, New York, and shipped to Charleston in pieces, where Allen assembled it. Unnamed, it was dubbed the *Best Friend of Charleston*, for it was charged with vastly increasing the city's trade. This locomotive was the first to both be built and regularly operated in North America. By Christmas Day 1830 6 miles of track (laid at the 4-foot, 8½-inch Stephenson gauge) out of Charleston had been completed, and the engine drew coaches with two hundred citizens—plus a flatcar complete with a cannon and gunners to fire salutes—along the line.

The *Best Friend* worked well for a time, but on 17 June 1831, while the engineer was away, a fireman who had become tired of the noise tied the safety valve down, causing an explosion that destroyed the locomotive and killed the fireman. Salvageable parts were used to construct a replacement, appropriately enough called the *Phoenix*. The company rewrote its rule book, requiring the engineer to remain with his locomotive at all times, and thereafter, to reassure the public, ran trains with a car full of cotton bales between the locomotive and coaches, advertising that this would "protect travelers when the locomotive explodes." Not *if*, but *when*!

The South Carolina Railroad was the first in North America to offer the public scheduled steam-hauled services. It was completed to Hamburg, across the Savannah River from Augusta, in October 1833, and was for a time the longest railway in the world.

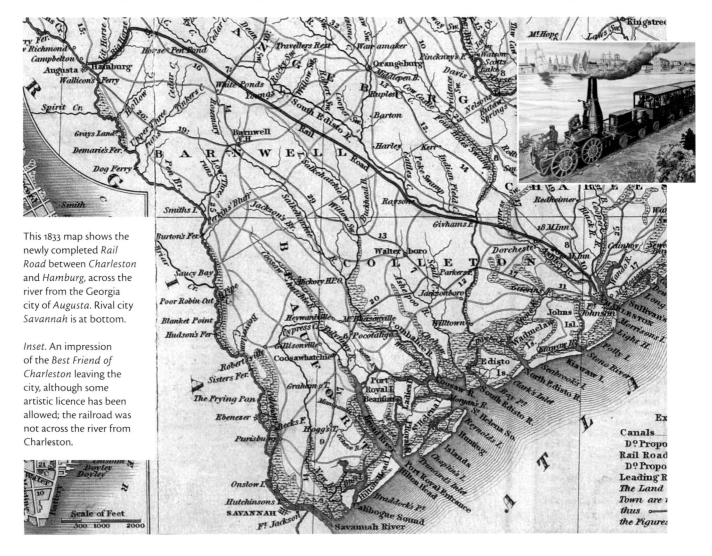

This 1833 map shows the newly completed *Rail Road* between *Charleston* and *Hamburg*, across the river from the Georgia city of *Augusta*. Rival city *Savannah* is at bottom.

Inset. An impression of the *Best Friend of Charleston* leaving the city, although some artistic licence has been allowed; the railroad was not across the river from Charleston.

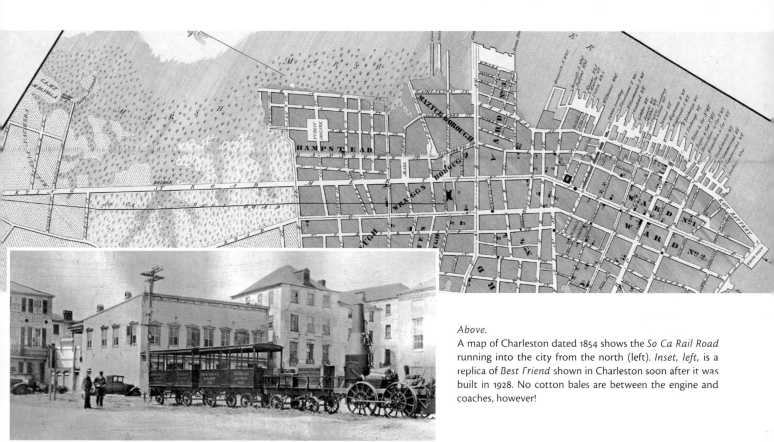

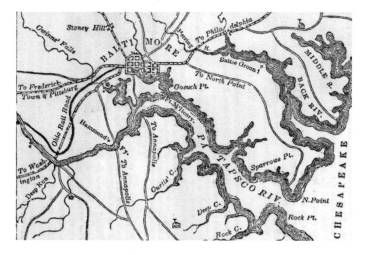

Above.
A map of Charleston dated 1854 shows the *So Ca Rail Road* running into the city from the north (left). *Inset, left*, is a replica of *Best Friend* shown in Charleston soon after it was built in 1928. No cotton bales are between the engine and coaches, however!

The Baltimore & Ohio

The citizens of Baltimore, Maryland, had a similar idea, but their vision was a bit wider. Not being located on a major river at all, they wished to funnel traffic coming east from the interior Mississippi River system through their city. Their idea was to connect Baltimore with the Ohio River, at Wheeling, then in Virginia, a distance of some 300 miles. The Ohio River was at that time the major northeastern interior path of commerce. This was a still a portage, though a rather long one. Philip E. Thomas and George Brown, entrepreneurs and bankers who had visited England in 1826 and examined railways there, headed a group of Baltimore businessmen who chartered the Baltimore & Ohio Railroad in 1827; it was thus correctly the first public railway in the United States, but it would begin operations only with horse traction.

Construction of the 4-foot, 8½-inch Stephenson-gauge line began in Baltimore on 4 July 1828. Ceremonies famously included Charles Carroll, the last surviving signer of the Declaration of Independence. By that time he was a millionaire and the largest investor in the railway. Carroll fully understood that what he was inaugurating that day would affect the lives of Americans almost as much as the Declaration of Independence.

In May 1830 service began over the first 13 miles of the line, from Baltimore to Ellicott's Mills, now Ellicott City, but this was using horse-drawn cars. The company had been discouraged from using steam locomotives by none other than Robert Stephenson, who doubted that they could negotiate the severe curves the route necessitated. The idea of using steam came from Peter Cooper, an inventor and entrepreneur who had purchased large tracts of land in Maryland after becoming convinced that the Baltimore & Ohio would increase land prices there. He

Left. A map of the environs of Baltimore surveyed in 1831 but not published until 1837 shows the [Baltimore &] *Ohio Rail Road* entering the city from the west.

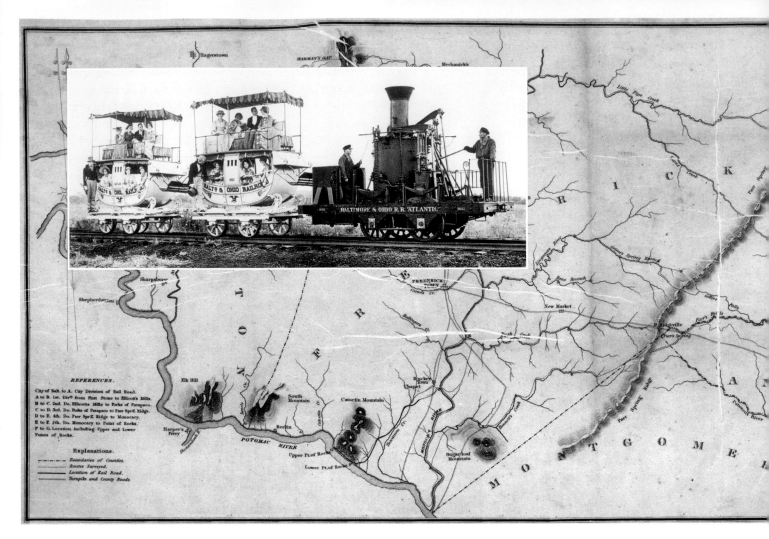

Below.
A replica of *Tom Thumb*, slightly larger than the original. The replica was built for the "Fair of the Iron Horse," the Baltimore & Ohio Railroad Company's centenary celebration in 1927.

Above.
This 1831 map shows the survey for the Baltimore & Ohio Railroad from Baltimore to *Upper Pt. of Rocks*, on the *Potomac River*. The line was surveyed by Army engineer (and western explorer) Stephen Long. The solid black line represents tracks laid, while the dotted lines show surveys. The railroad used the valley of the *Patapsco River* before traversing higher ground to the Potomac. *Ellicott's Mills* is shown close to *Baltimore*, at right. *Harper's Ferry*, at the confluence of the *Shenandoah R.* and the Potomac, is at bottom left; the line would be opened to that point in December 1834 following the resolution of a dispute between the railroad and the Chesapeake & Ohio Canal Company, which was also building west along the Potomac.

had found iron ore on his land and established the Canton Iron Works in Baltimore, and he hoped to sell iron rails to the railway. Cooper assembled a small makeshift vertical-boilered 1-ton steam locomotive in 1830 from many bits and pieces, including musket barrels. Dubbed *Tom Thumb*, it worked well, in July 1830 becoming the first steam locomotive to be used on a public railway in the United States, though it was too small to be used for regular service. It drew the directors' car at 18 miles per hour. The line as far as Ellicott's Mills was double tracked, and this prompted a local stagecoach company to challenge *Tom Thumb* to a race. The steam locomotive was winning until a belt slipped off a pulley powering a blower, at which point power was lost and the engine slowed, allowing the horse to win. Nevertheless, the race had demonstrated the engine's superior power; the directors became convinced that steam locomotion was the way forward, and investors rushed to purchase company stock.

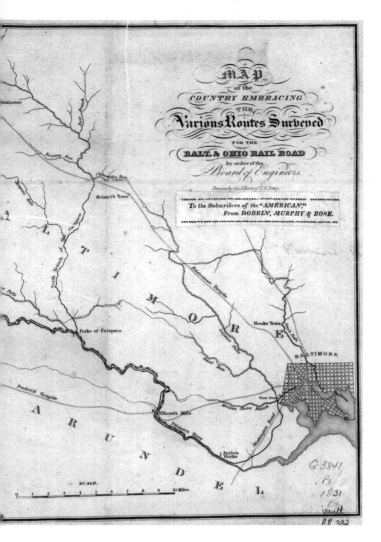

The following year the company held trials to find the best locomotives, getting the idea from the Rainhill Trials, which had been widely reported in the United States. Five locomotives were entered, though for some unknown reason they did not include *Tom Thumb*. The winner was *York*, designed and built by Phineas Davis in York, Pennsylvania, hence the name. *York* thus became the first locomotive in regular service and was capable of hauling 15 tons at 15 miles per hour on the level and could reach speeds of 30 miles per hour. Another of what became known as the "Grasshopper" type engines, the *Atlantic*, was added in 1832. The vertical-boilered type of American-designed locomotive was never quite as efficient as the Stephenson type but nevertheless lasted in service into the late 1830s.

Top left, inset on map.
The early style of train on the Baltimore & Ohio is illustrated by this replica at the 1927 centenary. The locomotive is the *Andrew Jackson*, first built in 1836 and rebuilt in 1892 to resemble the *Atlantic*, the first Grasshopper design that entered service in 1832.

Above.
A depiction of the race between a horse and *Tom Thumb* in 1830.

Right, centre.
A replica of *York*, originally built in 1831, which won the locomotive trials held in 1831. It was sold for $121,000 in 2016.

Right.
The converted *Andrew Jackson*, now displayed as *Atlantic*, as it is today at the Baltimore & Ohio Railroad Museum.

The Mohawk & Hudson

The Mohawk & Hudson Railroad was a 14-mile-long line between Albany, New York, on the Hudson River, and Schenectady, on the Mohawk River. It was conceived as a means of speeding up the transfer of passengers to and from the Erie Canal to avoid a tiresome long set of locks that brought the canal down to the level of the Hudson River. It was thus designed from the beginning for passengers rather than freight, for which time was not so critical.

The railway was chartered by the New York State Legislature in December 1825. It was the idea of a local entrepreneur, George Featherstonhaugh, who the following year sailed to Britain to gather information. Construction did not begin until 1829, however, and the railway was completed two years later. The locomotive-worked part of the line ran between the tops of inclined planes at each end as the line descended the cities. The track was rough, made of wood with metal strips nailed to the top surface, and when the company tried out a locomotive (named *John Bull*) made by Robert Stephenson & Company, it tore up the track and proved near useless. The track had been laid down at the 4-foot, 8½-inch Stephenson gauge to fit this locomotive. The company engineer, John Bloomfield Jervis, then designed a lighter locomotive, which was made by West Point Foundry; the gauge was retained. The resulting 3-ton engine was named the *DeWitt Clinton* after the governor of the state.

A ceremonial opening of the railroad took place on 9 August 1831, and regular service began the following day. Wood was used as fuel initially to try to get the locomotive's fire to draw better. The line was intended to be steam worked, but horses were sometimes used—there was a pathway for them in the centre of the track—and service was suspended for periods during the winter when the Erie Canal froze, thus delivering no passengers.

Above.
A replica of *DeWitt Clinton*, built in 1893 for the World's Columbian Exposition in Chicago that year, re-enacting the inaugural train of 9 August 1831. Five stage-coach bodies were mounted on flanged wheels to form the passenger accommodation.

Gentler grades at each end of the line were constructed in 1843 and the inclined planes abandoned the following year because of a new competitor, the Schenectady & Troy Railroad, which had opened in 1842 using gentler grades. The pioneer Mohawk & Hudson went on to become a link in the New York–to–Buffalo route, the so-called and much-advertised water level route of the New York Central Railroad.

In 1832 Jervis designed another locomotive for the Mohawk & Hudson to work better with uneven or tightly curved track. Apparently at the suggestion of Robert Stephenson, Jervis replaced the front wheels with four-wheel bogies to guide the locomotive around bends. The two wheels on the outside of the curve would press against the rail and provide better stability on uneven track. It worked, and the bogie design was widely adopted in the years following. The locomotive was built at the West Point Foundry and was initially named the *Experiment* (illustration, *right centre*). Later its name seems to have been changed to *Brother Jonathan*, but whether this was an official name or just a nickname is unclear; "Brother Jonathan" was an impolite way of referring to the English at the time!

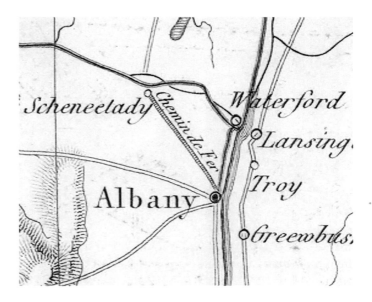

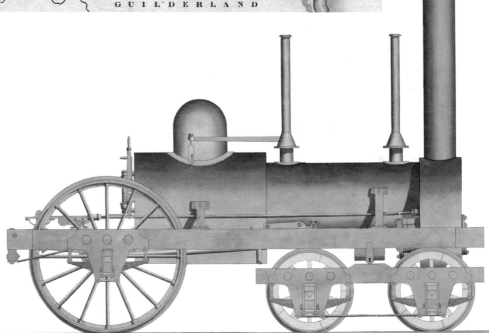

Left, bottom right.
Part of a French map published in 1834 shows the Mohawk & Hudson Railroad as *Chemin de Fer* from *Albany* to *Schenectady*.

Left, bottom left.
This 1834 poster advertises the joint service of passenger packet boats on the Erie Canal connecting with the Mohawk & Hudson at Schenectady.

Above.
By 1845, the date of this map, the inclined planes at either end of the line had been bypassed and are labelled *Abandoned R.R.* The new lines were now able to be worked by more powerful locomotives.

Right.
John Jervis's drawing of his bogie locomotive *Experiment*, or *Brother Jonathan*, built in 1832 to better deal with tightly curved and uneven track.

The Camden & Amboy

Colonel John Stevens in 1815 was the first person in the United States to receive a railway charter. His New Jersey Railroad Company was to run from New Brunswick, New Jersey, to Trenton, providing what was essentially a portage connection between two rivers and the two cities of New York and Philadelphia.

At that time he could not attract enough investment, so the idea was shelved, but in February 1830 his sons, Robert and Edwin Stevens, revived the idea, chartering the Camden & Amboy Railroad on a similar route. They had first to deal with a competing project, the Delaware & Raritan Canal, which wanted to build a connection from the Raritan River (which flows into New York's Lower Bay) and the Delaware River. A compromise varied the routes of both.

Above. The Camden & Amboy's first locomotive, the *John Bull*.

The railway opened in October 1832 between Hightstown, New Jersey and Bordentown, using horse traction and a connection to Philadelphia down the Delaware River by steamboat and a stagecoach connection from Hightstown to South Amboy. The line was completed from South Amboy to Camden in December 1834.

The Stevens brothers intended to use steam locomotives and in October 1831 had imported, in parts, an engine made by Robert Stephenson & Company, which was named *John Bull*, the classic name for an Englishman at the time (and not the locomotive with the same name as built for the Mohawk & Hudson). It was assembled by the Camden & Amboy's engineer, Isaac Dripps, but it kept coming off the roughly built track, built as so many British lines with cast-iron rails on stone blocks (and which was 5-foot gauge rather than the Stephenson standard 4 feet, 8½ inches) and so Dripps modified it by adding a two-wheeled pilot frame that would guide the locomotive around sharp bends. It also featured a pilot, or cowcatcher, and its invention is often attributed to him. Dripps added an oil-burning headlight and a bell, items that would become standard on American locomotives. And Robert Stevens seems to have introduced the T-shaped iron rail to America. The railroad also had another "first"— the death of a revenue passenger. On 8 November 1833, near Hightstown, a car pulled by *John Bull* broke an axle, derailing the train. Two passengers died and most of the others were injured, including Cornelius Vanderbilt, who swore never to travel by train again—yet went on to own the New York Central Railroad and make a fortune from railways.

A parallel and competitive line to the Camden & Amboy, the New Jersey Rail Road & Transportation Company, was chartered in 1832, and first services began between Newark and Jersey City in 1834. The two companies were merged in 1867 as the United New Jersey Railroad & Canal Company, and the railroad was leased to the Pennsylvania Railroad four years later.

Right, top to centre.
Camden & Amboy track, iron rails on stone blocks; *John Bull* in the Smithsonian National Museum of American History; and at Vancouver, BC's Steam Expo in 1986—the author's sons watch.

Below, left, and *below, right.*
Two details of a map published in 1850 showing the northern terminus of the Camden & Amboy at South Amboy's *R.R. Depot,* where steamboats connected with Manhattan, and a delightful illustration of a branch of the railway opened in 1839 just north of *Martinsville,* New Jersey.

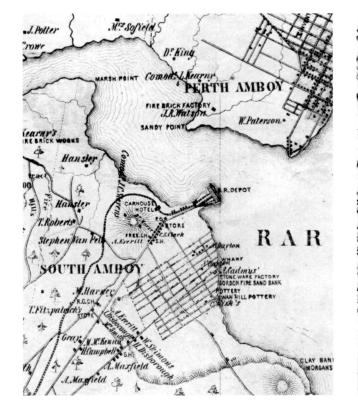

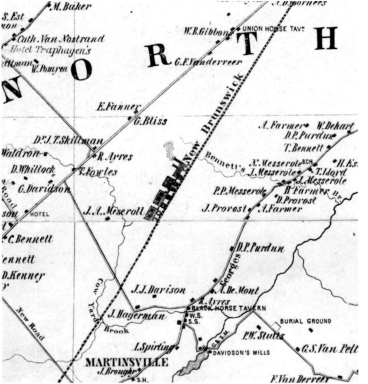

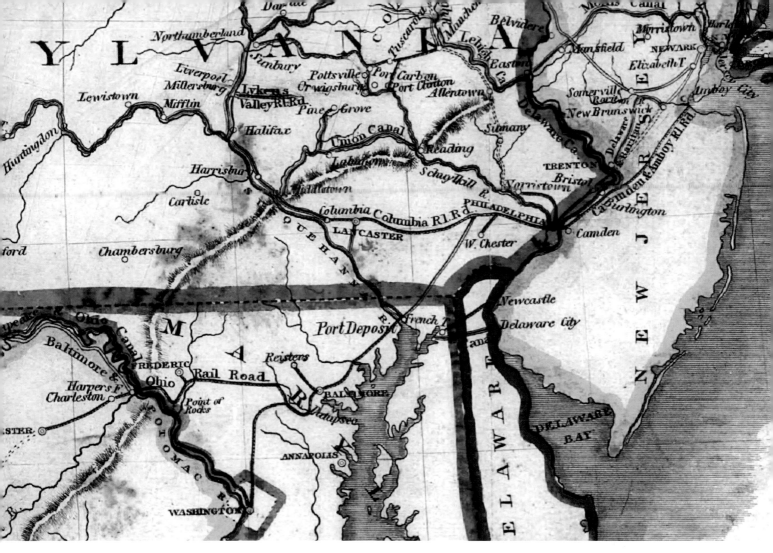

Above.

Both the *Camden & Amboy Rl.Rd.* and the *Delaware & Raritan* Canal are shown on this 1834 map, both permitting travel across the New Jersey peninsula, both connecting New York with *Philadelphia.* The canal, as its name implies, ran from the Delaware River to the smaller but navigable lower *Raritan R.,* which flows into Raritan Bay and allows an easy water connection with New York Harbor. Also shown is the *Baltimore & Ohio Rail Road,* including its branch to *Washington,* actually completed in 1835. Running into Philadelphia from the west is the *Columbia Rl.Rd.,* the eastern rail link in the Pennsylvania Main Line system. A line from *Winchester,* Virginia, to *Harpers F*[erry] on the *Potomac* is also on this map. The Baltimore & Ohio reached Sandy Hook, across the Potomac River from Harpers Ferry, in 1834. The Winchester & Potomac Railroad, built to connect Winchester with the Baltimore & Ohio system, reached Harpers Ferry in 1836, and a bridge across the Potomac completed the connection a year later.

Below. John Bull and train on the Camden & Amboy. Note the large pilot truck at the front of the locomotive to guide it around curves.

Lines from Boston

New England was the first American region to build something that might be thought of as a network, with a number of routes radiating from Boston.

The Boston & Worcester Railroad, chartered in 1831, opened its first section, to Newton, now a suburb of Boston, in April 1834; the rest of the 40-mile-long line to Worcester opened in July 1835 (map, *right*). The Boston & Lowell Railroad was also chartered in 1830 and was intended to service the textile mills in Lowell in much the same way as the Liverpool & Manchester had done with Manchester's. Despite being primarily planned as a freight railway, it soon became popular with passengers—just the same, again, as the Liverpool & Manchester. The railroad is notable for its initial solid granite roadbed, which jolted both passengers and freight so much it was soon converted to wooden sleepers or ties, the practice eventually adopted by all railways.

Before the coming of the railroad the preferred method of travel to New York from Boston had been by stagecoach to a port on Long Island Sound and then by boat to New York. The railroad initially duplicated this practice. The Boston & Providence was chartered in 1831 and completed in 1835, and the New York,

Above.
The beginnings of the New England railroad network are shown on this 1836 map. The *Boston* to *Providence* line opened in 1835, and from South Providence to *Stonington* two years later. Here passengers embarked by steamer down Long Island Sound to *New York*. The Boston to *Worcester* line opened in 1835, and *Springfield* was reached in 1839. The Boston & *Lowell* was completed in 1835, and the Eastern Railroad to *Salem* in 1838 and on to Portsmouth by 1840.

Providence & Boston Railroad completed a link from Providence to Stonington, on Long Island Sound, two years later. It was not until 1852 that an all-rail route to New York was completed, and even that used ferries across the river estuaries.

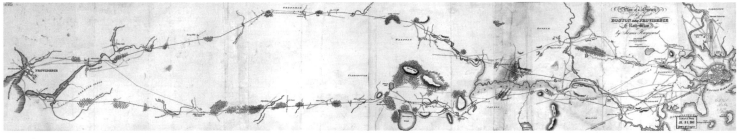

Above.
This 1828 survey for the Boston & Providence Railroad is one of the earliest U.S. railroad surveys. It shows two possible routes from *Boston*, at right, to *Providence*, at left. Both lines stop short of Boston itself. The route is actually oriented northeast to southwest.

The Allegheny Portage Railroad

As a counter to New York's Erie Canal, completed in 1825 (and soon aided by the Mohawk & Hudson Railroad), Pennsylvania's state officials, driven by the desire to enhance the competitiveness of its principal city, Philadelphia, planned a series of canals right across the Allegheny Mountains to Pittsburgh, on the Ohio River. The lesson of the Baltimore & Ohio, however, encouraged the state to incorporate railways into the system. At the eastern end, the Philadelphia & Columbia Railroad was completed in 1834 to connect Philadelphia with the Susquehanna River (map, *right, bottom*). To cross the highest parts of the Appalachians, another railway, called the

Allegheny Portage Railroad, was built that incorporated five inclined planes on either side of the mountains, rising 1,400 feet on the west side and 1,175 feet on the east. Between the planes was a railroad operated at first with horses and, after 1835, by steam locomotives. Canal barges, some specially built in sections, were placed on flatbed trucks to be hauled on the railroad.

The project included the first railroad tunnel built in North America, the Staple Bend Tunnel, a 900-foot-long bore located 4 miles east of Johnstown, Pennsylvania. The whole system of railways and canals was known as the Main Line of Public Works, and it was unusual in that it incorporated state-sponsored railroads, whereas almost all other railroad building in the United States was by commercial interests.

The Main Line was not a commercial success. It incorporated canals that froze in the winter, and it was cheaper to ship to the East Coast via the Mississippi River than the Main Line system, which required many transhipments from rail to water and vice versa. The State of Pennsylvania constructed a new route, known as the New Portage Railroad, completed in 1856, but by this time the Pennsylvania Railroad had completed an all-rail line from Philadelphia to Pittsburgh, in 1854.

Right.
Part of an 1829 map of Pennsylvania shows the Allegheny Portage Railroad as a *Rail Road* (and highlighted in red) between the two sections of canal at *Johnstown* and near *Hollidaysburg*. Although the railroad was built between the two ends of the canals, the route was not completely as shown on this map; its route as built is shown in the map *below*.

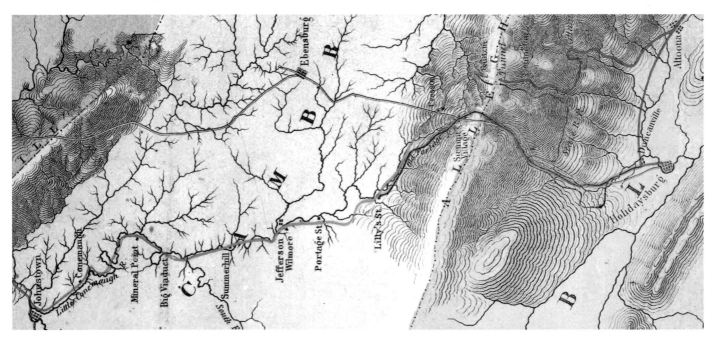

Above.
This was part of an 1855 map of the Pennsylvania Railroad, which was completed across the Allegheny Mountains the previous year and is shown in blue-green here. Highlighted in red and labelled *Old Portage R.R.* is part of the Allegheny Portage Railroad, which then follows the route of the Pennsylvania down the valley of the *Little Conemaugh R.* to *Johnstown*. Also shown (as a black line) is the New Portage Railroad, completed by the state in 1856 and labelled *State R.R.* This includes a tunnel through the summit just south of the Pennsylvania's Gallitzin Tunnel.

Below.
The state-sponsored *Columbia and Philadelphia Rail-Road* is shown on this map of the *West Philadelphia Rail-Road* dated 1835. The latter line was not built then and was taken over by the state in 1850 to replace the Philadelphia & Columbia's 2,800-foot-long Belmont *Inclined Plane*, shown rising 187 feet from the Schuylkill River. The plane (also shown in the illustration *inset*) was in 1836 the scene of an experiment that saw *George Washington*, a steam locomotive from the William Norris works in Philadelphia draw a loaded train up the incline, thus proving that inclined planes were not necessary.

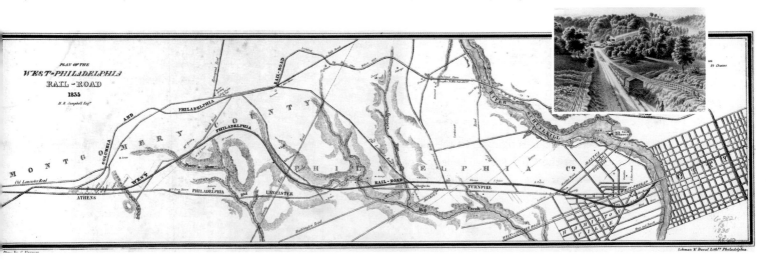

First Continental

Britain's nearer neighbours also quickly adopted railways with steam locomotives, sometimes building to their own design and sometimes simply importing British ones. By 1840 at least twelve continental railways had imported locomotives built by the company that had become the premier locomotive builder in the world, Robert Stephenson & Company of Newcastle, though other manufacturers also supplied engines. The increase in speed and efficiency over horse travel was so dramatic it simply could not be ignored anywhere.

Above.
Marc Seguin's 1829 steam locomotive for the St.-Étienne–Lyon railway, using his 1828 patent for a multi-tubed boiler. The tender housed a massive blower fan to feed the draft in the locomotive. The cylinders were vertical. This is a model in the Musée des Arts et Métiers in Paris.

The first steam locomotives had been built as early as 1816, in Berlin, then in Prussia. These were the two Blenkinsop rack-type engines that, for reasons not related to the locomotives' design, were never used beyond demonstration runs (see page 115).

France

The early railways of France were, like those in Britain, designed to link, or provide a pathway to, navigable waterways (map, *right, top*). The first steam railway in Europe was in central France, from St.-Étienne to Lyon. A horse-drawn railway had been opened in 1827 to connect the coalfield around St.-Étienne to the Loire River at Andrézieux. Copying British practice, the railway used cast-iron fishbelly-type rails on stone blocks. This line was extended downriver to Roanne in 1832 because navigation on the Loire above that town was difficult. At the same time, steam locomotives were introduced, one of which was built by Stephenson.

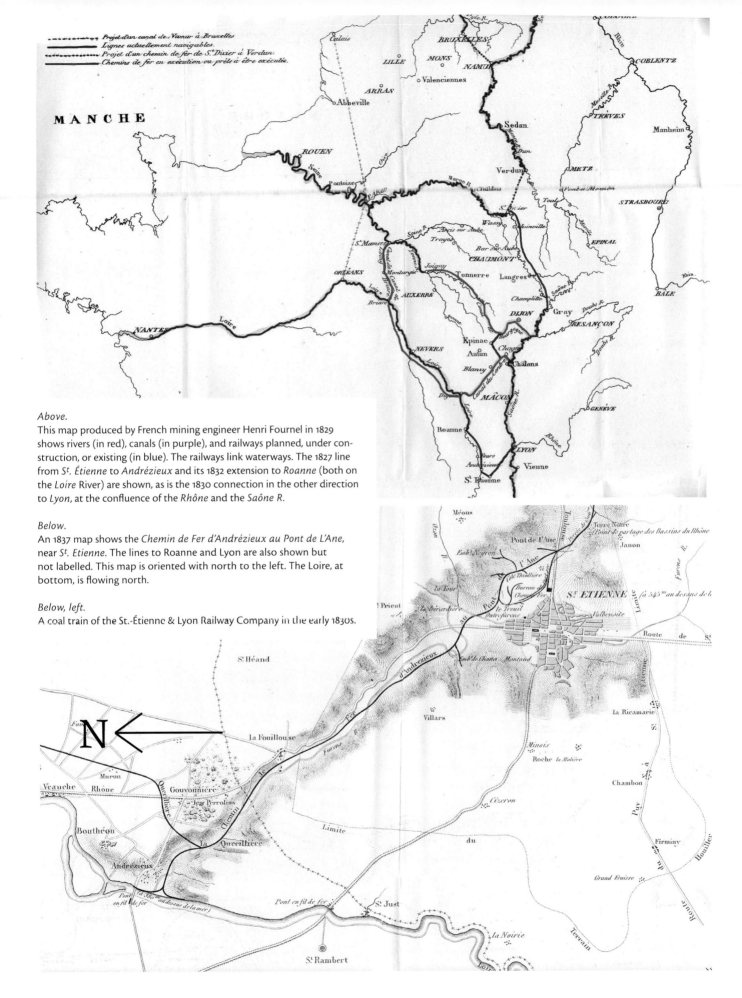

Above.
This map produced by French mining engineer Henri Fournel in 1829 shows rivers (in red), canals (in purple), and railways planned, under construction, or existing (in blue). The railways link waterways. The 1827 line from *St. Étienne* to *Andrézieux* and its 1832 extension to *Roanne* (both on the *Loire* River) are shown, as is the 1830 connection in the other direction to *Lyon*, at the confluence of the *Rhône* and the *Saône R.*

Below.
An 1837 map shows the *Chemin de Fer d'Andrézieux au Pont de L'Ane,* near *St. Etienne.* The lines to Roanne and Lyon are also shown but not labelled. This map is oriented with north to the left. The Loire, at bottom, is flowing north.

Below, left.
A coal train of the St.-Étienne & Lyon Railway Company in the early 1830s.

A wonderful gallery of original early French locomotives preserved in Cité du Train, the French national railway museum, in Mulhouse, Alsace. *Above, left:* Stephenson locomotive No. 6 *L'Aigle*, 1846, Compagnie d'Avignon à Marseille; *above, right:* Buddicom locomotive No. 33 *St. Pierre*, 1844, Compagnie de Paris à Rouen; *below, left:* Cail Crampton–type locomotive No. 80 *Le Continent*, 1852, Compagnie de Paris à Strasbourg; *below, right:* Hallette locomotive No. 5 *Sézanne*, 1847, Compagnie de Montereau à Troyes.

The line from St.-Étienne to Lyon was opened in 1830. Like its British counterpart, the Liverpool & Manchester, it was intended to carry goods, in this case coal, to market in the city of Lyon but soon attracted passenger traffic (illustration, *below*). The first steam locomotives in France were run here. In 1829 inventor Marc Seguin, who had previously visited England and seen George Stephenson's *Locomotion*, delivered two engines of his own design to the railway (photo, *page 244*), which, like Robert Stephenson's *Rocket*, had multi-tube boilers to extract greater heating power from the fire. Instead of using Stephenson's blastpipe, Seguin had large mechanically driven blower fans mounted on the engine's tender to provide draft to the fire, a design that worked quite well and enabled his locomotives to achieve speeds of 25 miles per hour. The railway did not exclusively use steam locomotives at first; some trains were horse drawn. The line from St.-Étienne to Lyon, much changed, of course, today carries the TGV, the *Train à Grande Vitesse*, the French high-speed train.

A horse-drawn passenger train on the St.-Étienne–to–Lyon railway in the early 1830s.

France's first main-line railway intended principally for passengers opened in 1837, a 12-mile-long line from Paris to St.-Germain-en-Laye, which actually ended at Le Pecq, on the other side of the Seine River (map, *right*). It was financed by the Rothschild banking family and was immensely popular: in its first two years it carried over 2 million passengers, creating, in effect, France's first commuter railway. An extension up the hill to St.-Germain as an atmospheric railway, powered by a vacuum in a tube, opened in 1847.

The widespread use of railways in France was slowed by the existence of a better network of roads and wide canals than in Britain. In 1837 the French public works minister, Louis Legrand, drew up a program for the development of a French network, with lines radiating out from Paris, using a combination of state and private enterprise; the government would plan the route and create the trackbed, while private companies would lay the track

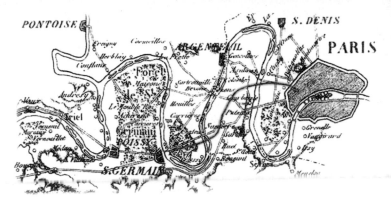

Above. The 1837 line (in red) from *Paris* to *Le Pecq*, across the river from *S. Germain*.

and provide and operate the trains. Concessions were granted, from which six major companies emerged. Nevertheless, by 1840 France had only 350 miles of short and unconnected lines, compared with 2,000 miles in Britain by that date.

Ireland

Not surprisingly, the railway made an early jump across the Irish Sea to Ireland, then still part of the United Kingdom. The first railway was a line from Dublin to Kingstown, now Dún Laoghaire, some 7½ miles south of the Irish capital. A new harbour had just been completed there, as the port of Dublin itself was difficult for sailing ships. In 1831 the Dublin & Kingstown Railway was authorized by Parliament, and it was completed three years later. Charles Vignoles was the engineer, and the line was built to George Stephenson's "standard" 4-foot,

8½-inch gauge. (This was converted in 1857 to what had emerged as the standard Irish gauge of 5 feet, 3 inches.) Stephenson and Joseph Locke visited the railway when it was under construction in 1832. The railway was partly built on a causeway (map, *below, bottom*), and the land behind it was soon filled in.

The railway was a huge success, developing Kingstown as a suburb of Dublin and as a fashionable place to live; commuter traffic soon became a significant source of revenue. Ten million passengers were carried in the first eight years. Trains met mail packet ships from Holyhead, making the route the preferred one for fast travel between Great Britain and Ireland, which it still is.

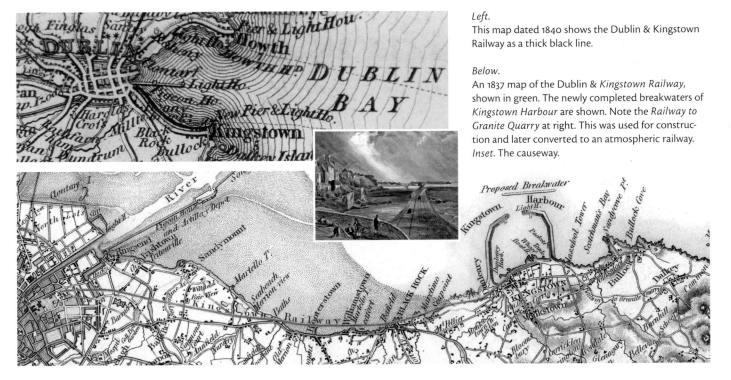

Left.
This map dated 1840 shows the Dublin & Kingstown Railway as a thick black line.

Below.
An 1837 map of the Dublin & *Kingstown Railway*, shown in green. The newly completed breakwaters of *Kingstown Harbour* are shown. Note the *Railway to Granite Quarry* at right. This was used for construction and later converted to an atmospheric railway.
Inset. The causeway.

Belgium and the Netherlands

Belgium was the third European country to open a steam-hauled railway, but it did it differently from all the others. Here it became a state enterprise, planned and initially built by a central agency. Belgium had become a country independent of the Netherlands only in 1830, and the government saw railways as a great way to bind the new country together as well as stimulate economic growth. There was also the possibility of capturing interior European trade that was then being funnelled down the Rhine and through Dutch ports, and diverting it to Antwerp. There were also military considerations. A network, then, was planned from the start.

The enabling legislation was passed in May 1834 for a line from Mons to Antwerp, via Brussels, and on 5 May 1835 the first section, between Brussels and Malines (Mechelen in Flemish) was opened, with George and Robert Stephenson in attendance; they had been hired as advisors. Two years later both attended the opening of the next section, to Ghent. Both were awarded medals by King Leopold. By 1836 the railway was completed to Antwerp.

CHEMIN DE FER DE BRUXELLES A MALINES.

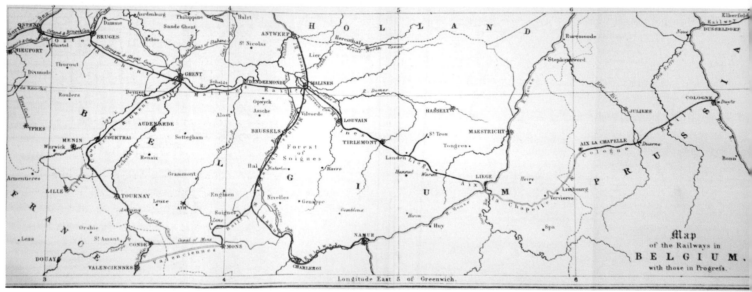

Map of the Railways in BELGIUM. with those in Progress.

Above, top.
A representation of the inaugural train on the first section of the Belgian railway network from Brussels to Malines, 5 May 1835.

Above.
The incipient Belgian railway network is shown on this map published in a travel guide in 1843. The first line, opened in 1835, ran from *Brussels* to *Malines*.

Left.
The first Belgian locomotive, *La Belge* ("the Belgian"), was built in the country for the Brussels–Malines line and pulled the inaugural train (*above*). It was a Patentee type, a design of Robert Stephenson & Company, and was licensed from that company.

Above.
One of the first two Dutch locomotives, *De Arend* ("The Eagle"), a Patentee type built in England by R.B. Longridge & Company of Bedlington. This is a 1939 replica, built for the centenary of Dutch railways, in the Nederlands Spoorwegmuseum (Dutch National Railway Museum) in Utrecht. The other locomotive was named *Snelheid* ("Speed").

In the Netherlands the situation was entirely different. Railways were not particularly appealing because the country was already covered with a considerable network of canals, required for drainage in any case. The Netherlands was not very industrialized either. Attempts to raise investor interest for railways failed until 1839, when the Hollandsche IJzeren Spoorweg-Maatschappij (Holland Iron Railway Company) opened a line between Amsterdam and Haarlem, a distance of about 12 miles. The inaugural train ran on 20 September 1839.

Reflecting the relative ease of waterborne transport for freight, the railway was a completely passenger one, where speed was of greater value. Most of the Dutch railway network, which developed slowly, had passenger traffic in mind. It was eight years before the railway reached Rotterdam.

One railway was built principally for freight, however. This was the Rhenish Railway, planned even before the opening of the Holland Iron Railway to connect the Rhine to the sea. It would reach Germany in 1856. Dutch railways were initially built to a unique broad gauge of 6 feet, 4½ inches, but they were converted to the Stephenson standard in 1866 when it was realized that they needed to be compatible with the lines of neighbouring countries.

The Netherlands ultimately had a network one-third the size of that of its neighbour Belgium, the difficulty of constructing railways being a major influence. The land was level, for sure, but it also tended to be boggy, and there were many waterways to be crossed, all of which needed to allow waterborne traffic to pass, so bridges either had to be high or movable; all this added tremendously to construction costs.

Right.
A train on the Amsterdam–Haarlem line enters Haarlem across a bridge in this 1852 scene painted by Dutch painter Jakob Theodor Abels.

Germany

As we have seen (page 13) the area now covered by Germany was the birthplace of several hand-propelled railways. In 1816 and 1818, Blenkinsop rack-type engines had been tried out, the 1818 attempt with some success (see page 115). The Prince William Railway, a 4½-mile-long horse-drawn line considered to be the first iron railway in Germany, was opened in 1831; the rails were initially wooden with iron strapping. The line was in the Ruhr, the German coal-mining region, and ran from Kupferdreh, now part of Essen, to Langenberg, now in Velbert. It was not until 1847 that steam traction was used on part of the line.

The first public steam railway in Germany was a line opened in 1835 from the Bavarian city of Nuremberg

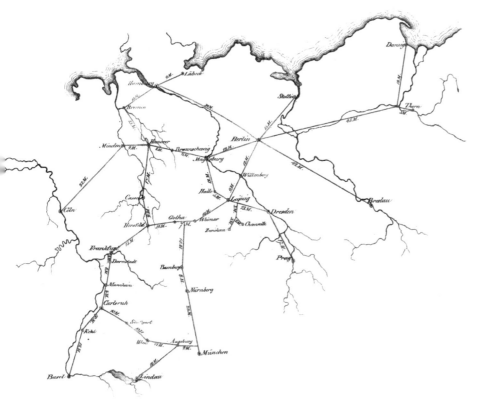

Left.
Events in Britain had not escaped the attention of innovators in Germany, and the advantages of a rail network were even more apparent because at this time Germany was still non-existent, with multiple states in the region, the largest being Prussia and Bavaria, that would come together in 1871 to create a German nation. The leading promoter of railways in Germany was an economist, Georg Friedrich List. He was a supporter of pan-European aspirations and was considered by some a forefather of the European Union. He saw that railways would be useful for defence, would help prevent "excessive fluctuation in the prices of the necessaries of life," and would "promote the spirit of the nation, as it has a tendency to destroy the Philistine spirit arising from isolation and provincial prejudice." The iron rails, he wrote, "become a nerve system," strengthening public opinion at the same time as the power of the state for police or governmental purposes. This is a map of a proposed German rail network drawn in 1833 by List. His route suggestions were widely adopted.

Above, top.
A replica of *Adler* ("Eagle"), the first German steam locomotive to go into regular service, in 1835 on the Bavarian Ludwig Railway from Nuremberg to Fürth, is displayed in the Deutsche Bahn Museum in Nuremberg.

Right.
The route of the Ludwigs-eisenbahn is shown as a straight thick black line paralleling the road, depicted as a double thin line. The railway runs from *Nuernberg* to *Fürth* on this 1840 map, starting just outside the southwest corner of the city walls; the tower at this location is shown on the illustration and photo *overleaf.*

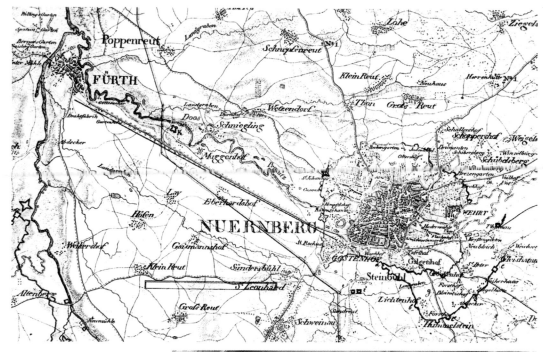

to Fürth, a distance of a little over 4 miles (1 on outline map). The line had received royal approval in 1834, perhaps because the promoters intended to name the railway the Ludwigsbahn, after the king. The railway was built by Nuremberg citizen Johannes Scharrer and paralleled the busiest road out of the city, so that it could be relied upon to attract a major portion of that traffic, which it did. Labourers or foreigners were not allowed to stay in Nuremberg overnight, a medieval-originated defence strategy, and so Fürth had grown up as a dormitory for such workers and ensured that heavy commuting took place, creating ideal traffic for a railway.

The Ludwigseisenbahn opened on 7 December 1835 with an inaugural train and much pomp and ceremony. The railway had purchased a locomotive from Robert Stephenson & Company named *Adler*, German for "Eagle," and it was operated by a driver also provided by Stephenson, William Wilson. Wilson became a bit of a celebrity, and his initial eight-month contract was repeatedly extended. The line was very successful, and its steam- and horse-drawn trains together carried 450,000 passengers in the first year and paid investors annual dividends of 20 per cent. *Adler* operated only two trains a day, the rest being horse drawn. Surprisingly, perhaps, the Ludwigseisenbahn was never extended and never connected with the rest of the emerging German railway system; it was closed in 1922 and replaced by trams.

Above.
A three-dimensional rendering of the inaugural train leaving Nuremberg on 7 December 1835. This view is on one side of a commemorative monument for the railway (photo, *overleaf*).

Below.
A model of *Adler* with its train in the Deutsche Bahn Museum in Nuremberg.

Left, top.
A contemporary view of the Ludwigsbahn. *Adler* is seen departing from Nuremberg with a passenger train. A tower, part of the medieval town wall, is in the background.

Left, centre.
The same location today. The railway closed in 1922. One of the trams shown here has the name "Adler" featured prominently on its front. The medieval tower is in the background of this view, too.

Left, bottom.
The monument to the Ludwigsbahn, which now stands on Fürther Straße, on the route of the railway. It was moved from its original location in front of the Nuremberg station.

Below.
Another view of *Adler*, in the DB Museum standing next to the front part of an ICE-3 (Inter-City Express) high-speed train, introduced in 2000.

Above. A replica of *Saxonia*, the first German-designed and -built steam locomotive, which pulled the third train on the opening day of the Leipzig–Dresden Railway, behind two British-built locomotives, *Robert Stephenson* and *Elephant*.

Economist Georg Friedrich List was the foremost promoter of early German railways, even planning a route network that crossed the borders of the German states (map, *page 250*; Germany was not united until 1871). List considered the route between Dresden, the capital of Saxony, and Leipzig, its largest city, to be ideal for a railway. The government of Saxony, while interested in the line, was not persuaded by List's arguments that it could be extended to create a German network, as it thought Saxony would

Far left, with three details, *left.*
A pictorial map of the Leipzig–Dresden Railway published in 1839, the year the railway opened. The centre detail shows the Oberau Tunnel.

Below. A train at Althen in 1837 on the first part of the Leipzig–Dresden Railway to be completed. A train departs, headed by one of the company's first four locomotives, all imported from Britain.

Left.
The Oberau Tunnel on the Leipzig–Dresden Railway. It was the first continental European tunnel for a standard-gauge railway. It is shown on the map on the *previous page.*

Below.
This engraving of a train on the Leipzig–Dresden Railway clearly displays the railway's aspirations of reaching Berlin.

Below, bottom.
Replica of the locomotive *Beuth* displayed in the Deutsches Technikmuseum. The original was built for the Berlin–Anhalt Railway in 1844. The line connected Berlin to the Magdeburg–Leipzig Railway at Köthen, via Wittenberge, and had been completed in 1841.

lose power to larger states such as Prussia. But the businesspeople of the two cities saw its merits, and investment was forthcoming. Scottish engineer James Walker, who had surveyed the Leeds & Selby Railway (see page 212) was hired to survey a line. By now well-established British railway practices were adopted, including the Stephenson standard gauge of 4 feet, 8½ inches, and locomotives were purchased from Britain. The railway was completed from Leipzig to Althen, a distance of about 6 miles, and opened on 24 April 1837, but it took another two years to complete to Dresden, working from both ends of the route (2 on the small outline map, *page 250*). It was almost entirely hand built using labourers drawn from neighbouring villages. The entire 75-mile-long line opened on 7 April 1839—with inaugural trains driven by British drivers. It is considered to be the first trunk railway in Germany and was the first that exclusively used steam traction. It also encompassed the first continental European standard-gauge railway tunnel, a 560-yard-long structure at Oberau dug by more than 500 miners from Freiberg between 1837 and 1839. It was converted into a cutting in 1934.

The Leipzig–Dresden Railway, as the first of many long-distance railways, proved several of List's predictions. Not only did it stimulate industry in Saxony, but it also proved to be the start of a network of railways that would encourage economic interdependence between the German states and push Germany towards unification.

Another long-distance railway was planned in 1838—a line from Berlin to Magdeburg. The first section, from Berlin to Potsdam, about 15 miles west of Berlin, opened on 29 October 1838, becoming the first railway in Prussia (3 on the small outline map). The 100-mile route through to Magdeburg, on the Elbe River, was not completed until 1846.

The year 1838 also saw the opening of the initial part of the first German state railway, a line from Brunswick (Braunschweig), 90 miles south of Hamburg, and Wolfenbüttel, a few miles further south. This was the Duchy of Brunswick State Railway. The government decided to build this line to pre-empt the state of Hannover's building a line from Hannover to Magdeburg that would bypass Brunswick. But railway mania was about to engulf Germany, and by 1840 many more lines were planned and under construction. By 1843 the (German) Rhenish Railway Company had completed a line to the Belgian border, thus linking with the Belgian line to Antwerp and creating the first international line.

The routes of all the early German railways, and those in parts of the surrounding countries, are shown on the large map, *pages 258–59*.

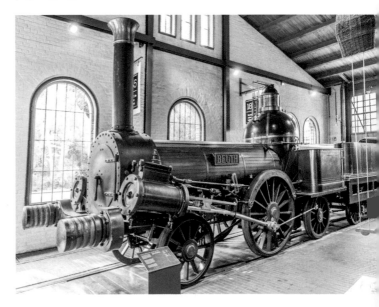

Other European Countries

Right. A superb model of the American locomotive manufacturer William Norris's steam engine *Austria*, a type first made in 1837 and later built in Austria. This type of locomotive was much used in Austria but was also exported to other European countries. Its front four wheels were on a pivoting bogie, which gave it the ability to deal with tight bends and steep inclines on mountain railways.

Railways spread rapidly to the rest of Europe, though beyond France, Belgium, and Germany they were later for various reasons ranging from topography, the distribution of industrial activity, and even the distrust of autocratic rulers.

The first railway in Switzerland was not built by a Swiss company at all but by the French, with a line from Mulhouse, in Alsace, to a station outside the walls of Basel in 1844. The first Swiss-built railway was the 10-mile-long Schweizerische Nordbahn (Swiss Northern Railway), from Zurich to Baden, opened on 9 August 1847 (1 on outline map, *above*), with the inaugural train pulled by *Limmat*, shown on *page 257*, built at the Kessler works in Karlsruhe, Germany. It soon became known as the "Spanisch-Brötli Bahn," literally the Spanish sandwich railway, because the well-to-do of Zurich developed the habit of sending their servants to Baden to collect prized Baden bakers' rolls, which could now be delivered in half an hour!

In Austria, where Salzburg was the home of what may be the world's first railway, the Reißzug (see page 13), a rail line was opened in sections between 1828 and 1836 from Budweiss, in Bohemia (the home of the famous beer in what is now České Budějovice in the Czech Republic), south, via Linz, to Gmunden (2 on map). The railway was horse drawn because the curves were considered too severe for locomotives. When the Czech section opened in 1828, it became the first public railway in continental Europe. The railway discontinued service in 1872.

The first steam railway in Austria was called the Emperor Ferdinand Northern Railway and was intended to link Vienna with salt mines at Bochnia, near Krakow, in Poland.

The first 8-mile-long stretch was completed in 1837 from Floridsdorf, in the northern part of Vienna, to Deutsch-Wagram. It was extended into Vienna the following year, to Brünn in 1839, and completed as far as Oderberg (Bohumín) in 1847, never reaching Bochnia or Krakow (3 on map).

Also shown is a railway from Vienna to Trieste, the Austro-Hungarian empire's outlet on the Adriatic Sea, begun in 1839, with the first section between Baden (bei Wien) and Vienna completed in 1841. A Norris locomotive (*above*) was purchased for this line. The first mountain railway, the Semmering Railway, over the eastern Alps via a tunnel under

Above.
The line from *Budweis* to *Gmunden,* built between 1828 and 1836, is shown on this enlarged part of the map on *pages 262–63.* The mountain section north of *Linz* was operated by horses; the *inset* shows a train leaving Linz.

Right.
The same 1849 map shows the short *Zürich-to-Baden* line in Switzerland, opened in 1847. The 1844 French line to *Basel* is also shown.

Semmering Pass, was built between 1848 and 1854 (4 on map) and provided a vital link; it is shown as a gap on the 1849 map (*pages 258–59*). Trieste was finally reached in 1857.

A competition similar in idea to the Rainhill Trials (see page 186) was held in 1851 to find a locomotive powerful enough to haul trains over the Semmering route. Entrants included an articulated design by Wilhelm von Engerth in which the fuel and water were distributed over the engine and tender so as to provide greater weight—and thus adhesion—on the driving wheels. Other articulated designs such as Fairlie's (see page 90), grew out of this design. The Semmering Railway is now a UNESCO World Heritage Site.

Italy, like Germany at this time, was not yet unified. Railways developed earlier in the northern part of the country than they did in the southern, poorer, part. The first, however, was in the south, a 4¾-mile-long line in the Kingdom of the Two Sicilies, between Naples and Portici, opened on 3 October 1839 (5 on outline map). It was the first part of a concession to a French railway promoter, Paul-Armand Bayard de la Vingtrie. An 8-mile-long line from Milan to Monza, in the Kingdom of Lombardy–Venetia, opened the following year, and a line from Milan to Venice was also begun in 1840. The section from Padua to Mestre was completed in 1842, and the whole line, including the 2½-mile-long causeway to Venice, in 1846 (shown on the map *overleaf*).

Also shown is the first railway in Poland, built by the Upper Silesian Railway Company from Breslau (Wroclaw) to Brieg (Brzeg); it was completed in 1842.

The Tsarskoye Selo Railway was the first public railway line in Russia. It ran for 17 miles from St. Petersburg to Pavlovsk through nearby Tsarskoye Selo (6 on the outline map). Construction began in May 1836, and the line was officially opened on 30 October 1837, when a train was hauled by a steam locomotive built by Thomas Hackworth (brother of Timothy, locomotive superintendent to the Stockton & Darlington Railway) between St. Petersburg and Tsarskoye Selo. In 1842 Tsar Nicholas I announced that the state would build a 400-mile-long line to connect St. Petersburg with Moscow, and after almost ten years of construction and financial problems the line finally opened on 1 November 1851. The Russians deliberately chose a gauge of 5 feet so that invading armies could not easily use the train.

In Denmark a line from Altona (close to Hamburg) to Kiel was opened in 1844 (7 on the outline map) to permit freight transport across the Danish peninsula (shown on the map, *overleaf*); this was lost with all of Holstein to Prussia in 1864. A line from Copenhagen to Roskilde, about 22 miles west of

Above.
The inaugural train on the Naples–Portici Railway, 3 October, 1839.

Below.
This 1857 map shows the completed line from Moscow to St. Petersburg (shown as a thick line with two thin lines), with the Tsarskoye Selo Railway and another short line from St. Petersburg also shown completed, plus other lines contemplated.

Below, left. The opening of the Tsarskoye Selo Railway in 1837.

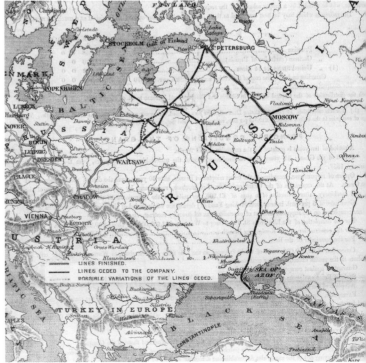

the capital, was completed in 1847 and was the first railway in what is Denmark today.

The other Scandinavian countries, Norway and Sweden, came later to railways, opening their first lines in 1854 and 1856, respectively. Norway was then part of Sweden. Norway's first line, the Hovedbanen, opened in 1854 from Christiania (now Oslo) to Eidsvoll, 38 miles to the north. It was engineered by Robert Stephenson, who, of course, introduced British standards. It was initially intended to transport lumber to the capital but soon attracted passengers. In 1853 Sweden's government decided that the country's railways should be state built and run, but in fact only about a third of them were. The first Swedish railway was an 11-mile-long private line from Nora to Ervalla, 100 miles west of Stockholm. Two short state-built lines serving Malmö and Göteborg (Gothenburg) opened later in 1856. The first trunk line, between Göteborg and Stockholm, was not completed until 1862.

Other latecomers were Spain and Portugal, poorer countries with fewer resources and less industry than most. Spain's first railway, from Barcelona to Mataró, 22 miles up the coast,

Above. A train on the Spanish Barcelona-to-Mataró railway in 1848.

Below. A one-third scale model of *Limmat*, the first Swiss steam locomotive, in the Verkehrshaus der Schweiz (Swiss Museum of Transport) in Luzern. The model was built in 1945 for the centenary celebrations two years later.

opened in 1848 (8 on the outline map), Portugal's not until 1856. Spain chose a wider gauge than the rest of Europe and later lived to regret it when interconnectivity became more important for trade. The choice of a wider gauge for main lines also resulted in many narrow-gauge lines being built, to save money.

Right.

A map of German railways, and those of adjacent countries, published in 1849. By this time a network of trunk lines was emerging. Place names are, of course, in German. The 1837–47 line north from *Wien* (Vienna) to *Brünn* and *Oderbg* (Oderberg; Bohumín) is shown and was extended to connect with *Prag* (Prague) in 1845. The first Polish railway from *Breslau* (Wrocław) to *Brieg* (Brzeg), completed in 1842, is a little farther to the north, then in Prussia. The extension north to *Warschau* (Warsaw) was completed in 1848, just in time to allow the Russian Tsar to dispatch 200,000 soldiers to Vienna and Budapest to put down a revolution. Dutch railways now reach from *Amsterdam* to *Haarlem* and south to *Rotterdam*, connected in 1847; and east to near the Dutch border, though Germany would not be reached until 1856. The originally Danish line from *Altona* (near *Hamburg*) to *Kiel* was completed in 1844. This map shows Schleswig-Holstein as Prussian, but it was part of Denmark until 1864. The *Leipzig–Dresden* Railway is shown and has been extended by several routes west, and also connected to the *Berlin–Potsdam–Magdeburg* line. *Berlin* was connected to *Hamburg* in 1846. In Italy, the line from *Mayland* (Milan) to *Venedig* (Venice) is shown; it was completed in 1846. The lone stretch of railway in Switzerland, from *Zürich* to *Baden*, opened in 1847, has been extended a few miles to *Brugg*; it would be 1854 before the track would reach *Basel*. The first railways of Austria—*Budweis* (České Budějovice)–*Linz* (1828–36); and France—*St. Etienne–Andresieux* (Andrézieux; 1828), *Andrézieux–Roanne* (1832), and *St. Etienne–Lyon* (1830)— are still isolated, though there is a planned connection from *Lyon* to *Paris*. The main line from Paris to Marseille via Lyon was opened in 1856. The line from *Wien* (Vienna) to *Triest* (Trieste) still shows a gap where the Semmering Tunnel was under construction. The comparative density of railways in the northern part of Germany compares with the lower density evident in France at this time (1849).

Below.

Preserved in the DB Museum in Nuremberg is *Phoenix*, one of the last Crampton-type locomotives, built in 1863 for the Baden State Railway. A French Crampton locomotive is shown on *page 250*. Thomas Russell Crampton was an English engineer who worked with Brunel on the Great Western Railway and developed this type of locomotive, which had its main driving wheel behind the firebox. The design, first built in 1846, was widely used on French and German railways, and to a lesser extent in Britain.

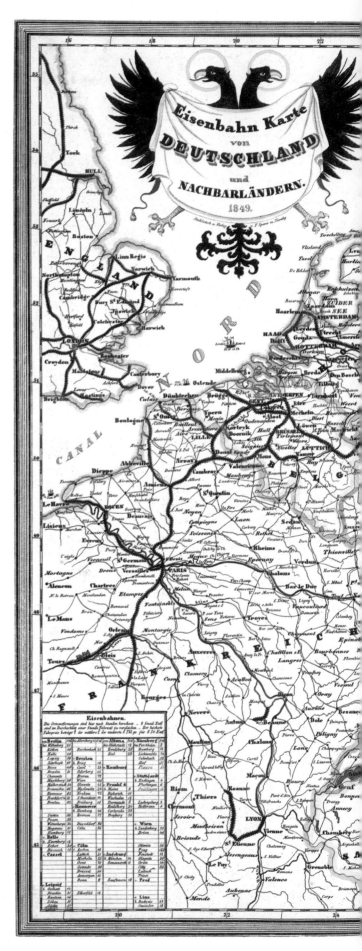

Map and Illustration Sources

Maps and illustrations not otherwise credited are from the author's collection.
Source information is given in some captions and is not repeated here. Old routes are typically marked on Ordnance Survey period base maps. Some outline base maps are from freevectormaps.com.
All photographs are by the author unless otherwise credited.

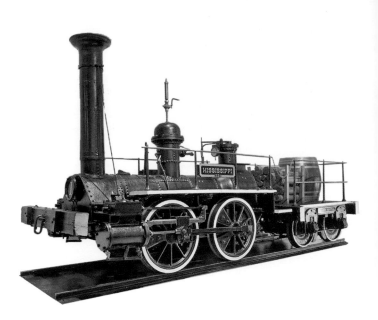

Right. Mississippi, built in England by Braithwaite & Ericsson in 1834 and exported to the United States as a kit of parts. It was used for a while on the only part of the Mississippi Railroad to be completed, a line between Natchez and Hamburg, becoming the first steam locomotive in the central South. It was used in the Civil War, first by Confederates and then, after being captured, by the Union Army. Later it was bought by the Illinois Central Railroad and in 1893 was exhibited at the World's Columbian Exposition in Chicago. It then spent 80 years in the Museum of Science & Industry in Chicago before being sold for $220,000 in 2015.

Title page
Plan of the Rivers Tyne & Wear with the Collieries, Waggon-ways & Staiths, thereon And the Principal Roads & Villages, also a Plan of Newcastle upon Tyne
D. Akenhead & Sons, 1807
North of England Institute of Mining and Mechanical Engineers NRO 3410/Bell/3/12-13

Contents page
Plan of Long Benton Estate Belonging to Lord Carlisle
1749
North of England Institute of Mining and Mechanical Engineers Watson 20A/9

Page 8 (top)
Map of the Inland Navigation, Canals and Rail Roads with the Situations of the various Mineral Productions throughout Great Britain
J. Walker, 1830
National Railway Museum 2001-625

Page 8 (bottom)
General Railway Map Engraved Expressly for the Official Guide of the Railways and Steam Navigation Lines of the United States
1918
Library of Congress G3300.1 P1 1918.N3

Page 11
Plan of the Waggon Rail way from Collieries near New-bottle in the County of Durham
1817
Sunderland Museum

Page 15 (both)
Map of Berwell [sic, Benwell] showing names and tenure of fields
Roger Wills, 1637
UK National Archives MR1/28/1

Page 16
A Plan of the Town and Port of Neath in the County of Glamorgan Being Part of ye Estate of Sir Humphry Mackworth
M.O Conner, c. 1697
Page 17 (top left)
Map of East Lothian Surveyed by Mr. J. Adair, F.R.S.
J. Adair, 1737
Royal Geographical Society

Page 17 (top right)
Haddingtonshire

William Forrest, 1799
British Library

Page 17 (centre left)
Map of the County of Haddingtonshire
William Fowler, 1824–25
National Library of Scotland

Page 17 (bottom right)
Plan of the Town of Alloa from Actual Survey
John Wood, 1825

Page 18 (left)
An Actual Survey of Bath in the County of Somerset and of Five Miles Round
Thomas Thorpe, 1742
Harvard College Library
Page 19
Plan of the Town and Harbour of Whitehaven
J. Howard, 1799
Carlisle Public Library

Page 21
A Plan of Tanfield Moor
1761
Northumberland Archives
SANT-BEQ-09-01-03-64
Courtesy Society of Antiquities of Newcastle-upon-Tyne

Page 22
Plan of the Collieries on the Rivers Tyne and Wear also Blythe, Bedlington and Hartley
John Gibson, 1788
Science and Society Picture Library

Page 23
Plan of Long Benton Estate Belonging to Lord Carlisle
1749
North of England Institute of Mining and Mechanical Engineers Watson 20A/9
Pages 24–25
Plan of the Collieries on the Rivers Tyne and Wear also Blythe, Bedlington and Hartley
John Gibson, 1788
Science and Society Picture Library

Pages 26–27
Neptune Shipyards wooden trackwork, 2013
Paul Jarman, Beamish Museum

Pages 28–29
Plan of the Rivers Tyne & Wear with the Collieries, Waggon-ways & Staiths, thereon And the Principal Roads & Villages, also a Plan of Newcastle upon Tyne
D. Akenhead & Sons, 1807
North of England Institute of Mining and Mechanical Engineers NRO 3410/Bell/3/12-13

Page 34 (top)
Murdoch model steam vehicle, 1784
Birmingham Museums Trust

Page 37
Index to Nichols & Company's Six Sheet Map of the Inland Navigation and Rail Roads of Great Britain
From: *Historical Account of the Navigable Rivers, Canals and Railways Throughout Great Britain.*
Joseph Priestley, Second Edition, 1830

Page 39 and page 41
Map of the Country Twenty Miles Round Mansfield
George Sanderson, 1835
University of Nottingham Library

Page 42 (top left) and page 43 (bottom)
G. Bradshaw's Map of Canals Situated in the Counties of Lancaster, York, Derby & Chester
G. Bradshaw, n.d. (c. 1833)
Borthwick Archives, University of York

Page 44
Bugsworth Basin
From survey by Manchester, Sheffield & Lincolnshire Railway, 1889
Canalmaps Archive (www.canalmaps.net)

Page 45 (main map)
Map of the Inland Navigation, Canals and Rail Roads with the Situations of the various Mineral Productions throughout Great Britain
J. Walker, 1830
National Railway Museum 2001-625

Page 45 (insets, left and right)
Ordnance Survey Map, 1849

Page 46
G. Bradshaw's Map of Canals Situated in the Midland Counties of England
G. Bradshaw, 1830
Borthwick Archives, University of York

Page 121 (bottom)
Plan of the Coal District on the Rivers Tyne & Wear
R. Pellington, 1826
Beamish Museum

Pages 122–23 (bottom) and page 127 (top)
Plan of the Waggon Rail Way from Collieries near Newbottle in the County of Durham
1817
Sunderland Museum

Pages 124–25
Steam Elephant (oil painting, artist and date unknown)
Beamish Museum

Page 125
Plan of the Coal District on the Rivers Tyne & Wear
R. Pellington, 1826
Beamish Museum

Page 126 (centre, left and right)
Plan of the Rivers Tyne & Wear with the Collieries, Waggon-ways & Staiths, thereon And the Principal Roads & Villages, also a Plan of Newcastle upon Tyne
D. Akenhead & Sons, 1807
North of England Institute of Mining and Mechanical Engineers NRO 3410/Bell/3/12-13

Pages 128–29
George Stephenson's 1816 steam engine
William Strickland, 1825
Beamish Museum

Page 129 (top)
Killingworth Waggon Way
Undated
North of England Institute of Mining and Mechanical Engineers Watson 3/55/156

Page 130
Design of a Losh and Stephenson Locomotive Steam Engine
c. 1817
National Railway Museum

Pages 134–35 and page 136 (bottom)
A Description of the Hetton Rail Road, in England
From: *Columbian Centinel* (newspaper), Boston, MA
1 February 1829

Page 135 (top)
View of the Railway at Hetton Colliery
1822
Beamish Museum

Page 139 (top)
Drawing of Losh–Stephenson patented rail
William Strickland, 1825
Beamish Museum

Page 139 (bottom)
Plan of the Coal District on the Rivers Tyne & Wear
R. Pellington, 1826
Beamish Museum

Pages 140–41 (top and bottom)
Steam Conveyance on a General Iron-Rail-Way
From: Thomas Gray, *Observations on a General Iron Rail-way*, 1822

Page 142 (top)
Plan of Rail Ways to connect Bolton and Bury with Liverpool
William James, 1802

Page 142 (bottom left)
Plan of a General Iron-Rail-Way for Ireland
From: Thomas Gray, *Observations on a General Iron Rail-way*, 1822

Page 142 (bottom centre)
Plan of a General Iron-Rail-Way for Great Britain
From: Thomas Gray, *Observations on a General Iron Rail-way*, 1822

Page 143 (top)
Plan of the Lines of the Central Junction Rail-Way or Tram-Road
William James, 1820
From: Ellen Paine, *The Two James's and the Two Stephensons*, 1861

Page 143 (bottom right)
Map of the rail lines projected by Robert Stevenson
From: David Stevenson, *Life of Robert Stevenson, Civil Engineer*, 1878

Page 145 (top)
A Plan of the River Tees and of the Intended Navigable Canal from Stockton by Darlington to Winston in the Bishoprick of Durham
Robert Whitworth, 1772
From: *The Gentleman's Magazine*, August 1772

Page 145 (bottom)
Durham for the Agricultural Survey
J. Bailey, 1810

Page 146 (all)
Plan of an Intended Rail or Tram Road from the Collieries Near West Auckland by Darlington to Stockton
George Overton, 1818 (deposited 30 September)
Durham Record Office Q/D/P 2b

Pages 148–49 (all)
Plan of the Intended Railway from Stockton to the Collieries in the Neighbourhood of West-Auckland
[George Overton] Unsigned, undated; deposited 3 April 1819
Durham Record Office Q/D/P 4/1

Pages 150–51
Darlington Railway, 1819
Unsigned map of possible railway routes presumed to be by Robert Stevenson
Stevenson papers, reproduced by permission of the National Library of Scotland
Acc. No. 10706 / 455

Pages 152–53
Plan and Section of the Intended Railway or Tramroad from Stockton by Darlington to the Collieries near West Auckland with several intended Branches (base map)
(Overton's line compared with Stevenson's line).
Base map dated 1820
Stevenson papers, reproduced by permission of the National Library of Scotland
Acc. No. 10706 / 453

Pages 154–55 (all)
Plan and Section of the Intended Railway or Tram Road from Stockton by Darlington to the Collieries near West Auckland with several intended Branches
David Davies and George Overton, 1820; deposited 30 September 1820
Durham Record Office Q/D/P 7

Page 156
Plan of the Darlington Railway
Prospectus map, 1820 or 1821
UK National Archives RAIL 1075/199

Pages 158–59
Plan and Section of the Intended Railway or Tramroad from Stockton by Darlington to the Collieries near West Auckland in the County of Durham with several intended Branches . . . and also of the Additional Branch of Railway or Tramroad Proposed to be Made
W. Miller (engraver), 1822
UK National Archives RAIL 1037/3/10

Page 160 (bottom)
A Plan of the Railway or Tramroad from the River Tees at Stockton to Witton Park Colliery . . . And Also a Plan and Sections of Several New or Additional Branch Railways or Tramroads
Robert Stephenson and John Dixon, 1823
UK National Archives RAIL 1037 3/12

Page 161 (right)
Plan of the Coal District in the County of Durham, 1829
North of England Institute of Mining and Mechanical Engineers NRO 3410/Bell/2/421

Pages 160–61 (top), page 161 (bottom left), and page 162 (inset, top)
From: James Adamson, *Sketches of Our Information as to Rail-roads: Also an account of the Stockton & Darlington Rail-way*, 1826
National Railway Museum B1/72

Page 166 (bottom)
Map of the Inland Navigation, Canals and Rail Roads with the Situations of the various Mineral Productions throughout Great Britain
J. Walker, 1830
National Railway Museum 2001-625

Page 167 (bottom)
Plan and Section of the Intended Branch Railways From the Stockton & Darlington Main Railway to the River Tees
Thomas Storey and Richard Otley, 1827
UK National Archives RAIL 667/267

Pages 168–69 (bottom)
Large plan of the Canterbury & Whitstable Railway
Creator unknown, c. 1970s
Canterbury Heritage Museum

Page 169 (top)
Map of the Inland Navigation, Canals and Rail Roads with the Situations of the various Mineral Productions throughout Great Britain
J. Walker, 1830
National Railway Museum 2001-625

Page 169 (centre)
Plan of the proposed Line of Rail Road from Whitstable to Canterbury set out by me
William James, 29 October 1824
From: Reginald B. Fellows, *History of the Canterbury and Whitstable Railway*, 1930.

Pages 172–73 (top)
Plan and Section of an Intended Railway or Tramroad from Liverpool to Manchester
George and John Rennie, and Charles Vignoles, 1826
UK National Archives MPC 1/177

Railways in 1830

Bibliography

Addyman, John, and Victoria Haworth. *Robert Stephenson, Railway Engineer.* Hull: North Eastern Railway Association, and Robert Stephenson Trust, 2005.

Anon. *Le Grand Atlas des Trains et Locomotives: 200 ans d'histoire ferroviaire.* No location given [Paris]: Editions Atlas, 2004.

ArcHeritage. *Silkstone Waggonway, South Yorkshire.* Sheffield: ArcHeritage, 2012.

Bailey, Michael R. (ed.). *Early Railways 3. Papers from the Third International Early Railways Conference.* Clare, Suffolk: Six Martlets Publishing, 2006.

Bailey, Michael R. *Loco Motion: The World's Oldest Steam Locomotives.* Stroud, Gloucestershire: The History Press, 2014.

BaltimAAore & Ohio Railroad. *The Catalogue of the Centenary Exhibition of the Baltimore & Ohio Railroad 1827–1927.* Baltimore: Baltimore & Ohio Railroad, 1927.

Baxter, Bertram. *Stone Blocks and Iron Rails.* Newton Abbot: David & Charles, 1966.

Bennett, G., E. Clavering, and A. Rounding. *A Fighting Trade: Rail Transport in Tyne Coal, 1600–1800.* 2 vols. Vol. 1: *History;* Vol. 2: *Data.* Gateshead: Portcullis Press, 1990.

Bick, D.E. *The Gloucester & Cheltenham Railway and the Leckhampton Quarry Tramroads.* Lingfield, Surrey: Oakwood Press, 1968.

Boyes, Grahame (ed.). *Early Railways 4. Papers from the Fourth International Early Railways Conference.* Clare, Suffolk: Six Martlets Publishing, 2010.

Briggs, Asa. *A Social History of England.* London: Weidenfeld & Nicholson, 1994.

British History Illustrated. *Railway Special, 1825–1975.* London: Historical Times, 1975.

Bryan, Tim. *The Great Western Railway.* Botley, Oxford: Shire Publications, 2011.

Carlson, Robert E. *The Liverpool & Manchester Railway Project, 1821–1831.* Newton Abbot: David & Charles, 1969.

Casserley, H.C., and C.C. Dorman. *Railway History in Pictures: The Midlands.* New York: Augustus M. Kelley Publishers, 1969.

Clinker, C.R. *The Leicester & Swannington Railway.* Bristol: Avon-Anglia Publications, 1977.

Collins, Paul (ed.). *Stourbridge & Its Historic Locomotives.* Dudley: Dudley Libraries, 1989.

DB Museum. *Ein Jahrhundert unter Dampf: Die Eisenbahn in Deutschland, 1835–1919.* Nuremberg: DB Museum, 2009.

———. *Der Adler: Deutschlands berühmteste Lokomotive.* Nuremburg: DB Museum, 2011.

Dendy Marshall, C.F. *A History of British Railways Down to the Year 1830.* Oxford: Oxford University Press, 1938.

———. *A History of Railway Locomotives Down to the End of the Year 1831.* London: Locomotive Publishing Co., 1953.

Donaghy, Thomas J. *Liverpool & Manchester Railway Operations, 1831–1845.* Newton Abbot: David & Charles, 1972.

Dott, George. *Early Scottish Colliery Wagonways.* Westminster: St. Margaret's Technical Press, 1947.

Duffy, Michael C. *Electric Railways, 1880–1990.* London: Institute of Electrical Engineers, 2003.

Ellis, Chris, and Greg Morse. *Steaming through Britain: A History of the Nation's Railways.* London: Conway/Anova Books, 2010.

Emmerson, Andrew. *The London Underground.* Botley, Oxford: Shire Publications, 2010.

Ewans, Michael Christopher. *The Haytor Granite Railway and Stover Canal.* Dawlish: David & Charles, 1964.

Fairbrother, Martin. *The Kilmarnock & Troon Railway: Child and Orphan of Plateway Technology.* York: University of York Institute of Railway Studies & Transport History, 2005.

Fellows, Reginald B. *History of the Canterbury and Whitstable Railway.* Canterbury: J.A. Jennings, 1930.

Francis, John. *A History of the English Railway: Its Social Relations and Revelations, 1820–1845.* London: Longman Green Brown & Longmans, 1851; reprinted edition. Newton Abbot: David & Charles, 1968.

Freeman, Michael, and Derek Aldcroft. *The Atlas of British Railway History.* London: Croom Helm, 1985.

Gibbon, Richard. *Stephenson's Rocket and the Rainhill Trials.* Botley, Oxford: Shire Publications, 2010.

Gibbs, Ken. *The Steam Locomotive: An Engineering History.* Stroud, Gloucestershire: Amberley Publishing, 2012.

Goslin, G.W. *London's Elevated Electric Railway: The LBSCR Suburban Overhead Electrification, 1909–1929.* Colchester: G.W. Goslin, 2002.

Griffin, Trevor, David Bunting, and Brian Key. "The Butterley Gangroad." *Derbyshire Archaeological Journal,* Vol. 134, pp. 221–52, 2014.

Guy, Andy. *Steam and Speed: Railways of Tyne and Wear from the Earliest Days.* Newcastle: Tyne Bridge Publishing, Newcastle Libraries & Information Service, 2003.

Guy, Andy, and Jim Rees. *Early Railways, 1569–1830.* Botley, Oxford: Shire Publications, 2011.

Guy, Andy, and Jim Rees (eds.). *Early Railways. A Selection of Papers from the First International Early Railways Conference.* London: Newcomen Society, 2001.

Gwyn, David (ed.). *Early Railways 5 Papers from the Fifth International Early Railways Conference.* Clare, Suffolk: Six Martlets Publishing, 2014.

Gwyn, David. *Welsh Slate: Archaeology and History of an Industry.* Aberystwyth: Royal Commission on the Ancient & Historical Monuments of Wales, 2015.

Hadfield, Charles. *Atmospheric Railways: A Victorian Venture in Silent Speed.* Newton Abbot: David & Charles, 1967.

Hadfield, Charles, and A.W. Skempton. *William Jessop, Engineer.* London: David & Charles, 1979.

Hayes, Derek. *Historical Atlas of the North American Railroad.* Berkeley, CA: University of California Press, 2010.

Hayes, Geoffrey. *Beam Engines.* Botley, Oxford: Shire Publications, 2003.

Haywood, Richard Mowbray. *Russia Enters the Railway Age, 1842–1855.* Boulder, CO: East European Monographs, 1998.

Holman, Printz P. *The Amazing Electric Tube: A History of the City and South London Railway.* London: London Transport Museum, 1990.

Holt, Geoffrey. *The Ticknall Tramway.* Ticknall, Derbyshire: Ticknall Preservation & Historical Society, 1994.

Hughes, Stephen. *The Archaeology of an Early Railway System: The Brecon Forest Tramroads.* Aberystwyth: Royal Commission on Ancient & Historical Monuments in Wales, 1990.

Hylton, Stuart. *The Grand Experiment: The Birth of the Railway Age, 1820–1845.* Hersham, Surrey: Ian Allan, 2007.

Jackson, Alan. *Volk's Railways, Brighton: An Illustrated History.* London: Light Railway Transport League, 1993.

James, Leslie. *A Chronology of the Construction of Britain's Railways, 1778–1855.* Hersham, Surrey: Ian Allan, 1983.

Jeans, J. Stephen. *Jubilee Memorial of the Railway System: A History of the Stockton & Darlington Railway and a Record of Its Results.* London: Longmans, 1875.

Johnson, Peter. *An Illustrated History of the Snowdon Mountain Railway.* Hersham, Surrey: OPC/Ian Allan, 2010.

Jones, Mark. *Discovering Britain's First Railways: A Guide to Horse-Drawn Tramroads and Waggonways.* Stroud, Gloucestershire: History Press, 2012.

Jones, Robin. *The Dawn of Steam.* Wellington, Somerset: PiXZ Books, 2009.

———. *Brunel's Big Railway. How the GWR Stretched from Paddington to Penzance . . . and New York!* Horncastle, Lincolnshire: Mortons Media Group, 2013.

Kirby, Maurice W. *The Origins of Railway Enterprise: The Stockton & Darlington Railway, 1821–1863.* Cambridge: Cambridge University Press, 1993.

Leboff, David, and Tim Demuth. *No Need to Ask! Early Maps of London's Underground Railways.* Harrow Weald, Middlesex: Capital Transport Publishing, 1999.

Lee, Charles. *Narrow-Gauge Railways in North Wales.* London: Railway Publishing, 1945.

———. *The World's Oldest Railway: 300 Years of Coal Conveyance to the Tyne Staiths.* London: Newcomen Society, 1946.

———. *The Swansea & Mumbles Railway.* Oxford: Oakwood Press, 1988.

Lewis, M.J.T. *Early Wooden Railways.* London: Routledge & Kegan Paul, 1970.

Lewis, M.J.T. (ed.). *Early Railways 2. Papers from the Second International Early Railways Conference.* London: Newcomen Society, 2003.

Moody, G.T. *Southern Electric, 1909–1979.* Fifth edition. Hersham, Surrey: Ian Allan 1979.

Ripley, D. *The Peak Forest Tramway.* Locomotion Papers 38. Second edition. Lingfield, Surrey: Oakwood Press, 1972.

———. *The Little Eaton Gangway, 1793–1908.* Locomotion Papers 71. Lingfield, Surrey: Oakwood Press, 1973.

McDougall, C.A. *The Stockton & Darlington Railway, 1821–1863.* Durham: Durham County Council, 1975.

McGowan, Christopher. *The Rainhill Trials: The Greatest Contest of Industrial Britain and the Birth of Commercial Rail.* London: Little, Brown, 2004.

Macnair, Miles. *William James (1771–1837): The Man Who Discovered George Stephenson.* Oxford: Railway & Canal Historical Society, 2007.

Marshall, John. *The Cromford & High Peak Railway.* Newton Abbot: David & Charles, 1982.

Martin, Don. *The Monkland & Kirkintilloch and Associated Railways.* Glasgow: Strathkelvin District Libraries & Museums, 1995.

Matheson, Rosa. *The GWR Story.* Stroud, Gloucestershire: The History Press, 2010.

Maxwell, Eric, and Neville Whaler. *The Bowes Railway: A souvenir of Britain's only surviving rope worked railway.* Springwell, Gateshead: Bowes Railway Company, 2011.

Messenger, Michael. *Slate Quarry Railways of Gwynedd.* (Chacewater, Cornwall:) Twelveheads Press, 2008.

———. *The Bodmin & Wadebridge Railway, 1834–1983.* (Chacewater, Cornwall:) Twelveheads Press, 2012.

Middleton Railway Trust Museum. *A History of the Middleton Railway, Leeds.* Eighth edition. Leeds: Middleton Railway Trust, 2004.

Moody, G.T. *Southern Electric, 1909–1979.* Fifth edition. London: Ian Allan, 1979.

Morgan, Bryan. *Early Trains.* New York: Golden Press, 1974.

Norris, John. *The Stratford & Moreton Tramway.* Guildford: Railway & Canal Historical Society, 1987.

Owen-Jones, Stuart. *The Penydarren Locomotive.* Cardiff: The National Museum of Wales, 1981.

Paine, Ellen (as "E.M.S.P.") *The Two James's and the Two Stephensons, or, The Earliest History of Passenger Transit on Railways.* London: G. Phipps, 1861

Pollins, Harold. *Britain's Railways: An Industrial History.* Totowa, NJ: Rowman & Littlefield, 1971.

Priestley, Joseph. *Historical Account of the Navigable Rivers, Canals, and Railways throughout Great Britain.* Second Edition. New York: Augustus M. Kelley Publishers, 1968. (Original edition 1830.)

Proud, John H. *The Chronicle of the Stockton & Darlington Railway to 1863.* Hull: North Eastern Railway Association, 1998.

Ransom, P.J.G. *The Archaeology of Railways.* Tadworth, Surrey: World's Work, 1981.

———. *The Archaeology of the Transport Revolution, 1750–1850.* Tadworth, Surrey: World's Work, 1984.

Rattenbury, Gordon. *Tramroads of the Brecknock & Abergavenny Canal.* Oakham, Rutland: Railway and Canal Historical Society, 1980.

Rattenbury, Gordon, and M.J.T. Lewis. *Merthyr Tydfil Tramroads and Their Locomotives.* Oxford: Railway & Canal Historical Society, 2004.

Rigg, Michael. *The Innocent Railway: The Birth of Edinburgh's First Railway and Its Life to "Hasten Slowly."* York: Institute of Railway Studies, University of York, 2003.

Robertson, C.J.A. *The Origins of the Scottish Railway System.* Edinburgh: John Donald Publishers, 1983.

Rolt, L.T.C. *George and Robert Stephenson: The Railway Revolution.* Stroud, Gloucestershire: Amberley Publishing, 2009.

Rosen, William. *The Most Powerful Idea in the World.* New York: Random House, 2010.

Schofield, Reginald B. *Benjamin Outram, 1764–1805 An Engineering Biography.* Cardiff: Merton Priory Press, 2000.

Semmens, P.W.B. *Stockton & Darlington: One Hundred & Fifty Years of British Railways.* London: New English Library, 1975.

Simmons, Jack (ed.). *Rail 150: The Stockton & Darlington Railway and What Followed.* London: Eyre Methuen, 1975.

Simmons, Jack. *The Railways of Britain: A Journey through History.* Moorebank, NSW: Mallard Press/Transworld Publishers, 1990.

Simmons, Jack, and Gordon Biddle. *The Oxford Companion to British Railway History.* Oxford: Oxford University Press, 1997.

Skeat, W.O. *George Stephenson: The Engineer and His Letters.* London: The Institution of Mechanical Engineers, 1973.

Smith, George. *Wylam: 200 Years of Railway History.* Stroud, Gloucestershire: Amberley Publishing, 2012.

Smithsonian. *Train: The Definitive Visual History.* New York: DK Publishing, 2014.

Spaven, David, and Julian Holland. *Mapping the Railways.* London: Times Books, 2011.

Stead, Christopher. *The Birth of the Steam Locomotive: A New History.* Haddenham, Cambridgeshire: Fern House, 2002.

Stevenson, David. *Life of Robert Stevenson, Civil Engineer.* Edinburgh: Adam & Charles Black, and London: E. & F.N. Spon, 1878.

Tanel, Franco. *An Illustrated History of Trains: From Steam Locomotives to High-Speed Rail.* Newton Abbot: David & Charles, 2010.

Tasker, W.W. *Railways in the Sirhowy Valley.* Headington, Oxfordshire: Oakwood Press, 1992.

Thomas, R.H.G. *The Liverpool & Manchester Railway.* London: B.T. Batsford, 1980.

———. *London's First Railway: The London & Greenwich.* London: B.T. Batsford, 1986.

Tomlinson, William Weaver. *The North Eastern Railway Its Rise and Development.* London: Reid/Longmans Green, 1915; new edition Newton Abbot: David & Charles, 1967.

Turnbull, Les. *Railways Before George Stephenson: A Study of the Waggonways in the Great Northern Coalfield, 1605–1830.* Oxford: Chapman Research and the North of England Institute of Mining & Mechanical Engineers, 2012.

Wall, John. *First in the World: The Stockton & Darlington Railway.* Stroud, Gloucestershire: Sutton Publishing, 2001.

Warren, J.G.H. *A Century of Locomotive Building by Robert Stephenson & Co., 1823–1923.* Newcastle upon Tyne: Andrew Reid & Co., 1923; new edition New York: Augustus M. Kelley Publishers, 1970.

Webb, Brian, and David Gordon. *Lord Carlisle's Railways.* [Cheltenham:] The Railway Correspondence & Travel Society, 1978.

White, John H. *American Locomotives: An Engineering History, 1830–1880.* Baltimore: Johns Hopkins Press, 1968.

Williams, Alan. *Southern Electric Album.* London: Ian Allan, 1977.

Wolmar, Christian. *The Subterranean Railway.* London: Atlantic Books, 2005.

———. *Fire & Steam: A New History of the Railways in Britain.* London: Atlantic Books, 2007.

———. *Blood, Iron and Gold: How the Railroads Transformed the World.* London: Atlantic Books, 2009.

———. *The Iron Road: An Illustrated History of the Railroad.* New York: DK Publishing, 2014.

Young, Robert. *Timothy Hackworth and the Locomotive.* Reprint of original 1923 edition. Shildon: Stockton & Darlington Railway Jubilee Committee, 1975.

Index

Entries for place names, rivers, canals, railways, loco names etc **other than the UK** are followed by their abbreviated country of origin in brackets

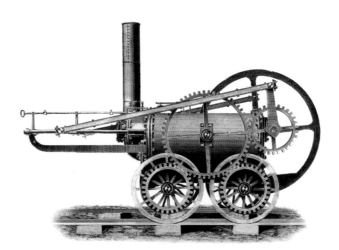